A SURVEY OF THE

SOCIAL SCIENCES

GARY D. BROWN
UNIVERSITY OF DELAWARE

DUANE BROWN
UNIVERSITY OF NORTH CAROLINA, CHAPEL HILL

McGRAW-HILL BOOK COMPANY
New York
St. Louis
San Francisco
Auckland
Düsseldorf
Johannesburg
Kuala Lumpur
London
Mexico
Montreal
New Delhi
Panama
Paris
São Paulo
Singapore
Sydney
Tokyo
Toronto

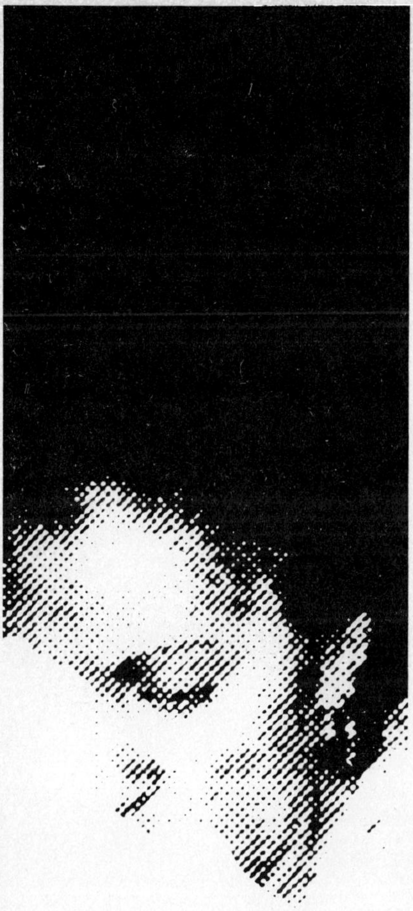

A SURVEY OF THE SOCIAL SCIENCES

A SURVEY OF THE SOCIAL SCIENCES

1234567890DODO798765

This book was set in Helvetica Light by Black Dot, Inc.
The editors were Lyle Linder, Janis M. Yates, and Phyllis T. Dulan; the designer was Anne Canevari Green; the production supervisor was Charles Hess.
The drawings were done by J & R Services, Inc.
R. R. Donnelley & Sons Company was printer and binder.

Library of Congress Cataloging in Publication Data

Brown, Gary D
A survey of the social sciences.

Bibliography: p.
1. Social sciences. I. Brown, Duane, joint author. II. Title.
H61.B677 300 74-22299
ISBN 0-07-008195-6

to our parents

CONTENTS

PREFACE

This book is intended to serve as the basic text in a one- or two-term introduction to social science course. The different sections are designed so that they are self-contained and thus can be covered in any sequence. Further, no area in the social science field has been given special emphasis. Therefore, the specific thrust of the course will be determined by the supplemental materials chosen by the instructor.

The idea for the book grew out of the frustrations experienced by the senior author and his colleagues while developing a general social science course at Meramec Community College in St. Louis, Missouri. Like most instructors, this group wanted to find a text which would provide the student with an introduction to social science methodology and also the fundamental concepts used by social scientists to explain the functioning of humanity and its organizations. A review of other texts in the field revealed nothing particularly suited to the typical community college class. The diversity found in this group demands a different approach than that typically employed in the four-year college or university class. It should be noted that as college and university classes become more heterogeneous, traditional approaches will have to be abandoned at that level also.

In the evolution of *A Survey of the Social Sciences* many of the materials were used as handouts at Meramec Community College in an attempt to bridge the gap between what was available in current textbooks and what was desired in course content. The negative feedback received from students convinced the authors that a textbook must be used with community college students to help them integrate the diverse materials covered in the course. This book was developed to fulfill this purpose.

The book was written with one other specific purpose in mind. The authors believe that education should assist students to understand the day-to-day events of their lives and assist them to deal more effectively with these events. Too often introductory texts are filled with facts and figures and generalized abstractions. A genuine attempt has been made to avoid this approach.

While this text may help the instructor deal with a diverse population of students, it cannot and should not serve as the sole vehicle for presentation of the social sciences. It has been emphasized throughout the text that the material in the area is too vast to cover in a single book. The instructor should also engage the resources of his students, his institution, and his community as a social science laboratory for in these real-life situations the social sciences take on true meaning.

It is impossible to acknowledge all those who contributed to this book. However, we would be remiss if we failed to recognize the students who used and reacted to certain parts of it, those colleagues who read the manuscript and made many useful suggestions, and the editorial staff of McGraw-Hill who were important in determining its final form.

Gary D. Brown
Duane Brown

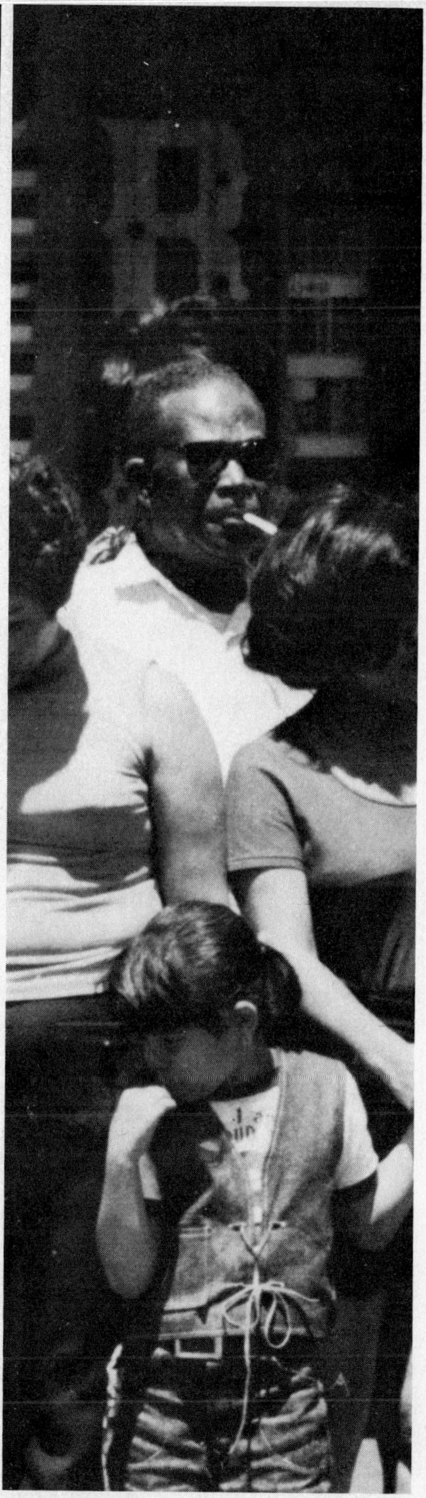

CHAPTER ONE
THE STUDY OF THE SOCIAL SCIENCES

IDEAS AND CONCEPTS

people
the subject matter of the social sciences

scientific method
truth or knowledge is found through direct observation

hawthorne effect
response of people to being studied

technology
application of knowledge to perform some task

normative
deciding whether one thing is preferable to another

GLOSSARY

amoral not concerned with moral standards; neither moral nor immoral

census when all the items in the population are used in a scientific investigation to determine the characteristics of the population

empirical process a process of acquiring knowledge based on the philosophic doctrine which asserts that knowledge is found through direct observation

fallacy of composition the assumption that what is true of the parts is true of the whole when this is not the case

false analogy when one attempts to prove something by comparing it to something which is not comparable

hawthorne effect when people respond to being involved in an experiment rather than to what is being done in the experiment

intellectual experiment the use of abstract models instead of actually conducting a real experiment

normative social science the part of the study of social science that deals with "what should be"

population in scientific investigations population refers to all the items or people in the group being studied

positive social science that part of the study of social science that deals with "what is"

post hoc ergo propter hoc a mistaken assumption that when one event follows another then the first caused the second

pragmatism an indigenous American philosophy which asserts that change is the essence of reality and that reality is constituted of mass interaction of man with his environment

real income income measured in terms of actual goods and services as opposed to money

sample when only part of the items in the population are used in a scientific investigation to estimate population characteristics

technology the application of knowledge by man in order to perform some task he wants done

Why is it illegal to have more than one wife or husband at a time in the United States? Why is the male expected to provide the economic support for the family? Why do you have to go to school? What causes people to develop the types of behavior that they do? Can an individual ever be free from the influence of his past environment? Why do people feel "guilty" or "good" when they do certain things? How does a society decide which goods and services to produce? What or who determines the pattern of distribution of goods and services in a society? What should be the proper role of government in a society? Who can be elected President of the United States? What will society be like by the year 2000? These are the types of questions which are of interest to social scientists and society generally.

Common element of the social sciences The very diverse topics of social science all have one common element: they are all concerned with people and/or their organization. *Organization* refers to any patterned way of interaction of people. The organization of a group of people is for the purpose of carrying out some specific function or functions. The functions include such diverse things as the provision of protection from other groups, the rearing of children, and the providing of recreation for the members of the group. The organization of any particular group of people varies from very simple to extremely complex. For instance, the organizational pattern which exists in the United States for dealing with casual acquaintances is very loose and informal, whereas the organizational structure which has been developed to perform the functions of government is very complex and involves the interaction of very diverse units.

The type of organization which exists in a society influences the way different functions are performed and is a particularly important determinant of the patterns and types of change which can occur without severely disrupting societal organization. The social scientist attempts to discover the patterns of organization in a society and to explain how these affect the people within the society, as well as the ways in which any single organization influences the general functioning of the society. Even in societies with relatively simple social organization there is a great deal of interdependence of the people and their organization.

It is essential that the social scientist always include consideration of this interdependence when studying some specific aspect of a society. For example, any explanation of the rapid growth of the role of government in society in the United States in the twentieth century would have to include consideration of changes in the structure and functions of the family during this time period. An explanation of changes in the structure and functions of the family, in turn, would have to include consideration of changes in the labor needs of the economy, etc. In some form or another each aspect of the organization of a society influences every other part of the way the society is organized, and at the same time it is affected by all the other organizational aspects of the society. In the interrelationship between the family and government, for instance, government uses its power to force children to go to school, to make them receive immunizations, to prevent family vendettas, and to rescue the family from the need to care for its aged.

Physical environment Social scientists as social scientists are not interested in the physical environment in which man lives per se. For instance, we do not attempt to explain what causes different weather conditions or the nature of the forces that have influenced the geologic evolution of the earth. However, we are interested in the relationship between the social development of people and their physical environment. People's ability to control or adapt to their physical environment is a very important element in the determination of their behavior and the organizational patterns they will develop to perform different functions. As an example, the current famine in Volta and the nearby countries in Africa resulting from temporary changes in weather patterns has attracted the attention of many social scientists.

Specialization in the social sciences Social scientists are also very interested in learning which aspects of people's behavior and potential for performing different types of tasks is genetically determined, ie., inherited, and which are learned. There is considerable disagreement among the experts on this question. This question serves as the framework for the discussion in the section on the Psychological Person. Because of the complexity of people and their organizations, it is impossible to study all facets of people and their organization simultaneously. The general areas of specialization serve as the basis for the structure of this book. The areas of specialization identified for this purpose are: (1) social person, (2) psychological person, (3) economic person, and (4) political person. No one of these areas can be identified as the exclusive domain of any one of the social science subjects taught in college, that is, sociology, anthropology, psychology, political science, economics, and geography. History is included in the social sciences by some colleges and in humanities by others.

The major advantage of specialization is that it enables an individual to develop an expertise necessary to conduct the research needed to expand our knowledge of people and their organization. The major disadvantage of specialization is that it tends to lead to a compartmentalization of knowledge. When this happens, we end up with an explanation of people's political activities and an explanation of their economic activities, social activity, and so forth, but no adequate explanation of the relationship between their economic activities and their political activities, etc.

The relatedness of the different social sciences can easily be discerned when one looks at any real world conflict that is of interest to social scientists. The analysis of the different aspects of this problem requires the expertise of social scientists with different areas of specialization. To what extent is this conflict one of sociology—social class conflict, cultural conflict, group ethnocentrism on both sides, a reflection of the need of develop a new self-image, a study of social movements,

The struggle between California farm interests and the United Farm Workers, led by Cesar Chavez, is an example of social conflict in which economic, political, and psychological factors are interrelated. *(Bruce Anspach/Editorial Photocolor Archives, Inc.)*

and/or a comment on charismatic leadership? The psychologist's special skills are needed to determine to what extent the conflict stems from other problems—rationality versus emotionalism, efforts to overcome inferiority, and/or Anglo and Chicano as psychological types. The skills of the economist are needed to analyze such issues as the consequences of strong unionization, why the economic struggle between the two sides is unusually bitter, how the public might have a vested interest in low wages for farm workers (what happens to the prices of products in the stores if farm workers get higher wages?), and how an economic system can be highly discriminatory even in a democratic society. The political scientist is needed to provide answers to such questions as: To what extent does the situation present a failure of governmental institutions? Has government provided the farm workers with a sense of participation? Are there any legitimate channels of redress for injured parties? Which side has access to the sheriff and courts? Finally, what are the techniques by which powers can be attained by people outside the political system? (Remember the boycotts of California farm products?) Thus, anyone who wishes to fully understand the conflict between the California farm interests and the United Farm Workers must analyze all aspects of the problem and discover how social, psychological, economic, and political factors interact to influence the behavior of the parties involved. A study of all aspects of the problem frequently reveals that behavior which appears irrational at first glance is in fact very rational.

METHODOLOGY OF THE SOCIAL SCIENCES

The method or technique used by a discipline to collect and evaluate knowledge is very important. To a large extent the methodology used determines the types of information which will be collected and of that collected which information will be accepted and which will be rejected. The methodology of the social sciences is the scientific method which is an empirical process. It is based on the philosophic doctrine which asserts that truth or knowledge is found through direct observation.

The nature of the scientific method The importance of the scientific method as a process for gaining knowledge becomes apparent when it is compared to techniques which are rejected by the scientific process. Those rejected include pure logic, revealed knowledge, common sense, and appeal to authority.

The scientific method consists of the following steps:

1. Selection of specific questions or hypotheses for investigation.
2. Design of an investigation or experiment.
3. Collection of information; i.e., conducting the investigation or experiment.
4. Organization and classification of the data.
5. Development of generalizations based on the data.
6. Verification of the results, i.e., checking the data and generalizations.

The adoption of this process as a technique for acquiring knowledge has been one of the major factors which has contributed to the rapid growth in scientific knowledge during the past century.

APPLICATION OF THE SCIENTIFIC METHOD

Prejudice is a problem the social scientist might study using the process previously described. The first step would be to determine the specific aspects of prejudice to be studied and to develop hypotheses. For example, do you want to study racial prejudice, ethnic prejudice, etc., or do you wish to attempt to find out if there are some common elements in all types of prejudices? The problem might be restricted even further for purposes of research to something such as studying how much reduction in prejudice can be found between the college generation and the parental generation. The second and third steps would be to design an experiment or investigation and to carry it out. The difficulties of these two steps when you are dealing with a problem such as prejudice will be discussed in a later section. It is sufficient now to say that this would involve the development of a technique to measure the aspect of prejudice being studied and a system to collect accurate data based on the technique of measurement developed. The fourth step is to organize and classify the data so that it can be analyzed. The types of things which can be done at this stage of the process are determined by the way the second and third steps are carried out. However, for a problem such as prejudice the data would likely be classified by various demographic characteristics such as age, sex, race, and birthplace. This will make it possible to analyze the data in several different ways. Various statistical tests may be run at this stage to provide the investigator with additional information to use when interpreting the data. The fifth step is to look at the data and develop generalizations which are suggested by data. These generalizations might be in the form of statements that some age groups or races seem to show more of the type of prejudice being studied than others. The final step is verification of the results. This involves the rechecking the first five steps to make certain that they have been carried out properly. Whenever possible, the investigation or experiment will be repeated to verify the validity of the results. In any case, the knowledge obtained through the scientific process is never considered final. It is always viewed as tentative and subject to refutation. Obviously, the longer tentative knowledge withstands attempts to refute it, the greater the confidence scientists have in it.

GOALS OF THE SCIENTIFIC PROCESS

The goals of the scientific process are generally classified into three categories: (1) understanding, (2) prediction, and (3) control. Understanding a problem or question implies a comprehension of all the variables which have an important impact on the problem, the relationships of these variables, and the way they interact. This involves discovering the cause-and-effect relationships associated with the problem. Scientists assume that all events can be explained in terms of preexisting relationships and earlier events. This does not mean that the scientists believe that at any given time enough knowledge will exist to explain all events in this manner, but only that all events are explainable in this manner.

Once a problem is understood, it becomes possible to engage in prediction. Prediction is not as accurate in the social sciences as in physical and biological sciences. In a sense prediction in the social sciences is at a stage similar to weather forecasting, i.e., we are able to predict future weather only in terms of probabilities. For example, a typical forecast might be that for a future date that there is a 20 percent chance of rain. This means that in the past when conditions similar to the existing ones were present it rained 20 percent of the time. Prediction in the social sciences is frequently a process of enumerating the possible outcomes. In some instances, it is possible to specify the probability associated with each potential outcome.

The last goal of this scientific process, control, is not as generally accepted in the social sciences as in the biological and physical sciences. The question as to the extent to which there should be control of people and their organization has not yet been resolved. Of course any society controls people, but the problem is one of determining what methods should be used and how extensive the control should be. One of the major difficulties involved in controlling individuals is the determination of how extensive individuals should be controlled for the "good of society." Control should certainly stop short of the type envisioned in Aldous Huxley's *Brave New World* where individuality is obliterated for community ideals—a world in which human beings are produced in test tubes and graded according to intelligence.

The scientist is supposed to seek knowledge without consideration of the moral implications of the knowledge. Science is often viewed as "amoral," i.e., the scientist does not view his work as good or bad from an ethical point of view. This approach works quite satisfactorily in the area of "pure" science which is primarily concerned with understanding and prediction. However, it is not very satisfactory in "applied" science which emphasizes control. This problem will be discussed later in this chapter.

MEASUREMENT AND EXPERIMENTATION IN THE SOCIAL SCIENCES

There are two aspects of the scientific method that present difficulties when it is applied to the social sciences. These are measurement and experimentation. The variables with which the social scientist works are frequently difficult to quantify, i.e., assign numerical value to.

Use of samples For instance, suppose an investigator wanted to measure people's attitudes concerning trial marriages. First it would be necessary to specify the population whose attitudes were to be measured. The term *population* is used in scientific investigations to refer to all the items or people in the group being studied. If the population is a large one, it will likely not be possible to directly include all the items in the population in the investigation, and the investigator will have to rely on a sample. When all the items or people in the population are directly used in the investigation, we say that we are using census data, and it is possible to derive population characteristics directly from this data. However, if a sample is properly drawn, it is possible to make reliable estimates of the characteristics of the population from the sample. A properly drawn sample will accurately represent the characteristics of the population being studied.

Problem of measurement The next step is to design a technique to measure the population's attitude toward trial marriages. Additional complications arise at this stage because it will be necessary to specify just what is meant by the concept of a trial marriage. It is likely that there are many people who would favor some forms of trial marriage and oppose others. Also, it will be necessary to determine the types of responses that will be accepted. Should there be two responses (favor or opposed) permitted or should there be a series of alternative responses accepted (e.g., strongly opposed, moderately opposed, neutral, etc.)? The difficulty of this aspect of measurement is frequently present even in situations where the values of the variables are expressed in numerical values. A good example of this is the unemployment rate, a variable whose value is measured regularly. What does it mean when someone says that the unemployment rate is 6 percent? To an economist it immediately implies that 6 percent of the labor force is unemployed. The *labor force* is defined as those people working in the market or actively seeking work in the market. Thus, large segments of the population such as housewives and students are excluded from the labor force. There are two ways to become unemployed. One way is for an individual to lose the job at which he is currently employed, and the other is for someone not currently in the labor force to start looking for a job. On the other hand, there are two ways to cease to be unemployed. One way is to find employment, and the other is to quit looking for a job, which means you have dropped out of the labor force and therefore are no longer counted as a part of the unemployed. This is not the end of the problem. There is also the question of deciding how much an individual has to be working before he is considered employed. A person is considered to be employed if he is working fifteen hours a week or more. People are also considered employed who have jobs but were off because of vacation, illness, labor disputes, bad weather, and various other reasons. There is frequently a serious danger of poor communication when concepts such as unemployment are used without fully understanding their meaning.

Measurement in the social sciences is also more complicated than in areas such as chemistry because of the lack of constancy in the variables with which one works from one time period to another and from one group (or place) to another. Once a chemist has isolated an element, the chemist can assume with a high degree of certainty that it is basically the same today as it was a hundred years ago and that it will be the same for some time to come. Also, the chemist can assume that the element is the same in the United States as in China. Social scientists cannot make such assumptions. The social scientist must discover similarities when and where they exist, but he must be cautious when drawing conclusions from the existence of such similarities.

Difficulty of experimentation Experimentation also poses difficulties for the social scientist because experimentation involves exercising control over the variables with which the experimenter is working. Thus it is almost impossible to control people and their organizations, which is the focus of study of the social sciences. Because of the inability to control people and their organizations for purposes of experimentation, alternative techniques have been developed for studying the potential impact of the manipulation of different variables on humans and/or their organization.

Lower animals One such technique involves the use of lower animals such as rats, dogs, cats, and so forth, in the experimental situation. This technique has been used extensively by psychologists. In fact, much of our current knowledge of human behavior has resulted directly or indirectly from insights gained from experimental situations using lower animals.

The intellectual experiment Another technique that has been developed is often referred to as the intellectual experiment. The intellectual experiment involves the use of abstract models. With this approach, a real-world problem in which the social scientist is interested is selected, and a model is abstracted from this problem. The model is a simplification of the real world problem. However, it is necessary to include all the important variables which influence the problem in the model, and the relationships of these variables must be accurately represented. Once the model is constructed, it is possible to manipulate the variables in the

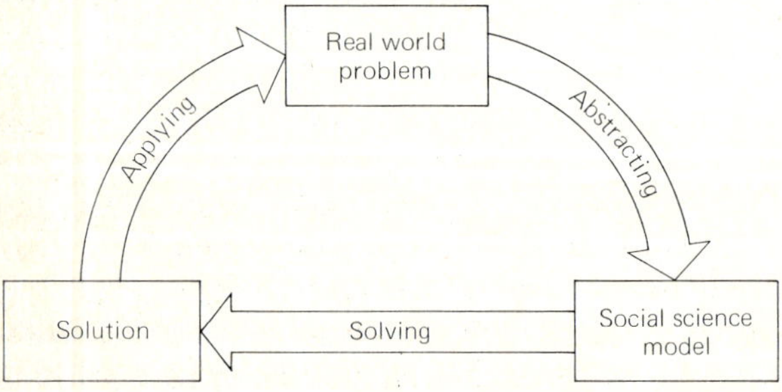

Figure 1-1 The intellectual experiment.

model and then to solve the model and apply the solution to the real world problem. This process is represented in Figure 1-1 below:

The above approach can be used to analyze a problem such as the relationship between population-growth rate and the rate of consumption of natural resources. To do this, a model would be constructed which shows the relationship between population growth and the rate or use of natural resources. With the use of estimates of the availability of different natural resources, this model can be used to generate estimates of how long the available natural resources can support different combinations of resource consumption and population growth. Such experimentation provides policy makers with information they need for planning.

In order for the intellectual experiment to be of value, it is crucial that the model be abstracted accurately. The model is, in fact, a theoretical explanation of the existing relationships in the real world. The models used by social scientists range from simple classification models to highly complex mathematical ones designed to explain something as complex as the operation of the U.S. economy. This technique of experimentation is used most extensively by economists. An example of the potential benefits of this approach can be seen by examining the uses of a model of the United States economy. If the model has been constructed properly. it is possible to predict in advance the effect that a reduction in individual income taxes will have on such things as savings, individual expenditures, the purchase of various categories of goods and services, and government tax revenue.

Human responses to experimentation Even when the social scientist is able to conduct experiments directly on the population being studied, he still faces problems that are difficult to overcome. First of all, complete control of the experimental situation is never possible. For instance, we know that identical twins raised in the same home have different environmental experiences. Also, the social scientist is faced with a situation in which the things he is working with (people and their organizations) respond to all types of alterations in their environment. Thus, people who are involved in an experiment respond not only to manipulation by the experimenter or the variables being studied, but also to the very fact that they are being studied. It is frequently difficult to separate the effect on responses associated with the manipulation of the variables being studied from the effect on responses which result from the fact that the people are being studied.

One type of response of people to being studied is often referred to as the Hawthorne effect.[1] This effect is so named because it was discovered in an experiment being conducted at Hawthorne Works of the Western Electric Company in the 1930s. The company was experimenting with different variables in the work environment of employees who assembled electrical relays. Higher pay and shorter hours led to increased output by the workers. The investigators also found that improved lighting and ventilation, rest breaks, and refreshment periods all tended to increase the level of output of the workers. Each time the investigators manipulated a different variable, the production of the workers tended to increase. In fact, when the original work conditions were restored, the output of the workers still continued to improve. The investigators concluded that much of the change in output of the workers was a result of improved morale or feeling of importance of the workers because the company was showing an interest in them. Today, improvement in performance by individuals as a result of special attention is often referred to as the Hawthorne effect.

Social scientists frequently use both the intellectual experiment and real experimentation when studying a problem. This is currently the situation in which efforts are being made to determine the impact of a guaranteed annual income for families. A guaranteed annual income would involve having the government provide all families whose incomes are below a specified level with a large enough subsidy to raise their income to the guaranteed level. For instance, if the guaranteed level was

Like all scientists, social science investigators employ the scientific method of testing their questions about human functioning and in conducting their experiments. *(Vika Zahn/ Medical World News)*

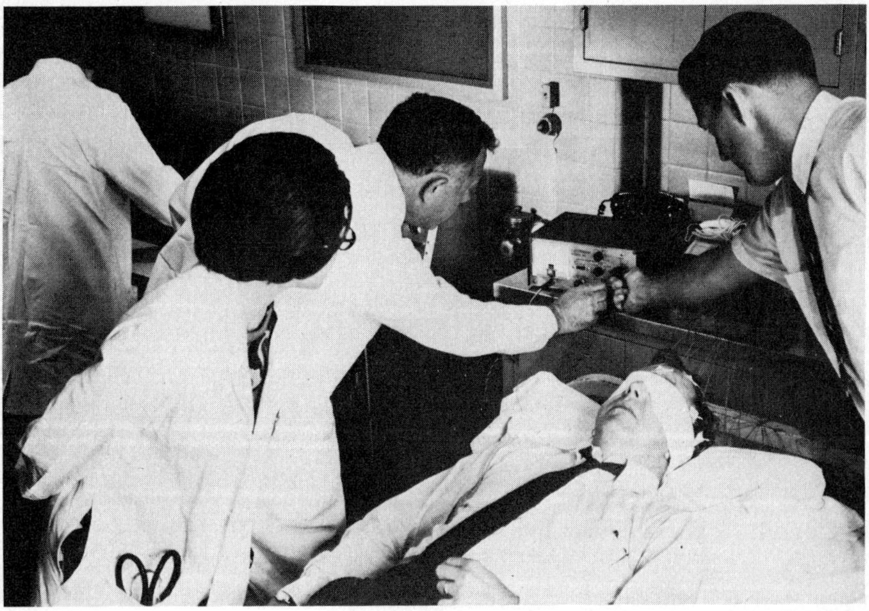

$5,000 per year, a family with an income of $3,000 would be given an income subsidy of $2,000. The two major aspects of interest to those studying this problem are the impact that such a program will have on the amount of labor that the recipients of the subsidies will supply in the market, and how effectively the additional income will be used by those who would receive additional income under such a program. In addition to these two aspects, the investigators are interested in determining the impact that such a program would have on those marginal individuals whose incomes are just above the guaranteed level. However, most of the studies that have been conducted and which are currently being conducted do not attempt to measure the effects associated with this third aspect of the problem.

Several quantitative models have been developed to attempt to determine the impact of a guaranteed annual income. The effects of such a program will be determined in large part by the technical aspects of the program; e.g., will the recipients receive the subsidy with no strings attached, or will they be required to participate in some type of training program or public employment project? Needless to say, alternative methods of providing the guaranteed income should be considered in order to determine the best program.

In addition to the theoretical attempts to explain impact of a guaranteed annual income, a major experiment has been conducted by the Institute for Research on Poverty at the University of Wisconsin. The results of this study, the New Jersey–Pennsylvania Graduated Incentive Experiment, which was designed to measure the amount of labor supplied by households given a guaranteed annual income, are not what popular belief would have predicted. This experiment, which took place from 1968 to 1972, involved some 1,350 experimental and control families in four cities (Trenton, Paterson–Passaic, and Jersey City, New Jersey; and Scranton, Pennsylvania) found that, overall, the labor supply response to the various negative income tax plans was small. There was no negative effect on the amount of labor supplied by black families. In fact, the labor supplies by black husbands increased. There were small negative effects for white and Spanish-speaking families. These negative effects consisted of a reduction in the number of hours of labor supplied by white male heads, an increase in the unemployment rate of Spanish-speaking male heads, and a large relative reduction in the labor force participation of white wives.[2] Those conducting this experiment caution that conclusions drawn from their results must be viewed as tentative. However, the results are in direct contradiction to the belief held by many people that a guaranteed income would lead to dramatic reductions in the labor supplied by households receiving the guaranteed income.

CHANGE AND THE SOCIAL SCIENCES

Change is one of the most important elements with which the social scientist is concerned. Pragmatism, an indigenous American philosophy, asserts that change is an essential part of reality and that reality is constituted of mass interaction of people with their environment. From the point of view of pragmatism, people create their own reality to the extent that they affect their environment and influence the way that they interact with it. As long as change is relatively slow, people are able to make the adjustments in their views as to the nature of reality which are dictated by the change without any serious disruptions. However, as the rate of change accelerates, as it has during the past century, the adjustment process is complicated. In the twentieth century, more changes which effect humanity's existence have taken place than occurred during its entire previous existence. As a result of the rapid rate of change, many parents and children frequently find it difficult to carry on effective communication today because they encountered radically different social and physical environments during their formative years. This effect has been labeled the "generation gap."

Social scientists are interested in understanding the forces which generate change and predicting the direction of change and its effect on people and their organization. In addition, there is the problem of determining whether or not efforts should be made to control the course of change. The following section is devoted to a discussion of technology, a factor to which much of the change that has occurred in the United States during the twentieth century is attributable.

TECHNOLOGY

Why has the role of government in the United States changed so drastically in the twentieth century? What caused the feudal system of Europe to collapse? What force is so strong that it can cause people to set aside or radically alter values which they have held for centuries? The answer to such diverse questions as these must include technology as a major explanatory variable. Technology is the application of knowledge by people in order to perform some task they want done.

Technology as a cause of change Breakthroughs in technology frequently lead to dramatic changes in people's existence. It was the development of more efficient production techniques in agriculture that created the necessary food supply to permit part of the people to engage in specialized tasks which contributed to the improvement in humanity's existence. In fact, historians often identify the development of a steady food supply as the necessary first step in the development of a civilization.

The importance of the use of the wheel in transportation is well known. Also, the importance of such things as the printing press, the longbow, gunpowder, and navigation instruments to humanity's development has been well documented by historians. However, technological change is not simply a series of inventions, but rather it is a process which is continually occurring. The rate of change of technology has been increasing at an accelerating rate. The nature of humanity's existence tends to change in accordance with the rate of technological change. The industrial revolution is often identified as the period during which the current rapid rate of technological change started. The industrial revolution occurred in the United States in the middle part of the nineteenth century. It was a technological revolution during which developments in techniques of economic production greatly increased people's potential productivity. Since the industrial revolution, enormous changes in transportation and communication systems have occurred as a direct result of technological developments, and these have greatly influenced people and their organization. Examples of technological developments during the twentieth century which have dramatically altered the nature of society are: the auto, radio, nuclear warfare, television, space travel, and developments in medical care such as the ability to transplant human organs.

In order to demonstrate the scope of the impact of technological change, one has only to examine the effects that the adoption of new techniques of production during the industrial revolution has had in the United States. The production techniques associated with the industrial revolution required a cheap method of transportation, a cheap source of power, and a readily available labor force. The first two of these needs determined the location of production facilities, and the latter meant that there would have to be large concentrations of people living near the production sites. An additional concentration of people near the production site was required to supply those engaged in industrial production of goods and services.

Throughout the nineteenth and the first part of the twentieth century, the migration into the city continued at a rapid rate. Technological developments during this period required even larger concentrations of people. Large industries developed which supplied other industries. Production was no longer characterized by individual production units, but rather by interdependent units which compromised an industrial complex. The need for a cheap source of power and cheap method of transportation dictated that these industrial complexes would be geographically concentrated. Thus, the new technology provided the impetus for the urbanization of United States society which has had a profound influence on nearly every aspect of our lives.

Good or bad? Changes in technology were largely responsible for the development of cities, and it is developments in technology that are in large part responsible for the deterioration of the cities which is occurring in the United States today. That is, there have been developments in technology which make it possible to decentralize many of the activities that had been earlier concentrated because of technological needs. New developments in technology now make it possible to take power to the factories, rather than having to build factories near the source of power. In addition, the development of the trucking industry has made it possible to locate production facilities in geographic areas far removed from either supplies or markets. However, an even more important technological factor has been the development of the automobile and the accompanying highway system which makes it possible for workers to move out of the city. Technology has also shortened the work day and the work week, which time-wise makes the location of the residence outside the central city feasible.

A second factor which tends to support the decentralization made possible by the technological development is the rise in real income. The higher level of real income makes it possible for people to support the higher costs associated with the movement out of the central city. We can now afford the expensive highway system and high costs of operating automobiles which accompany the pattern of living associated with the urban areas.

The other major decentralization force is the movement out of the central city of those engaged in providing services, along with those to whom they are providing the services. Just as the food stores, clothing stores, etc., moved in, they are moving out as the workers are moving out.

Technology has not really been the cause of the movement out of the central cities. It has only made it possible to escape from the disadvantages which were associated with the growth of industrial cities. From the very early days of the industrial city there were mixed feelings about the city as a place to consume. The concentration of large numbers of people create large markets, which make it possible to provide many goods and services at relatively low costs, many of which it might not have been economically feasible to otherwise provide. These include such things as museums, symphony orchestras, and utilities. However, there are many disadvantages to consuming in the city. There is a reduction in the spacial area where people live, which lowers the satisfaction associated with many activities and the consumption of many goods. Housing is an example of a good that yields a greater utility when consumed in a spacious setting. In addition, the satisfaction associated with city consumption is less because of the existence of external diseconomies from production. The production process has tended to pollute the environment, which creates a problem when consumption must take place in the same geographic area. The classic example of this is the one in which the housewife hangs her clothes out to dry on the line and the polluted air gets them dirty again before they can dry. Perhaps a less obvious but more important example is larger medical bills which result from living in a polluted environment.

Until recently in the United States technology has been viewed as humanity's benefactor. Although there have always been some people who bemoaned the loss of the "good old days," there has been a general belief that technological change represented progress and that progress was good. In fact, in the United States, progress and technological change have generally been viewed as being synonomous. However, in the last few years, there has been an increasing number of people who have been questioning this concept of progress. Ecologists have pointed out that we have developed a pattern of living in the United States that is not sustainable on a world-wide basis given the resource stock of the earth and the constraints of the ecological (environmental) system within which we live. For example, if the rest of the world developed its economies in such a way that it requires as many resources to function as are required by the United States economy, it would require 75 times as much iron, 100 times as much copper, 200 times as much lead, 75 times as much zinc, and 250 as much tin as is currently being used in world production.

Some people react to the developments which are associated with modern technology by condemning technology. This is a naive approach to the problems associated with technology. Technology is neither good nor bad; it is neutral. It is the way people use the available technology that determines its impact. Thus, the problem is to develop techniques to control the use of technology so that it will provide the greatest possible benefit to humankind. This implies controlling the types of social change which can occur to the extent that change is effected by technological change. The question of controlling people and their organizations is a topic of the next section in this chapter.

VALUE JUDGMENTS AND THE SOCIAL SCIENTIST

Even though the scientific method emphasizes that scientific knowledge should be sought without consideration of the moral implications of the knowledge, the scientist cannot avoid involvement with moral considerations. There are times when the scientist is forced to make decisions which are based on value judgments. In order to differentiate between those aspects of the work of the social scientist that involve value judgments and those that do not, the terms *positive* and *normative* are used. Positive refers to situations in which the social scientist is attempting to understand and/or make predictions related to existing phenomena. The normative aspects refer to occasions when the scientist makes a decision that one thing is preferable to another.

Positive versus normative It is frequently necessary for social scientists to deal with both positive and normative considerations in their work. However when social scientists study a problem, it is very important that they avoid becoming so involved with the normative aspects of the problem that they lose their ability to see issues as they are. A common error made when normative issues interfere with a person's ability to positively analyze problems is the overemphasis of those aspects of the problems which tend to support one's personal views. This must be avoided because overemphasizing certain aspects of a problem can lead to a distortion of the real issues associated with the problem.

Poverty is an example of a problem that a social scientist might study which would probably involve both positive and normative considerations. When social scientists study the nature of poverty and the impact that it has on the poor and the rest of society, they are dealing with the positive aspect of the problem. They are, in fact, simply attempting to understand poverty as it is and possibly to predict the impact that the current situation will have on the future if no changes are made in the existing situation. However, if the social scientists suggest that poverty is bad and that something should be done to alleviate it, they then attempt to deal with the normative aspect of the problem. For example, they might suggest that it is the responsibility of the government to remove poverty. When they do this, they are not acting as social scientists but as informed citizens. However, it is the function of social scientists *as* social scientists to suggest possible ways of solving existing problems.

Normative considerations are necessarily involved when decisions are made to control something. The basic normative assumption associated with a decision to control something is that things will be better off with control than without it. In many situations today, we are faced with the decision of whether to impose deliberate limitations or to rely on automatic checks which arise out of the constraints imposed by existing conditions. The issue involved, of course, is whether the overall results which would be associated with deliberate checks are preferable to those which would be associated with automatic checks. Such an evaluation frequently involves value judgments. The treaty signed in 1972 which banned the development and use of bacteria warfare is an example of a world-wide agreement to deliberately check an activity that was deemed undesirable. The automatic check in this instance could well have been the destruction of mankind or at least millions of people. For this same reason it is argued that similar restrictions should be placed on the development and use of nuclear weapons. Decisions to deliberately restrict other types of activities such as the production and use of automobiles, the way land and water are utilized, etc., are more difficult to support because automatic checks are not so dramatic. Those who oppose such restrictions frequently argue that the very act of controlling the activities is potentially more harmful than the results associated with the automatic checks.

Controlling change The rapid growth of knowledge in the twentieth century has provided humankind with an ability to exercise controls over its environment and perform feats that would have seemed like fiction a generation ago. The knowledge which has been acquired provides great potential, if used properly, for helping people to solve many of the problems that have plagued them all during their existence on this planet; or if used improperly it could conceivably terminate their existence here. Thus, it is crucial that we exercise caution in the application of the power that has resulted from the knowledge accumulated during the last century.

The social scientist has an important role to play in determining how best to use the powers acquired from scientific developments because the major criterion, in determining how to apply scientific knowledge or whether or not to even use it, "should be" the impact that its use will have on people and their organization. One of the difficulties associated with determining the impact of many scientific and technological developments is to distinguish between short-run effects and long-run effects. For example, much has been written about the impact of developments in mass communication, especially television, on American society. We know that television has greatly influenced family life, political campaigns, etc., but we are just now beginning to be able to evaluate the long-run impact of television on people's attitudes and behavior. This is because television did not really become widespread in the United States until the 1950s, so the first "full television generation" is just reaching maturity. Even now it is difficult to determine the specific impact of television, because it is only one of many variables in the environment which have contributed toward the development of people's attitudes and behavior.

In summary, the question of controlling the course of change is really a question of whether to rely on automatic checks which result from existing social organization or to attempt to deliberately guide the course of change. Should we attempt to directly regulate the way land is used in the United States, or should we rely on the forces currently operative in dictating land use on the assumption that the latter will lead to a more preferable pattern of land utilization than could be achieved by direct controls? Historically, in the United States we have tended to assume that it was usually better to rely on the forces operative within the existing societal structure to make such decisions. This approach has been taken in the past on the assumption that regulation was a form of restricting individual freedom, and it has always been an American idea that individual freedom should be restricted as little as possible.

However, it is important to recognize that in many instances the proper use of regulation can result in greater freedom. For example, imagine how difficult and dangerous it would be to drive in the United States if the traffic was not regulated. It is quite possible that uncontrolled development and use of technology could turn the world into a place in which individual freedom has little meaning.

ERRORS IN REASONING

Many of the misunderstandings about social phenomena can be traced, either directly or indirectly, to certain errors in reasoning. Most of these errors fall into one of five general categories. The five are: (1) generalizing from too small and/or unrepresentative sample, (2) use of false analogies, (3) fallacies of composition, (4) improper use of syllogistic reasoning, or (5) *post hoc ergo propter hoc,* i.e., the incorrect assumption that an event was necessarily caused by an event which preceded it.

Generalization from too small or unrepresentative sample is perhaps the most common mistake made by people in their efforts to explain things. The most common example of this is the individual who attempts to explain everything in terms of personal experiences. There are also problems associated with relying on those with whom we have direct contact because they are rarely representative of the population generally.

The *false analogy* error results when one attempts to prove something by citing a similar (analogous) situation or problem. All too often the analogous situation or problem is not similar enough to the one under consideration to make the comparison relevant. The danger of the false analogy increases the greater the time span which separates the two things being compared. This results because institutional organization changes over time, and this alters the nature of cause and effect relationships. For example, the role of the stock market in the United States economy is very different today than before the 1930s. This became very obvious in 1969–1970 when there was a drastic drop in the value of securities traded in the stock market without any significant effect on the real economy. This would have been almost impossible before the 1930s. However, due to changes in institutional organization, today it is possible to have large fluctuations in the prices securities in the stock market without any major effects on the real economy. This means that if one is trying to understand the role of the stock market in the United States economy today, it is necessary to be very careful when comparing the current role with anything that existed before the 1930s.

The *fallacy of composition* results when one generalizes about the whole from its parts because what is true of the parts is not necessarily true of the whole. From Benjamin Franklin ("A penny saved is a penny earned"), we know of the merits of an individual's saving. But if all individuals as a group attempt to save too much, there will be fewer goods and services produced and made available for sale than if less saving had been attempted. As a matter of fact, it is impossible for an economy as a whole to save. If people stop buying the goods and services which are being produced (in order to save), the goods and services will not be saved; rather they will not be produced. This results because individual saving represents the refraining from exercising claims the individual has against current output. Since, then, all goods and services currently being produced will not be purchased by those who have acquired claims against them, producers will reduce their output. Thus, if individual saving occurs, it will be necessary to get some individuals to purchase more goods and services than those against which they are currently acquiring claims. The transfer of current claims from one individual to another is carried out in part through financial institutions. (In this reference, "individual" may be a business or government.) If someone does not exercise the claims against current output that someone else is refraining from exercising, the output of the economy will be reduced because the goods and services will not be produced.

The fourth type of error in reasoning, *the improper use of syllogistic reasoning,* results when incorrect conclusions are drawn from two premises (a major and minor premise) that are both correct. Below is an example of an improper use of syllogistic proof:

(Major premise): All cats have tails.
(Minor premise): Albert has a tail.
(Conclusion) Therefore, Albert is a cat.

Here, the conclusion is not necessarily correct even though both the major and minor premises are correct. Although Albert has a characteristic which all cats have, he is not necessarily a cat because cats are not

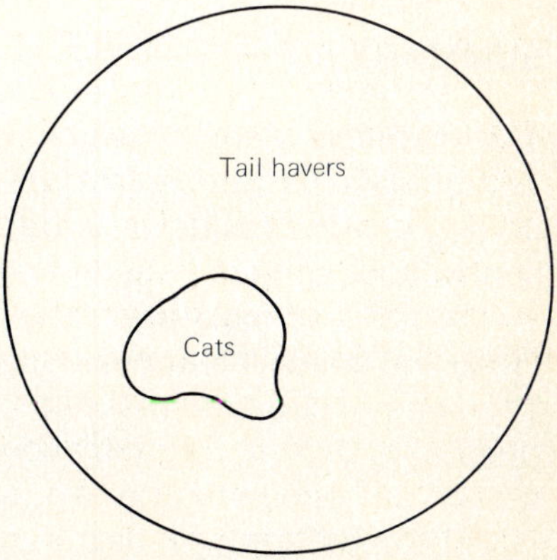

Figure 1-2 Fallacy of the undistributed middle.

the only animals which possess this characteristic. Technically, this error is called the "fallacy of the undistributed middle." The major premise provides us information about only one group of "tail havers;" it does not, however, give us information about the entire class of things which possess tails. As is shown in Figure 1-2, we know that there is a general class of things which have tails and that cats are a subclass of this general class. We also know that Albert is in the general class, but we cannot be certain that he is in the subclass. Here is an example of improper use of syllogistic reasoning that your social science teacher might take:

(Major premise):	Some employees of the university are geniuses.
(Minor premise):	The social science teachers are all employees of the university.
(Conclusion):	Some social science teachers are geniuses.

Post hoc ergo propter hoc The error in reasoning results because people have a tendency to assign a causal relationship when two things occur together. For example, many people attributed the Depression of the 1930s to Herbert Hoover because he was President when the Depression was precipitated by the crash of the stock market in 1929. Today few historians infer any causal relationship between the Depression of the 1930s and actions of Hoover.

There is also a tendency to assign a causal relationship between events which occur together in several different situations because statistical techniques can be used to "prove" a statistical correlation between events of this type–and there is a very strong temptation to assume some type of causal relationship between things which are statistically correlated. The existence of a statistical relationship, however, does not necessarily imply a causal relationship. Strong statistical relationships have been found to exist between such things as the length of women's skirts and movement of prices in the stock market.

SUMMARY

The common element which is found in all the diverse topics of social science is people and/or their organization. Social scientists are particularly interested in understanding the impact of social organization without seriously disrupting societal organization.

Social scientists are interested in the physical environment only to the extent that it influences people's social organization and/or behavior. The general structure of this book is based on four overlapping facets of people and their organization: (1) social person, (2) psychological person, (3) economic person, and (4) political person.

The methodology of the social sciences is the scientific method which is based on the philosophic doctrine which asserts that knowledge is found through direct observation. The goals of the scientific process are: (1) understanding, (2) prediction, and (3) control. The latter raises some rather serious ethical questions for social scientists. Measurement and experimentation are two aspects of the scientific method which pose problems for social scientists. The difficulties of measurement stem from problems of specifically defining the thing to be measured in a form which can be quantified and due to the absence of constancy in the variables which social scientists study from one time period to another and from one group of people to another. Experimentation presents difficulties because of the need to control the variables being studied, i.e., people and their organization. To overcome this problem, social scientists frequently use lower animals in their experiments or rely on the intellectual experiment which involves the use of abstract models. Experimentation is also complicated by the presence of the Hawthorne effect.

Change is one of the most important things with which social scientists are concerned. The rapid rate of change in the twentieth century has presented serious adjustment problems for people and their organization. A large part of the change in the twentieth century is attributable to changes in technology which have occurred during this century. The impact of technological developments on the pattern of residence and the accompanying changes in life styles is a dramatic example of the effect of technological change on people. Some people have responded very negatively to technology because of some of the undesirable effects that have been associated with it. However, technology is neither good nor bad per se, it is the way people use it that determines its impact.

The scientific method frequently emphasizes that scientific knowledge should be considered amoral, i.e., it should be viewed as a process of discovering how things are without taking on any moral connotations. This is fine up to a point; but once the knowledge is discovered and put to use, it can no longer be classified as morally neutral. The application of scientific knowledge implies an attempt to change something which in turn implies that someone has decided that something "should" be different than it is currently. Such decisions obviously involve value judgments. In order to differentiate between those aspects of the social scientist's work that involve value judgments and those that do not, the terms positive and normative are used. The latter implies that value judgments are involved.

Misunderstandings about social phenomena frequently result because of certain errors in reasoning. These errors fall into five general categories: (1) generalizing from too small and/or unrepresentative sample, (2) use of false analogies, (3) fallacies of composition, (4) improper use of syllogistic reasoning, and (5) the assumption that when one event follows another the second is necessarily caused by the first.

REVIEW QUESTIONS

1. What is the common element of the diverse topics which are the concern of social scientists?
2. What is it that social scientists are attempting to discover in their work?
3. How do social scientists view the role of the physical environment?
4. What is the advantage of specialization in the social sciences?
5. What is the methodology of social science? Describe the process associated with this methodology.
6. Discuss the three general goals of the scientific process. Which one of these goals is somewhat controversial? Discuss.
7. How does the problem of measurement complicate the use of the scientific method in social science?
8. Why does experimentation pose problems for social scientists? What two techniques do social scientists use to overcome these problems?
9. Describe and evaluate the intellectual experiment.
10. What is pragmatism?
11. How does the rate of change effect pcoplc and their organization?
12. What effects does technology have on people and their organization? Give examples.
13. How are many people reacting to technology today? Are their reactions justified? Explain.
14. Distinguish between the positive and normative aspects of the work of social scientists. Give examples of each.
15. Why is the question of controlling the course of change essentially a normative one?
16. What are the five errors in reasoning which frequently lead to misunderstandings about social phenomena? Briefly define and give examples of each.

款
會
館菜
Louie's
FINE CUIS
49
MILE

PART ONE
SOCIOLOGY

In the three chapters which follow, the general area of sociology will be covered. An attempt will be made in these chapters not only to expose the readers to a social science discipline, but to raise their awareness of the number and severity of the problems in our society.

Sociologists study the origin and evolution of society and thus the study of how and why societies develop has long been a focal point. This is an interest jointly held with anthropologists. As a society grows and develops, sociologists are concerned about the way social classes develop, how certain social institutions such as education evolve, and the mechanisms utilized by the society to transmit its culture to succeeding generations. Sociologists also concern themselves with how present-day societies modernize themselves and the entire process of social change.

In Chapter 2, an overview of sociology will be presented. At the outset the general endeavor of sociology will be examined. This will be followed by an exploration of the most basic of social processes, socialization. *Socialization* is, for the sociologist, the means by which a society passes on its values to the new generation. More importantly, the socialization process is instrumental in the development of personality. As we shall see, a variety of factors enters into socialization and, hence, there are a number of ways by which a society may fail to impart its values into its new members.

The introduction to Chapter 3 deals with social change and social movements. We know from casual observation that there are forces at work which seek change just as counterforces attempt to retard change. Most of us recognize that many changes are called for in our society, but we are often in disagreement about the direction of change. Shall we go forward into a great tomorrow, or shall we go backward to the "good old days"? In fact, the answer to this question will not be provided in Chapter 3, but hopefully the student will come away with a better understanding of the process.

In the remainder of Chapter 3 some of the problems confronting our society will be examined. Specifically, the problems of the family, women, and our growing population will be reviewed. Some lay people and professionals alike have predicted the demise of the family as a viable institution in our society. There certainly are indications that the family as it presently constituted is having difficulties. Some societies have developed alternate forms of child rearing because of their social needs. It may well be that some alternate forms of family structure will need to be considered for our society as well as new approaches to child rearing.

A part of the family problem is the role of women in our society. Women have been discriminated against by a male-dominated society since the beginning of our country. While it seems unlikely that this abuse will come to an end immediately, the situation is changing. As women assume their new role as coequals, their traditional role in the family must change. Although no one is ready to say what changes will occur, we can consider the possibilities. Hopefully, sections of Chapter 3 will be helpful in this regard.

At this point in time, the population growth in this country is difficult to forecast, although we do know that certain parts of the rest of the world are experiencing staggering increases. In the last section of Chapter 3 various population projections are examined and their potential impact discussed.

Chapter 4 is in some ways a continuation of Chapter 3. In Chapter 4 the societal problems of work, drugs, crime, and poverty are examined. The position is taken that we will continue to be a working society for the foreseeable future. Many trends in the world of work are examined and their implications discussed.

Drugs are a problem of great concern to our society. Alcoholism is our greatest drug-abuse problem, but the new trends of using barbituates, amphetamines, and the continued use of heroin are receiving considerable attention at this time. Theories of drug abuse are considered in Chapter 4 and the scope of the problem is examined.

The United States has an extremely high crime rate when compared to other countries, such as Canada or England. Sociologists are interested in why this crime rate has developed and possible solutions to the problem. A variety of potential causes and solutions are presented in Chapter 4.

Poverty is an ageless social problem. However, the question is raised repeatedly: "How can we have so much poverty in a land of plenty?" Efforts to solve the poverty problem have been launched from time to time, but without marked success. We know that the impact of poverty upon the person is severe. We cannot, as a society, be self-content with halfway measures to solve the problems of the poor. Yet, as is the case with most social problems, the solutions are not always clear. Hopefully, in the last part of Chapter 4 some sensitivity to the plight of the poor will be developed.

GLOSSARY

aggregate a group of people close together characterized by a random interaction pattern

anomie a state of normlessness; without internalized values

assimilation absorption of the culture and tradition from a smaller group into a larger culture

caste system a social system characterized by no upward mobility

category a number of persons who have characteristics in common but do not have established patterns of communication or interaction

class system a social system

based upon wealth, expertise, power, and social status; this system is characterized by upward mobility

commune a societal or small-group pattern of living characterized by collective ownership and use of property; usually members of a commune hold similar values and are regulated by similar norms

conjugal family husband and wife

custom traditional practice viewed as unwritten law

demography the statistical study of population trends with emphasis upon size and density of population

discrimination an overt act against a person or group presumably because of prejudicial feelings

egalitarian family family characterized by democratic climate

ego the part of the personality which develops out of basic instincts for the purpose of dealing with the real world

estate system a social system characterized by little upward mobility; stratification is primarily based on land holdings

faith belief in the doctrines of a particular religion

folkways societal standards of behavior regarding manners, dress, etiquette, etc

group two or more people who have a feeling of belonging and share common norms and values to which all must adhere

hallucenogens a class of drugs which result in visual, auditory, olfactory, or other sensory distortions

in-group a group to which persons feel they belong and with whom they feel comfortable; opposite of an out-group

institution installation as a societal component of structure

job alienation a state of hopelessness regarding one's job of which symptoms may be extreme boredom and absenteeism

junkie a drug user addicted to heroin

kibbutz a communal form of living developed in Israel

matriarchal family a family in which the mother or other female is the dominant person.

monogamy marriage with one person at a time

mores the implicit or explicit societal standards of behavior pertaining to sexual habits, marital patterns, the treatment of property of others, etc.

narcotic drugs a class of extremely addictive drugs including heroin, morphine, codeine, and other opium derivatives

norms societal standards of behavior

nuclear family family members including husband, wife, and children

patriarchal family family structure dominated by the father

physical dependence certain drugs cause the body to create antibodies. Withdrawal from the drugs produces real physical symptoms in the form of pain and nausea

polyandry marital state characterized by wife with several husbands

polygyny marital state characterized by man with several wives

power ability to control the behavior of others

prejudice an inner feeling against a person or group

primary group groups characterized by a high degree of interpersonal intimacy

proaction a theory of social change that anticipates needs

psychological dependence after continuous use of certain drugs, the individual must have the drug to produce certain types of psychological states such as happiness or contentment

reform social movement a social movement which seeks to make changes within the existing structure

revolutionary social movement a social movement which attempts to bring about change by overthrowing the existing structure

ritual an established form for ceremony; an attempt to show the relationship between doctrine and life

secondary group a group characterized by lack of intimacy; task-oriented

sedative drugs drugs that cause a reduction in anxiety level, drowsiness, and may produce a state of well-being; in street language, these are the "downers"

social differentiation the differences between groups, social positions, or individuals which evolve in the process of social interaction

socialization the process by which the values of a culture are inculcated, norms are taught, roles are learned, etc., resulting in the development of personality

social strata groupings of persons who hold positions of same or similar rank in a society

sociometry the study and measurement of interpersonal relations in groups

stimulants drugs that "pep up" the individual; "uppers" as they are sometimes called may produce high levels of activity and various ecstatic psychological states

subculture a subgroup of a culture that differs in norms, values, customs, or in some other significant manner

superego that part of the personality which develops to provide moral guidelines; this part of the personality is often called the conscience

theology a set of beliefs or doctrines about the nature of God, the nature of reality, and the nature of being

tolerance a bodily state that requires larger and larger dosages of drugs to produce effects

underemployment being employed below one's educational level or below an individual's potential level of functioning

values beliefs or attitudes, intrinsically held, which serve as guides to behavior

white-collar crime nonviolent crimes, often job related, committed by middle-class Americans; another characteristic of these crimes is that they are not pursued as a basic means of earning a living

SOMETHING TO THINK ABOUT

How can sociology be differentiated from the other social sciences?

What is culture? What is a subculture?

What are the different types of groups? What is the function of each?

Is social mobility possible in this country? Why or why not?

What causes social change?

Is the family a viable child rearing institution? Why or why not?

What is the future of the family in the U.S.?

What are your own views of the role of women? Men?

What is "Women's Liberation?" What are its goals? How does it differ from women's rights movements? How is it similar?

What is your stand on abortion? Justify the stand.

Other than earning a living, why do people work?

What are the trends in the area of employment of college graduates? Is there a general picture?

What are the causes of crime in our society? Do you believe that we are living in a criminal society? Why or why not?

Can poverty be eliminated in our society? Why or why not?

Are the poor happy?

FOR FURTHER READING

Sociology is not a field of study which is limited to the textbook. Modern literature abounds with references which will help you broaden and deepen your understanding of the field.

Francois Duchene's *The Endless Crises* is a series of readings which depicts the problems confronting America today and your reading might begin there. Similarily, Alvin Toffler's *Future Shock* may be used as a starting point to sensitize you to the impact of rapid change upon our society. Toffler's premise is that we must adapt to this change. Robert Theobald takes a different view in *An Alternative Future for America II.* He believes that we must change our American system.

The family is the basic sociological unit and even a casual review of current literature reveals that a wide variety of people are concerned about this institution. Louise Howe's *The Future of the Family* illuminates the problems of the family as no short treatment can do. *The Baby Trap* by Ellen Peck discusses the stresses which having children places upon a marriage, and *The Second Wife* by Jean Baer provides insight into an ever-increasing family situation, the second marriage. Robert Rimmer's *The Harrad Experiment* provided a blueprint for many of today's experimental approaches to marriage. Any or all of these will help the reader to understand more completely the situation of the family today.

A companion problem to the family structure is the place of women in our society. Books such as *Sexual Politics* by Kate Millett, *The Silenced Majority* by Kristen Amundsen, and *The Female Eunuch* by Germaine Greer all discuss the plight of women.

Our Criminal Society by Edwin M. Shur will help the student gain a better perspective of the rising crime rate in our country, as can *Violence in America. Getting Busted,* edited by Ross Firestone, gives detailed accounts of what it means to be arrested in this country, and *Outside the Law* by Bruce Jackson is a criminal's report of his own "education".

For a greater appreciation of the American Indian, read Dee Brown's *Bury My Heart at Wounded Knee, The Death of A Great Spirit* by Carl Shorris, or *Disinherited* by Dale Van Every. Similarly, Gunnar Myrdal's *The American Dilemma* or *Manchild in the Promised Land* can help you to understand what it means to grow up black in America. For a look at what white middle-class schools can do to black children, read Herbert Kohl's *36 Children.*

Other readings in your exploration of sociology might include *The Poorhouse State,* a picture of what it means to be on welfare by Richard Elman, or *The Workers* by Kenneth Lasson which looks at the alienation of the blue-collar worker. *Taming Megalopolis,* edited by Wentworth Eldridge, will provide valuable information about the complexities of dealing with cities.

CHAPTER TWO
INTRODUCTION TO SOCIOLOGY

IDEAS AND CONCEPTS

anomie a state of normlessness; without internalized values

culture behavior characteristic of a given society

socialization the process by which the values of a culture are inculcated, norms are taught, roles are learned, etc. resulting in the development of personality

social strata groupings of persons who hold positions of same or similar rank in a society

institution installation as a societal component of structure

Today as never before we are concerned about the structure and fiber of our society. The mass media bombard us with social happenings which to the casual observer must appear to be chaotic. Governmental scandal, unemployment resulting from the energy crisis, the attempt of women to gain equality in our society, and many other current events appear as part of the larger social situation. The question of what these apparently isolated events mean and how they fit into an overall picture is the knotty problem faced by sociologists.

Sociology defined Sociology might simply be defined as the attempt to study and explain these human events, but that would be a gross oversimplification. In fact, defining sociology may well be the most difficult task undertaken in this book.

Rosenberg[1] points out that even now, some hundred years after Auguste Comte founded sociology, it may be premature to rigidly define the boundaries of sociology. However, as Faris[2] so aptly points out, sociology began because of humankind's wish to understand and explain those events which occur in its environment. He goes on to indicate that it is the role of the modern day sociologist to organize the knowledge that it has at hand and to apply systematic tests of the principles that have been developed regarding human interaction. The ideas expounded by Faris are in keeping with the tradition of sociology. Although Comte is known as the "Father of Sociology," Herbert Spencer popularized the idea of studying sociology. Emile Durkheim went one step further and collected data and attempted to analyze social problems using the scientific method. For this reason, Durkheim is often referred to as the first true sociologist.

Sociology can roughly be defined as the scientific study of human interaction. The sociologist wants to know what influence is exerted by two or more people upon the various groups to which they belong and, conversely, the influence of the group upon the behavior of the individual. Most sociologists do not believe that it is possible to explain human functioning solely by studying the individual. Rather, as Faris[3] points out, the search for causation of behavior must also focus on a human culture, the organization within that culture, and how these impinge upon people. Only by understanding the individual and the way he or she interacts with various groups can meaningful principles about the functioning of people be derived: this is the stance of the sociologist.

Sociology contrasted to other social sciences Sociology can be quite neatly distinguished from the other social sciences. For example, history is the study of unique human events. A historian may write about the great wars in history. The historian will, however, report the battles, the people involved, the dates, and the times, even some of the interaction. However, the sociologist is interested in studying those factors which cause war to recur in our society—not in the specifics of the events themselves. The sociologist may very well examine the societal structure at the time which wars occur, the nature of the government, and the types of people in power at the time of war, but in this study the sociologist will attempt to determine those things—those generalized factors—which can be used to explain the events. Economics, another social science, places its focus upon business cycles and upon the things which are produced, exchanged, and consumed. In essence, economics takes a very narrow look at human interaction. Sociologists, on the other hand, take a very broad view and the economics of society are but one of the many factors which they examine. Similarly, political science looks at the functions of power and authority within a society. Although a sociologist would be interested in the idea of power and authority, this would be simply one of the factors which would be examined. Psychologists are concerned with studying the individual. Sociologists, as was indicated earlier, concentrate more on groups and organizations and their impact upon the individual.

Anthropology is undoubtedly the social science most closely related to sociology. The anthropologist focuses primarily upon developing societies and very often upon primitive societies. Sociologists deal with modern societies and try to derive laws which will enable them to make predictions about their functioning. To a very large degree, sociology contains components of all of the other social sciences, but like other social sciences it has its own tools, approaches, and to a very large extent its own subject matter areas.

Divisions of sociology Sociology as a discipline has subdivided itself into several areas, each of which will be considered to some degree in this and the following chapter. A major subdivision of sociology examines the socialization of the individual. Sociologists who specialize in this area are concerned about what society does to the individual. For example, some questions posed by sociologists in this area are: What is the impact of sociology upon the personality of the individual? How are sex roles determined? How does the individual acquire values? And, how do the *mores* of the society affect the overall functioning of the individual?

A second broad division of sociology deals with collective behavior. As the name indicates, this area is concerned primarily with the organizations and the social groups within society. The area of collective behavior focuses upon the rise of new societies and new social units and seeks to explain why these things come into being. The whole area of social movements comes into consideration in the study of collective behavior. A third area, social institutions, is a natural outgrowth of collective behavior because most social movements terminate in the establishment of institutions. For example, our society's concern about the education of its members has resulted in the establishment of public and private schools and with the founding of institutions of higher learning. Other social institutions are the family and the church. Government can also be viewed as a social institution.

Race and culture is also a major division of sociology. Sociologists in this area are concerned about the impact of factors such as race which have subdivided people and which has an impact upon their functioning. Culture can be defined as a set of values or ways of behaving that are inherent in a society and are transmitted to new members of that society. A value is presumed to be an internalized causal agent of behavior in sociological thought, although Blake and Davis[4] point out that this may not always be the case. An individual may value education for example, but this may not necessarily dictate that this person will pursue self-education or foster it in the family. Most individuals in our society value the preservation of human lives, yet this value does not stop us from killing others during wartime nor does it stop us from recklessly obliterating thousands of people each year on American highways. Therefore, it may be more useful to think of *norms,* or standards of behavior, when looking at cultural differences. Culture is studied as a means of examining how a society develops and controls itself.

Human ecology, another division of sociology, deals with people in their physical setting. Human ecology is becoming a major concern to members of our society. We are increasingly disturbed at this time with the growth of population, not only in this country but in the world. We are also concerned about humankind's pollution of its environment and the impact that this will make upon its functioning, not only at this time but in the future. The rush to our cities has made a vast impact on our society. Sociologists are concerned about problems raised by the increased density of population in such centers such as New York and Los Angeles. Do people function differently when they are crowded together, when most of their history has been such that they did not live in close proximity to other people? The whole area of human cooperation is of interest to the sociologist who studies human ecology. However, the sociologist may focus more on the physical factors which lead to this cooperation and less on the human components of this interaction.

Finally, a major branch of sociology has to do with the entire field of social problems. This area is sometimes called applied sociology. A sociologist whose primary interest is applied sociology is concerned with methods by which sociological data can be utilized to find practical solutions to current social problems. A sociologist might, for example, focus attention upon the problem of school integration and how it can be resolved with a minimum of conflict. An applied sociologist might also be interested in how we can overcome the boredom inherent in much of the work in our society. Practical solutions are also sought to situations such as overcrowding in our cities, overpopulation, high suicide rates in certain populations, and social problems such as crime and delinquency.

In the foregoing discussion, sociology has been depicted as consisting of a series of subdivisions, and in fact, these subdivisions do exist. However, it is quite possible and as a matter of fact probable that a sociologist may be interested in one or more of these areas since they are related. For example, most social scientists find it very difficult to separate the theoretical from the practical and therefore most sociologists would be concerned with the practical implications of their work. Sociology has therefore been characterized as consisting of a series of subdivisions merely for explanatory purposes.

The sociologists To this point, sociology and sociologists have been discussed and perhaps the reader is asking what a sociologist does. One thing that may have become clear is that many sociologists are involved in research, but few sociologists are engaged in research as their sole activity. The majority of sociologists teach, primarily at the college level. However, there is an increasing trend to offer sociology courses at the high school level, and it appears that this trend will continue. Other sociologists engage in consultation with government agencies and with organizations and attempt to determine the nature of organizational problems. Still another group of sociologists is involved in administration of organizations such as businesses, community agencies, and so forth. They are selected for these areas because of their recognized knowledge in the understanding of human interaction. A sociologist should not be confused with a social worker who, in fact, applies many of the principles that are derived from sociological research. However, social work is a specialized area that requires intensive training in social work methods.

SOCIETY AND THE INDIVIDUAL

The word *society* has been used often in the introductory paragraphs of this chapter. At this point the idea of society and its impact upon the individual will be examined somewhat more carefully. Society can be defined in a number of ways, but perhaps the best definition is one that emphasizes that society is a group of individuals which have definite ties to one another and which interact on a regular basis. For the most part, the interaction patterns result because members of a society have a type of interdependence among its members, and as Lenski points out society is a form of organization which has a relatively high degree of specialization. For example, the society which has evolved in the United States establishes its own laws, has formed organizations which are designed to protect the society from outside forces, has established its own government, etc. We are, in fact, an autonomous group. Lenski[5] puts all of these facets of a definition of a society together as follows:

> A society exists to a degree that a territorially bounded population of animals of a single species maintains ties of association and interdependence and enjoys autonomy.

Formation of societies A society is formed for a variety of reasons. We have already pointed out that there is interdependence among the members of a society, so one of the functions of a society is to provide services to the members of that society. However, the basic reason for the formation of societies is to assure the survival of the members of the society. Because of this basic fact a society establishes laws, customs, rules, and regulations which are aimed at assuring that the society perpetuates itself. Because these rules and regulations are established for the protection of the society, they change rather slowly—though it should be emphasized that a society is not static.

Individuals within a society are greatly affected by the society, regardless of their like or dislike for it. The so-called radical individual is as much a product of society as is the highly conforming individual. The major difference between the two individuals is that because of the circumstances brought to bear upon them, they act in different ways. Martin Luther King's nonviolent method of dealing with racial discrimination grew logically out of a socialization process as did those of the militant black leaders who killed police officers and set fire to the racial enclaves in our cities. All had been socialized.

Socialization Generally *socialization* is the influence which varying groups bring to bear upon an individual within a society which enables a person to adopt a set of social patterns which will be acceptable to the society. In the event that the socialization process fails, the society develops means by which an individual can be taken out of the mainstream of society. For example, criminals are placed in institutions which have been designed for the purpose of caring for people who have not been properly socialized. Similarly, institutions for the insane have been established to insure that individuals who do not conform to the *norms* of the society are withdrawn from the society.

It should be recognized that the entire process of socialization is one which is continuously at work. We are not fully socialized at the age of six, sixteen, or sixty, for although there is an overall socialization process which occurs in our society at large, each subgroup within that society not only contributes to the overall socialization process but also has its own process which is designed to allow an individual to fit into that particular group. There are acceptable standards of behavior in a hippie commune, just as there are in other kinds of subgroups within our society. The adaptation to that subgroup is a socialization process.

Culture can perhaps be described as the glue which binds a society together. We have already defined culture as a set of values or norms. At this point an attempt will be made to define it somewhat more broadly. E. B. Taylor (1889) defined culture as that complex whole which includes knowledge, belief, art, morals, law, custom, and any other capabilities and habits acquired by a person as a member of society. Contemporary sociologists are inclined to view culture as the knowledge and beliefs and customs or ways of doing things that are common to the society and transmitted from one generation to another. With this in mind, we can see that the object of the socialization process is to pass the culture from one generation to another and we know by studying evolving cultures that this process is to a large extent successful.

Some sociologists believe that there is only one culture for each society and indeed in this country we share certain cultural beliefs regarding monotheism, democracy, belief in education, nuclear family and many others.[6] Other sociologists have theorized that no single culture can be pervasive, particularly in a society as diverse as ours. As a result, the concept of subculture has arisen. Subcultures are in a very real sense a part of the dominant culture, but they usually have redefined certain basic cultural ideas.

Anderson[7] points out that because of the diversity of religions, races, ethnic backgrounds, and occupational structure it is possible to enumerate many distinct *subcultures* in our society. He lists five distinct ethnic and class subcultures: white Protestant upper class, Jewish upper middle class, black lower middle class, Catholic working class, and white Protestant lower class. Another subculture which is frequently mentioned in our society is the youth group. An apparent cultural difference between youth and the dominant culture lies in the area of dress, but there are also basic differences in sexual behavior, use of drugs, approaches to work, and other areas. What differentiates the youth subculture from the others mentioned is that it is obviously specific to an age group. The very process of aging provides the impetus for assimilation of the subculture members into the dominant culture.

While subcultures exist as a part of the dominant culture it is also possible for a separate culture to exist in the midst of, but apart from, the dominant culture, although we shall see that the pressures for absorption of that culture are great.

Socialization Many native Americans or American Indians as they are usually called still maintain much of the cultural identity of their ancestors. This cultural tradition involves worshipping ancient gods, rejection of the work ethic, maintenance of a noncompetitive societal structure, and establishment of differing roles for children to name but a few aspects. The junior author was amazed when he observed Sac and Fox Indian children choosing up sides for a game of baseball (an obvious adoption from the dominant culture). However, children were not chosen because of their athletic prowess but because they were friends or obviously needed to be included. The playing of the game was also quite different. They did not keep score!

The reaction of some Indians to the work ethic is embodied in a nineteenth-century speech by Smohalla, religious leader of the Dreamer religion. Smohalla was a member of the Nez Perce tribe.

> My young men shall never work. Men who work cannot dream, and Wisdom comes in dreams.
>
> You ask me to plow the ground. Shall I take a knife and tear my mother's breast? Then when I die she will not take me to her bosom to rest.
>
> You ask me to dig for stone. Shall I dig under her skin for bones? Then when I die I cannot enter her body to be born again.
>
> You ask me to cut grass and make hay and sell it, and be rich like white men. But how dare I cut off my mother's hair?
>
> It is a bad law, and my people cannot obey. I want my people to stay with me here. All the dead men will come to life again. We must wait here in the

Some American Indians have resisted the pressure from the dominant American culture to conform to its customs. This family practices skills handed down for generations. *(Courtesy of the American Museum of Natural History)*

house of our fathers and be ready to meet them in the body of our mothers.[8]

What has been the reaction of the dominant culture to the rejection of its cultural standards? At first, attempts at out-and-out genocide. Books such as Dee Brown's *Bury My Heart at Wounded Knee* have made it apparent that the strategy employed in the nineteenth century was apparently to obliterate the Indian from our society. Atrocities against the Indian have few parallels in history. Since that time, attempts to stamp out the Indian culture have been more subtle. Religous groups have tried and succeeded in many instances to convert the "heathen" from "erring" ways. The Bureau of Indian Affairs is viewed by many as an instrument of the dominant culture and through education and other means has attempted to acculturate the Indian.

The impact of the cultural clash has been devastating for the American Indian. Graves[9] found the intake of alcohol of the Indian is three times that of a Spanish American group which he studied, and seven times that of a white control group. Indians admitted to being drunk seven times as much as whites and nine times as often as Spanish Americans. Ferguson[10] found that 30 percent of the Navaho people drink excessively. Bahr[11] reports that the homocide rate among Indians was 16 times the average national rate, and other crime rates were considerably higher than the national average. The average income of an American Indian family is 50 to 75 percent below the national average and hence many live in abject poverty. Infant mortality is twice the national average[12]. The Indian has paid dearly for adherence to heritage, and the dominant culture in our country has done little to ease the situation.

Some people are at long last beginning to see some of the wisdom inherent in Indian culture. Their egalitarian society, their child-rearing techniques and their basic concern for the environment are now receiving attention. However, many sociologists predict that it is too late to save the Indian culture, and indeed some Indian tribes have already become acculturated. What will happen to those Indians that cling to the remnants of their cultural heritage remains to be seen.

Role of socialization in personality development While the general goal of socialization is the passing on of culture, the specific objective of the process can be characterized as the development of personality of the individual. Through the process of absorbing the culture, the individual develops a personality. Each personality is different because of the differing socialization forces which come to bear upon the individual. Although the personality can be defined in a variety of ways, one point central to any definition is the idea that a feeling of self, a feeling of individuality, develops. This feeling of self is, of course, in reference to others from a sociological point of view. According to sociologists, this feeling of identity in relation to others is the basis of being human for sociologists believe that it is this ability to relate one to another that is a unique characteristic of the human species.

Personality development is a dynamic process because socialization is unending. However, as an integral part of our personality development, society demands that we learn certain kinds of skills, attitudes, and ways of behavior. For example, as a part of socialization process an individual must learn a series of *roles*. A role can be generally defined as a position filled by an individual which has distinct expectations and a requirement attached to it. For the most part, these requirements are behavioral in nature. For example, a boy must learn to fill the typical masculine role as a part of the socialization process. Throughout his life, he must learn to fill other roles, however. For example, he learns prior to and during marriage the role a husband must assume. He also learns the role of a worker, a responsible member of society, and a variety of others. The learning and acquiring of roles is important to any culture for it is the accepting and fulfilling of roles that allows individuals to specialize within our society. Different workers, for example, fulfill different roles and fit into the interdependent pattern which must develop in a society if it is to survive. Roles also serve as a means of cultural or societal control. Because there are specific behavioral expectations attached to roles, individuals who step out of their roles in particular situations may be chastized. Each society develops a variety of mechanisms to enforce its role expectations.

One of the problems and sources of frustration to the individual is that conflicts develop between and among the roles. An individual's role as a father dictates that he spend time with his children. At the same time, his role as a businessman may dictate that he spend increasing numbers of hours away from his family. This specific role conflict is also particularly acute for many women at this time. There are a number of conflicts which grow out of our religious roles. How can one embrace the Judeo Christian ethic on one hand, and yet participate in an occupational role that dictates ruthless, aggressive behavior? Conflicts also develop between civilian roles which dictate respect for human lives and military roles which demand the taking of lives. These conflicts appear to develop not because of inconsistencies in individuals so much as the impingement of the roles of others upon them and other constraints. An individual who adheres to the Judeo-Christian ethic in one sphere may discriminate against minority groups because of a supervisor's views. One knows that one will lose employment if one treats all people equally. Similarly, a soldier may kill because of the consequences of not killing, both in terms of reactions from peers and superiors and also the fact that the soldier may be killed which enters strongly into the picture. Resolution of the role conflict may lead to alteration of one or more roles or the abandonment of a role altogether.

In addition to roles, an individual must learn discipline as a part of the socialization process. Discipline has to do with the formation of certain habits or means of behaving which allow the individual to live within society. In one respect these could be called basic skills for living. In our society, for example, an individual must learn self-discipline in terms of the ways of dealing with people. It is unacceptable for an adult, for example, to assault another adult as a means of solving their problems, although this is often permissible among young children. The individual must also learn social skills such as table manners and proper means of addressing people.

During the socialization process the individual is also expected to acquire certain socially acceptable aspirations. In our country's society one of the aspirations held is that each individual should become a productive member of society. This usually means that an individual must aspire to some kind of work role. Another common aspiration in our society is to be successful. Again, this very often means the accumulation of money or at least holding down a successful position. In conjunction with the aspirations an individual should also learn skills. Skills are the means by which the individual can achieve aspirations. If,

In our society many think that knowing how to sew is an expected part of the female role. Learning this skill may be fun for these little girls in kindergarten, but it is also part of the socialization process. *(Marcia Weinstein)*

for example, an individual sets as an aspiration the acquisition of wealth, skills must be learned which would enable the achievement of that goal. Another aspiration of our society involves achievement of a successful marriage. This, of course, involves learning quite a different set of skills.

Socialization and conformity In reading the foregoing paragraphs about the socialization process, one may very legitimately become concerned about the socialization process and the pressures brought to bear upon the individual with regard to conformity to societal standards. As was stated at the outset, socialization has as its general objective the integration of the individual into society and that to do this the individual must develop socially acceptable behavior. Although the social system does have influence upon the individual, the reverse also occurs. It should also be noted that while the individual does come to share a variety of goals, aspirations, values, and morals with the group or with the society, there is considerable opportunity to develop independent or autonomous elements of personality. If one considers the diversity of our societal structure with the interrelationship of small groups such as families to large groups such as governmental structures, one can readily see that the complexity of human behavior cannot be determined strictly by societal norms. There is adequate opportunity for the development of autonomous behavior within our society and within all societies. This is true because although our society does pose certain standards for the individual, within the culture in this country a certain amount of independence is expected and reinforced.

Finally, there is little evidence to support the idea that culture has a pervasive enough influence that it can shape the total personality of the individual. This is true probably because of the nature of our society and because of the different reference groups to which an individual is exposed throughout life. This may also be true because of certain characteristics of the organism which are biological and perhaps psychological in nature. Because cultural influences are not uniform and because of the variations in socialization processes which occur throughout an individual's life, culture can only be partially effective in determining the personality of an individual.

To further illustrate the socialization process, let us consider varying influences within the process. First and foremost there is the biological makeup of the individual. Each person is a unique person with certain kinds of biological predispositions which will interact differently with environmental circumstances. An individual may have a greater or lesser intelligence level, for example, and this in itself will greatly affect the way in which one matures and develops. One may have physical handicaps, or one may have outstanding physical attributes, which also will affect the socialization process. Even the prenatal care which one's mother experiences may determine the way in which the child comes into and untimately views the world. Early in a person's childhood the family may decide to use either a very permissive or very authoritarian approach of rearing the child. This will undoubtedly have an impact upon the personality of the developing infant. While growing older the child may be exposed to a Protestant, Roman Catholic, Jewish, or even atheistic philosophy of life. These, too, will have some impact upon a young personality. As the person matures, the developing personality will be exposed to a variety of adults: aunts, uncles, grandparents, and teachers will come into close proximity with the individual. They in themselves will bring a variety of information and forces to bear upon his personality. The person also will have a peer group. Although there is some disagreement about what the individual will learn from a peer group, there can be littlc doubt that they have some impact upon the way an individual functions. Of course there will be a variety of exposures to other various agencies of socialization throughout the person's life. We already mentioned the school, but there are other social agencies such as the church, colleges and universities, welfare agencies, and so forth which will impinge upon the socialization process. In short, the variety of socialization agencies in themselves lobby against the possibility of developing a highly uniform group of individuals.

The anomic personality Some sociologists believe that because of certain aspects of our culture an anomic personality type is developed. This *anomic* personality is the result of a culture which is in constant upheaval and dramatic change according to Durkheim. The individual, according to this theory, is constantly exposed to situations in which traditional values and mores provide little assistance in making important life decisions. Further, because of the apparent disintegration of the family and because of the change in traditional social institutions, such as the church, the individual has little opportunity to participate deeply in social groups. Because of these upheavals individuals are unable to internalize the norms of their culture. The poor have often been characterized as being more susceptible to anomie because of economic insecurity and because the norms of the predominant middle class are not entirely appropriate for them. However, Rosenberg[13] pointed out that anomie is not restricted to a single socioeconomic class as did Anderson.[14]

In an anomic condition an individual is likely to react in an extreme manner. Durkheim[15] believed that anomie was one of the basic reasons for suicide. Fromm[16] suggests that the individual is more likely to seek some powerful external source for direction such as a dictator. Rigidity, conformity, inflexibility, and authoritarianism are characteristics of the person in the anomic condition.

GROUPS—A FOCUS IN SOCIOLOGY

Because a person is a social being people have formed together in clusters or *groups.* A group can be defined as a number of people (two or more) who have a feeling of belonging and the realization they are separate from other clusters of people. Groups also have definite roles for members to play, statuses assigned to and assumed by members within the group, and patterns of communication. These patterns of communication are largely based upon the status and roles played by various members of the group. For example, a person who is a leader in the group may be the object of a great deal of communication and may, in fact, control the communication that occurs within the group. Other group members who have less status may be the object of much less communication and may be, to a large extent, left out of group interaction.

Another characteristic of a group is that they have a commonly held set of *norms* and *values* to which all members adhere. In fact, all members must adhere to the values to remain as a part of the group. The role the individual has in a group may be viewed as the assignment of a set of expectations by other group members. Generally, these expectations are assigned because the individual has certain kinds of characteristics. An individual who is assigned the role of a leader is expected to conform to certain kinds of standards and act in a certain kind of way. In some groups the leader is expected to be a forceful, dynamic individual who is able to make decisions and act upon those decisions. Leaders in other groups may be expected to perform differently. Group members also have similar values as we have pointed out. A *value* is a set of moral beliefs to which the members of a group subscribe. Some groups such as religious groups have a very specific set of values, whereas other groups may have loosely defined sets of values. However, the important concept in understanding groups is that group members are expected to conform to the values of the group. Charles Manson, a convicted mass murderer, during the late 1960s collected a series of individuals who became known as his family. Some of the values of the group which Charles Manson developed had to do with disregard for human life, importance of the leader, and disdain for societal structure. The family also had a specified set of *norms.* A norm as was discussed earlier is a set of behaviors which are expected in specific situations. One of the norms of Manson's group was the taking of human life.

Other types of groups have much different types of norms. The norms established in a convent may be for daily prayer and meditation, service to others, and basic humility in dealing with people. A sorority or fraternity may have norms of scholarship and service or expectations of campus involvement and social activity. These two types of norms are not mutually exclusive, however.

An individual who does not follow a specific expectation of other group members in a specific group situation may find that he or she either loses a place in the group or is unable to function as before in the group and his or her role may change. A role has been defined previously as a position which can be filled by an individual and to which distinctive behavioral expectations and requirements are attached. A leader who does not function in an appropriate manner may find that he or she has been supplanted by another member of the group.

Groups should not be confused with two other terms common to sociological thought. A *category* is a number of persons who have characteristics in common but who do not have patterns of communications established, roles and norms. A category of people would be adolescents, divorcees, aged, etc. Groups should also not be confused with aggregates. An *aggregate* is a number of people in close proximity, such as those to be found in an auditorium viewing a play. In these groups there may be random interaction patterns and certain types of communication which occur, but they in fact do not have assigned norms, values, or roles. Another example of an aggregate is the typical college class. There is often very little interaction between and among the various members in this situation. However, if a class were to be subdivided into discussion groups and these subgroups were given an opportunity to know each other, establish patterns of communication, set norms, and establish values, they would become a group in the formal sense of the word.

Types of groups Groups may be classified in a variety of ways, but perhaps the most important classification for our consideration are groups which are classified as *in-groups* or *out-groups*. An in-group is one to which an individual feels one belongs and in which one feels comfortable. The family is perhaps the best example of an in-group. An out-group, of course, is just the opposite. This is a group of people to which an individual feels no attachment, no belonging. In fact, an out-group may be classified as one toward which the individual may feel hostility or resentfulness. An individual may belong to a number of in-groups at the same time. For example, a black student might feel like a member of the in-group in a predominantly black area and might view the white students within that neighborhood as a part of the out-group. However, a series of black and white students could form an in-group and other black and white students might find themselves viewed as an out-group, depending upon the neighborhood or situation.

Primary and secondary groups Two important types of groups are *primary* and *secondary* groups. This distinction is made upon the degree of intimacy within a group, with the primary groups feeling the most

The motorcycle is a unifying focus of shared interest that reinforces the loyalties and psychological needs of this in-group. Conformity in dress, length of hair and life-style is an expression of adherence to the standards of the group and a way for members to maintain approval of the group. *(Andrew Sacks/Editorial Photocolor Archives, Inc.)*

intimacy and the secondary group members less intimacy, or having no strong ties to one another. Again, the family may be viewed as an example of the primary group, while a committee of college students working on the drafting of regulations governing the student body would usually be a secondary group. The primary group is usually small, so that the members come to know each other relatively well. However, size alone is not necessarily a condition for the formation of a primary group. The main reason why a group becomes a primary group is the satisfaction and pleasure that they derive from the behavior of one another. Although it is not necessarily the case, primary groups are more likely to be democratic in nature, highly stable, and maintain themselves over a relatively long period of time. The family has been used as an example of a primary group, but there are a variety of primary groups which can form. Peer groups often take on the characteristics of a primary group.

The primary group has a tremendous amount of influence upon the behavior of its members. Very strong values are adopted, norms and roles are assigned to individual members, and the group develops means by which the behavior of its members can be controlled. The primary group is of great importance in the maintenance of the societal structure, since it is in the pirmary group that much behavioral control occurs.

There are many secondary groups or formal groups within our society. Typically these groups have impersonal social relationships and a formal structure that is characterized by orderliness and general lack of spontaneity. Unlike primary groups which have as one of the functions the support and general welfare of its members, the formal group is primarily interested in certain kinds of goals and it concerns itself primarily with utilitarian concerns. Performance and efficiency become the main criteria. Most business organizations fall into the category of formal groups, as do governmental agencies. Other examples of secondary groups are social clubs and church organizations.

Sociologists utilize *sociometry* as a means of studying social structure within groups. Sociometry can give important clues as to group membership, status, and certain other aspects of group action.

SOME SOCIAL INSTITUTIONS

In the paragraphs which follow, certain institutions within our society will be discussed and their impact upon our society examined. Among these, the family is perhaps the most important group of our society, for this is the primary group which we have discussed and which plays such an important role in the maintenance of the fiber of our society. The church and the school are also important societal institutions. All of these institutions have in common that they have been established to perform certain basic functions in society. Because of space, only the family, the school, and the church will be discussed here.

The concept of an institution is an abstraction, that is, it is a representation of a set of values, norms, and mores, held by society or a subgroup within society. We could not, for example, study a single church and generalize from it to other churches. Rather, what would be found is a group of people that have established a church, but we would be unlikely to find the stereotypical church which we might expect. Similarly, we cannot look at a single family and fully understand the institution known as the family.

The family The family is perhaps the primary agency involved in the socialization process and because of this has received a tremendous amount of attention from sociologists. A family is, as has been stated, a social group in our society and is usually characterized by a common residence, a certain amount of economic cooperation, and reproduction. It typically includes adults of both sexes and children who are the result of a socially approved sexual relationship. In our society the family is a *monogamous* union, which means that only one spouse is acceptable. In other societies polygyny or polyandry are practiced. *Polygyny* is where a husband has more than one wife. *Polyandry* is where a wife has several husbands.

There are two family organizational structures which can be easily distinguished. In our society we have a *nuclear* or *conjugal* family which consists of the marital partners and the children, as the most common type. In other societies and at times in our society there is a consanguineal structure, which consists of two or more nuclear families. In this type of family structure persons related by blood ties are joined in some manner. For example, a newly married couple may live with the mother and father of one of the marital partners. The extended or consanguineal family is found with increasingly less frequency because of the mobility of our society.

The family has a variety of functions which it plays in the socialization process. For example, the child learns usually from the like-sex parent the typical sexual role. The child also develops conceptualizations of the idea of family living. From these, it may generalize to society at large and in this sense the family is a microcosm of the society for the developing child. Additionally, the child develops basic ideas about interpersonal functioning from the relationships which it observes in the immediate family. Although there are other opportunities for the child to learn new patterns, it becomes very obvious that much of what it learns in the family structure is, in fact, carried with it into society.

The family serves a variety of other functions which are not related directly to the socialization process. For example, the family serves an economic function in that it is the basic unit of economic consumption. At one time the family was also the primary unit of economic production, but in modern society this function is considerably less important. However, farm families still are a major unit of economic production in some sections of the country.

Reproduction is, for the most part, the proper function of the family. Each society must determine means by which it will replenish itself and most societies, including ours, have chosen the family as a means of doing it. There are, of course, births ouside of the family, but these are not societally sanctioned and must therefore be viewed as a deviation from the regular pattern. In our society since postmarital sexual intercourse is the only sexual union which is officially sanctioned, the family also serves as a means of controlling sexual drives. Parents are expected to regulate their children and of course regulate themselves because of the monogamous nature of American families. The number of premarital pregnancies, the skyrocketing veneral disease rate and the incidence of extramarital affairs resulting in divorce or separation would make it appear that the family is not being highly effective in this area.

There are common definitions and common purposes which families take in all societies. There can also be vast differences in family structure. For example, the authority structure in a family can differ vastly across and within a society. A family may be *patriarchal,* where the father is the primary authority figure; *matriarchal*, where the mother is primarily the authority figure; or *egalitarian*, where dominance and authority are fairly equally distributed. In few cultures has the egalitarian family been truly a fact. However, in modern American culture the egalitarian family is emerging as a primary family structure.

Families also may differ in things such as roles assumed by members of the family, child-rearing patterns, and in other important aspects. At one point in the evolution of our culture it was unacceptable for women to be breadwinners within a family structure. At this point, however, there is an increase in the number of women working (particularly married women) and nearly 40 percent of the work force is comprised of women. Increasingly because of divorce and other factors, women are becoming the heads of households.

Child-rearing patterns also are quite diverse within the family structure. Typically the middle-class family has a permissive approach to child-rearing, whereas lower-class families are likely to adopt an authoritarian approach to rearing the children. Upper-class parents may have less direct contact with their children because of the presence of nurses, maids, and governesses.

Education Historically, schools were organized for the purpose of socializing the young—to teach them the morals and mores of the culture and to inculcate in the children of society the traditions and beliefs of their society and culture. Although some educators disagree with this concept, there can be little doubt that schools developed primarily for

At the University of Wisconsin, Madison, buildings were blown up, vandalized, or seized during the student riots protesting U.S. involvement and military action in Southeast Asia. *(United Press International Photo)*

this purpose. Educational institutions have other functions which are also related to the sustaining of the society. One of these is the provision of trained laborers. This is, of course, a very vital function for a complex culture such as ours where the increasing specialization has become necessary. Because of this specialization we have come to rely heavily upon our educational institutions for the development of skills in our societal members. Education is also viewed by members of society as a means of solving society's problems. Universities in particular have been assigned a research role which relates to the problems found in society.

From time to time society at large believes that educational institutions are not serving its purposes. During the late 1960s students reacting to the Vietnam war and the insensitivities of colleges and universities, rioted. Because these events were dramatized through the mass media, some members of society became outraged. People believed that the institutions were no longer serving the best interest of society and were sowing the seeds of anarchy, which might in fact lead to a weakening of society. The result of this concern was a decrease in the amount of support for higher education. This in turn led university administrations to sharply curtail student activities and to take stronger policies to suppress students who might become involved in activist practices. Administrators also adopted different approaches to dealing with students and perhaps for the first time in our history students were beginning to be treated as mature individuals. Also, it is almost certain that the lowering of the voting age to eighteen and the consequent enfranchisement of youth in our society was a direct result of the turmoil on the college campuses.

Education also functions in the area of personal development. Society at large has assigned education the task of developing certain kinds of societally acceptable behavior. Various programs such as counseling, the provision of psychological services, and so forth are now providod thorugh tho educational institution primarily as a means of promoting personal development of the individual.

In summary, the educational institution rose and still functions as a means of promoting societal interests. Whenever society becomes concerned that it is not fulfilling this function, certain sanctions are levied against the educational institution, such as the reduction of funds. This typically diverts the institution back to its primary role.

The religious institution Religious institutions have developed because of people's belief in the supernatural being and a feeling for a need for relationship with this being. These needs and beliefs have been institutionalized in the form of what we know as the church. The church plays a vital role in our society and has as its primary tools *theology, faith,* and *ritual.*

Theology is a set of beliefs or doctrines about the nature of God, the nature of reality, and the nature of being. These beliefs or doctrines are usually codified in some way. The Bible, for example, is a codification of Judeo-Christian beliefs or theology. In keeping with the theology, certain rituals are developed. Ritual is defined by Webster as an established form for ceremony, a system of rites, a ceremonial act or action, or any formal and customarily repeated act or series of acts. Religious rituals attempt to show the relationship between doctrine and a person's life. For example, the ritual baptism originally began in the immersion of prospective Christians to show that sins or transgressions against the Holy Being were being cleansed or taken away.

Faith is also an important part of religion. Faith is the belief that one has in what must be viewed as an intangible subject. Faith is measured by one's commitment and one's behavior as they are related to the beliefs which are set forth in the religious doctrine.

Certain basic religious sects in this country have as one of their rituals the handling of poisonous snakes. Their belief is that if your faith is strong enough you will not be bitten or if you are bitten it will not result in death. The behavioral manifestation of faith is the handling of the snake. Although few religious sects have expectations of its membership that are as dramatic as snake handling, certain behaviors are expected. Certain religious groups, such as the Friends or Quakers, expect that the individual will assume nonviolent ways. The Amish reject modern technology and expect its members to act accordingly. These are but a few examples of how faith is transmitted into action.

It should be noted that the extent to which religion and the church have an impact upon an individual's life is primarily the result of the socialization process; therefore, to an extent, the church or religion is an extension of the family. However, the church may affect the individual's socialization in other ways. Since the church is primarily a device by which the morality of a culture can be transmitted, it may act to influence laws or practices which come to bear on the individual. For example, some states have blue laws which prohibit the sale of a variety of products on Sunday. These stem from religious beliefs that people should worship God on the seventh day and other practice is blasphemy. These laws influence people whether or not they believe they should in fact keep the seventh day as the sabbath. Another example of this situation can be found in abortion laws. The Roman Catholic Church has lobbied strenuously against laws which allow abortions to occur, believing steadfastly that the taking of the fetus is the same as taking a life. This contention has in the past kept many states from passing abortion laws and has therefore had an impact on the lives of many people who do not subscribe to the Roman Catholic faith. Recent Supreme Court action regarding the rights of the individual have dramatically altered this situation, however.

Of course, many people are much more directly affected by the church because of their own belief systems. Although this varies considerably with the individual, it can be said that the religious institution and its doctrines do have a considerable impact on individuals in our society.

There are two major types of institutions which impinge upon the individual. These are the political and economic institutions. Because political science and economics will be discussed at some length, these will not be considered at this point to any great degree. However, political institutions develop for the purpose of preserving the social order, as do the other institutions. They also serve the function of protecting the society which develops them. Political institutions may also regulate economic institutions for the protection of society. Economic institutions are established as a means of serving the needs of that society for material goods. Primarily, economic institutions produce goods, distribute those goods, and assist in the consumption of the products which have been produced.

Institutional interrelationships To this point social institutions have been discussed very much as though they operate independently in our society. This is not the case. It was mentioned that the church impinges upon the family, but the church also interacts with business, government, and other social institutions and has varying impact upon them. Government, perhaps the most influential institution in our society, influences the actions of families, churches, business and industry, education and all other institutions.

Let us consider some examples of institutional interrelationships. Businesses in our country hire ex-military leaders to serve as lobbyists in Congress in hopes of influencing legislation. Educational groups act in a similar manner for the flow of federal dollars into education is a tremendous source of revenue. Governmental budgets regarding the space program led to dramatic decreases in the space industry and laws regarding education of the poor have influenced educational policy and programs.

Because of the interface of institutions, conflict can arise although it is not a necessary product of the interrelationship. Church-state relations are set forth in our Constitution, but in areas such as abortion, military service, taxability of church property, these institutions frequently clash. If an effort were made to drain off defense money for ecological improvement it is certain that the defense industry and government would enter into a serious conflict. Certainly the family and education come into conflict in a variety of issues including sex education and teaching about racial equality. Other examples could be given at this point, but perhaps it will suffice to say that conflict does and will continue to occur among institutions.

SOCIAL STRATIFICATION

Although there may be times when we would like to believe that because of the nature of our society there is in fact no differentiation between and among classes, sociological studies such as those conducted by Warner and Hollingshead emphasize that this is not the case, and we do in fact have a variety of social classes in our society. Sociologists have found that these social classes have certain characteristics which help to identify them and set them apart as separate groups. Roughly we can classify the social classes in this country as being upper, middle, and lower. Some sociologists have differentiated between and among these groups, and some have indicated that there may in fact be nine separate social strata which exist in our society: (1) upper-upper; (2) middle-upper; (3) lower-upper; (4) upper-middle; (5) middle-middle; (6) lower-middle; (7) upper-lower; (8) middle-lower; (9) lower-lower. Each social strata is a group of persons who occupy a similar rank in our society.

Anderson[17] asserts that income or wealth is the most important criterion of social class. He indicates that this is true because wealth determines educational limits which is a major factor in occupational choice. These two factors—education and occupational choice—influence life style, societal prestige, choice of friends, personal identity

Several communities of middle and upper-class blacks are located in Atlanta, Georgia, and its environs. While almost 50 percent of Atlanta's population is black, only a small percentage live in such an affluent neighborhood as Collier Heights in northwest Atlanta. *(Photographic Services of Atlanta and courtesy of the Atlanta Daily World)*

and the relative power one holds in society. While there is much to be said for Anderson's ideas, there are also some contradictory evidence. A teacher or a minister may have considerably less income in our society than a plumber or truck driver but belong to a higher social class. Anderson does point out that occupation is the most frequently used component of social status, however. In summary, social class is determined by a variety of factors which can roughly be enumerated as (1) economic status, (2) power or influence, (3) information—skill or knowledge and (4) social status or deference.[18] While, as Anderson pointed out, one or two of these may be prepotent, a social class cannot be determined by looking at a single factor.

Why social stratification occurs Why do social classes arise? Mayer and Buckley[19] provide a graphic description of this process. According to these authors *differentiation* occurs in the nonhuman world because of hereditary factors. In the bee world, differentiation among workers, drones, and queen bees is solely because of inherited characteristics. Of course human beings inherit certain traits such as mental capacity, sex, age, and physical traits and these may form the basis for differentiation in very primitive societies. As we shall see, social differentiation in modern societies is dependent upon factors other than these inherited traits.

In the developing society the basis for stratification seems to be the assumption of *power* or control over the lives of others. However, as Mayer and Buckley[20] indicate, for power to serve as the basis for social stratification, it must be *institutionalized.* The selection of a chief or witch doctor would be an institutionalization of a position.

Another prerequisite for social stratification is numbers.[21] Unless there are sufficient numbers of people in a tribe or group, it is unlikely that the social organization will continue to rest upon age, sex, and physical attributes.

Finally, social stratification depends upon an economic system that will enable the group to produce an economic surplus. Whenever there is a surplus, individuals can compete and maintain a disproportionate share of the wealth. This wealth can be transmitted to family members and offspring and thus the institutionalization of social strata is achieved.

Three general types of stratification systems have developed: *caste, estate,* and *class.* A caste system can best be characterized as one which has little or no social mobility, that is, a person born into a particular caste is likely to stay in that social strata. The untouchables in India are an example of a lower caste, although this system is being modified by time. The caste system is characterized by slow technological change and an economic system that allows the upper castes to maintain substantial differences in power and wealth.

An estate stratification is based primarily on land holdings and power derived from military service. Medieval Europe was stratified in this way. This system differs from the caste system in that limited mobility can occur. A nobleman could marry a peasant's daughter or a peasant could better his lot either by his wits or as a result of benevolent acts from the upper class.

In a class system such as we have in this country, social stratification is based upon the factors previously mentioned: wealth, expertise, power, and social status. The class system, unlike the caste and estate systems, is characterized by great social mobility or at least the potential for mobility.

Hollingshead[22] conducted a classic study of a Middle Western community of 10,000 which he referred to as Elmtown. He discovered that Elmtown was composed of five social strata. In Hollingshead's study the class-one families were the "old" rich, the people who had primarily inherited their status and their wealth from their fathers or mothers. The persons in class two were aware of the difference between themselves and class one, but made every effort to identify themselves with the upper-class families. In class two, income was earned largely by the male head who operated a business or engaged in an executive or enterprise owned by one of the class-one families. Class-two persons were more likely to be involved in power-wielding associations, such as the Chamber of Commerce or Rotary, usually owned real estate, and almost always owned their home. The adults of the class-two family were the most highly educated in the community and education was viewed as a requisite to success in business and in the professions, according to Hollingshead.

In class-three in Elmtown, Hollingshead found that the income was most likely to derive from profits, fees, and salaries earned by both father and mother. The men were likely to own small retail businesses or medium-sized farms, or in some instances pursue the lesser professions. Some were highly skilled craftsmen, and others were foremen in the mills or clerks in the banks of the town in which they lived. In the class-three families it was not uncommon for the wife to be employed outside of the family.

Persons in class-four in Elmtown realized that they occupied an inferior position in the prestige hierarchy. They discriminated between themselves and those who were apparently socially ambitious. Class-four members worked for wages on the farms, mines, in the mills, and in the shops of Elmtown.

Class-five families were not usually found in the leading residential areas. They were shunted aside into the undesirable areas of town. Family dwellings were likely to be small and unattractive. Members of these families were not active in organized community activities, although a few men did belong to veterans' organizations.

In summary, Hollingshead found that even in a small Midwestern city social classes existed. Other studies, such as those conducted by Warner in looking at Yankee City, and other more contemporary sociological studies have resulted in findings similar to those of Hollingshead.

Social mobility It has long been the American dream that the poor boy can rise from the wrong side of the tracks into the upper classes and there are enough instances of this occurring to perpetuate this belief. Let us look for a moment at how realistic this idea is within our society.

In 1965, Otis Dunkin[23] published a study of the occupational mobility in the United States in the *American Sociological Review.* He looked at the upward social mobility in the United States for 1932, 1942, 1952, and 1962. He concluded that an examination of the most recent period shows that there is, in fact, more of the upward mobility, particularly into salaried professionals and technical positions, than at any previous time in the history of this country. He also found that there is less downward mobility, that is, less people are moving from middle and upper classes into the blue-collar and farm occupations than in previous periods.

Perhaps the major reason for increased mobility in this country is availability of educational opportunity. To a very large extent one's social class is determined by one's occupation, although family background, family wealth, and a variety of other factors also are determinants, as we have seen. In our society, education has been made available to a wide variety of people and therefore the increased opportunity to increase one's social status. It seems certain that this trend is likely to continue in our society because of the changing occupational structure. According to the Manpower Report of the President for 1972, the area in which there will be the greatest expansion for occupational opportunities will be in the professional and technical areas. These are, of course, highly prestigious types of jobs.

While there can be little doubt that there is opportunity for upward social mobility in our society, there should also be no doubt that there are a number of barriers to this movement. There still exists in our society barriers against minority groups and even recent legislation which has mandated that certain types of occupations hire a proportionate number of minority groups does not keep these groups from being the last hired and first fired. It should also be noted that although education is a means by which an individual can be upperwardly mobile in our society there seems to be a cumulative effect in our society. By this is meant that education tends to have a great deal of impact upon the social mobility of the child. This, of course, could be the result of a variety of factors, but for the most part the parents in minority groups are the least well-educated members of our society. Because of this lack of education they hold down the lowest types of jobs and are thus unable to provide financial resources needed by their sons and daughters to secure an education. Additionally, because of their failure they often do not equip their children with the values which are necessary to succeed in an educational situation. This often means that the children very frequently fail to secure the skills which will enable them to take full advantage of the opportunities that society provides to them.

Social class differences One can readily observe that social class has an important impact upon our society and upon individual members of our society. The most obvious impact is in the economic area, for lower classes are less likely to be able to take advantage of the overall wealth of our society. Simply put, the lower classes are often unable to secure the goods and services available to most members of our society. Perhaps even more important than this is the fact that members of lower classes cannot even attain the necessary health care which they need, cannot properly house or cloth themselves, and in fact must live as substandard citizens in a society which has the resources to eliminate most of their problems.

It has also been found that the incidence of physical and mental problems is directly related to social class. The higher the social class the individual has the longer one is likely to live and the more likely to enjoy sound physical and mental health. Members of the middle and upper classes are also more likely to attend school for a longer period of time and to get more from their schooling. As we have already seen, members of the middle classes particularly view education as important and emphasize it in their own lives and in the lives of their children. It is also of interest that the possibility of one being drafted and killed in war is directly related to one's social class. The state of West Virginia has had the highest number of persons killed per 100,000 population in the last three major wars. It is no accident that many of the people in West Virginia are from the lower classes.

The basic pattern of the family is also affected by the social class that the family occupies. The higher the class the fewer the children per family, although this has been changing with the increasing use of birth-control devices. It has also been discovered that boys and girls from higher-class families are married at a later age and are less likely to get a divorce after marriage. There is also less likelihood of being arrested, tried, and convicted if one belongs to the higher class in our society. This does not mean that less crimes are committed by upper-class individuals, only that there is less likelihood of prosecution and incarceration if these people are caught committing crimes.

The life-style of social classes also varies greatly. Lower-class people are less likely to become involved in civic activities and more inclined to use relatives and neighbors as social contacts. Citizens from the upper classes more often vote in elections and support liberal issues in our society. Class can even affect political party. Lower classes are more likely to belong to the Democratic party, while the Republican party is more favored by the upper classes. Morality is also likely to be affected by the class to which one belongs. The lower classes are more likely to condone early sexual intercourse, while the middle classes disapprove of this type of activity.

While sociologists have long been interested in the impact of social class upon life-style in this country, the most accurate statement is that there are probably no clear-cut differences attributable to social classes in this country. There are, as Anderson[24] puts it, ". . . a number of cultural tendencies within certain layers of American society." To be sure, the presence or lack of wealth has a considerable impact upon the lives of individuals as we have already seen. But the significant lack of variation among the classes is perhaps the most striking characteristic of American society.

ETHNIC AND RACIAL GROUPS

Because of the diversity of our society, some consideration must be focused on ethnic or racial groups as separate entities. It should be stated at the outset that ethnic groups and social classes are not—and cannot—be equated. While it is true that members of some ethnic and racial groups are predominantly members of certain social classes, there cannot be a one-to-one relationship established between ethnic origin and social class. An ethnic group can be defined as individuals who view themselves as being essentially similar and who are viewed as a group by others in our society.[25] Ethnic groups may be composed of members of similar races, the same national origin, or of the same religion. However, as Phillips[26] points out, an ethnic-group member may belong to such a group because he is defined as such by others. Phillips uses the example of the Jewish parents who adhere to the Zen Buddhist religion, but because they are viewed as Jewish by other members of their society, they belong to that particular ethnic group.

There are three types of racial groups which can be classified according to their skin color. These are *Mongoloid, Negroid,* and *Caucasoid*, which are predominantly yellow, black, or white, respectively. There are, of course, a variety of problems regarding this classification system. The major one is that there are large numbers of people in the United States and in the world who do not fit specifically into any of these three categories. If one examines skin pigmentation, the range is from the albino of a Caucasoid race to the extremely dark or black member of the Negroid race, with an infinite number of colors in between these two polar positions.

Ethnic groups can be distinguished more on the basis of cultural

Hassidic Jews, not withstanding cultural pressures, have maintained their strict observance of ritual law, their Orthodox customs, and traditional dress—frequently in the face of anti-Semitism. *(Michael Tzovaras/Editorial Photocolor Archives, Inc.)*

differences than by direct physical attributes. Irishmen, Italians, Jews, Germans, Scandinavians, and Swedes are all examples of ethnic groups in our society. These groups have very often been assimilated into our society but not without hardship. Glazer and Moynihan[27] detailed the plight of the Italian migration to this country which reached its peak between 1907 and 1913. The majority of this wave of immigrants came from poor southern Italy and Sicily. They trusted no one because of their experiences in the homeland. Because of this distrust, the new Italian American kept close to his neighborhood and his family. Because of this unity the outside culture had little influence on the new immigrant and the second generation, like the first, were laborers. In reality, the upward social mobility of the Italian American began after World War II, but importantly it was three decades before this process began on a large scale.

Basis for discrimination Racial and ethnic groups are the subject of study because in our society and in the societies of other countries they are the object of discrimination and social prejudice. Since there is no biological basis for the placing of these groups into inferior positions, discrimination and prejudice are social phenomena. The results of discrimination can take many forms, perhaps the most drastic one is genocide where one group tries to annihilate another. One of the most recent examples of this is during World War II, when Nazi Germany tried to exterminate the Jews in Western Europe. Although they were unsuccessful, over six million Jews died in concentration camps such as Auschwitz.

As was pointed out earlier, genocide was also practiced in this country during the late 1800s. Many people wanted to eliminate the American Indians so that their lands would be open to white settlers streaming West, and from time to time there have been other instances of one group trying to completely eliminate another. Certainly in modern-day Ireland there are certain radical Protestant and Catholic groups attempting to completely eliminate one another.

A far more common result of racial and ethnic discrimination is in the area of segregation. Most of our cities have sections designated as "Chinatown," "Little Italy," or "Nigger Town," which illustrate dramatically the idea of segregation. Of course, segregation can take place in other areas than in housing. Modern-day America is much concerned about de jure and de facto segregation because the courts of our society have determined that segregation has negative effects upon minority groups. An attempt is being made to integrate our public schools. This is being sought through busing and a variety of other means. Most of these are being resisted in at least some areas and segregation still continues because of the attitudes of people. It is likely that many forms of segregation will exist in our society in the foreseeable future.

Conflict is often the outcome of racial discrimination. In the late 1960s, places like Watts, Bedford Stuvyesant, and many other sections of our large metropolitan areas became overnight headlines when radical black members of our society struck out in rage and desperation at the society in which they lived. Today, there are a handful of extremist black groups which have as their intent inflicting some pain or damage to the majority group. Another goal of some of these groups is the founding of a black state, either in this country or another country. Although this idea had more support during the late 1960s, there are still numerous black people who would like to see the establishment of a black state. Partition would not be a new solution to problems of discrimination, however. Many other countries have seen violence break out and result in the establishment of new countries. An interesting turn in events has occurred in one militant black group—the Black Panthers in its new socially oriented stance. In San Francisco a member of the Black Panthers ran for mayor and was nearly elected. In Durham, North Carolina, and in other cities, members of the Black Panthers are establishing free ambulance service for the poor. Although it is difficult to identify specific reasons for a reversal from a posture aimed at violence to one aimed at service, hopefully the reason is that this group saw new promise in our society for the black man.

Discrimination Throughout the history our society various types of religious groups have been identified and at times have been discriminated against. Perhaps the Jews and Roman Catholics have been the groups which have been the object of more prejudice than any of the others, but certain Protestant sects have also been the object of discrimination in our society.

Forms of discrimination In the preceding paragraphs we have alluded to a variety of types of discrimination, but at this point we would like to make an attempt to identify more specifically the types of forms of discrimination. The major form of discrimination in this country is perhaps in the area of employment. The Manpower Report of the President in 1972, indicated that the unemployment rate among blacks was 9.9 percent, while that among whites was 5.4 percent. This rate is slightly below the historic two-to-one differential which the black man has experienced in the area of employment. However, when one considers the number of black workers who have become discouraged and quit looking for jobs, it is quite likely that at least the unemployment rate among blacks would reach the point it would be nearly doubled that of whites.

Unemployment rates do not, in and of themselves, tell the true story of occupational discrimination. When one examines the employment figures, it becomes quite evident that blacks represent a disproportionate number of workers in the unskilled and semiskilled areas and that they are only rarely represented in the professions.

At one time, the Supreme Court of the United States supported racial segregation in the public schools. Many states, particularly those of the South, had contended that as long as the schools to which black children were sent were equal to those of white children that there was in fact equality of education. However, evidence presented in the late fifties indicated to the Supreme Court that the separate-but-equal policy was not an equitable approach. When the evidence became clear that the separation of the races in public education was contributing to self-hatred and feelings of inferiority, the court struck down the separate-but-equal ruling and ruled that schools must be in fact integrated. However, since the early fifties the inequality of education for minority groups has not in fact been remedied. In the modern urban situation the schools with the poorest facilities, the youngest, least-qualified teachers, and those which in almost every sense have the poorest learning environment are located in inner cities where minority groups live. This inequality tends to reinforce the situation in which minority groups find themselves because they are unable to prepare for the modern world in which they must live.

Much has been made of residential segregation and its impact upon urban life. Most of us have been exposed to newspaper stories which told of the consequences of a minority-group member moving in an otherwise segregated neighborhood. The result has often been persecution, castigation, and outright physical abuse in some cases.

In some states it is still difficult for a member of a minority group to qualify to vote. These states require poll taxes or literacy requirements which uneducated minority-group members cannot meet. The Supreme Court has, of late, however, declared literacy tests unconstitutional. Court rulings along with the effects of certain groups such as black-power groups and attempts to organize the Chicano or Mexican American have given these groups much more political power in the United States. However, there can be little doubt that these groups are, to a very large extent, still discriminated against in our society.

Why discrimination? The reader may be asking himself at this point: Why does discrimination occur? At this point it might be well to distinguish between the ideas of *prejudice* and *discrimination*. Prejudice is an inner feeling or attitude against a person or group of persons. Discrimination is the behavioral manifestations of that attitude. Discrimination then occurs because members of the majority have developed attitudes which are principally based upon fears. Some of these fears have their basis in the economic area. The uneducated and unskilled white man may be afraid that the competition from the black worker will put him out of a job and thus endanger his economic position in our society. Similarly, white merchants may be fearful of the impact of an industrious Jewish merchant, and this fear may in itself lead to prejudice and discrimination.

Feelings of prejudice may also be based upon ideas that certain groups have ideological differences which are essentially wrong. Protestant groups have discriminated against Catholic groups because of the Roman conspiracy. This is purportedly an attempt by the bishop of Rome to take over all organized religion in the world. Similarly, Roman Catholics and Protestants have discriminated against Jewish people because of the belief that it was the Jewish people who crucified Christ and because of economic competition. In both instances, these are ideas based on misunderstandings, but nevertheless serve as the basis for prejudice. In most instances, bias and discrimination are the result of complexities of factors which are societal, economic, and personal. It should suffice to say at this point that they are irrational feelings in most instances.

SOCIAL DEVIANTS

In later chapters the idea of psychological deviation will be discussed in some detail. At this time the concept of social deviation will be examined. In an earlier part of this chapter the idea of conformity was presented. It was stated that to a very great extent the socialization process has as its aim the production of an individual which conforms to society's accepted standards. It was also indicated at that time that because of a variety of conditions it was impossible to produce a completely conforming person. Any failure to conform to society-set standards, goals, values, or norms can be classified as social deviation, but it should be stressed at this point that deviation is a matter of degree and that in fact all people are social deviates. It should also be stressed that the idea of deviation is neither good nor bad since deviation can be either. A mass murderer is one type of social deviate who can be classified as bad. Ernest Hemingway is another type of deviate who produced great literature, but few would classify Hemingway and his work as bad.

Definitions Defining social deviation is an extremely difficult task, and it should be pointed out that definitions change from time to time because the norms of groups and societies change. In the mid 1960s, smoking marijuana would have been a deviation on many college campuses among almost all groups. However, at this point in time smoking marijuana is not a deviation from the norms of many groups found on our college campuses. This change has come about because of different points of view by college students about smoking marijuana. Larger groups within our society also change their own expectations from time to time. In 1970, abortion was viewed as a deviation in all states within the United States and it was an illegal operation except under various well-defined circumstances. At this time a number of states either have laws which legalize abortion or are considering such laws. Clearly, abortion is not seen as a deviation from the norms in those, at least by the larger groups.

It should be noted that there is a difference between a cultural deviate and one who is classified as a psychological deviate. A person who is a psychological deviate differs from certain personality norms which have been established. A person who is culturally deviate may be one who simply dresses different from the norm of his society. Not long ago it was considered to be deviate behavior for women to go "braless." However, at this point the "braless" look is considered to be a cultural norm in many instances and the dressmaking industry caters to women who wish to go "braless." Although cultural and psychological deviates cannot be equated, people who are classified as psychologically deviate are done so because of cultural norms. For example, homosexuals have for many decades been considered as psychological deviates. However, some groups—including entire states—have redefined homosexuality and no longer consider it to be deviate behavior. In summary, social deviation is somewhat hard to define and must be viewed loosely as differing from the regular norms of a societal group or a society-at-large.

Social deviants as bad or good Sociologists have long been concerned with the causes of social deviation. Sociologists, like their social science colleagues, psychologists, have concentrated to a very large extent upon the negative aspects of deviation and have focused only occasionally upon those factors which give rise to positive deviation, that is, those things which will be useful and helpful to society. In their search for the cause of deviation, sociologists have concentrated their attention upon the socialization process. The family in particular has received a great deal of consideration in this process. Sociologists have also been concerned with deviation in the subcultures, such as youth groups, delinquent gangs, and so forth. Some of the research which is beginning to emerge in the area of drug abuse seems to point to the deviant subculture as a prime factor in drug abuse. However, it is doubtful that any single factor can be identified as being the cause of social deviation. Some sociologists believe that the normal course of events in a society lead to deviation. They indicate that because of a diversity of the groups within a culture various kinds of norms are established. Because of the difference in norms, conflict becomes a natural phenomenon for the developing individual. This conflict can result in the rejection of both sets of norms and the adaptation of a deviate pattern of behavior.

Perhaps the major factor in social deviation has to do with cultural expectations. Chinese American youths have in the past decades had the lowest juvenile-delinquency rates. As the Chinese became more integrated into American culture the incidence of juvenile delinquency has increased to the point that it is approaching the norm of the overall American culture. Other figures, such as a lower rate of alcoholism among Jewish people and substantially lower suicide rates among certain other ethnic groups, tend to support the idea that the cultural expectations to which one is exposed lead to social deviation or the lack of it.

Social order and deviation It is perhaps an obvious fact that each society must have a degree of order if it is to survive and it follows that only a certain degree of deviation can be tolerated. Therefore, each society develops its own means of enforcing its social norms which have been established within that society. The social controls which are exerted vary from society to society, but in our society they are quite diverse. Punishment of some type is the most frequently used means of bringing deviates back into line with the social expectations. Although there seems to be some doubt about the usefulness of punishment in the controlling of social deviation, it is still the primary method utilized. Because punishment is used to control deviant behavior, the result of deviation for the individual is very often pain.

Deviates may have some useful benefits to society, however. For example, deviates may bring social problems to the public attention. Certainly, the burning of the ghettos in the late sixties brought to the public the idea that certain minority groups were being misused. There can also be little doubt that the antiwar demonstrations which occurred in the late sixties and early seventies helped alter the government stand toward the Vietnam war. It should also be pointed out that even these deviations which had socially useful implications often had unfortunate consequences for those people who deviated. Persons who demonstrated against the Vietnam war by burning draft cards or not reporting for draft calls often found themselves incarcerated or forced to flee to other countries. Similarly, blacks who set fire to ghettos were arrested and punished for their acts. Thus, although our society like others does abhor the idea of social deviation, it does have a socially useful function in the evolution in a society.

SUMMARY

In this chapter the depth and scope of sociology have been explored. Sociology has been defined as the study of human interaction and numerous examples of types of interactions have been presented.

A society develops and differentiates in order to preserve the well being of its membership. The process of socialization takes place whenever a society passes on its values, norms, and customs to its children. The basic institution in the socialization process is the family. In a highly transitional society members may not have the opportunity to participate deeply in primary groups and the result may be anomie or a state of normalessness. This person may be characterized by highly diverse behavior and some sociologists believe that this is the basis for suicide.

Social stratification occurs in a society whenever members gain power and wealth is distributed in a disproportionate manner. In many societies, including our own, there are barriers to upward mobility for certain groups because of discrimination and other reasons.

Societies change in a variety of ways, but the development of technology, population growth and personal unrest are primary reasons for social change.

REVIEW QUESTIONS

1. Who was the "Father of Sociology"? The first true sociologist?
2. Why did sociology begin?
3. How can sociology be differentiated from the other social sciences?
4. What are the divisions of sociology?
5. Why are societies formed?
6. What is socialization? What is its ultimate goal?
7. What is culture? What is subculture?
8. What are typical roles learned by members of our society? How do they come into conflict?
9. What causes anomie? How does a person in an anomic condition act?
10. What are the different types of groups? What is the function of each?
11. What are the different types of family structures?
12. What are the different types of social institutions? Why do they develop?
13. How do social strata develop? What are the different social classes in this country?
14. Are social classes different? In what respects?
15. Is social mobility possible in this country? Why or why not?
16. Are ethnic groups members of social classes?
17. Why do people discriminate?
18. Are social deviants bad? Why or why not?
19. What are the different explanations of social change?
20. What causes social change?
21. What are the steps in a social movement?

CHAPTER THREE
SOCIAL CHANGE AND SOCIAL PROBLEMS

IDEAS AND CONCEPTS

communes
a societal or small-group pattern of living characterized by collective ownership and use of property; usually members of a commune hold similar values and are regulated by similar norms

esprit de corps
a set of ideas or propositions which attempt to explain some phenomena

patriarchal society
a society in which the family structure is dominated by the father

population control
the stabilization of population growth

theory
a set of ideas or propositions which attempt to explain some phenomena

This chapter will focus upon the process of social change and introduce three major social problems which confront our society. Social change is introduced first for the student should consider both the process of change and the magnitude of the problem of change before he begins to consider the complexities of the problems in our society. After reading the section on social change, the question that should be uppermost in the student's mind when considering the problems presented here and in the chapter to follow is: "How can these situations be altered?" Do not be dismayed if you come up with no ready solutions. Sociologists and politicians have in large measure failed and thus the problems persist.

The specific problems discussed in this chapter are those of the family and two companion difficulties, women's role in society and population.

There will be times while you are reading this chapter and the one to follow when you will be asking yourself: "How did *they* get in that condition?" Or, depersonalizing the problem even more: "How did the world get in this shape?" Unfortunately, that is the view often taken by members of our society. It will be helpful to you in learning from the material here if you will ask yourself: "To what extent am I a part of the problem being presented?" There will be some areas where you are automatically a part of the problem. By being alive you are a part of the population and thus consume scarce resources which are needed by others. You also create waste and pollutants which makes you a part of the human ecology concern. There certainly may be other areas where you contribute to the social probems confronting our nation and the world. Do you discriminate against other races and minority groups? What is your attitude toward equality for women? Have you committed a crime even though never arrested or incarcerated?

Perhaps even more important than considering your own role in contributing to or creating social problems, you should be considering what you can do about the situations being presented. It has long been the "cop out" by members of our society to say, "I am only one person and therefore what I do does not count." To a certain extent this is also a rationalization for continuing to drive to work during the energy crisis even though there is a car pool in the neighborhood. Also, if your actions are not really important, why not go ahead and discriminate against other people or drive while drunk? The fact is that your actions do count, that what you do with regard to social problems can make a difference.

In summary, our plea is a simple one. Do not read this section as though you were reading about another planet. You are reading about yourself and your world.

SOCIAL CHANGE

Sociologists have concerned themselves with the whole idea of social change since the inception of the sociological movement. However, it should perhaps be stated at the outset that at this point no definitive answers are available as to why change occurs in the social system. But a great deal of sociological research and sociological theorizing has brought considerable illumination to this entire area. In this section explanations regarding social change will be explored.

Theories of social change Since there are no answers available as to the exact reasons why social change occurs, the authors of this volume felt that it would be wisest to talk about the various theories that have been espoused regarding social change and its occurrence. A *theory* can be roughly defined as a set of ideas or propositions which attempt to explain some phenomenon—in this case social change. To be of value, a theory must have a number of characteristics. First, it must be parsimonious. A *parsimonious statement* is one that is succinctly stated; that is, it is put forth in the most economical means and in the simplest terms. Second, a theory must be *heuristic* to be effective, that is, it must give rise to research regarding the propositions to the theory if it is to be judged truly valuable. Third, the theory must be consistently stated and have its terms specifically defined. It is perhaps obvious that no theory should contain contradictions. Succinct, clear-cut definitions of social phenomenon are not easily developed; however, these definitions should relate the contents in the theory to observational data and make possible the study of the concepts in research and experimentation. If, for example, a theorist was seeking to explain the phenomena of urbanization, it would be necessary for the theorist to define such terms as mobility, urban, urbanization, and so forth, and these terms would have to relate to the entire movement from country to city. In the paragraphs which follow several theories of social change will be described. It should be pointed out that none of these theories meet the foregoing criteria.[1] However, at this point they represent the best thought of sociologists and anthropologists regarding the entire area of social change.

Evolutionary theory Evolutionary theory, as one might suspect from its title, was heavily influenced by Darwin's theory of biological evolution. Spencer[2] and Durkheim,[3] were the early advocates of this theory, although it has modern day proponents.

In 1859, Darwin published *The Origin of the Species,* his statement about the evolution of biological creatures. In 1880, he revised some of his earlier theories, but essentially they are reducible to a few propositions. These are: (1) tremendous variability exists among the species;

(2) the population of any given species tends to increase beyond its means of subsistence; (3) as a result, there is a struggle for existence within and among species; (4) in this struggle the strongest or most fit—the best adapted—survive in the long run; the weaker perish.

Because of this process of natural selection which occurs, animals evolve—according to Darwin at least—from a more simple state to an increasingly complex state. This somewhat simple idea became the basis for evolutionary theory of social change. Essentially, those people who adhere to this idea of social change indicate that societies start as rather primitive states and evolve in an increasingly complex manner. As society becomes more complex, according to the evolutionists, social interdependence becomes the rule and the need for strong integrating forces arise within the society. For some[4,5] this integrating force—or this force that holds the increasingly complex society together—is a strong central government. Others have speculated that the central force may be a strong patriarchal family or other types of strong central forces.

Evolutionary theory has been rejected by some modern day sociologists because for most sociologists the idea that societies necessarily become more complex is not always supported by the data. Some societies stay primitive. Others have declined from complex to primitive states. However, evolutionary theory of social change stands as an important contribution to modern sociological thought.

Conflict theory As was perhaps evident in the brief discussion of evolutionary theory, social change was seen as a highly orderly process. This is not so in conflict theory, which was first developed by Karl Marx. Marx believed that there could be no progress without conflict and he said that it was the history of all societies, at least all modern societies, that struggles between the classes or social strata inevitably occurred. Marx believed that in the modern industrial society goods and wealth would be increasingly usurped by the upper class, thus leaving the lower classes or the proletariat with few of the benefits that should accrue from an industrial society. He further believed that once these groups became clearly polarized the proletariat would revolt and overthrow the upper class or bourgeoisie. This would in turn result in a truly classless society. This, according to Marx, was the end result of societal development. It should perhaps be pointed out that Marxian theory served as the basis for the communist revolutions in Russia and China.

Although conflict theory does *not* have an important place in American sociological thought, there are a number of people who have redeveloped some of Marx's ideas and who espouse conflict theory of sociological change. Dahrendorf[6] rejects Marx's ideas of the development of social classes which ultimately conflict, but he postulates that society is subjected every moment to social change and that at all times in all societies social conflict exists. Dahrendorf believes that every element in the society contributes to the change process, but that society has a set of constraints which restrain part of its members. It is against these constraints that people react.

Dahrendorf's idea can perhaps be illustrated by thinking of a senior high school situation in which the students make up one group and the teachers and administrators another. The latter group makes rules and regulations and establishes standards of behavior for the students. According to Dahrendorf this sets the stage for continued conflict for these two groups. This conflict may take a variety of forms, but it need not be revolutionary in the Marxian sense. However, as a result of the conflict, change will occur. The type of change which occurs would be the result of a variety of conditions such as the relative power of the two groups, the tactics employed by the two groups, and others.

Cyclical theories Whereas the evolutionary theories were *unilinear* in nature—that is, they saw societies going from less complex to more complex—cyclical theories tend to look at developing societies as having the potential for either becoming more complex or less complex. Further, sociologists such as Spengler,[7] and historians such as Toynbee, believe that societies go through childhood, adolescence, maturity, and old age, and that these phases are the natural phenomena which occur in a society. This process, according to Spengler, takes approximately a thousand years. Rise-and-fall theorists rely primarily on the history of other cultures to support their ideas. Whether or not these theories are accurate is a moot point. It can be said, however, that they serve only relatively limited purposes in helping to explain recurrent process of social change.

Equilibrium theory The equilibrium theory, sometimes referred to as structional-functional theory of social change, is based upon the idea of homeostasis, which in itself seems paradoxical. Biological theories of homeostasis assert that the individual attempts to maintain his life systems at a level which is predetermined by genetic characteristics. For example, 98.6°F is the well-known, typical temperature for the human body and a variety of biological factors come into play to maintain this temperature. These factors are activated automatically, and unless they are successful the individual becomes very ill and may ultimately die. In equilibrium theory of social change much the same idea applies. A society, according to this theory, rests in a state of *equilibrium*, that is, that a system of relationships develop between and among the various elements of the society as it develops. Whenever one of these developments becomes unbalanced, mechanisms are automatically activated to return the system to an equilibrium state. Talcott Parsons is the major proponent of this theory in modern sociology.

Let us think for a moment of the developments in our society whenever an extremely high unemployment rate occurs. It should be pointed out that this condition may result from external forces such as foreign competition or from internal sources such as the impact of increasing automation. Regardless of the source of the problem our society typically activates a series of mechanisms designed to bring the system back into equilibrium, that is, in this case to bring employment back to those people who are unemployed. In some instances, this activation is merely the mobilization of structures already available in society. Congress might appropriate money for vocational-technical schools to provide free or inexpensive training for workers who are unemployed. This would be the utilization of an existing structure. When J. F. Kennedy was President he conceptualized the idea of the Office of Economic Opportunity which created a series of structures. However, the aim of these new structures was exactly the same as the mobilization of the existing structures—to provide opportunities for members of our society to be retrained, thus bringing the society into relative equilibrium.

It should be noted that there is one characteristic of equilibrium theory which is dominant. Whereas conflict theory holds that change is inherent in any social system, equilibrium theory has a much more conservative approach to the idea of social change. In fact, the theory asserts that social change is done only on a very limited basis and very slowly. It sees society as reactive, rather than proactive. This simply means that a society does not anticipate its problems and plan for them but rather organizes only after the need for social change becomes apparent. Indeed, many social activists on the modern scene have decried the fact that our society moves slowly toward solving the problems which are inherent in its fabric. Our movement toward solution of the human rights situation in this country attests to the accuracy of their statements.

Four brief looks at theories of sociological change have been presented in this section. The student should be aware that none of these represents the true picture of social change in our society but are only approximations of this picture. The true nature of social change cannot be ascertained by reading sociological theory, and perhaps observation of and direct participation in the process is the best means to learn of this process. However, there can be little doubt that these theories have had tremendous impact upon the world. Conflict theory alone may have changed the fate of many nations, while evolutionary theory had undoubtedly influenced the thinking of governments toward providing assistance to developing countries; that is, governments have given aid for primitive societies to continue to develop and specialize their own society, thinking that this was the developmental pattern which societies should take.[8] Similarly, equilibrium theory plays a tremendous role in

American sociology today. Perhaps what is needed is a *proactive* theory of social change which would take ideas from all the existing theories.

SOCIAL MOVEMENTS

Social movements can roughly be defined as collective behavior which is aimed at some form of social change in our society. Characteristically, social movements in our society have stemmed from two sources. These are either from basic unrest about personal conditions, such as was the situation in the movement to unionize labor, the civil rights movement, and currently the women's liberation movement, or dissatisfaction with certain of the conditions that exist in a society although they may not effect the persons involved in the movement directly. For example, there have been three great social movements to correct the conditions which exist in various parts of Appalachia. One of these movements was primarily the responsibility of the church, and the other two were primarily the result of governmental action. In no instance has there been a major social movement arising in Appalachia that was initiated by the people of Appalachia themselves. Perhaps this in itself is the basis for the failure of the movements thus far. In our discussion we will be primarily concerned with social movements which are the result of personal dissatisfaction and unrest.

Types of social movements There are at least three basic types of social movements and these can take at least two forms. One type of social movement is concerned with gaining power within the societal structure. This type of social movement may be typified by the formation of a new political party which has occurred frequently throughout the history of this country. The second type of social movement attempts to change the values of society and culture. The Satanists or Devil worshippers who exist in various parts of this country could possibly become a social movement and attempt to reorient the values of our society. On a lesser scale the present movement to gain acceptance for homosexuals is an example of such a movement. A third type of movement is one which provides rewards and gratification for the members who participate in it. To a certain extent all social movements have this component in them. However, the labor movement was primarily aimed at gaining additional money and better working conditions for unskilled and semiskilled workers in our society. Although it was also concerned with gaining power, unionization was primarily aimed at materially enriching the lives of the participants.

Two classifications of social movements are *reform* and *revolutionary*. A reform movement is one which seeks to achieve its goals by working in the existing system. An economic boycott, such as that which was levied against certain businesses which did not employ black members, is an example of a reform movement. The Communist takeover in Russia and China are examples of revolutionary social movements. Their tactics were to overthrow the existing social system and replace it with a new one. Although there have been no successful revolutionary movements in this country since the subjects of King George overthrew British rule, there have been many advocates of this particular approach. Certain black militant groups and others advocate a revolutionary movement to remedy the situation of the black man.

Bases for social movements Typically the prelude to a social movement is some form of social unrest. At the turn of the century workers were scandalously exploited by their bosses. This resulted in a social movement. Today poor people in this country are often unable to get the necessary food, clothing, and medical care which they believe to be their birthright. Minority group members of our society are still discriminated against in hiring practices and other aspects of our society. Both of the present conditions are causing unrest which is manifested by mass marches, demonstrations, and other nonviolent protest. However, these actions in themselves do not make a social movement.

In the initial stages of a social movement leaders or the founders of the movement may agitate in order to recruit participants in the movement. In agitation the leaders may point out the conditions which exist and provide a rationale for doing something about their conditions. Agitation may lead to strikes or even to civil disobedience, but agitation in itself does not provide the basis for the initiation of a social movement. The primary role of agitation is the recruitment of members, and if this fails the social movement will also fail.

Once a group of participants—no matter how small or large—has been recruited and interested in the social problem, *esprit de corps* must result. Esprit de corps may be characterized as a feeling of unity—a feeling of oneness as opposed to a feeling of separateness. It is a feeling of belonging and the feeling of purposefulness. Esprit de corps must be followed by the development of group morale if the movement is to continue. While esprit de corps gives the group a collective feeling of life and enthusiasm, group morale provides the persistency and determination to a movement.

The morale of a group seems to evolve from a set of convictions or ideas and a belief that these ideas or goals will be achieved. Once morale develops, the social movement is well on its way since the members have attained the feeling that they will succeed regardless of the length of the struggle. After this time ideology develops which consists of explanations as to why the social movement should continue and a program for action. Ideologies may be embodied in such

In the late 60s after one hundred years of discrimination and frustration many black Americans turned to violence. Here young militant blacks peacefully demonstrate for the release of their imprisoned leaders. (*Bruce Anspach Editorial Photocolor Archives, Inc.*)

simplistic ideas as slogans. "We shall overcome" became the slogan of the civil rights movement. These few words represented the social ills of the black man in our society to many people. In some instances ideologies of social movements contain basic errors. For example, Hitler convinced the German people that the basis for the economic depression they were suffering in the early thirties was the result of the eastern Jewish gold-hoarding establishment and that they were threatened by an impending Communist takeover. Although neither of these situations were true, the Nazi party was able to gain supporters and eventually take over the country of Germany.

There can be little doubt that social movements do produce social change in this and other societies. This change comes whenever the goals and ideologies of the movement are formalized in some way such as enactment into law and are included or institutionalized within our society. The labor movement in this country succeeded in having laws enacted which described unfair labor management and labor practices and which set up structures within our society to monitor business and its treatment of the laboring class. Similarly, the feminist movement has supported and it seems eventually will gain a constitutional amendment which will assure equal rights for women.

Other factors which bring about social change We have already discussed personal unrest as a potential factor in social change. There are, however, a variety of other factors which may also contribute to this process. Among the factors which are predominant in producing change in our society is our technological advancement. One need look no further than the agricultural industry in order to ascertain the importance of technology in our society. At the time of the Civil War we were largely an agrarian society. Today somewhat less than 5 percent of our population is involved in the production of agricultural goods and in fact less than one-half of these probably produce a majority of the agricultural goods in this society. Technology has an impact on other aspects of our society also. It has taken the drudgery of housekeeping chores and freed the American women to participate in the labor market. Technology has also allowed us to produce goods and services at an unheard rate.

There are the favorable results of technology. There are, of course, negative aspects of technology and these are the ones with which society must ultimately deal. Many jobs have been completely eliminated. For example, in one 12 month period nearly 400 elevator-operator jobs were eliminated in New York City alone. The U. S. Treasury went from 4,000 check writers to 4 when computerized check writing was installed. Assembly lines have become dull and meaningless work places, and members of our society find little pride in their work or little satisfaction in the products they produce. This unrest is beginning to manifest itself in absenteeism, in strikes, and in other kinds of protest movements. Clearly our society needs to work on the consideration of helping the worker find meaningful activities that are connected with his work.

Technology also affords government a means of monitoring the lives of the citizens of this country. As data collection procedures become more routinized and as electronic devices become more sophisticated, the Orwellian society of 1984 becomes more of a possibility. The potential for abuse of power also becomes more real. The Watergate case which began in the 1972 presidential election and resulted in the resignation of President Richard Nixon in August 1974 is a case in point. In this case members of the Republican campaign staff were involved in "bugging" the Democratic party national headquarters located in the Watergate Hotel in Washington, D.C. Other instances of electronic surveillance have made it clear that our society needs to deal with the problems inherent in technology.

The physical environment in this country and the relative population also may be determinants of change. In earlier paragraphs we have alluded to the urbanization trend in this country and there seems to be little evidence that the movement from rural to urban will cease in the near future. This concentration of population has caused many social difficulties which need to be attacked and solved for the welfare of members of our society. Transportation alone poses a major problem as do housing and health services.

Some people are alarmed by the increasing population of this country. There are at this time approximately 210 million people in this country. However, population predictions for the United States for the year 2000 range from 265 million to 392 million depending upon the birth rate used. It is already apparent that the resources of this country are strained by our present population. Further, it is folly to consider only the population of our country when considering the problems. Although countries such as Japan have reached zero population growth (ZPG), Latin American countries and certain African countries have staggering birth rates and it appears unlikely that this situation will be reversed in the near future. The United States can hardly continue to think of itself as an island with the advent of increasing world travel and with the likelihood of new coalitions developing among nations. The population of the world will undoubtedly impinge upon our existence.

In summary, three major causes of social change have been listed: technological growth, population growth, and personal unrest. These give rise to social movements which ultimately affect us all.

MARRIAGE AND CHILD REARING

"What God hath joined let no man put asunder" (Matthew 19:6). These are the words utilized by clergymen to admonish couples during the wedding ceremony that they are entering into a holy state. However, for hundreds of years individuals have put "asunder" their marriages. The skyrocketing divorce rate, the numbers of desertions, and other types of family disorganization have caused social scientists, the clergy, and other members of our society to focus upon this problem. This concern grows out of the importance attached to the family as an integrating force. As was pointed out earlier, it is the family that has the responsibility of transmitting cultural values, and many are concerned that it can no longer serve this purpose adequately.

Divorce rates The United States has the highest divorce rate among the Western countries. While divorce statistics vary, it is probably true that about 30 percent of all marriages will end in divorce court. It is also true that about 85 percent of these divorced persons will remarry, leading some persons to characterize the marital pattern in this country as *serial monogamy.*

Reasons for divorce While this country has a high divorce rate at this time, many countries have had divorce rates higher than ours at given periods of time. We may be able to draw some inferences about the reasons for our divorce statistics by examining the trends in these other countries. At the turn of the century, Japan's divorce rate was about two and one-half times that in this country. In fact, Japan's divorce rate has gone from 18.4 percent in 1900 to 8.1 percent in 1965. In this same period our rate climbed from 7.5 percent to 25.8 percent.[9] This seems a little paradoxical when you consider that Japan's society has increasingly been Westernized during this period. However, at the turn of the century mates were selected by the elders of the family. Whenever the bride came to live with her new family, it was incumbent upon her to adjust properly to the situation. If she did not, she was literally divorced by the family and sent back to her parents. Thus, one thing that is apparent, in Japan at least, is that increased personal choice led to a decrease in divorce rates.

Some countries such as Spain, Ireland, and Brazil do not permit divorce except in very special circumstances. In Chile marriages can be annulled, but it is a slow process. Legal constraints can, of course, decrease the divorce rate, but generally other means of resolving marital conflict are adopted. It was not uncommon practice for men of means in Italy to keep mistresses prior to the adoption of divorce laws (and it may still be common practice).

Perhaps the only fact that can be gleaned from the foregoing is that social conditions affect the marital state. War, for example, appears to have affected the divorce rate in this country. Goode[10] points out that divorce rates soared after the Civil War and after each of the world wars. Recent articles in magazines such as *Newsweek** seem to indicate that veterans of the Vietnam conflict are having marital problems, thus substantiating the idea that the involvement in war has a negative impact upon marital longevity. There is an alternate hypothesis that should be considered, however. It may be that the long period of separation is the primary factor resulting in the termination of the marriage, and not the involvement in war. Whether the trauma of war or the fact of the long separation is the contributing factor to marital discord and disintegration remains to be seen.

It has also been noted that different age and racial groups have varying divorce rates. Persons marrying under the age of 25 have a divorce rate that is nearly three times that of the overall rate. Since 1940, the percentage of nonwhites divorced has ranged slightly higher than that of whites.[11] However, divorce statistics among poor blacks and whites are misleading because one means of dissolving the family is through desertion. This is simply because neither group can afford the expense of a formal divorce.

* See, for example, "What Happens to Returned POW's?", *Newsweek*, Oct. 9, 1972, pp. 26–27.

The impact of religion and other social factors upon divorce has received considerable attention in this country and in others. Generally speaking, Jews and Catholics have lower divorce rates than do Protestants. Socioeconomic status also seems to have an effect upon marriage and divorce as does educational level. There is an inverse relationship with both of these variables. The higher the socioeconomic and educational level the less proneness there seems to be to divorce. There is one discordant fact when racial groups are examined separately however. Statements about education pertain only when the educational level of the couple is considered. There seems to be a curvilinear relationship for black females as far as education is concerned. Divorce rates increase rapidly as educational level increases from grade eight to grade eleven and decrease rapidly after that point.

An interesting aspect of marriage and divorce rates has to do with their relationship to the economic cycle. There are more marriages and divorces during economic prosperity and less of both during recessions in the economy.[12]

Many have been concerned about the impact of the Women's Liberation movement on marriage and, while it is too early to tell, there are two schools of thought. One view is that the new role of women will result in more divorces because of role conflicts which will develop in the home. However, another argument is that women will become more interesting and thus more attractive as a result of their new role which in turn will result in less divorces.

TABLE 3-1 FACTORS ASSOCIATED WITH PRONENESS TO DIVORCE[13]

Greater likelihood of divorce	Lesser likelihood of divorce
1. Low socioeconomic status	1. Middle or upper socioeconomic status
2. Low educational level	2. High educational level
3. Short courtship	3. Long courtship
4. Married at early age	4. Married at age over 20
5. From broken homes or unhappy marriages	5. From families with happy marriage
6. Dissimilar religious beliefs	6. Similar religious beliefs
7. Disagreement on role relationships	7. Agreement of role relationships
8. Urban background	8. Rural background
9. Economic instability	9. Economic stability
10. Emotional instability of one partner	10. Both partners emotionally stable

A summary of the characteristics which are associated with greater or less proneness to divorce is presented in Table 3-2.

Child rearing It should be pointed out that there are those who are greatly concerned about the child-rearing process, even in those families that stay together. These people admit the fact that children are only exposed to two models in the nuclear family, their mother and father, for guidance and training in their formative years. They also point out that because of these limitations children are denied the opportunity to learn ways of behaving and means of solving problems from a variety of sources. Social scientists such as Margaret Mead and Bruno Bettelheim appear to be suggesting ways by which some form of an extended family child-rearing approach should be reinstituted in this country.

Alternate forms Bruno Bettelheim[14] has spent much of his life working with emotionally disturbed children in the Orthogenic School at the University of Chicago and has concerned himself with better ways of child rearing. In 1970, he published a book entitled, *The Children of the Dream*, in which he described the *kibbutz* which is utilized in Israel as a child-rearing institution. Although Bettelheim does not unequivocally endorse the kibbutz as a means of child rearing, he believes that children raised in this system fare better than many of those raised in the poor families in this country and argues that even some of the children in middle-class homes probably do not do as well as the children raised in these institutions in Israel. Other countries have developed alternatives to child rearing other than the family. Along with a consideration of the kibbutz, the systems in Russia and China will be discussed here.

The Kibbutz Children have been raised communally in Israel for the past sixty years. Although only 4 percent of Israel's population lives on the kibbutzim, they play an important role in the structure of Israeli society. All Israel is proud of the brave Sabra building a new society on the kibbutz, although the average Israeli might not want to change places with him.

The life of the kibbutz child starts in the group practically from the moment of birth. At the age of four days he comes from the maternity home to the infants' house where he shares everything—toys, clothing, and the caretaker's love with his infant comrades. He is never alone, and for all practical purposes he will never be alone, at least as long as he remains in the kibbutz.

The child shares a bedroom with three other children; each bedroom is shared by two boys and two girls. In some kibbutzim the children are separated by sex when they reach adolescence, in others not until adulthood.

The infant is cared for by a metapelet. This person is roughly an overseer, a parent surrogate. His mother comes to visit him several times a day in the early months. Most kibbutz infants are breast-fed until the age of six months, at which time they are weaned directly to the cup. After the infant is weaned he sees his parents once a day when he goes to their room for the daily children's hour in the evening. The rest of the time he spends with the other children and the metapelet.

Group activity and sharing of belongings are encouraged from the start. The babies are put into large playpens, several children all together. For many hours of the day the children are left to their own devices while the metapelet is occupied with housekeeping chores. The children learn early how to amuse and take care of each other. If a child cries long and loudly, the metapelet will pick him up, but only for an instant. She generally puts him down again before his crying is fully stopped. This is because the child must learn how to get along in his group. He must learn not to depend on the interference of someone outside his group, whether parent or metapelet.

Bettleheim observes that by toddler age the children have learned to look upon each other as comrades rather than as competitors. "The spirit of helpfulness among them is much more evident than the desire for dominance."[15] Because the adults around him are so busy with their own affairs, the child learns to turn to his companions for comfort and security. The child derives his security, first, from the group to which he belongs and, second, from the kibbutz itself, rather than from his parents or other adults.

At the age of one-and-a-half to two the children move from the infants' house to the toddlers' house. They move whenever four to six toddlers are ready to make the move together, so the child remains a member of his group. Before this first move, however, he may have experienced several changes of caretaking personnel. Routinely at the age of six months to a year the metapelet takes over from the infant nurse. A metapelet may herself become pregnant, or her work assignment may be changed. Thus, the child learns early that the adults in his world are not necessarily permanent. The child forms close attachments to his peer group instead of to the adults in his environment.

The child moves to the kindergarten house at age four and to the house of the primary school children at age six or seven. Still he moves always with his group. The house in which he lives and the adults who care for him change; only the peer group stays the same. Bettelheim[16] feels that this arrangement has advantages for the child. He may achieve less security than the most fortunate middle-class children in our culture, but he has a great deal more security than the great numbers of our children who grow up under less than ideal conditions. Also, while the middle-class child derives a great deal of security from his parents, he must always live with the fear of losing them. The kibbutz child does not have to worry about who would take care of him if he should lose his parents. He knows that his life in the kibbutz would go on just the same.

The child's relationship to his parents is necessarily a much less intense one than that of the middle-class child in our society. The child sees his parents for a couple of hours each evening. These hours are devoted to the children and no other obligation is allowed to interfere. In good weather the child may play outdoor games or walk about the grounds with his parents. In bad weather he will spend the time in the parents' room where the parents have taken special pains to make things pleasant for him.

Since the children's hours are to be devoted to the children's pleasure, any worries or problems the parents may have are resolutely pushed aside during this time of the day. The child, too, learns not to bring his own problems to his parents for solution. Since the lives of the children are controlled by the kibbutz as a whole, there is little an individual can do to alter a situation about which his child complains. The only real control a parent has over the upbringing of his child is his voice in the general meeting of the kibbutz where all important matters are decided. Bettelheim believes that the children learn not to burden their parents by bringing them their emotional problems. This is not to say that the parents are unimportant to their children. Bettelheim feels they are more significant to the child than his teachers or metapelets:

> They are one of the three centers around which the child's life revolves and whose impact will shape his personality. But in my opinion they rank third in a hierarchy of importance in which the peer group comes first, the kibbutz itself second, and the parents only last.[17]

The children begin at an early age to work for the kibbutz. They have their children's farm where they raise animals and grow crops. Since farming is the main way the kibbutz supports its members, the child knows that his work is important in the eyes of the community. He is a contributing member of his society from an early age and from this he derives considerable security and a feeling of competence. While the parents and child may only get together once a day, the child does not have the feeling, so common in our culture, that they lead completely separate lives. He understands what his parents do all day and may even spend part of his own day in the same kind of useful activity.

The U.S.S.R. The Russian child's early experience is radically different from that of the child of the kibbutz. In infancy the Russian child is given a great deal of love and human warmth. Breast feeding is practically universal, and even when not being fed the infant is in his mother's arms most of the time. Thus, the Soviet child receives considerably more hugging, kissing, and cuddling than either kibbutz or American babies. The Russian infant is also confined more closely and given little chance to develop independence.

The main method of discipline in the U.S.S.R. is withdrawal of love. Mothers are urged to show their disapproval of the child's disobedience by a certain coldness in their attitude toward the child, making it clear to the child how much his action has hurt them.

Communal facilities for the rearing of children are common throughout the Soviet Union. Nurseries and kindergartens are readily available, as are boarding schools and "schools of the prolonged day" which are similar to boarding schools except the children go home around 6 P.M. and return early the next morning.

Children in Russian nurseries receive early experience in collective living. They are placed in large playpens, several children to a pen, which are raised to permit face-to-face interaction with staff members. There is one upbringer for each four children. The upbringer spends a certain amount of time each day stimulating each child and training him in sensory-motor functions. A great deal of emphasis is placed upon the development of self-reliance.[18]

From an early age the children are taught to share and to play peacefully together. Collective play is encouraged. The adult begins to withdraw in order to let the children learn to cooperate and discipline themselves. As the children grow, they are expected to develop more responsibility for themselves and others—serving at table, cleaning up, gardening, and so forth.

Child care in China In China a new mother usually goes back to work when her infant is 56 days old. Her baby may be cared for at home by a grandparent, but she may take him to a nursing room at her place of work. Factories, hospitals, and so forth, have nursing rooms where babies from 56 days to one-and-one-half years are cared for by "aunties," as they are called by the children. Most mothers breastfeed their babies and are allowed breaks twice during the working day for this purpose.

The aunties are warm and loving toward the children. They do not change jobs very often, so it is common that a baby will be cared for by the same group of aunties during his entire stay in the nursing room. The mother brings the child in the morning and takes him home at night; thus, he is with her during all her nonworking hours. Everyone, aunties as well as parents, agrees on the goals of child rearing in Chinese society. Thus, there is little conflict between parents and caretakers.

> Above all, children are taught "Wei renmin fuwu"—"Serve the people." They are taught to care for each other. They are trained to love Chairman Mao and to love their country. They are trained to love the workers, peasants, and soldiers, and to love physical labor. They are taught to keep only the public good in mind.[19]

The family, so important a factor in China's past, is obviously still a significant factor in the development of the child. Frequently three generations of a family will live together and the grandparents help to look after the children. Even when the nature of the mother's work forces her to enter her child in a boarding nursery, she will see him frequently and the ties between them remain close.

Experiments in this country Margared Mead[20] has suggested that there is an urgent need for both parents and children to develop new configurations for family living. She believes that these patterns should be so developed as to instill greater feelings of community among adults and to provide children with a greater sense of identity with other children and adults. She does not go so far as to suggest that families occupy single units and that communelike settlements be developed. She does suggest, however, that families who have common interests and are willing to work together in child-rearing enterprises move into clusters or into small communities where there can be interaction among the various families.

Although institutions which take responsibility for child rearing would be resisted in this country, there are experiments in progress that are attempting to utilize nontraditional approaches to the family and child rearing. Among these only communal forms of living will be discussed here.

Communes have received widespread attention in the popular press and have been studied to a considerable degree by sociologists who are

Meals together in a commune serve the same function as they serve in the traditional family structure . . . a time for sharing experiences and dealing with the realities and problems of day-to-day living. *(Susan Yevisaker)*

interested in aberrations in family patterns. Although the stereotype of commune is a group of long-haired, bearded, half-naked people indulging in unrestricted sexual activity, and on a continuous drug trip, this is far from typical. Communes develop for a variety of reasons. To a certain extent the Amish sect, which has settlements in Pennsylvania, Indiana, and other states, is a communal form of living. The primary purpose of these communes is to maintain a particular way of life as is the case with most communal systems.

However, many of the communes which are forming today are a reaction to modern society and a seeking means of finding a better pattern of living. Some communes are formed where the primary motivating force is a political belief. Prior to the end of the Vietnam war some communes formed as peace movements.

The structure of the family may take many forms in a commune. In some of the communes infidelity may not be permitted and in fact may be taboo. In these instances, monogamy is in fact being practiced in a communal system. In others, group marriages are formed where married couples share the same home, expenses, automobiles, and frequently exchange marital partners. It is also not uncommon that any type of pairing off or monogamous relationships is discouraged. In these situations every person is married to every other person and all of the children resulting from the marital relationships are everyone's children. In fact, in these situations there is usually no attempt to discover who the father of a child may be since he in fact belongs to the group.

One commune which has been in existence for five years and shows every sign of lasting is Twin Oaks in Virginia. Twin Oaks is an attempt to translate into practice the ideas expressed in B. F. Skinner's novel, *Walden Two*. Attempts to follow Skinner's model can be seen in the labor credit system for allocating jobs, the planner-manager system of government, and the use of positive reinforcement as a motivational device. Unlike the world of Skinner's novel however, which sometimes seems sterile and unreal, the Twin Oaks community is alive and real, with very real problems. The ideals and goals of Twin Oaks are reflected in its code, borrowed from *Walden Two*.

(1) We don't use titles. All members are equal in the sense that all are entitled to the same privileges, advantages, and respect.

(2) All members are expected to explain their work to any other members who desire to learn it. The purpose of this is to insure the opportunity to learn any available and appropriate work.

(3) We don't discuss the personal affairs of other members; we don't speak negatively of other members when they are not present, or in the presence of third parties.

(4) We don't publicly complain about things we think are wrong within the community. Gripes are best taken up with the appropriate manager.

(5) Members who may have unconventional or unorthodox views on politics, religion, or national policies stay clear of such topics when it's prudent.

(6) Seniority is not discussed among us. We wish to avoid prestige groups of any kind.

(7) We try to exercise consideration and tolerance of each others' individual habits.

(8) We don't boast of individual accomplishments. We are trying to create a society without heroes.

(9) We try to clean up after ourselves after any private or individual project; we try not to keep articles longer than we need them, and to return them to their proper places so that other members may enjoy them.

(10) Individual rooms are inviolate. No member enters another's room without permission.[21]

Twin Oaks plans to bring up its children communally although at last report there were no children in the community. Early in the history of the community there were difficult experiences with children. In one instance a new member had a small son. Since there was no children's house, he shared a room with his mother and wanted to be with her most of the time. Caring for the child was put on the labor credit system since there was no one who really wanted to do it. There were no other children in the community at the time, and the one little boy became a burden on everyone. A baby girl was born in the community some time later and the community felt it had the right to make decisions about her upbringing. The mother, however, wanted to care for the child herself. After much argument and conflict the mother took the child and left the community.[22]

The community banned families with children until three conditions should be met: (1) the money and labor to build a nursery, (2) membership stability so that the children could be taken care of by the same people, and (3) a group of parents who believed in the community's ideals and would not be likely to leave. These conditions have now been fulfilled.

Kincade discusses some of the goals Twin Oaks members have for their children:

> We do expect, however, to be able to teach the basic things we believe in, such as mutual consideration, and the peaceful settlements of disagreements. We are confident, also, that we can inculcate the capacity for day-to-day enjoyment, the pleasure in learning new things, the habit of imagining oneself in another's shoes. With the possible exception of noncompetition and nonagression, our goals for our children are not different from the goals most liberal Americans have for their children.[23]

Only time will tell whether Twin Oaks will succeed in raising a second generation. If it does, it will surely demonstrate a new way of raising children in the United States.

The future of the family Although many families are breaking up and there are numerous experiments going on in this country at this time with regard to new familial patterns, the majority of families still stay together, at least 70 percent of them at this point. Even within these so-called stable families there are a number of problems which cannot be ignored and which contribute to the overall view that the family as an institution is sadly in need of repair. For example, many families which have not dissolved externally have, in fact, dissolved internally. This means simply that although marriage may not have been broken by deaths, separation, divorce, or annulment, there in fact exists a physical arrangement rather than a social one. In these situations parents and children fulfill many of the obligations of the family, but the nurture needed for healthy socialization does not exist. Fathers and mothers may provide the family with adequate food, shelter, and clothing, but fail to provide those experiences which enable the children in the family to learn role-models necessary for their own developments. Parents in these types of arrangements may fail to be openly expressive towards one another or even the children, thus instilling in the offspring serious limitations with regard to their own abilities to establish families of their own. Although it is difficult to estimate the impact of this type of internal dissolution, some sociologists and psychologists believe that the impact of these families can be more debilitating than actual separation or divorce. This is, of course, an unsubstantiated hypothesis at this point, but it is not uncommon for children to have been a product of such marriages to openly state that divorce would have been a far simpler solution and alternative to the problems confronting their family.

When one considers the numerous problems that beset marriage and child rearing, one might assume that there would be a decline in the proportion of persons becoming married in our society. Glick[24] reports that there is a decrease in the number of persons under eighteen years of age entering into marriage. However, Glick reports that in the 1960–1965 period there was an increasing tendency for both blacks and whites to marry. This indicates, of course, that monogamy, although decried by many as an unworkable approach to marriage, has not been abandoned in our society.

Some institutions, particularly the church, have taken a different approach to the reform of the family in our society. Instead of searching for alternative forms, an emphasis is being placed on premarital counseling, much of which is being done by individuals with sociological backgrounds. In premarital counseling, the focus is upon having the individuals get to know each other and to anticipate the problems they will confront when they enter into a marital relationship. Some adolescents or adults are led astray by the romanticism present in our society and are ill-prepared to deal with the emotional and economic problems confronted after the marriage.

What is not clear at this particular point is the future of the family in American culture. While it is easy to criticize a monogamous marital relationship and the nuclear family, it is far more difficult to come up with viable alternatives to these traditional family forms. What makes the situation even more difficult is the fact that our society provides no opportunity for experimentation in this area, at least no opportunity which is socially accepted. Further, it seems unlikely that existing laws prohibiting multiple marriages are likely to change. What can best be said at this point is that powerful arguments can be mounted on both sides of the issue of marriage and child rearing. Perhaps what is needed are some socially approved experiments in the entire area of marriage and child rearing. One approach might be the polygynist approach among senior citizens—a family structure wherein the male has a number of female "wives." This approach has been suggested by some sociologists but has been rejected for the most part by our society. However, such an experiment would allow the collection of some data about a polygynist living arrangement in which children are not directly affected. Additionally, much research remains to be done with the children who are the products of the communes which have sprung up throughout the United States. Although it can be argued that these communes could have been better designed and better run if the principles of social science had been utilized in their establishment, the fact remains that these children are one of our first real opportunities to examine in a systematic manner the products of a communal approach to family living in our society.

Finally, it is safe to assume that marriage and child rearing will remain the focal point of much sociological thought in the coming decades. The problem is indeed a serious one when one considers the implication of the family structure for the fabric of society. The entire problem is not one that can be taken lightly.

WOMAN'S ROLE IN SOCIETY

Woman's role in our society has been mother, wife, and housekeeper, stereotypically at least. Today that role is not a satisfactory one for many. The changes in woman's role will have a significant impact upon the family. While the problems of women's rights and responsibilities are considered broadly in this section, the impact of changes in the traditional roles is also inherent in the presentation.

Women constitute about 53 percent of the population of this country and for this reason have been classified by many as the oppressed majority. Others point to the "soft" life of women resulting from the technological revolution that has lessened the burden of keeping house and child rearing. Yet, women make up 43 percent of the labor force and

The impact of the women's rights movement has led to an increasing number of opportunities in institutional and business structures as well as in occupational categories for women to have roles and hold jobs traditionally performed by men. *(United Press International Photo)*

it has been well documented that they work primarily because of an economic need. Either a woman is the primary breadwinner which is increasingly the case, or the husband does not have sufficient income to support the family: these are the primary reasons why women have worked. Increasingly, women work because the roles of mother and housewife do not provide sufficient stimulation for her. The impact of housewifery on many women has been alcoholism and mental illness.

Impact of discrimination The result of sexual discrimination has been very similar to that of racial discrimination: self-hatred, relatively low-level employment and economic disadvantage. Another impact of sexual discrimination has been uncertainty of women about their own sexuality. Examples of self-hatred can be found in everyday life. Women often disdain female political candidates and the accomplishments of their own sex. Research studies have demonstrated that females, when asked if they would prefer to be male or female, chose male in percentages ranging from one-quarter to one-half.[25,26] In one study ten times as many fourth-grade girls elected to be boys as did girls to be girls. Clearly the long history of discrimination has taken its toll on women's self respect.

The employment level of women has been well documented by the U.S. Department of Labor's Women's Bureau. Their *Handbook on Women Workers* shows that women hold jobs which are inferior in prestige and earnings to those held by men. Further, women hold jobs which are less likely to provide satisfaction to the worker. Seventy-eight percent of all women are employed as clerical service workers, sales clerks, and as factory workers. Forty percent of the men employed are in these types of jobs. Fifteen percent of women who work are in professional jobs, but most of these are in teaching and nursing. The traditionally male professions of lawyer, doctor, scientist, professor, and engineer are filled by less than 1 percent of the female labor force. Three percent of lawyers and seven percent of the physicians are female. These are, of course, our most prestigious professions.[27]

Women make proportionately less than do men. In 1968, their earnings were 58 percent of those of men *down* from 64 percent in 1955.[28] The Equal Pay Act of 1963 prohibits paying differential wages for equal work, but there is evidence that the practice persists. Investigations in colleges and universities throughout the country have shown that women hold lower professional ranks and are paid less than their male counterparts. This is interesting when one considers that on measures of productivity, such as publication, women do as well as men.

Women's concern about their own sexuality is the result of being viewed as objects of sexual attention rather than as mutual partners who should receive satisfaction from intercourse. In *Sexual Politics* Millett[29] provides many examples of how authors have perpetuated this idea in literature.

A patriarchal tradition which places men in dominant positions has led to the status of women as follows:[30]

1. Patrilineal—the line of descent is through the male. Women who bear "fatherless" children are held in disrepute and the children are termed illegitimate.

2. Most avenues of power are in the hands of males. Government officials, corporation presidents, school officials, etc., are all male.

3. Males dominate females—men who are dominated by females are viewed as something less than real men.

4. A woman's class is related to that of her husband's or father's. Men's class is unaffected by marriage.

5. The Deity is male. Mary achieved status through motherhood.

6. Characteristics of dominance, aggressiveness, and competitiveness are male and valued. Dependence, possessiveness, and emotional weakness "female characteristics," are traits often associated with mental illness.

7. Sexual segregation is common. Athletic programs in schools are primarily for males. Historically, we have had male and female prep schools, colleges and universities. Certain types of civic clubs are also predominantly male. Not until 1973 was it possible for females to belong to Phi Delta Kappa, an education honorary organization. This is particularly interesting when you consider that half of the female professionals are teachers.

8. Women are deprived of the control of their bodies. Prostitution rings are often male dominated. Women are raped and there is no male counterpart. The female is forced to have the abortion when there is a "mistake."

9. Women are economically dependent on men.

The women's movement The reaction to the patriarchal society and its subjugation of women has been a social movement usually titled the Women's Liberation Movement. Freeman[31] indicates that there are really

Members of various feminist groups and sympathizers join a demonstration on the steps of St. Patrick's Cathedral. New York City, to dramatize their feelings and grievances ranging from sexist advertisements to stereotyped roles for women. *(J. Paul Kirouac)*

two aspects of the feminist movement, reform and radical. One she dubs women's rights and the other women's liberation. The women's rights branch has concentrated on legal and economic issues and is more formally organized. The radical or liberation group is constituted quite differently, according to Freeman.[32] This branch is made up of small groups concentrating on a variety of issues. These groups initially had little contact with each other, and thus lacked the cohesiveness to sustain a social movement. However, that situation has changed and the liberation branch probably has greater participation than the rights group.[33] While both women's groups have been instrumental in bringing about change in our society, their goals are as yet unrealized—total equal rights for women. One indicator of the success of these groups was the passage of the Equal Rights Amendment on March 22, 1972.

Impact of Equal Rights Amendment Not all women are solidly behind the movement to provide equal status for women. A counterrevolution actually seems aimed at maintaining the status quo. Many women do not relish a world in which they are asked to compete on an equal basis with men. They have been taught for generations to believe that woman has a certain place, and essentially that place is in a subordinate position to men. The passage of the Equal Rights Amendment will erode certain

Women have adopted the strategy and tactics of other "minority" groups in lobbying for their rights. The National Organization for Women are shown here "taking their case" to the court of public opinion by an orderly demonstration in front of the White House. *(United Press International Photo)*

traditional roles and rights of women. The *Yale Law Journal*[34] listed the possible impacts of the act upon women. These are:

1. The amendment would greatly change the view of the military in terms of men and women.
   a. Assignments could no longer be made on the basis of sex.
   b. Deferment, in the event of a reinstitution of the draft, would have to take into consideration both parents since both would be eligible.
   c. No separate women's corps such as WACS—men and women would be assigned positions based upon individual characteristics.
   d. The provision that is now allowed male officers for dependents would be extended to women.
2. Criminal courts must invalidate laws not applicable to both sexes such as laws regarding sodomy or adultery with sex discriminating provisions.
   a. Laws such as statutory rape and using obscene language in the presence of women would not be allowed by the courts because they are based upon social stereotypes. Rape, for which there is no male counterpart, might be justified by the courts because of the physical abuse involved.
3. Domestic relations laws would be affected.
   a. States could no longer require that a child's last name be the same as the father's—or the mother's.

b. Presumptions and laws about custody based upon sex would be struck down. A court could no longer presume that because the child was female, the mother was the best possible custodian because she too was female *or* because mothers are best equipped to rear children.

c. Differential laws regarding legal age to be married would be struck down.

d. A husband could no longer gain a divorce because a woman refused to accompany him to a new home.

e. Nonsupport laws would apply equally to husband and wives. The journal points out that husbands and wives in Iowa are equally responsible for supporting their children.

f. Laws which place husbands as the managers of community property would be struck down.

g. Grounds for divorce would be the same for men and women.

h. Alimony might either be abolished or extended to both husbands and wives. It could not be viewed as a female right.

4. Labor legislation

   a. Occupational discrimination because of sex would be ended.

   b. Women would no longer be required to take maternity leaves.

   c. Unfavorable working conditions now imposed upon women workers would be abolished for all.

5. Miscellaneous

   a. Child care and child-rearing provisions of labor laws will be extended to men and women.

Some women feel that what they are losing is greater than what they are getting, and are thus fighting the adoption of the ERA. Others firmly believe that this amendment is the cornerstone of female equality and the only thing to be lost is an inferior status.

It is undoubtedly true that before equality for women is reached, many changes must take place. The family structure must become egalitarian, equal economic opportunity must come about, and sexist material in textbooks which portray women in traditional roles must be altered, along with a score of other remnants of the male oriented society. Anyone who has attempted to raise a liberated girl, as both authors have, will find it exceedingly difficult. Hopefully, it will be accomplished for the welfare of womanhood—and manhood.

POPULATION

The family is the unit of procreation in our society. As we shall see, in light of the population explosion, husbands and wives must consider the problem of child rearing as never before.

Densely populated cities such as Tokyo have aroused fears in social planners and demographers. Limited resources and a polluted environment threaten the quality of life of urban dwellers. (*United Nations/Phillips*)

An excerpt from the Report of the Commission on Population Growth and the American Future brings the problem of population into sharp focus:

> There is hardly any social problem confronting this nation whose solution would be easier if our population were larger. Even now, the dreams of too many Americans are not being realized; others are being fulfilled at too high a cost. Accordingly, this Commission has concluded that our country can no longer afford the uncritical acceptance of the population growth ethic that "more is better."[35]

Impact of population upon environment At the present time the population of the world is approximately 3¾ billion. This number is doubling approximately every forty years and therefore should reach 7½ billion by approximately 2010. This staggering number has caused considerable concern among scientists of all types, and social scientists in particular. Perhaps most important among the issues confronting the world with a population of 7½ billion, how will these people be fed and housed? Other important issues involve the impact of this number of people upon the general ecology of the world. At this time, a number of people support the idea of ZPG (zero population growth). This issue has raised a variety of moral, political, and social issues which will be discussed briefly in this section.

The population of the world and of the United States is determined by two important factors. First, and perhaps most obvious, is the birth rate. It takes about 2.1 offspring per marital union to maintain the population of the world, and in fact, the 2.1 figure has been reached in the United States. However, the average family expects to have 2.3 children in this country according to a survey by the Census Bureau. This expectation can be contrasted with expectations of 4.0 to 4.5 in certain

African and Asian countries. If these expectations are realized, there is little doubt that the 7½ billion population figure will be reached by 2010.

The death rate is the second factor influencing population of the world. It is common knowledge that the average man and woman in this country live longer than they did ten or twenty years ago. While longevity in this country increases by one or two years every decade, the expected life span of an Asian or African may be increased dramatically by the initiation of a vaccination program, and the utilization of insecticides to control mosquitoes and other types of disease-bearing insects. In short, the death rate in the entire world is being decreased by the application of modern medical practice. There is little doubt that this will be a long-term trend and thus the lower death rate will contribute to the population problem.

One of the difficult problems in discussing the actual numbers of people who will be habitating this planet is the difficulty in predicting both birth and death rates. Birth rates are influenced by economic trends, educational attainment, religious and ethnic background. We have also seen that the adoption of effective birth control devices, such as the pill and the IUD (intrauterine device), can have significant impact upon the birth rate. It seems certain that liberalized abortion laws will also decrease the birth rate in this country as it did in Japan and other parts of the world. The death rate could be greatly influenced by breakthroughs in the area of heart disease and other leading causes of death.

For the aforementioned reasons, differential population forecasts are made. As can be seen in Table 3-2, differential birth rates can have a considerable impact.

In making the projections found in Table 3-2, the demographers make a series of assumptions. First, it is assumed that the immigration rate of 400,000 would remain unchanged. Second, the projections also assumed that data collected from women who had entered the child-rearing period and had not completed it gave accurate information about the number of additional births expected. Third, it was assumed that mortality rates could be projected. Finally, the differential rates listed in Table 3-2 are projections of birth rates for women who have *not yet entered the child-bearing age.*

It can readily be seen that a 2.8 birth rate would bring this country to a population close to double that of its present size. The impact of a population of this magnitude would be staggering. For example, the Commission on Population and Growth foresees problems in the area of energy usage, water supply, availability of recreational facilities, food prices which would increase by 40 to 50 percent, pollution and other areas, if our birth rate is near the 3.0 figure. This same commission saw relatively fewer problems if a 2.0 birth rate were to be maintained.

TABLE 3-2 SUMMARY OF PROJECTIONS OF TOTAL POPULATION: 1960 TO 2020

Year July 1	Average number of births per woman upon completion of child rearing			
	2.8	2.5	2.1	1.8
1960		180,671,000		
1965		194,303,000		
1970		204,879,000		
1972		208,837,000		
Projections in Thousands				
1975	215,872	215,324	213,925	213,378
1980	230,955	228,676	224,132	221,848
1985	248,711	243,935	235,701	230,913
1990	266,238	258,692	246,639	239,084
1995	282,766	272,211	256,015	245,591
2000	300,406	285,969	264,430	250,686
2005	321,025	310,397	273,653	255,209
2010	344,094	318,156	281,968	259,332
2015	367,911	335,028	290,432	262,631
2020	392,030	351,368	297,746	264,564

Source: *Population Estimates and Projections* 1972, U.S. Dept. of Commerce Series P-25, No. 493, p. 1.

Population control The means by which population stabilization in this country can be permanently achieved are not clear. Our birth rate has fallen, but whether or not it will remain at the 2.1 rate remains to be seen. Suggestions have been made that perhaps income tax deduction should not be given for more than two children thus bringing social and economic pressure on persons having large families. As was previously noted, effective birth control devices have a significant impact upon birth rate and this research goes on. One of the interesting aspects in this area is the search for birth control devices which can be used by males other than the condom or submitting to a vasectomy. The male pill seems to be in the future but is a distinct possibility.

Perhaps the bitterest fights have arisen over the recent trend for the use of abortion as a means of lowering the birth rate. On one hand are many religious and other concerned groups who state categorically that the taking of a fetus regardless of the age is murder, and on the other hand are groups who believe that any child born into the world should be wanted and valued and therefore it is more humane to destroy the fetus in its early developmental stages than to have it born as an unwanted child. However, abortion as a means of ending pregnancy was accelerated by the 1972 Supreme Court ruling that state laws which prohibit abortion violate a constitutional right of privacy and therefore must be struck down. The court held that the right of personal privacy in the Ninth and Fourteenth Amendments permits a woman in consultation with a physician to make determinations about whether or not to have an abortion. In the third trimester of pregnancy, according to the court, the fetus becomes in essence a human being and therefore must be protected. This protection outweighs the individual rights of the mother.

There are, of course, other means by which the birth rate may be reduced. These include postponement of marriage, "birth" counseling, and the rhythm method which is advocated by the Roman Catholic Church as a means of limiting the size of the family. None of these appear to be viable solutions to what appears to be perhaps the most pressing problem of mankind at this time. It seems likely that the population issue will continue to be a major one throughout this decade and into the next at least so far as the world is concerned. In this country ZPG seems to be well within reach but we can ill-afford to ignore the population crisis that appears to be arising in the world because it must inevitably impinge upon the affairs of this nation.

SUMMARY

The theory and process of social change were introduced at the outset of this chapter. There are two major lessons to be learned from this discussion. First, there is considerable disagreement among sociologists about why change occurs. Second, we know that change which occurs in the form of social movements may have a variety of beginnings. Certainly, a single individual may be able to bring about social change as well as groups or institutions within our society.

The family is one institution in our society which is changing and it seems likely that the forces which have caused problems with our family will continue and accelerate. It also seems likely that either means of supporting the family similar to those adopted in other countries or new child-rearing approaches must be adopted if we are to provide children the environment needed during their early developmental years.

It is a certainty that women will continue to gain equal status in our society, but the struggle is likely to continue for a considerable period of time. As women assume a more important role in our society their role in the family will also change. This of course means that the traditional male role will be affected. It seems apparent that the assumption of equal status will be beneficial to our society in general, but its short range impact upon men and society in general is difficult to predict.

Finally, our population poses a major threat to our economic and perhaps societal well-being. Perhaps as women become more career oriented the problem of overpopulation will be eliminated because of the relationship of work and family roles. Regardless of our stand on birth control measures, the overall population problem must be of vital concern to us all.

REVIEW QUESTIONS

1. To what extent are you a social problem? What ideas do you have that might contribute to social problems in the future?
2. What appear to be the causes of divorce? How could you personally avoid the situations that you have listed?
3. Is the family a viable child-rearing institution? Why or why not?
4. What are the advantages of approaches to child rearing in Israel, Russia, and China when compared to those in the United States?
5. What is your reaction to communal living? List the advantages and disadvantages.
6. What is the future of the family in the United States?
7. What is Women's Liberation? What are its goals? How does it differ from rights movements? How is it similar?
8. What are your own views of the role of women? Men?
9. Do you agree that we have a patriarchal society? Why or why not?
10. Would you vote for the Equal Rights Amendment? Why or why not?
11. Should family size be regulated in the United States? Why or why not?
12. What is your stand on abortion? Justify the stand.
13. What are the different explanations of social change?
14. What causes social change?
15. What are the steps in a social movement?

CHAPTER FOUR
SOCIAL PROBLEMS: WORK, DRUGS, CRIMINALITY, AND POVERTY

IDEAS AND CONCEPTS

hallucinogens
psychodelic drugs which cause distortions of physical senses

crime
a violation of societal standards of behavior

guaranteed income
a supplemental income for families below subsistence level as determined by the government

pleasure ethic
a value system based on the attainment of personal happiness

In Chapter 3 population problems, the status of women and the family were discussed. This discussion of social problems continues in this chapter with a look at work, drugs, criminality, and poverty. At the outset of Chapter 3 you were urged to consider yourself as a present or potential social problem. Hopefully, that same introspection will carry forth as you read Chapter 4. While you read you may wish to consider whether or not you have made a wise career choice; or will you end up like millions of Americans, unemployed, underemployed or unhappily employed?

Other very personal considerations may involve drug usage and participation in our so-called criminal society. Most people know that drug abuse can have disastrous effects upon the individual but most have not considered the impact of millions of drug users. Similarly, an occasional theft from a drugstore or supermarket seems small; but what are the implications for our social structure when millions participate in some form of crime? Finally, the total picture of poverty must be considered as perhaps our most chronic social problem and, while it may be difficult to see what an individual can do about such a pervasive problem, a total social consciousness must be the forerunner to the solution of any major social problem.

WORK AS A SOCIAL PROBLEM

At this time, the unemployment rate stands at approximately 5 percent of the total work force. That means that approximately 4½ million people in this country are unemployed. This situation in itself poses a significant problem for our society because of the human misery and alienation from society that can occur whenever an individual has been denied an opportunity to work in a society where work is valued above all other activities. What may make the foregoing unemployment statistics even worse is the fact that some workers have become so discouraged that they have ceased to look for jobs and therefore are not counted among those who are actively seeking employment. Estimates by the U.S. Department of Labor indicate that as many as one million more people may have ceased to look for work because of past failures. This would, of course, mean that the unemployment figure is nearly 5½ million in our society. In this section this and other statistics will be employed and inferences for society drawn.

Trends in the labor force When unemployment figures are examined more carefully, some interesting facts become apparent. For example, in Table 4-1, the unemployment figures for individuals twenty years of age and older are presented and in Table 4-2 the employment rate for sixteen to nineteen year olds.

TABLE 4-1 PERCENT OF WORK FORCE UNEMPLOYED WHO ARE 20 YEARS OF AGE AND OLDER

Year	White male	White female	Black male	Black female
1969	1.9	3.4	3.7	5.8
1970	3.2	4.4	5.6	6.9
1971	4.0	5.3	7.2	8.7

Source: Manpower Report to the President, 1972

Several facts become obvious whenever these two tables are examined. First of all, there is a discrepancy between the unemployment figures for whites and blacks in our society and, at least for the year as given, this situation is relatively unchanging. What is even more evident is the sixteen to nineteen year old group is in deep trouble so far as employment is concerned. Generally speaking, teenage unemployment rates run from four to five times that of the twenty and older group and these figures tend to bear this out. Another fact crystallizes when one examines the figures: unemployment among females is considerably higher than that among males. This is the result of discrimination which has taken place in our society for the past two centuries.

The question which may have arisen in some minds is, "Is this situation likely to be self-correcting if there is a greater emphasis in our society in providing equality in the world of work?" The U.S. Department of Labor has made a series of predictions about what is likely to occur with regard to employment during the 70s and beyond. One other thing that is certain to occur is that the number of young adults in the society is going to increase dramatically. For example, the sixteen to twenty-four year old age group who will be entering the labor market will increase by about 19 percent while the twenty-five to thirty-four year old age bracket will increase 49 percent. This, of course, means keener competition for entry level jobs and an increased likelihood that the rate of unemployed juveniles and young adults may very well increase unless adjustments are made in our society.

The U.S. Department of Labor also predicts that the civilian labor force will increase in educational achievement. In 1965, 46 percent of the labor force had at least a high school education, while an additional 28 percent had some college. By 1975, it is anticipated that both of these percentages will increase somewhat. This, of course, means that the individuals in our society who are deficient in the educational area are likely to find it increasingly difficult to find appropriate employment. This situation will be worsened considerably by the fact that by the end of this decade less than 5 percent of the jobs in the labor force will be in the unskilled areas.

TABLE 4-2 UNEMPLOYMENT RATE FOR AGES SIXTEEN TO NINETEEN YEARS OLD IN PERCENT

Year	Total	White	Black
1969	12.2	10.7	24.0
1970	15.3	13.5	29.1
1971	16.9	15.1	31.7

Source: Manpower Report to the President, 1972

One of the unfortunate predictions being made by the U.S. Department of Labor is that blacks are likely to continue to lag behind the whites in the employment situation in the 70s. It is an established fact that blacks have made considerable gains in the amount of formal schooling completed. At this point 80+ percent of the white students leaving high school have completed the requirements for diploma and over 70 percent of the blacks have done likewise. But as is obvious from the employment figures this has had little impact thus far in the area of getting jobs. Some strides are being made by black workers in the area of professional, technical, clerical, and craft-type jobs, but on the whole blacks have not yet reached parity with whites. There is one bright spot in the overall employment picutre for blacks, however, and that is in the area of college graduates. Businesses, industries, governmental agencies, and educational institutions are all actively recruiting black workers for their establishment and black members of our society with college diplomas are able to demand and get wages equal to or superior to those of their white counterparts.

The influx of women into the work force will accelerate the situation that already exists in the American work force. There can be little doubt that a continuing number of women will enter the world of work during the 70s and 80s. At this point women make significant contributions to family income in this country. In fact, they contribute about one-quarter of family income at all economic levels. This is somewhat astonishing when one considers the discrimination that has occurred against women in professional areas. In 1972, 7 percent of the physicians in this country were female, while in countries such as Russia more than one-half of the physicians are women. In the law profession less than 3 percent of the lawyers are women—a statistic which has gone unchanged for the last fifteen years, and surprisingly there is a smaller percent of Ph.D.'s who are women today than there were two decades ago. The fact is that women will enter the work force and it is predicted that 100 million workers will be in the work force by 1980; of these 37 million will be women and of these 32 million will be married. Clearly our society must develop institutions and means by which child-rearing patterns can be changed. It is also clear that opportunities must be made available for women to work on parity with men in our society.

In looking at the employment and unemployment situation, one current phenomenon must be noted. Today for the first time there is unemployment and *underemployment* among persons holding the doctorate degree. Although reliable figures are unavailable at this time, there are in fact persons holding Ph.D. degrees who are unable to obtain unemployment in our society. There is a far greater number of persons holding a doctorate who are underemployed, that is, they are holding positions which could be filled with persons with a bachelor's and master's degree. If the National Science Foundation's estimates are correct, this situation is unlikely to change. The N.S.F. estimates that during the next decade there will be positions for between 270 thousand to 297 thousand social and natural scientists and engineers with Ph.D. degrees. Their estimates are that colleges and universities will produce between 315 thousand and 336 thousand of these individuals. This, of course, means that many individuals receiving the Ph.D. degree will be unable to obtain positions which are commensurate with their skills and training. This whole area points to a problem in our society which is just now beginning to receive appropriate attention. We know that somewhat less than 20 percent of the jobs in our society require a B.A. degree or higher, and yet the great American dream has been to educate large numbers of persons in our colleges and universities. In fact, in many areas we have overproduced and many individuals receiving the baccalaureate degree are unable to secure appropriate employment. This has caused a considerable amount of disorganization in the educational and working world. It seems likely that vocational-technical education and other types of subcollege training will become more in vogue in the years to come.

Worker alienation Although unemployment and underemployment are serious problems in the occupational structure, many members of our society are becoming increasingly concerned about the alienation of some members of our society from work itself. Although some people point to the young as being lazy and uninterested in working, the whole idea of job alienation goes far deeper than just a few young people who are unwilling or unready to enter into the labor market.

First let us examine the meaning of work to members of our society. In a study reported in a 1955 article in the *American Sociological Review*,[1] a study was reported that tried to ascertain what work means to people. For example, men were asked "If you inherited enough money to quit working, would you?" Eighty percent of those responding said no, they would not; only 20 percent said yes. These men comprised a national sample and therefore were representative of a cross section of our population. In 1971, a study was conducted at the Ohio State Center

Alienation results not only from worker dissatisfaction with his job but also from the value society places on his work. *(Charles Gatewood)*

for Vocational Technical Education entitled Worker Adjustment Problems: High School to Work.[2] Persons in this study were all under the age of twenty-five years. When they were asked if they were to become financially independent would they continue working, 85 percent responded affirmatively. Thus it seems that work in our society is tied up with more than earning a living. It seems that working is related to a feeling of self-worth, of belonging, and of being a productive member of society. If this assumption is true, as it seems to be, alienation can only lead to lower self-esteem and maladjustment. Let us examine for a moment some of the data to see if in fact workers are dissatisfied with their occupations. Table 4-3 shows the results of the 1955 studies of occupational satisfaction and dissatisfaction cited previously. Interestingly, persons in managerial positions were the most dissatisfied with their occupations. This group was followed by those in service occupations and then by those in unskilled occupations. Twenty to thirty-six percent of the individuals in these three occupational groups were dissatisfied with their occupations. Are these figures an indication that persons are alienated from their job? Although the data is not clear cut, they are certainly some support for this idea. In the Ohio State[3] study of young workers, 43 percent of these individuals expressed dissatisfaction with the jobs which they held and there was a direct correlation between the level of the job and the amount of dissatisfaction expressed. For example, those persons who were blue-collar workers on the lower end of the occupational scale were extremely dissatisfied with their jobs. Nearly 57 percent of this group indicated that they would like some type of a job change.

What does worker alienation mean in a society such as ours? It is increasingly clear that alienation has a considerable impact in a variety of areas. Perhaps the most famous case where worker satisfaction has manifested itself is in the Lordstown, Ohio, Vega plant. In this ultramodern factory designed by General Motors to produce its small subcompact car much of the work was so routinized by the automation that workers soon became bored and discouraged. Because of their boredom and alienation workers left their jobs and refused to return unless work could be made more interesting and satisfying. The automobile industry generally is faced with unusually high absenteeism rates, and some have reported as high as 13 percent of their work force absent on Fridays and Mondays.

Labor experts are unable to estimate the impact upon the quality of the product produced and upon the lower production because of worker dissatisfaction and alienation. However, as the November, 1972, issue of *Industry Week* reports, worker productivity in this country has gone up approximately 3 percent per year, while that in Japan has increased at a rate of about 12 percent per year. There can be little doubt that worker attitude has some impact upon American business.

There can be no easy solution to the problems that have been brought about by worker alienation. Technology will continue to be an important force in the American working situation, but technology in some instances has impact of lessening the importance of man in the work environment—thus contributing to his alienation. Certainly the advent of large corporations with thousands of workers has also contributed to this situation. The alienation of being a number rather than a person has been experienced by most of us in modern-day society. It seems unlikely that we will stop technological advances or reduce the size of our corporations; however, alienation has also resulted because *workers no longer see the products of their labor*. Rather, they see some small portion of it and therefore can take no pride in the product they produce or help to produce. Again, the assembly line has become so much a part of American industry that it is hard to visualize its abandonment or modification, particularly if it lessens productivity.

Just as there are no single causes for the problem of worker alienation, there can be no easy solutions to the situation. Shorter work weeks have been proposed and this seems to be in the offing. We have gone from 40 hours a week to 38.5 hours and can be expected to reach approximately 35 hours by the end of this decade. The theory here, of

TABLE 4-3 PERCENT SATISFIED AND DISSATISFIED WITH THEIR JOBS BY OCCUPATIONS

Class	Very satisfied	Satisfied	Dissatisfied
Middle			
Professional	54	36	10
Managerial	23	41	36
Sales	46	36	18
Working Class			
Trades	32	57	11
Operatives	25	60	15
Unskilled	25	54	21
Service	19	50	31

Source: American Sociological Review 1955, 20, pp. 191–198.

course, is to reduce the boredom and alienation by forcing the worker to spend less time on the work situation. Other industries have attempted to adopt Japanese procedures where the workers are made to feel a part of the company. The Toyota company has worker bowling leagues, worker recreation areas, worker housing developments, and every attempt is made to make the employee feel that he is an integral part of the company. Few can doubt that the Japanese have been successful in motivating their workers to produce superior products. Whether or not this approach can be utilized in this country remains to be seen. Still another approach that can be utilized is to rotate workers through jobs, particularly those involved in routine tasks. A worker may, for example, hold down a chore no more than one week before he rotates to another, and in a series of four weeks he may hold down four different jobs and then begin the rotation again. This has not significantly helped the problem where it has been tried, but it is one of the many solutions being attempted at this particular time in American business and industry.

What is feared by many people in this country is that the work ethic which has served as the cornerstone of American philosophy will be completely scrapped. Some have pointed to ancient Rome where work was abandoned by Romans and the culture existed on the labor of a group of slaves. Some say this led to the demise of the Roman Empire. This is, of course, conjecture. Other sociologists have suggested that the work ethic should in fact be abandoned and that a new leisure ethic be adopted in our culture. This would mean that the centrality of work in our society would be replaced by a focus upon assisting its members to learn how to use their time in other ways than producing goods and services. It seems unlikely that this will occur in the near future, but what seems equally likely is the problem will continue to receive considerable attention among sociologists and industrial people throughout this country.

GLOSSARY

acidhead Frequent user of LSD
bag Packet of drugs
barbs Barbiturates
bennies Benzedrine, an amphetamine
bindle Packet of narcotics
blast Strong effect from a drug
blue angels Amytal, a barbiturate
blue velvet Paregoric and Pyribenzamine mixed and injected
bombita Amphetamine injection, sometimes taken with heroin
buttons Sections of the peyote cactus
cap Capsule
chipping Taking narcotics occasionally
cokie Cocaine addict
cold turkey Sudden withdrawal of narcotics (from the goose flesh, which resembles the skin of a cold plucked turkey)
coming down Recovering from a trip
crystal Methedrine, an amphetamine
cubehead Frequent user of LSD
cut Dilute drugs by adding milk, sugar, or other narcotics
deck Packet of narcotics
dexies Dexedrine, an amphetamine
dirty Possessing drugs
dollies Dolophine (also known as methadone)
downers Sedatives, alcohol, tranquilizers, and narcotics
dynamite High-grade heroin
flash Initial feeling after injecting
flip Become psychotic
floating Under the influence of drugs
freakout Bad experience
gage Marijuana
goof balls Sleeping pills
hash Hashish, the resin of Cannabis
hay Marijuana
hearts Dexedrine tablets
hophead Narcotics addict
horse Heroin
joint Marijuana cigarette
jolly beans Pep pills
junkie Narcotics addict
kick the habit Stop using narcotics (from the withdrawal leg muscle twitches)
layout Equipment for injecting drug
lemonade Poor heroin
maintaining Keeping at a certain level of drug effect
manicure Remove the dirt, seeds, and stems from marijuana
meso Mescaline, the alkaloid in peyote
meth Methamphetamine (also known as Methedrine, Desoxyn)
narc Narcotics detective
nickel bag $5 packet of drugs

O. D. Overdose of narcotics
on the nod Sleepy from narcotics
pop Inject drugs
pothead Heavy marijuana user
purple hearts Dexamyl, a combination of Dexedrine and Amytal: (from the shape and color)
quill A matchbook cover for sniffing Methedrine, cocaine, or heroin
rainbows Tuinal (Amytal and Seconal), barbiturate combination in blue and red capsule
red devils Seconal, a barbiturate
roach Marijuana butt
satch cotton Cotton used to strain drugs before injection
scag Heroin
skin popping Injecting drugs under the skin
smack Heroin
snorting Inhaling drugs
snow Cocaine
speed Methedrine, an amphetamine
speedball An injection of a stimulant and a depressant, originally heroin and cocaine
speedfreak Habitual user of speed
stick Marijuana cigarette
tracks Scars along veins after many injections
turps Elixir of terpin hydrate with codeine, a cough syrup
twenty-five LSD (from its original designation, LSD-25)
works Equipment for injecting drugs
yellow jacket Nembutal, a barbiturate

DRUG ABUSE

Drug abuse is not a new sociological problem. So far as anthropologists can determine, practically every society, no matter how primitive or how highly developed, has utilized various forms of drugs. However, the present preoccupation with drug abuse stems from at least two facets. The first consideration is the overall scope of the problem. Although the exact nature of this will be investigated further in this section, there is a widespread belief that has been substantiated to a degree that a large number of people are involved in some form of drug abuse. A second source of the concern regarding drug abuse is that it now appears to be rampant among the young age groups. The utilization of drugs by youth is, of course, a violation of societal values and norms. This arouses fears that drugs may tear the very fabric of society.

The first question that must be answered of course is: "What is a drug?" A drug may be roughly defined as any substance that has a potential of altering the homostatic condition of the body or the mind. This, of course, means that a wide variety of substances may be classified as drugs. Caffeine is a drug widely utilized by persons in the

American society and is absorbed in the form of coffee. Caffeine stimulates the overall body functioning. Similarly, alcohol and tobacco are two widely used drugs in American culture today. Although it is likely that alcohol consumption and alcoholism is a primary drug problem in the United States today, the present preoccupation with drugs has not focused upon the alcoholism problem, although there is deep concern about this situation. Perhaps the reason for alcohol not being included in the present thrust to eliminate drugs from our culture is that it is to a very large extent already highly regulated in each state, and in many instances local towns and cities have laws which regulate the sale and use of alcoholic beverages. Additionally, society has established means for the overall control of the person who overuses alcohol and it has gone so far as to establish treatment programs for the alcoholic. For the most part, this has not been done for other drugs with the possible exception of heroin.

Types of drugs There are at least five categories of drugs which are the focus of attention in America today. The first of these drug categories is *hallucinogens* or psychodelic drugs. This category of drugs includes peyote, mescaline, and LSD among a variety of others. LSD, or lysergic acid, has received perhaps the most attention in our society. LSD is noted for producing strong and often bizarre mental reactions in people. These reactions for the most part take the form of distortions of physical senses—vision, touch, smell, and hearing. Hallucinogens may also produce other mental reactions such as hallucinations. Marijuana, the most commonly used of the hallucinogens and probably the most commonly abused of the drugs to be discussed in this section, also has a mind-altering property. Hashish is the dark brown resin that is collected from the top of the marijuana plant and is at least five times stronger than the marijuana leaves and stems.

Little is known about the long term impact of the usage of hallucinogens, although there have been many documented cases of persons involved in accidents because of impaired judgment resulting from the usage of these substances. There have also been instances of suicide and murder because of the impairment of the senses or the psychological reaction produced by the use of these drugs. There is a strong belief that even the usage of marijuana may affect the personality of a heavy user. However, this has not been documented and is under intensive study at this time.

Another broad category of drugs in common use in American society today can be classified as *stimulants*. The use of a stimulant may produce the effect of overconfidence and alertness, or may induce a false sense of security in the user, depending upon the type of drug taken and the extent of the use. The stimulants in common use include cocaine, amphetamines, benzedrine, dextroamphetamines, and metaamphetamines. Stimulants are also known as "uppers" or "pep" pills and at one time it was common for college students and others who were required to be awake over long periods of time to utilize stimulants to increase their functioning. As was mentioned previously, coffee is a widely used stimulant in our society, but as compared to the impact of some of the aforementioned drugs it is extremely mild.

Stimulants as a category of drugs must be viewed as extremely dangerous. Amphetamines are known to produce a *psychological* or *physical dependence*, or in some instances both—depending upon the amount and period of usage. It is also known that the body develops a *tolerance* to amphetamines, thus requiring a heavier and heavier dosage to produce the original effect. Cocaine, another stimulant, has been imported in this country from South America where it has been used for centuries by Indians. Cocaine, sometimes known as "snow," is increasingly part of the drug scene in the United States. In large dosages cocaine produces hallucinogenic effects and may produce many of the same effects as amphetamines. After prolonged use of cocaine, the individual builds up a strong dependence upon the drug, thus increasing the likelihood that he will continue to utilize it. It has also been fairly well established that cocaine has a personality-altering property and the long-term use of cocaine may lead to a variety of severe psychological disturbances.

Sedative drugs have been widely utilized in this country in a variety of ways. Doctors have prescribed them for hyperactive business men and housewives to reduce their anxiety and many of these drugs have been utilized in the treatment of high blood pressure, ulcers, spastic colitis, and other types of disorders. Commonly utilized sedatives are pentobarbitol, secobarbital, phenobarbital, thiopental, and a variety of others. These drugs are marketed under the names such as Nembutal, Seconal, and Luminal.

The response from the use of barbiturates is that of depression of the central nervous system. Typically, the individual feels drowsy or sleepy, but there is also an accompanying sense of well-being, which develops with the usage of these drugs. Individuals on "downers," "sleepers," or "goof balls" as they are commonly categorized run the risk of habituation because the body quickly builds a tolerance to barbituates and other types of sedative drugs. This habituation may lead to addiction and thus to the most serious of drug problems, since addiction must roughly be defined as a physical dependence upon a drug. Whenever this occurs, withdrawal from the drug is usually extremely difficult and may be extremely painful. It also should be noted that barbiturates are commonly used in suicides, and accidental overdoses of these drugs which result in death are not uncommon. This is another of the dangerous qualities of the barbituates.

An extremely dangerous category of drugs although in relatively small use are the volatile substances. These substances are absorbed by sniffing and such commercial solvents as Benzine, Naptha, acetone, carbontetrachloride and others may be utilized to produce the effect of the inhalents. Common airplane glue at one time would produce the symptoms of nausea, dizziness, shakiness, and muscle spasms on the physical side, but might also produce a dreamlike state of drunkenness and sleepiness accompanied by hallucinations and delusions. Most manufacturers of this substance have removed those chemicals which produce these reactions, but other common aerosols and anesthetics—such as chloroform—may also be utilized to produce these effects.

Generally, sniffers are quite young, although there have been documented cases of adults who were sniffers. It should be noted that sniffing can be an extremely dangerous activity and in some instances the result is death because the substances contained in the material inhaled cause damage to the internal organs, particularly the liver and, of course, the lungs.

The final broad class of drugs are those generally termed as narcotic. Narcotic drugs are extremely addictive and heroin is undoubtedly the best known of these drugs. Demerol and Methadone are also narcotic drugs, as are codeine, opium, morphine, and other opium derivatives. All opiates are derived from the juice of the opium poppy, which is produced for the most part in the Near East. The United States entered into contracts with the Turkish government to destroy the opium plant before it is processed into raw opium, but these were renounced by Turkey in 1974.

Heroin has a variety of street names, such as "Smack," "Scag," "Horse," "Junk," and "H" and is the most commonly sold narcotic drug in this country. The heroin addict gets "*hooked*" which means that very rapidly a physical dependence upon the drug occurs, and since the body builds up a tolerance to heroin, what is required is an increasingly heavy dosage to maintain the effects of the drug. Because heroin must be obtained illegally and because of the expense of the habit an individual needs increasingly large amounts of money to support his habit.

Seymour[4] in *The Young Die Quietly* describes the life of an addict as follows:

> 7:49 AM . . . Raymond reaches toward the table beside his bed and takes a small glassine bag, eye dropper and hypodermic needle he left there the night before. He pours white powder from the bag into a few drops of water in a bottle top and then holds a lighted match under the mixture. When the heroin is dissolved he takes it up in the eye dropper, pushes the needle into an artery into his arm and injects the fluid.
>
> Another day has begun. The same as yesterday and the same as tomorrow, if Raymond is still lucky or unlucky enough to be alive.
>
> "A wake-up" morning shot of heroin to calm his anxieties. And to taper off the feeling of nausea.

> 10:24 AM . . . Raymond forces open the door of apartment 12A, in a luxury building on the East side. He rummages quickly through the bureau in the bedroom, finds the jewelry box, and scoops up three rings and a bracelet. He picks up the television set from the bedroom table, moves out the door again, pulls it closed, and heads back down the stairs to the building service entrance.
>
> 12:18 PM . . . Raymond approaches his "connection" on 112th Street. "I want aid," he says quietly as he walks past the man. He enters the hallway of a tenement building down the block, leaves $40.00 between banisters on the staircase, and goes back out into the street. He watches the pusher enter and leave the building, then he goes back into the hallway and picks up the glassine bags, stuffs them into his pocket, and hurries off. Soon he will have another shot of heroin coursing through his veins and the world will be all right again for a few hours.
>
> The rest of Raymond's day follows a familiar pattern: Empty activity and a growing anxiety about finding enough money to keep supplied with heroin. During the afternoon a cheap movie. Then another shot. This time with some friends on a rooftop. In the evening, Raymond and two companions stake out a darkened side street in the West 70's. After a short wait they spot their quarry—a grey haired man walking alone down the block. Raymond holds a knife to his throat while one of the others seizes his wallet. A sharp kick in the small of his back sends the panic stricken man sprawling toward the gutter. The three addicts run down the street, around the corner, and duck into a subway.
>
> Another shot before going to bed. Then Raymond carefully arranges his works on the bedside table ready for that first shot of heroin when he wakes up the following morning—to get him "straight" for another day.

The female addict may lead quite a different life from that described for Raymond. While it is increasingly common in larger cities throughout the United States for females to be involved in violent crimes, it is far more likely that the female would turn to a life of prostitution to support her habit, a habit which may run up to $100 or more a day in some instances.

Heroin may be injected directly into the vein—called *mainlining*—or placed just under the skin, or sniffed through the nose. No matter how it is taken, the effects generally appear to be the same, that is, it takes the edge off reality and removes the individual from the problems that he must face on a day-to-day basis. The addict who is unable to obtain his supply begins to experience withdrawal symptoms within twelve to sixteen hours and these symptoms become progressively worse, but within a week the individual is usually free from his symptoms.

The life of a "junkie" is an uncertain one. Because heroin tends to reduce the sex, thirst, and hunger drives, it is not uncommon for these individuals to become highly undernourished. Another common problem is the incidence of hepatitis and other blood infections because of the use of unsterile syringes and needles. Tuberculosis, venereal disease,

This teen-age prostitute makes her contacts on the street. She is likely to have a history of drug addiction, venereal disease, and arrests. Poverty, poor housing, and broken homes are other factors contributing to prostitution among the young. (*United Press International Photo*)

and other types of medical problems are also common problems of the "junkie."

Theories of drug abuse Brotman and Suffet[5] in *Youthful Drug Use* attempt to identify the various causes for drug abuse in our society. They put forth a variety of theories as to why drug abuse occurs. The theories they discuss are of three types: societal, interactional, and personality theories. One of the theories put forth by Brotman and Suffet and one found in a variety of other references is that drug abuse is the result of our society blocking young people from fulfilling their goals and desires in socially approved ways. In this theory, since youths have neither legal or illegal means of achieving the trappings of the adult world, they develop a retreatist attitude and drugs are the instrument for that retreat. According to this explanation drugs are in effect a withdrawal from society.

A second theory outlined by Brotman and Suffet[6] is somewhat similar to the first. This theory asserts that youthful drug users turn to marijuana and other types of drugs as a visible means of dissent. According to this theory, drug use is in fact a rejection of the values and life-styles of the adult culture.

A third societal level theory indicates that the use of drugs is the forerunner of the new pleasure ethic. Those who hold this theory assert that the old work ethic of our society is gradually breaking down and we are on the verge of a pleasure or hedonistic ethic in our society. Drug abuse is simply one of the new means by which gratification may be obtained. Proponents of this theory point to new experiences in the area of music, sex, and the overall leisure movement that is occurring in this country to provide support fór their argument.

Brotman and Suffet[7] point out that the interactional theories of drug abuse have several components. The first component of these theories is that drugs must be available before they can be utilized. This, of course, is ridiculously obvious. Persons who hold this point of view also indicate that the use of new drugs or the use of drugs at all is determined primarily by the association with people who are users themselves. This presupposes, of course, that the individual has been accepted into a group and that he will not report the activities either to parents or local law enforcement groups.

The third component of the interactional theory points out that individuals may begin to use drugs primarily as a response to their peer group. It is, of course, quite common to note, particularly among early adolescents, the high degree of conformity in the area of dress, music, language, and so forth. Theorists who hold an interactional point of view note that the more highly motivated an individual is to join a particular group the more likely he is to behave as do the members of the group. The availability and the peer group in themselves are not sufficient to lead to drug abuse according to the interactional theorists. For the most part, members of our society have been socialized to the extent that drug abuse is viewed unfavorably. Interactional theorists note that the third step to drug abuse must be an erosion of these negative attitudes, or at least a neutralization of them. The individual must ultimately begin to define drug abuse as a positive experience rather than a negative one. This experience, of course, takes place with an individual who is to a large degree dependent upon group activities. Once the individual has defined drug use as a positive experience, he has taken the first step toward drug abuse.

A fourth theory of drug abuse hypothesizes overuse of drugs is the result of some type or types of personality development. Specifically, this particular theory attempts to explain drug abuse by looking at underlying emotional problems and neurotic conflicts. There is a degree of support for this type of theory. As early as 1958, Ausubel,[8] in a study of thirty addicts, found that there exists a certain personality pattern. He found that addicts typically have a low tolerance of anxiety and frustration and are eager to use props of any type whenever they are available to them. Ausubel described the potential male addict as one who is suffering from a weak ego structure, a weak superego, and one who has an inadequate masculine identification. It is probably impossible to outline the personality traits of the potential drug abuser. However, the U.S. Department of Justice has attempted to alert the public by portraying a "typical" drug abuser.

In all likelihood an adequate theory of drug abuse would have to take into consideration all three of the approaches listed here. There can be no doubt, however, that drug abuse is an important problem in our society and that explanations need to be searched for by the sociologists and other scientists.

The extent of drug abuse Is the current alarm of drug abuse justified? Are there statistics which support the furor which is presently seen in our society? In a study of drug use in New York City schools, the Fleischman Commission on Education[9] found that the problem was the most serious of all problems of youth in that city. They found that 45 percent of high school students were using some "psychoactive drugs." They cited additional statistics and indicated that most of these were probably underestimates of the true situations. A part of these statistics indicated that at least 20 percent of those in lower grades were using some types of drugs. Interestingly, this same commission found drug use among only 25 percent of high school students in New York State schools outside of New York City. This study attempted to look at the so-called undercover users of marijuana and other so-called soft drugs. It did not examine the problem of hard-core addicts. Whether or not this is a true estimate of the problem in New York City cannot be substantiated, but there can be little doubt that the use of drugs among adolescents is rampant at this time.

A great deal of attention has been focused upon drug abuse at the colleges and universities. DeFleur and Garrett[10] studied marijuana usage at a land-grant university. They found that only about 13 percent of their sample had used marijuana and only about 5 percent had used it extensively. This hardly substantiates the idea that there is a great drug problem among the university students. However, this type of data is very hard to come by, and it must be conjectured that the usage is probably a lot higher than these statistics indicate.

Another indication of drug abuse in our society may be found in the statistics regarding the number of new addicts reported from 1952 to 1970. (See Table 4-4.) It can be seen, for example, that in the 1969–1970 period the number of reported drug addicts under twenty-one years of age increased rapidly, as did the number of addicts in other age categories. It can also be seen by looking at this data that most of these drug addicts were on heroin or some type of opium derivative. While some indicate that there can be no clear-cut relationship between the use of so-called soft drugs and hard drugs, there is considerable evidence to support the idea that there is, in fact, a progression which occurs from soft to hard drugs. If the 1969–1970 figures are any indication, the use of drugs in our society is increasing rapidly, although it should be noted that there was a drop off in 1970, over the 1969 figures.

Again the question must be posed, "How serious is the drug problem?" Horace Sutton[11] in an article entitled "Drugs: Ten Years to Dooms Day?" quotes Dr. Nils Bejrot of Sweden. He is that country's leading expert on drug addiction and he states:

> We live in a dramatic age and everything moves far more quickly now than when the Roman Empire met its fate. I believe that at best we have ten years to prevent a social catastrophe at worst; it may already be too late.[12]

Whether or not Dr. Nils Bejrot is a prophet cannot be determined at this time. It can be seen, however, that the prevention and control of drug abuse must occupy an important place in our society in the near future.

Prevention and control of drug abuse Drug abuse is not a problem in the United States alone. Many countries find they must fight this problem. So serious is the concern for the problem of drug abuse that the World Health Organization of the United Nations[13] has set up a council to study measures for prevention and control of drug abuse. They have outlined a program which is aimed at the prevention and control of drug abuse. They have established as their goals: (1) to prevent individual, public health, and social drug problems associated with the use of dependence-producing drugs; (2) a. to reduce the availability of dependence-producing drugs for self-administration, b. to reduce unhealthy interest in and demand for dependence-producing drugs, c. to minimize human discomfort, antisocial activity, and economic loss or other social harm related to drug taking, and d. to minimize the possibility of people beginning to use dependence-producing drugs while uninformed of their broad effects.

The first step, according to the World Health Organization, is to limit the availability of drugs. This, of course, can be done by cutting off the source of drugs. In the case of heroin, this must be done in countries such as Turkey or Red China, where the heroin is produced.

Additionally, the United States government has gone to extensive lengths to limit the influx of drugs into this country. Cooperative arrangements have been established with the Mexican government in order to eliminate fields of marijuana growing there which are destined primarily for this country. Similarly, the custom agencies and other law enforcement agencies in this country have tried a variety of methods to ascertain and eliminate the influx of drugs. There are, of course, the

TABLE 4-4 REPORTED NARCOTICS ADDICTS—SUMMARY: 1953 TO 1970

["Addict" defined as a person reported to Bureau of Narcotics and Dangerous Drugs by police or hospital authorities as physically addicted to narcotics use. Average age of active addicts as of Dec. 31, 1970, was 30.5 years]

Item	New addicts reported									Active addicts, Dec. 31, 1970[1]
	Annual average, 1953–1970	1963	1964	1965	1966	1967	1968	1969	1970	
Addicts, total	8,170	7,456	10,012	6,012	6,047	6,417	7,219	14,606	12,201	68,864
Reporting agency:										
Federal	1,122	815	870	543	509	515	569	1,186	744	5,382
State	1,071	1,525	3,415	788	864	572	955	1,789	1,991	11,252
Local	5,977	5,116	5,727	4,681	4,674	5,330	5,695	11,631	9,466	52,230
Race:										
White	3,949	3,847	5,258	3,562	3,467	3,585	3,785	7,553	6,813	35,275
Negro	4,132	3,538	4,720	2,419	2,559	2,817	3,425	7,008	5,315	33,348
Other	89	71	34	31	21	15	9	45	43	241
Age:										
Under 21 years	1,352	1,037	1,358	1,053	1,150	1,361	1,458	3,380	2,923	5,714
21–30 years	4,758	4,139	6,085	3,538	3,610	3,775	4,411	8,476	6,874	35,542
31–40 years	1,464	1,712	1,970	1,088	993	1,054	1,069	2,095	1,720	19,311
41 years and over	596	568	599	333	264	227	281	655	684	8,297

Sex:										
Male	6,630	5,946	7,850	4,954	4,962	5,342	6,135	12,429	10,313	58,445
Female	1,540	1,510	2,162	1,058	1,085	1,075	1,083	2,177	1,858	10,419
Drug used:										
Heroin	7,540	6,562	9,166	5,430	5,497	6,009	6,824	14,133	11,706	66,040
Morphine	201	188	169	117	138	77	98	101	104	697
Opium	29	13	9	2	6	16	20	37	83	173
Dilaudid	92	128	94	63	63	83	51	59	28	367
Demerol	110	149	174	110	112	104	82	70	52	489
Methadone	29	14	12	16	6	11	25	46	75	167
Codeine	64	110	120	147	107	70	69	69	49	423
Eucodal	16	77	56	44	31	10	9	13	7	87
All other	89	215	212	83	87	37	41	78	97	421

[1] 20,596 addicts, originally reported during 1953–1965, remained active during the 5-year period, 1966–1970.

Source: U.S. Bureau of Narcotics and Dangerous Drugs, *Drug Abuse* and *Law Enforcement Statistics*.

stimulant and depressant drugs which are produced in this country, however, and these pose a special problem. For example, many medical practitioners unwittingly prescribe drugs in an irresponsible manner. This is done either by prescribing unneeded drugs or prescribing quantities of drugs which go beyond the needs of the patient. The World Health Organization recommends that at every step an effort be made to control the manufacture, distribution, and prescription of drugs. This means that tighter security must be placed on drug manufacturers and distributors, and that medical practitioners must be fully educated to the effects of overprescription of drugs. Increasing the amount of education in this area in medical schools and a reeducation of medical practitioners in this country are steps in this direction.

The control of drug abuse in this country also must fall in the hands of legislatures and law enforcement agencies. Legislatures must be involved in developing laws which will actually contribute to the reduction of drug abuse. Many legislatures have seen this as their mission and most drug abuse laws have undergone revision during the past five years. For the most part, these laws have taken the form of making the sale and distribution of drugs a more serious crime and reducing the penalty for drug use. At this writing the tendency is for recommendations to increase the penalties already being placed on illicit drug distributers. Some have gone so far as recommending life penalties for illicit drug distributers. Police must also be trained in methods by which they can identify the flow of narcotics, narcotic users, and potential narcotic distributers.

This country has often tried to decrease the consumption of alcohol by raising the prices through taxation upon alcoholic beverages. Because drugs come to the public for the most part in an illicit manner, there is no similar means which can be employed for the control of drugs. Because of this fact, the supply of drugs must be stemmed or laws must be established which will prevent persons from becoming involved with drugs. There can be little doubt that additional measures are needed if we are to solve the drug situation which exists in this country.

The old adage that "an ounce of prevention is worth a pound of cure" applies directly in the drug situation. There can be little doubt that preventing individuals from taking drugs can be far more effective than either controlling their assumptions or curing them after they have become dependent or habituated to drugs. For the most part, the general education program in this country has taken two forms. One of these which is obvious to most is the attempt to educate the general public through the mass media. Television commercials, bill boards, radio programs, and even thirty minutes to one hour programs which expose the potential problems of drug abuse have been undertaken as a means of informing people about the potential danger of drug abuse. No success or failure can be directly attached to this type of effect. The theory of this approach is simply that if individuals know the problems involving drug abuse, they will be less likely to become involved in this type of practice.

The second approach to informing individuals about the problem of drug abuse comes through public education. Schools are seen as a means by which the youth of this country and other countries can be reached. Health education, science education, and many other courses now incorporate programs regarding drugs. The problem with these types of programs is that many teachers are as ignorant about the problems of drugs and drug abuse as are parents and students. This means, of course, that they must be educated and therefore the attempts to educate the general public about drug abuse is a longer-term situation than most realize.

The last approach to prevention and control of drug abuse mentioned by the World Health Organization is the so-called social measure. In this approach, teams of psychiatrists, social workers, and others deliberately seek out addicts on their own ground. This approach may also involve the running of an open youth-guidance clinic or, as has commonly been done in this country, the establishment of a so-called drug hotline where persons concerned about a drug problem can reach help if they deem it necessary. Again, there are no hard data about the impact of such a community intervention program, but at this point those interested in the prevention and control of drug abuse simply say that every possible means must be utilized in the control of the drug problem in the country. You may wish to investigate the impact of this program in your area.

CRIME AND JUVENILE DELINQUENCY

The Report of the National Commission on Violence accentuates the extent to which crime has become a problem in the United States. That Commission reported that 50 percent of the women and 20 percent of the men surveyed were afraid to walk outdoors at night, even near their homes. The Commission also reported that nearly one-third of American families keep guns to protect themselves against burglars or other persons who might be entering their home and that this same number, one-third, of the residents in urban areas wish to move from their present locations. The situation has gotten so bad in many areas that merchants close their shops early so as to prevent robberies, and many all-night attendants at service stations will not carry change and accept only the correct amount or credit cards. The Commission on Violence brought its findings into bold relief in a statement in the introduction of its report. It stated,

> We solemnly declare our conviction that this nation is entering a period in which our people need to be as concerned about the internal danger to our society as by any probable combination of external threats (p.xxiv).[14]

Perhaps the best way to dramatize the problem that this country faces is to let us look at some comparative statistics with regard to other countries. The homicide rate in the United States is nearly double that of Finland, the country with the second highest homicide rate and is nearly 16 times that of certain Iron Curtain countries. However, homicide is not the only area of criminality in which the United States leads. Our forcible-rape rate was found to be 12 times that of England and Wales and three times that of Canada. The number of robberies in this country is 9 times that of England and Wales and nearly double that of Canada. Similarly, our aggravated-assault rate is twice that of England and Wales and 18 times that of our next-door neighbor.[15] There can be little doubt that crime is one of the major social problems in this country. In the next section the possible causes of crime and some suggested solutions will be presented.

Causes of crime and delinquency Crime can roughly be defined as a violation of societal *norms.* Norms have previously been defined roughly as directions for behavior established by our society. The result of breaking norms even in childhood is usually some kind of punishment. The most important norms in any given society are called *mores.* They are implicit or explicit rules widely held in a given society. Cannibalism, rape, and murder are violations of the mores of most Western societies and are responded to by moral indignation and severe punishment. *Folkways* are norms regarded as less important behavior in a society. Folkways concern manners of dress, etiquette, and rules of fair play and business and personal transactions. Folkways, like mores, may be codified and made into laws. Breaking of these laws involving folkways, while punishable, usually carry less severe penalties in our society. A criminal or juvenile delinquent can then be viewed as an individual who has violated the mores or folkways of a society which have been codified into some type of legal structure. The major determining factor between a juvenile delinquent and an adult criminal is usually age. However, some states make distinctions on the basis of crimes committed. In West Virginia, for example, a youthful offender who commits a murder may be bound over to a regular criminal court and tried as an adult, depending upon the circumstances surrounding the homicide.

In the remainder of this section an attempt will be made to examine the various ideas about why people become juvenile delinquents or criminals. Perhaps the most pervasive idea about the etiology of criminal behavior was developed by E. H. Sutherland.[16] His explanation of criminal behavior deals almost exclusively with sociological and cultural factors as the causation of crime. The cornerstone of Sutherland's explanation of criminal behavior is that criminal behavior is learned. By this he simply means that criminality is not an inherited characteristic. At one time in sociological history it was a common belief that a criminal type was inherited directly, but this is no longer an acceptable hypothesis in sociological thinking. However, some sociologists still contend that while criminal behavior is learned, there are in fact certain tendencies which are inherited which may contribute to criminal behavior. For example, some individuals may inherit certain basic aggressive drives which may make them more prone to commit criminal acts than other individuals. This group would maintain that while criminal behavior is learned through interaction with one's environment and with one's culture, these inherited traits may in fact be a determining factor in the production of criminal behavior.

Sutherland maintained as a part of his theory that the major part of learning criminal behavior occurs within intimate personal groups. Sutherland asserts that the acquisition of criminal behavior occurs in groups such as the family, peer group, or some other type of intimate group structure. Support for Sutherland's ideas can be found in basic sociological theory and in basic definitions of the socialization process. As was discussed earlier, during socialization basic groups such as the family play a major role in the learning of behavior. However, those that take exception to Sutherland's ideas indicate that there are probably some factors which contribute to criminal functioning other than basic reference groups. Glueck and Glueck[17] found that only 56 percent of the delinquents in their study were found to belong to gangs. McCord, McCord, and Zola[18] report a study of 253 boys of criminal parents. They found that in most instances persons who had been criminals and had sired and raised children did not produce offsprings who were criminals. These findings do not rule out the hypothesis that Sutherland advanced since it can be contended that criminals who have been incarcerated for their crimes may have learned other values which were in turn transmitted to their children.

Sutherland goes on to hypothesize that even the techniques for committing crimes are directly learned from basic groups. Substantiation for this idea can be derived from reports of juvenile delinquents who have been incarcerated. They often report that they have learned new techniques for shoplifting, committing robberies, and other crimes from their association with other inmates. The fact that criminals do learn from one another is one of the bases for our present system of separating different types of offenders. In our society today we have maximum security prisons for rapists, murderers, and those who commit armed robberies for example, and at the other end of the continuum we have detention homes which attempt to approximate home environments for first offenders who are juveniles.

Sutherland asserts that an individual becomes delinquent because of his association with basic groups which define violation of the law as favorable as opposed to defining violation of the law as unfavorable. This idea is very similar to some of the sociological explanations of drug abuse which contend that drug abuse comes through association with basic groups which define drug abuse as positive and they themselves begin to define the experience as positive as a result of their interaction. It should be noted that although Sutherland's sociological theory of criminality has been rejected on several bases, it stands as perhaps a major sociological theory of delinquency and criminality in modern day thought.

There are in fact a number of other theories of delinquency and criminality which have been advanced. For example, Merton in 1964[19] and in earlier papers advanced the idea that a condition of anomie or normlessness accounts for various kinds of deviant behavior in our society. In delinquency and criminality according to Merton there is a clash between the values held by society and the means by which the society allows for the individual to achieve the values. Specifically, members of the American culture value the acquisition and possession of various kinds of economic goods, but the opportunity to acquire these goods is denied many members of society. Whenever an individual is denied an opportunity to acquire those goods valued by society, a state of normlessness results and deviant behavior (criminal behavior) may result. Merton's ideas like those of Sutherland have been disputed by numerous sociologists.

Another explanation of criminality, lower-class theory, has also been found somewhat wanting as an adequate means of explaining delinquent and criminal behavior. This theory hypothesizes that lower-class delinquents grow up with a set of values which are contrary to middle class and as a result of these values turn to crime and delinquency. There is, in fact, no satisfactory explanation of criminal behavior that has yet been advanced. However, it is likely that all theories have a kernel of truth which should be considered.

The incidence of crime in our society At this point it might be useful to look at the incidence of crime in our society. The statistics utilized in this section were taken from the Uniform Crime Reports,[20] 1972 *Preliminary Annual Release* issued by L. Patrick Gray, III, then Acting Director of the Federal Bureau of Investigation. Before the statistics are presented, a brief discussion of crime statistics is in order. Cressey[21] points out that the statistics on crime and delinquency are perhaps the most unsatisfactory of all social-science statistics. He lists several criticisms of these statistics; for example, true statistical data on the crime rate cannot be compiled at any given time primarily because it is impossible to ascertain the amount of crime in a specific locality upon any given date or upon any given year. This is true because not all crimes are discovered or reported or in certain instances not recorded in an official way that will appear in a set of crime statistics. Cressey points out that a variety of conditions affect the publication of crime rate. An overzealous police chief who is attempting to assure the public that he is doing an adequate job may not report all of the crimes in his particular district. Similar circumstances can occur at the city, state, or national level. It has been estimated that only about one-half of all crimes committed appear in crime statistics.

It is also true that certain types of crimes are not reported as judiciously as are others and are not reflected accurately in crime statistics. White-collar crime, for example, is difficult to detect and is not reported on the same basis as are violent crimes. It is also undoubtedly true that so-called white-collar criminals receive preferential treatment before the law. Let us look briefly at this problem.

Schur[22] defines *white-collar crime* as "occupational and related offenses committed by persons of high socioeconomic status. . . ." He goes on to identify several types of white-collar crime among which are nonprofessional fraud, embezzlement, forgery, amateur shoplifting, tax evasion, and a variety of others. Schur identifies nonprofessional fraud as fraud not directly related to making a living. Corporation heads may agree to fix prices in order to enhance the economic status of their corporations. Pharmaceutical companies may prematurely market a wonder drug or make undue claims for a new medicine which they produce. These are crimes of a very real nature, but are the people involved brought to trial? Their corporations may be fined large sums of money but they go literally untouched in many cases. It is impossible to judge the extent of the involvement by members of our society in white-collar crimes, but some sociologists believe that the practice is extremely widespread.

A final criticism of crime statistics levied by Cressey was that because crime and delinquency are not well defined it is almost impossible to get adequate indices of the incidents of crime and delinquency. At the outset of this section some very rough definitions of crime and delinquency were given, but Cressey's criticism is well taken. Legislatures are forever defining and redefining what a crime is and its seriousness. Legislatures have recently redefined the crime of possession of marijuana. Courts have eased previous restrictions about pornography, thus making the showing of X-rated movies legal. In the 1950s a similar showing would have brought a lengthy jail term.

The incidence of crime An attempt will be made to present an overall picture of crime in the United States as it is reported. In Table 4-5 it can be seen that the total of all crimes reported decreased 3 percent from 1971 to 1972 while violent crimes went up 1 percent. During this period of

TABLE 4-5 CRIME INDEX TRENDS

(Percent change 1972 over 1971, offenses known to the police)

Population group and area	Number of agencies	Population in thousands	Total	Violent	Property	Murder	Forcible rape	Robbery	Aggravated assault	Burglary	Larceny $50 and over	Auto theft
Total all agencies	5,821	164,859	− 3	+ 1	− 3	+ 4	+11	− 4	+ 6	− 2	− 3	− 7
Cities over 25,000	841	89,497	− 5	− 1	− 6	+ 4	+10	− 5	+ 4	− 4	− 6	− 9
Suburban area	2,295	52,857	+ 2	+13	+ 1	+11	+19	+ 9	+14	+ 2	+ 1	− 1
Rural area	1,221	18,953	+ 4	+ 9	+ 4	− 2	+ 1	+10	+11	+ 4	+ 5	− 3
Over 1,000,000	6	18,805	−12	− 4	−14	+ 4	+12	− 9	+ 4	−11	−19	−14
500,000 to 1,000,000	21	13,728	− 7	− 6	− 7	+ 2	+ 3	−10	− 2	− 6	− 7	−11
250,000 to 500,000	31	10,788	− 2	+ 2	− 3	+ 4	+12	+ 3	− 1	− 1	− 3	− 4
100,000 to 250,000	93	13,418	− 2	+ 3	− 3	+ 5	+ 4	+ 2	+ 4	− 2	− 3	− 5
50,000 to 100,000	240	16,937	+ 1	+ 9	—	+ 8	+14	+ 7	+11	+ 1	—	− 2
25,000 to 50,000	450	15,822	+ 1	+13	—	+ 3	+26	+ 8	+17	+ 2	− 1	− 2
10,000 to 25,000	1,104	17,636	+ 4	+ 9	+ 4	+ 4	+21	+10	+ 8	+ 4	+ 4	− 1
Under 10,000	2,357	11,069	+ 5	+ 4	+ 5	− 9	+19	+11	+ 2	+ 3	+ 6	+ 2

Source: Crime in the United States, Uniform Crime Reports 1972 (Preliminary Annual Release)

time murder went up 4 percent, forcible rape went up 11 percent and aggravated assault 6 percent. Crimes against property, robbery, burglary, larceny, and auto theft also declined during this period. It is interesting to note that crime in cities over 25,000 decreased by 5 percent while crime in the suburban and rural areas increased. Similarly, in areas over 1,000,000 crime decreased by 12 percent but in those areas under 10,000 the largest increase in total crime was noted. In Table 4-6 the crime index trend by geographic region is reported and in Table 4-7 the crime index trends over the period of 1966 to 1971 are reported. As can be seen in Table 4-7, crime in the 70s has been increasing at a *decreasing* rate until 1972. Table 4-8 is a presentation of certain selected cities with a population of 100,000 or more with regard to their crime statistics. In Washington, D.C., for example the decrease in the total number of crimes was dramatic while cities such as Gary, Indiana, showed only a slight decrease. Many other cities stayed at about the same or showed slight increases in the 1971–1972 period.

In examining these statistics Cressey's criticisms of crime indexes should be noted. It is impossible to ascertain whether or not these figures represent true decreases in the crime rate or are merely manipulations of crime statistics reporting. Regardless of how one considers them, they are little comfort to the average citizen because they still place the United States at the forefront in terms of the incidence of crime. Consider for example that eleven serious crimes are committed each minute in this country and every thirty-nine seconds there is a murder, forcible rape, robbery, or assault with intent to kill. A burglary occurs every thirteen seconds in our society and an auto theft every thirty-three seconds. It is little wonder that law-and-order has become a major issue in the political arena in our country.

Control of crime and delinquency in our society Although most sociological theories attribute crime and delinquency to factors inherent in the fabric of our society, most efforts at control of crime and delinquency have been aimed at suppression and at rehabilitation of offenders. Suppression has for the most part involved putting more policemen or law enforcement officers on the streets and upgrading the use of technology in law enforcement. In 1971 there were 2.4 law enforcement employees per 1,000 inhabitants in the United States, an increase of 4 percent over 1970. There has also been an attempt to modernize police forces by giving them the most up-to-date equipment and communications devices. There have also been considered efforts to attract more highly educated and skilled law enforcement officers at all levels of law enforcement by raising salaries and fringe benefits. To a certain extent these efforts are being offset by the increasingly hazardous duty of law enforcement officers. In the 1962–66 period 270 law enforcement officers were killed, but the number escalated to 452 in the 1967–71 period.[23]

TABLE 4-6 CRIME INDEX TRENDS BY GEOGRAPHIC REGION (1972 over 1971)

Region	Total	Violent	Property	Murder	Forcible rape
Northeastern States	− 8	− 1	−10	+ 6	+19
North Central States	− 3	− 1	− 3	− 2	+ 7
Southern States	− 2	+ 1	− 2	+ 4	+ 6
Western States	+ 2	+ 7	+ 1	+11	+13

Region	Robbery	Aggravated assault	Burglary	Larceny $50 and over	Auto Theft
Northeastern States	− 8	+ 9	− 8	−11	−10
North Central States	− 5	+ 5	− 3	− 1	− 7
Southern States	—	+ 1	+ 1	− 2	− 8
Western States	+ 3	+ 9	+ 3	—	− 3

Source: Crime in the United States, Uniform Crime Reports 1972 (Preliminary Annual Release)

TABLE 4-7 CRIME INDEX TRENDS

(Percent change 1966–1971, each year over previous year)

Years	Total	Violent	Property	Murder	Forcible rape
1967/1966	+16	+15	+16	+13	+ 8
1968/1967	+17	+19	+17	+14	+15
1969/1968	+11	+11	+11	+ 7	+16
1970/1969	+11	+12	+10	+ 8	+ 2
1971/1970	+ 6	+ 9	+ 6	+10	+ 9

Years	Robbery	Aggravated assault	Burglary	Larceny $50 and over	Auto theft
1967/1966	+27	+ 8	+16	+16	+17
1968/1967	+30	+11	+13	+21	+18
1969/1968	+13	+ 8	+ 6	+21	+12
1970/1969	+17	+ 7	+10	+14	+ 5
1971/1970	+10	+ 8	+ 8	+ 5	+ 1

Source: Crime in the United States, Uniform Crime Reports 1972 (Preliminary Annual Release)

TABLE 4-8 OFFENSES KNOWN TO THE POLICE, 1971 AND 1972

(Cities over 100,000 population)

			Crime Index total	Murder, non-negligent man-slaughter	For-cible rape	Rob-bery	Aggra-vated assault	Bur-glary break-ing or enter-ing	Lar-ceny $50 and over	Auto theft
Albany	N Y	1971	3,678	6	17	282	111	2,012	390	860
		1972	2,803	6	17	223	97	1,377	445	638
Atlanta	Ga	1971	30,056	230	268	2,207	1,935	13,726	7,656	4,034
		1972	33,213	255	256	3,074	2,143	14,676	8,659	4,150
Cedar Rapids	Iowa	1971	1,932	5	10	34	15	683	842	343
		1972	1,859	3	8	31	22	625	769	401
Columbus	Ohio	1971	26,579	69	269	1,873	943	10,025	8,176	5,226
		1972	24,049	59	292	1,464	890	9,641	7,647	4,056
Detroit	Mich	1971	127,245	577	853	20,753	5,400	51,531	25,361	22,770
		1972	107,199	601	818	17,170	6,120	42,563	19,405	20,522
Gary	Ind	1971	11,716	52	87	1,396	436	4,723	2,040	2,982
		1972	11,284	81	90	1,253	519	4,673	1,909	2,759
Indianapolis	Ind	1971	22,874	60	264	2,109	927	9,480	5,537	4,497
		1972	19,207	66	275	1,398	726	8,267	4,817	3,658
Kansas City	Kansas	1971	7,330	34	85	461	572	3,618	923	1,637
		1972	7,374	21	83	571	457	3,712	1,015	1,515
Los Angeles	Calif	1971	183,867	427	2,062	14,147	14,674	74,812	41,506	36,239
		1972	176,916	499	2,205	14,241	15,056	72,458	38,737	33,720

Miami	Fla	1971	24,895	100	137	2,829	3,014	9,258	6,299	3,258
		1972	22,429	78	99	2,555	2,656	8,294	5,949	2,798
Minneapolis	Minn	1971	23,865	35	228	1,646	1,037	10,039	5,884	4,996
		1972	24,294	39	308	1,908	1,358	10,495	4,960	5,226
New Orleans	La	1971	35,375	116	325	3,391	2,109	10,705	10,381	8,348
		1972	30,000	163	261	3,001	2,040	8,428	8,984	7,123
New York	N Y	1971	529,447	1,466	2,415	88,994	33,865	181,331	124,752	96,624
		1972	434,303	1,691	3,271	78,202	37,130	148,046	90,098	75,865
Omaha	Nebr	1971	11,408	24	122	482	1,085	3,706	3,097	2,892
		1972	13,234	24	125	692	1,092	4,064	4,237	3,000
Philadelphia	Pa	1971	61,340	435	546	9,243	4,970	20,914	7,387	17,845
		1972	58,584	413	588	9,710	4,603	21,182	6,048	16,040
Pittsburgh	Pa	1971	26,467	65	279	2,556	1,910	9,489	5,636	6,532
		1972	23,550	49	298	2,646	1,827	7,824	4,778	6,128
Salt Lake City	Utah	1971	11,179	16	64	409	292	4,159	4,387	1,852
		1972	10,057	12	79	446	350	3,935	4,035	1,200
San Francisco	Calif	1971	57,538	102	512	6,584	3,101	18,264	16,130	12,845
		1972	46,620	81	505	4,573	2,665	14,519	13,201	11,076
Washington	D C	1971	51,256	275	615	11,222	3,972	18,818	7,622	8,732
		1972	37,446	245	714	7,751	3,897	12,801	6,217	5,821

Source: Crime in the United States, Uniform Crime Reports 1972 (Preliminary Annual Release)

Rehabilitation efforts have been in the form of the development of basic educational skills, vocational skills development programs, early release programs, counseling, and other enlightened correctional approaches. This rehabilitation effort seems to be well focused since many of the offenders arrested each year are repeaters. Actually, over 69 percent of persons arrested in 1971 had been arrested previously. It should be noted that younger offenders show a greater frequency of repeating their crimes than do older offenders. Repeat offenders under twenty were rearrested on the average of every four months while those between the ages of twenty and twenty-four were rearrested every nine months and those twenty-five to twenty-nine every fourteen months. This can be contrasted with the repeaters between the ages of forty and forty-nine years of age who were rearrested every twenty-eight months and those over fifty years of age who were rearrested every thirty-eight months.

It is difficult to ascertain whether or not the placement of more police officers on the streets of our cities and suburbs will serve as a deterrent to further crime. It also seems apparent that our attempts at rehabilitating offenders in our correctional institutions have thus far not been highly successful. This is not to say that these attempts should not be pursued and intensified. It seems however that if our society is to have an impact upon the crime and delinquency rates, there must be a restructuring of societal values and opportunities for the achievement of society held goals must be made available to all. It seems likely also that institutions which are charged with the task of socializing the young must be strengthened. This, of course, means the family must take a leading role in the control of delinquency and crime in our society.

POVERTY

Poverty has been a part of America since its earliest beginnings. Many of the settlers who came to this country did so in an effort to flee economic deprivation. America was known as the land of opportunity where even the poorest peasant could get a piece of land, a living wage, and human dignity in the bargain. For some this American dream of the good life and human dignity has proven to be an unfulfilled promise. The impact of poverty in this country will be examined in this section.

Poverty may be narrowly defined in economic terms. A poor person is a have-not; he has little or no ability to secure goods and services because of his lack of personal resources. There are some problems involved in determining what a poverty level is in this country on purely economic terms. We know, for example, that a subsistence level of existence costs more in New York City (or any city) than it does in rural America. One of the factors here is the ability of some rural Americans to

The most concrete fact of a slum is its physical ugliness—the vermin, the dirt, the dilapidation —resulting from cramping too many people into an area too small. Such conditions brutalize the spirit as well as the body of an individual. *(Charles Gatewood)*

produce fairly large quantities of certain types of food at relatively little cost. There is also the difficulty of determining impact of family size upon economic needs. Although most indices of poverty have tried to account for number of family members, some would argue that few if any have been successful.

While we may think of poverty in strictly economic terms, it is also useful to consider the cultural implications of poverty. In Chapter 2 we introduced the idea of social stratification and discussed briefly the impact of class upon values and behavior. In terms of that earlier discussion, we are talking about the lower-lowers in American society when we refer to the poor. They are at the bottom-most rung of our societal ladder.

Describing the poor Blum and Rossi[24] reviewed the literature regarding the poor and attempted to develop a composite picture of the poor. They found that certain characteristics stood out when considering this group. The poor must suffer through long periods of unemployment and employment, when it comes, is intermittent and consists of the most menial jobs in our society. Blum and Rossi also found that marital instability characterized the poor. Symptoms of this instability were high divorce and desertion rates, households headed by females, illegitimacy rates higher than the general population, and generally superficial interpersonal relationships as a whole.

However, unemployment and marital problems are not the only characteristics of the poor. This group participates at a marginal level in our society and to a certain extent is alienated from it. They have lowered self-esteem and as a result a sense of helplessness. Personality traits such as authoritarianism and low need for achievement are common. The poor are also more likely to have superstitious beliefs, undoubtedly stemming from their inability to control their own circumstances.[25]

The picture of poverty in this country is not a pleasant one. Some people have hypothesized that the condition of poverty gives rise to greater spontaneity, but a statement by a friend of the authors while visiting in a home of an obviously wealthy man sums up the situation. He stated, "The virtues of poverty are greatly overrated."

There is considerable disagreement about how many poor people exist in this country. The extreme of this argument was noted in a recent statement by a government official that we have two groups in this country: the poor and the nonpoor. For him, poor people were all those with family incomes below $15,000 which would be considerably more than 50 percent of our population. While few would agree with this statement, it illustrates a point—poverty must be viewed in degrees. However, for our discussion we will attempt to give some estimates of the number of poor people.

The President's Commission on Income Maintenance Programs[26] reported that in 1966, 30 million of the nearly 194 million people living in this country were poor. This same commission reported what they considered to be poverty thresholds for the year 1968. These are provided in Table 4-9.

TABLE 4-9 1968 POVERTY THRESHOLDS[27]

Number of persons	Urban	Rural
1	1748	1487
2	2262	1904
3	2774	2352
4	3553	3034
5	4188	3577
6	4706	4021
7 or more	5789	4916

Even a cursory glance at these figures would cause most of us to wonder if they are not too low, and this is why some estimates of poverty-stricken people run as high as 40–50 million people for the period studied by the Commission.

The question which must be in the mind of the reader at this point is: "What progress have we made?" To be sure, family incomes have gone up steadily since the late 1960s. But the cost of services has also increased dramatically. If one takes a conservative estimate of a 5 percent inflation rate for the years 1968 to 1975, the poverty threshold for a nonfarm family of four would have risen from $4188 in 1968 to $5888 in 1975. When one considers the employment situation of the poor, it is hard to imagine that this group's income kept pace and in all likelihood the proportion of poor may have increased in this country.

The poor have been described generally, but at this time let us consider what groups make up this segment of our population. In this country you are more likely to be poor if you are either young or very old, nonwhite and live in an urban area. It should come as no surprise that many older people are in the poverty class since this is a time of declining incomes, but the fact that many victims of poverty are young (under eighteen) may come as a shock to many. Racial and ethnic group discrimination has taken its toll and has relegated many to poverty. Finally, city dwellers, because of reasons already mentioned, are likely to find themselves in poverty if they cannot cope in our society.

Solutions of poverty Ridding our nation of poverty has occupied many social scientists and solutions have been put forth. In the early sixties, manpower development programs were instituted and these became the forerunners of the War on Poverty which was launched fully in the mid-sixties. This so-called war was scarcely a skirmish when one considers the small impact it had on this problem.

Welfare, in one form or another, has been our answer. Welfare programs have succeeded only in providing a subsistence existence for many, but it is a start. Some people and groups oppose welfare and their objections are raised on bumper stickers that state "I fight poverty—I work," and in charges of misuse of welfare funds by high governmental officials. In fact, welfare money is rarely abused in our society. Some estimates of the misuse of these funds run from 1 to 3 percent, while others run somewhat higher. Another objection to welfare is that it merely perpetuates the cycle of poverty, and while there is some empirical support for this view, a question must be raised about alternatives. What can we do to a family that already has substandard health care, inadequate housing, and perhaps even insufficient food? The answers are hard to discern.

One solution to the poverty problem that has been offered from time to time is a guaranteed income. This plan would set minimum incomes required by families and individuals in different situations in much the same way that poverty thresholds are established. Those families not coming up to these levels would be provided money to supplement other sources of revenue so that this minimum level of income could be attained.

Finally, it is believed by some that the poor must pool their collective political power and elect officials who will assist them to climb out of the basement of our society. Thus far, no such movement has been forthcoming.

SUMMARY

Some sociologists have hypothesized that we will cease being a work-oriented society. That view has been disputed in this chapter, although the amount of time spent on the job will undoubtedly decline. In the foreseeable future, our career will be our means of livelihood and a major source of our self-satisfaction. For this reason, the problems of the unemployed and the unhappily employed must be considered as a major social concern.

Whether or not drug abuse is a symptom of a greater societal illness is difficult to determine. There are some encouraging signs with regard to the use of so-called hard drugs, but the abuse of alcohol and other types of drugs is still on the increase. The results of drug abuse are well documented and what is needed are better explanations as to why abuse occurs and how people with drug problems can be handled.

The crime wave in our society surges on. Perhaps the important concern for the student and the social scientist should not be the statistics, for they are woefully inadequate indicators of the true picture, but the morality of a society that produces vast numbers of lawbreakers.

Poverty has been a part of the American scene since the beginning of this country. What is called for are bold ideas, but those have either not come forth or they have been inadequately supported. However, the idea of 30 to 50 million poor in the midst of plenty should be of primary concern for every citizen in this country.

DISCUSSION QUESTIONS

1. How many people are unemployed in this country?
2. What groups are most likely to be unemployed?
3. Other than earning a living why do people work?
4. What is your view of the so-called leisure society? Do you agree with the authors' ideas?
5. What are the trends in the area of employment of college graduates? Is there a general picture?

6. What are the different types of drugs and what is their impact upon people?
7. How can drug abuse be prevented?
8. What are the various explanations as to why drugs are abused?
9. What are the trends in drug abuse?
10. What are the causes of crime in our society? Do you believe that we are living in a criminal society? Why or why not?
11. What is your estimate of the incidence of white-collar crime?
12. What are the trends in the area of crime? In light of what you know about crime statistics how do you react to the figures in this section?
13. Can poverty be eliminated in our society? Why or why not?
14. Are the poor happy?
15. How do poor differ from others in our society other than economically?
16. What is the best way to end poverty?

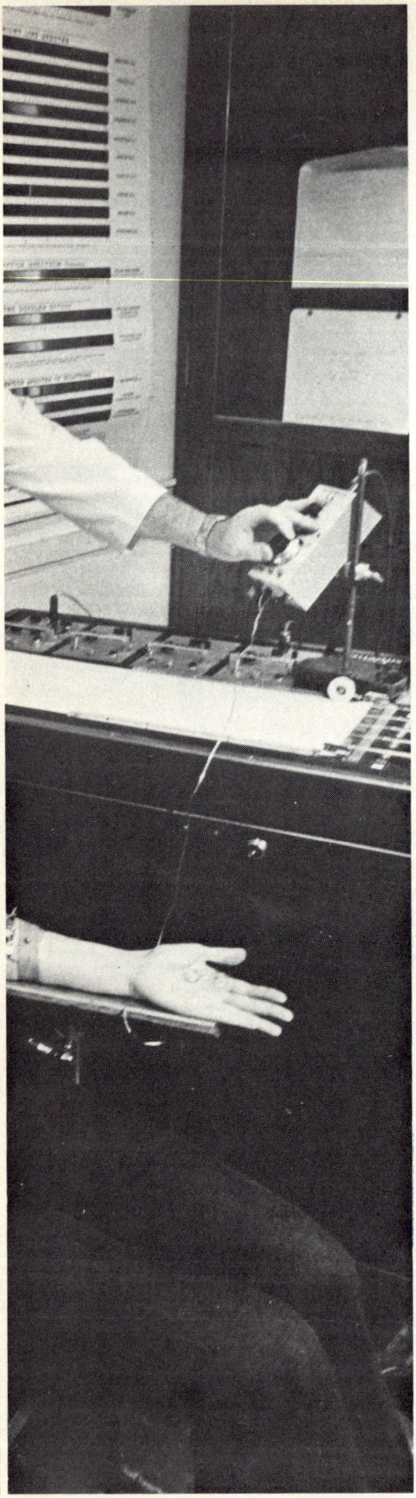

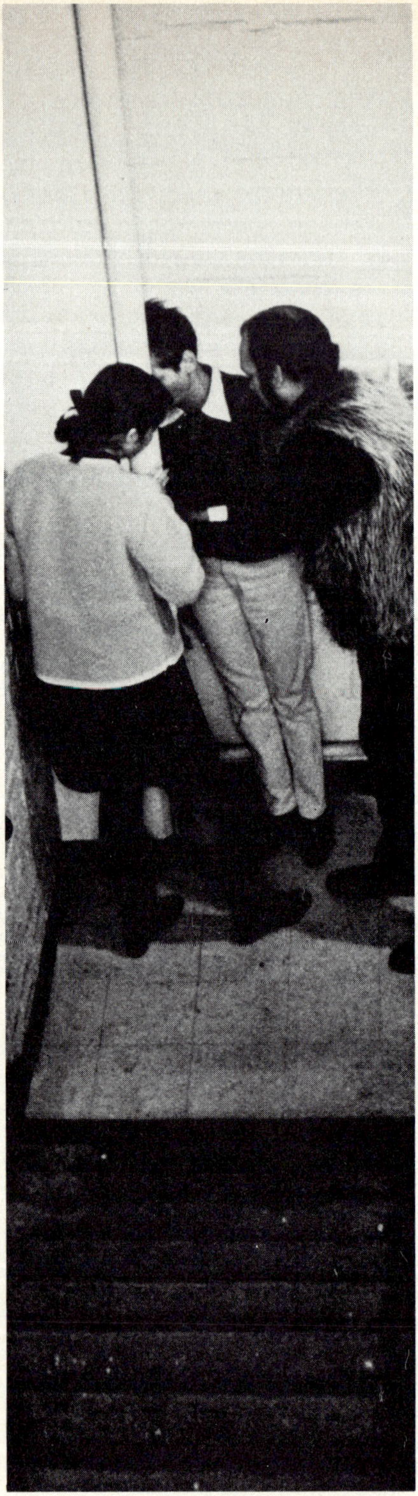

PART TWO
PSYCHOLOGY

The four preceding chapters discussed generally the area of sociology and delved into the myriad of social problems confronting our society. In those chapters, the focus was upon people as they function collectively. Thus the family, social groups, social institutions, and society in general were discussed at some length. In Chapters 5, 6 and 7, the thrust will be toward looking at a person as an individual. Psychology, the study of human behavior, will be explored in some detail in these chapters.

The psychologist is as interested in the problems of our society as is the sociologist, but the approach to solving these problems is quite different. The theories, and usually the research, are aimed at explaining how the individual develops and why he acts as he does. The general posture assumed by the psychologist is: if these phenomena can be unraveled, the key to unraveling our societal problems will follow.

In Chapter 5 we will examine the field of psychology as a general endeavor. We will see that there are many kinds of psychologists with widely varying roles. We will also see that psychologists, like sociologists, do not agree on many aspects of psychology. In this chapter we will look briefly at abnormal and normal functioning. In reading this chapter, the reader should keep in mind the concepts of socialization, for this is the basic process through which the individual develops in sociological thought. This view should be contrasted with the more molecular view of psychologists. It should also be noted that psychologists take greater pains to label and explain the various aspects of individual functioning.

In Chapter 6, intrapsychic explanations of people's functioning will be reviewed. It is the purpose of this chapter to give students alternative explanations for the phenomena which they observe in daily life. A secondary aim is to introduce the reader to the disparity in psychological thinking. In this chapter, Sigmund Freud will be presented as a starting place for the student's thinking. This Viennese physician shook the Victorian world with his theories of human development that included the ideas about the pervasiveness of sexual drives. The repercussions from his early twentieth-century writings are still felt in modern-day psychology and, indeed, the psychoanalytic practices developed by Freud are still in vogue in many places.

In Chapter 6, other explanations of human functioning will be presented. Alfred Adler, an early colleague of Freud, will be discussed as will the newer third force or humanistic psychology. Adler deviated from Freud on a number of philosophical points, and was a forerunner of many modern-day psychological theories. The third force in psychology developed as the middle ground between Freudian psychology, which depicted an individual as driven by sexual instincts, and the behaviorists, who believed that man's behavior is determined by environmental consequences. The humanistic psychologists take an optimistic view of the human race in that they believe that the individual has the ability to transcend both environment and instinctual drives.

In Chapter 7, the behavioral explanations of human functioning will be examined. B. F. Skinner has played a major role in popularizing this approach, but this movement has many devoted followers and may well be the primary force in psychology today.

The reader may very well be confused by the different ideas presented in these chapters, for the differences are often intricate. Perhaps, the logical starting place for evaluating the data is yourself. What do you believe about people and how they function? How do you explain why people behave as they do? And how do the ideas presented agree with your own ideas about human behavior? This, of course, is not the end of your personal dialogue. If you are a serious student, you will want to dig deeper into the vast amount of psychological literature in order to illuminate your thoughts and feelings. This material will serve as a point of departure for what could be an exciting journey.

FOR FURTHER READING

This section is written with the explicit purpose of helping you to provide explanations of the events of your life and hopefully by providing insight to make your life experiences more meaningful. The readings which are suggested here have been selected to amplify the material in the text and to aid you to further your exploration of self and psychology.

A number of recent books have had the dual purpose of explaining various psychologies and enhancing self-knowledge. *Games People Play* by Eric Berne and *I'm OK—You're OK* by Thomas Harris are two examples. Harry W. Hepner's *Psychology Applied to Life and Work* is perhaps not as entertaining as the two books already mentioned, yet serves much the same purpose, as does John T. Wood's *How Do You Feel?: A Guide to Your Emotions.*

Abnormality has always been of prime importance to psychologists. *The Far Side of Madness* by John W. Perry gives us some valuable insight into the internal processes of schizophrenics. *Voices from the Asylum* edited by Michael Glenn gives both a view of mental illness and the institutions which care for the mentally ill. *Suicide: The Gamble with Death* should help the reader understand why people take their own lives and *The Gay World* by Martin Hoffman looks at the problems of homosexuality and bisexuality.

More and more people in our society are turning to growth groups, counseling, and psychotherapy. *Black Rage* by W. H. Grier and P. M. Cobb is two psychiatrists' report of how racism corrodes the fabric of the black life in America. *Face to Face* by Gerald Egan is a guide for those who are considering participating in groups.

Several outstanding psychologists and their works are mentioned in the three chapters which follow. Sigmund Freud's own *An Introduction to Psychoanalysis* provides a good overview of his work and Carl Jung's ideas are contained in *The Portable Jung*, edited by Joseph Cambell. *Walden Two* by B. F. Skinner not only gives a model for communal living, but along with *Beyond Freedom and Dignity* by the same author gives us a chance to see how modern behaviorism might be implemented in a planned society. In this same vein, *Self Directed Behavior: Self Modification for Personal Adjustment* by D. L. Watson and R. G. Thorp provides an outline of how behavioral principles can be used to help oneself. Finally, *The Family Council* by Rudolf Dreikurs, Shirley Gould, and Raymond Corsini can help you understand how the psychology of Alfred Adler can be implemented.

GLOSSARY

amnesia partial or total loss of memory

anxiety reaction a neurotic state characterized by personal apprehension, irritability, and nervousness. Physical symptoms may accompany this reaction

archetype a memory trace inherited from man's ancestral past

asthenic reaction a neurotic state characterized by mental and physical fatigue. Also called neurasthenia

aversive stimuli pain and threats are negative or neutral stimuli. When these follow a behavior, they tend to repress it.

behaviorist a psychologist who subscribes to principles of behaviorism or the propositions that man is basically determined by his environment

causality explanation of behavior that holds that behavior results (is caused) by past experiences

collective unconscious the storage place of all archetypes

conditioning a form of learning based upon trial and error behavior rather than logical problem solving; the basic process through which behavior is acquired

conversion reaction the development of a physical symptom such as blindness without an organic cause

countertransference a phenomenon which occurs in psychoanalytic therapy where the therapist develops emotional states directed at the patient

defense mechanisms devices developed by the ego to protect itself from being overwhelmed by the id and the environment

delusions false beliefs which are defined against all logic

determinism philosophy of humans that holds that one's behavior is controlled or determined by instincts or environment

discrimination the ability to break generalizations down into smaller units

ego portion of the personality which deals with reality

empathy ability to perceive another's thoughts and feelings as that person does

existentialism a diverse school of psychological thought that focuses upon people's potential and experiences. Most believe that people cannot be reduced to a set of empirical equations or in fact studied objectively with any degree of success.

family constellation picture of family that involves birth order of children and relationship of parents, grandparents, and other relatives to children.

free association a technique utilized by psychoanalytic therapists where the patient is asked to talk about anything that comes to mind

functional psychosis severe mental illness resulting from psychological conditions

generalization the process by which an individual recognizes elements in a new situation which are common to other situations

hallucinations sensory aberrations that may take the form of hearing voices, seeing visions, smelling odors which are not present, etc.

id portion of personality which operates on pleasure principle. Center of sexual impulses.

indeterministic philosophy of humans that holds one is basically self-controlling

insight the process by which the individual analyzes the total parts of the problem and logically comes to a conclusion

intelligence a term in psychology which originally meant mental capacity, but now is usually interpreted more narrowly as ability to succeed in academic work

interval reinforcement a schedule of reinforcement based on time

intermittent schedule of reinforcement schedule for delivering reinforcers which approximate chance

intrapsychic view a position regarding the nature of man that holds that they are more than the sum total of their behavior—that there are factors that cause behavior that are not directly observable.

intrinsic positive reinforcement rewards which are derived from satisfaction such as doing a task well

inventories psychological instruments utilized to measure typical performances in areas such as interest or personality development

involutional psychotics- psychotic state characterized by depression. These persons are extremely dangerous to themselves

learning change in behavior not attributable to maturation

life-style sum total of a person's behavior, resulting from personal goals, beliefs, values, etc.

modeling the process by which a behavior is demonstrated and then imitated

negative reinforcement the removal of an aversive stimuli, thus resulting in the strengthening of a response

neurosis a less severe state of abnormal behavior usually characterized by anxiety

neurotic depressive a neurotic state characterized by general unhappiness and a feeling of worthlessness

neutral stimuli stimuli which are of no importance to the person

obsessive-compulsive reactions a neurotic state characterized by obsessive thoughts about having to do something. These thoughts may be translated into compulsive acts such as washing hands, having all drawers closed, etc.

operant conditioning process by which emitted responses, that is responses not arising from biological or psychological states, are strengthened through reinforcement

organic psychosis severe mental illness resulting from organic or physical causes

paranoid reaction a psychotic state characterized by an exaggerated feeling that the individual is being spied on or threatened in some way

persona Greek word for mask

personality the consistent pattern of emotions, feelings, and behavior experienced and exhibited by an individual

phenomenology school of psychology that holds that each person has a unique view of the world

phobic reaction unrealistic fears of specific situations

pleasure principle self-gratification is the basic rule of operation. Associated with the id.

positive stimuli reward or reinforcement

primary reinforcer biological reward such as food or water

private logic personal way of viewing the world

psychoanalysis school of psychology associated primarily with Sigmund Freud

psychology the study of human behavior

psychosurgery attempts to alter psychological functioning through alterations of the brain

ratio schedule of reinforcement a schedule of reinforcement based upon numbers of performance

reality principle dealing with the world as it really is by recognizing consequences of behavior for self and others

respondent conditioning Pavlovian idea that behavior is paired with basic biological drives. In this type of conditioning, respondent behavior is conditioned.

schedule of reinforcement systematic procedure for delivering reinforcers

schizophrenia a category of

psychotic behavior characterized by delusions and hallucinations

secondary reinforcer materials or events which have acquired the properties of a reward such as money

self personality structure that contains all thoughts, feelings, and ideas about oneself

self-actualizing people normal persons who have the ability to transcend environment

shaping the developing of complex behavior from small units of behavior

social reinforcer a reward growing out of human contact

sociopathic personality a personality with a poorly developed conscience

superego part of personality that deals with moral behavior; conscience

teleology refers to idea that behavior is goal-directed

tests psychological instruments utilized to measure a student's maximum performance in areas such as scholastic aptitude and achievement

transferance a phenomenon in psychoanalytic therapy where the patient attaches emotions for other people to the therapist

traumatic experiences-experiences which are extremely emotionally upsetting such as death of a close friend or other emotional shocks

SOMETHING TO THINK ABOUT

Do you know of any instances where psychology or psychologists have helped people?

What do you know about Sigmund Freud? Do you agree or disagree with him?

What is your personal belief about why persons behave as they do?

How should our society care for psychological deviates?

What is normal behavior? Abnormal behavior? Are you normal?

Do humans have free will, that is, in control of behavior?

Are humans subject to the same psychological laws as lower animals?

What psychological traits, if any, do humans inherit?

How do you feel about the use of surgical techniques to alter psychological functioning?

Do you believe that it is possible to develop the psychological technology to develop a society which has near perfect control over the behavior of its members?

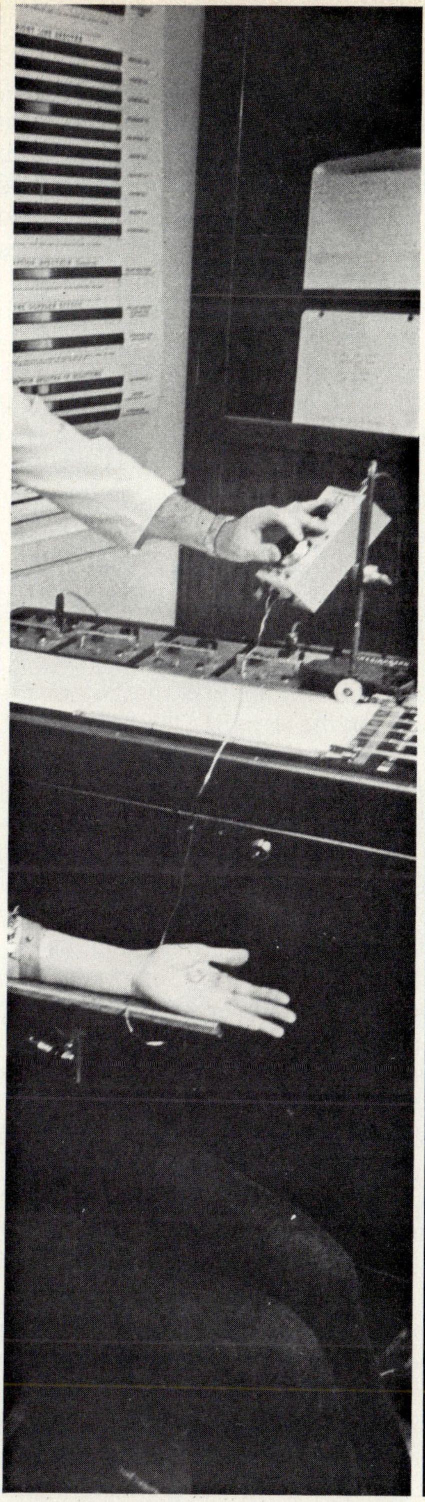

CHAPTER FIVE
INTRODUCTION TO PSYCHOLOGY

IDEAS AND CONCEPTS

euphoria
a state of well-being not caused by external events

learning
any change in behavior which is not directly attributable to maturation

methodology
a system of rules and procedures which serve as guideline for investigating a particular discipline

neurosis
a disorder in which some type of anxiety is present

personality
an individual's pattern of characteristics, traits, or attributes which persist over time

From time to time most of us have asked ourselves, "Why did I do that?" or, "Why do I act as I do?" Perhaps a more frequent question is: "Why do others behave as they do?" After having a frustrating fight with our parents, our wives or husbands, our girlfriends or boyfriends, or perhaps our peers, these and other questions come to mind and many times the answers are not always obvious. All of us would like to understand ourselves and others better.

Most of us are also faced with some other very difficult questions in our modern, technological society. For the young married college student it may be, "How do I rear my children so that they will be normal, healthy individuals?" Many students are determined not to raise their children as they were raised, but find, much to their chagrin, that they fall into the all too familiar child-rearing patterns of their parents. Unmarried students are concerned with, "How do I select a future husband or wife?" With over 30 percent of all marriages ending in divorce, this is a very realistic question and one that needs a well-considered answer. Other serious questions such as, "What career field should I enter?" and "What role should I take in community activities?" are also questions confronting us all.

It would be a gross error to lead the reader to believe that the answers to these questions will be given in these pages for they will not. However, *psychology*—the study of human behavior—is a field which focuses upon these and other problems confronted by people in our society. Psychologists are attempting to unravel the intricacies of human behavior. Their goal is to explain and predict how people will behave.[1] In all likelihood, this goal will never be completely realized, but psychology can give people a better understanding of how they and others function and thus assist them to better deal with their life situation.

Psychologists, like their natural science counterparts, rely upon research as their basic tool for exploring the human condition. Carefully controlled psychological research has been going on in this country with animals and human beings since the turn of the century and started in Britain, Germany, Russia, and other countries prior to 1900. The result of this research is a tremendous amount of scientific data about animal and human behavior. The problem in psychology comes not so much in the collection of data, but in the explanation of the data themselves. The reasons for this problem are rather complex, but an attempt will be made at this point to clarify them.

Nature of people The question about the nature of people is to a large extent a philosophical one, but nonetheless these philosophical arguments impinge upon the explanation of psychological data. The crux of the issue among psychologists is simple. One group of psychologists contends that people are *indeterministic*—that is, they are self-controlling and self-directing. To this group, people are clearly higher animals that because of their basic intellect and innate qualities are able to make decisions and act upon them despite factors which occur either within the individual person's self or within the person's environment. Another group contends that a person is *deterministic*, or stated differently, that one is an animal whose behavior is determined not by one's own abilities and powers but by one's drives, instincts, or environment. To this latter group people must be considered in the same category with lower animals because they are subject to the same psychological principles.

To illustrate how the nature of people can influence the interpretation of data, let us consider a hypothetical situation where a psychologist has completed an experiment in which this scientist used candy to reward small children who paid attention to their teacher. The psychologist found that this increased the amount of time students spent looking at and listening to the teacher. Philosophically, the scientist might conclude that small children are subject to environmental control; that is, the rewards which were offered caused the children to perform as they did. A second psychologist might concede that indeed candy could be used to entice small children to attend to their teacher, but if the children *decided* that candy was not important to them they could reject the reward and act in a manner which they *believed* more appropriate.

Theoretical differences Psychologists, like all scientists, are theory builders. A *theory* can be roughly defined as a set of interrelated principles which are designed to provide a plausible explanation for a set of events. A theory is a hypothesis or set of hypotheses about why something such as human behavior occurs in a particular manner. Theories give rise to ideas which can be researched and in turn the data from the research must be incorporated into the theoretical framework. For example, a psychologist's belief that learning takes place because of repetitive practice might lead to the building of a theory which defines learning and repetitive practice, and might include ideas about specific situations under which repetitive practice should take place. The psychologist could then design a research project which would test this theory. Finally, the data could be utilized to examine the value of the theory.

To continue this train of thought let us suppose that the psychologist in the foregoing paragraph did indeed design an experiment to prove the point and then found that repetitive practice did not significantly affect the learning of nonsense syllables such as agr, epz, gsp, etc. A psychologist who believes that learning takes place on a one-trial basis could use these data to support this theory. However, the experimenter might legitimately contend that the subjects were not motivated to learn nonsense syllables and thus the experiment was not a true test of the theory.

In summary, psychologists may disagree about the meaning of data because of differing theoretical or philosophical positions. However, psychologists are dedicated to expanding the frontiers of knowledge and the results of the aforementioned debates have, in fact, led to hundreds of experiments designed to ascertain the nature of people and the learning process. These types of disagreements have undoubtedly been a driving force in the rapid development of psychology as a science.

Types of psychologists To this point, psychology has been discussed as a science and perhaps the implication has been made that psychologists are of one particular type. Actually, there are a number of different fields within psychology and a variety of specialists within these fields.

Clinical psychologists are concerned primarily with the identification and treatment of behavioral and emotional problems. Specifically, clinical psychologists work with the mentally ill, the brain-injured, and the retarded. They may also elect to work with normal persons who are having adjustment problems, and many college and university counseling centers have clinical psychologists on their staffs. The clinical psychologist should not be confused with the psychiatrist, who is trained as a medical doctor. Although both are likely to work with the same types of patients, the psychiatrist is able to prescribe medicines and perform in other areas which are reserved for physicians.

Clinical psychologists perform a variety of functions among which counseling and psychotherapy probably lead the list. In order to be a skillful therapist a clinical psychologist typically must learn a variety of interviewing skills, how to use measurement devices such as personality inventories, and many specific treatment strategies designed to assist people with adjustment problems. Clinical psychologists often are involved in teaching and research, either in addition to their work as therapists or as their total job. This is because many clinical psychologists are hired by universities and colleges to train other psychologists and to do research in the psychological area.

Experimental and physiological psychologists are another large group of psychologists. Usually this group is primarily concerned with research but they, like the clinical psychologists, may do teaching because of university affiliations. The experimental psychologists may be concerned with the impact of physiological processes upon human functioning. Experimental psychologists might, for example, be concerned with the amount of retention of material learned through mass practice (cramming) versus practice conducted periodically over a long period of time. Physiological psychologists might concern themselves with the enzyme balance in *schizophrenics* hoping to discover a physiological explanation for this supposedly psychological state.

It is perhaps obvious that the experimental and physiological psychologist must have excellent research skills. They must know how to set up carefully controlled experiments so that the data obtained will be free from experimental bias. Research design, statistics, and the design and use of experimental equipment are all important tools for a well-prepared researcher.

Developmental psychologists are concerned with the behavior of human beings at various ages. They are concerned about such topics as age of walking, talking, development of eye-hand coordination, etc. Some developmental psychologists focus upon children while others may be interested in adolescents, early adulthood, or the aged. Research is a basic tool of developmental psychologists, but they—like other psychologists—are often involved in some teaching activities because of their university affiliation.

A group not often attached to universities is industrial psychologists. As the name implies, these people are hired by industry to assist in determining means by which worker productivity and morale can be boosted, to assist in designing training programs, and to consult with management on the psychological aspects of marketing and advertising.

There are a variety of other types of psychologists. Social psychologists focus on the behavior of people in groups and are closely akin to sociologists because of their interests. Educational psychologists work primarily in educational settings. Their job is to do psychological evaluations of students and consult with teachers about treatment of specific individuals. Statistical psychologists, personality psychologists, and engineering psychologists are also found in our society.

The number of psychologists is likely to increase dramatically in our society during the coming decades. The 1972 *Manpower Report of the President* estimates that there will be an increase of nearly 60 percent in this decade alone. However, it should be pointed out that psychologists are a highly educated group with many of them holding the Ph.D. degree and that the opportunities for attaining a Ph.D. in psychology are limited to a relative few.

METHODOLOGY OF PSYCHOLOGISTS

Psychologists, like other social scientists, have methods by which they collect data. Because psychologists are concerned primarily about the causes of human behavior, they have designed or borrowed from the natural sciences a series of methods which will allow them to collect information that will illuminate this subject.

The observational method At first thought, the idea of collecting data about people via direct observation seems ridiculously simple. All of us are able to observe others and make reports upon what we observe. The question that comes up, however, is with regard to the accuracy of the observation. Most of us have been involved in situations such as accidents that involved eye witnesses. The varying accounts of eye witnesses at the scene of an accident attest to the fact that most people are not trained observers.

Persons can be taught to make accurate, scientific observations which correlate to a high degree with the observations of others. This is the first step. Once this type of behavior is learned it can be utilized to collect data about animals or human beings in a fashion that enables us to attach validity to the data and thus increase our information about human functioning.

Tests and other assessment devices Psychologists use instruments to collect data about people which are called *tests* or *inventories*. All students have taken teacher-made tests but these are rarely used by psychologists. However, most of the readers have also taken standardized tests such as achievement batteries, intelligence tests, and other similar instruments throughout their elementary and secondary school years. Additionally, students who wish to attend college usually take tests for college admission such as the Scholastic Aptitude Test (SAT) of the College Entrance Examination Board, or the American College Test (ACT). These types of tests can give us information about how well an individual has done or will do in school and about other areas of one's functioning. However, reliance upon tests such as the ACT or CEEB as the sole criteria for admitting students to colleges and universities has come under heavy fire. Most so-called scholastic aptitude tests or tests that purport to predict academic achievement have biases which favor middle-class whites and thus discriminate against nonwhites. As a result, most colleges and universities consider other data in the admissions process.

Psychologists also frequently use interest inventories or personality inventories to explore human functioning. These instruments are called inventories because they are in no way an attempt to measure how well a person can do. Rather, they are designed to determine how a person typically feels, thinks, or reacts to a variety of ideas or situations. A person cannot do poorly on an inventory.

Other instruments commonly used by psychologists are questionnaires, sociometric devices, and attitude scales. Questionnaires are utilized to gain opinion type data such as that collected by pollsters at election time. Sociometrics is a means by which the structure of a group can be ascertained. Specifically, sociometrics are used to ascertain the social value of a person in a specific group. Attitude scales are used to infer feelings and thoughts about subjects such as racial prejudice, sexual stereotyping, and other similar areas.

The experimental method Like all scientists, psychologists attempt to conduct research which will enable them to prove or disprove their hypotheses about human functioning. The experimental method allows them to do this. In the experimental method there are at least two groups. One group called an experimental group is given a treatment of some type. The second group called a control group is untreated. The purpose of this design is to determine whether things which occur are due to the treatment or due to other factors.

A psychologist might, for example, want to ascertain whether or not a high level of noise has any effect upon work efficiency in an industrial situation. In order to determine this, the scientist would set up two identical work situations. In one, the workers would be assigned to chores and the noise (experimental condition) would be introduced. In the control group, the workers would be assigned to identical tasks without the noise. If the psychologist found that workers were less productive whenever the noise was present, one would be able to say with some certainty that noise negatively affected worker productivity. If, however, the hypothesis about noise was not verified, the researcher would have to design other experiments which would isolate other variables that have potential impact on productivity.

Case history method Some psychologists may study individuals or groups of individuals via the case study approach. Essentially, this approach involves the collection of data from the family, the school, and perhaps the work situation of the individual. Such data as health records, school records, test scores, and peer ratings might be consulted. Generally, the psychologist is trying to get some idea of how the individual or group being studied developed and perhaps identify certain factors which gave rise to present behavior or behaviors.

AREAS OF PSYCHOLOGICAL INVESTIGATION

To this point the idea has been promoted that psychologists are concerned with the total realm of human functioning and this is true. However, there are some major topics upon which psychologists. focus. These will be presented and discussed at this point.

Learning Learning can be simply defined as any change in behavior which is not directly attributable to maturation. Literally thousands of experiments have been conducted which were aimed at discovering the nature of the learning process. Today there is probably no clear cut agreement among psychologists as to exactly why or how learning takes place. However, two major explanations of learning have been identified.

Learning by insight *Insight* is the process by which the individual is able to utilize thought processes to solve problems. A person is, as Fitch[1] indicates, "a thinker first and doer second," according to those who subscribe to the insight explanation of learning.

The insight process itself is characterized by mentally "trying out" a variety of explanations or solutions and is at times characterized by an "aha" phenomenon when the individual finally sees the *gestalt,* that is, the relationship among the various components of the problem with which he is confronted. Most of us have experienced this situation whenever we have seen the principle behind the mathematics problems we were working, or realized that there was a pattern in the puzzle we were working.

Insight, of course, does not occur automatically, as most people can verify. At times, insight involves some trial and error processes, that is, alternative solutions are tried and rejected. The essential ingredient in the trial and error process is that the individual benefits from the experience and that there is an orderly progression toward the solution.

Conditioning The other major explanation of learning is that it occurs through some sort of *conditioning* process. In insight, the central nervous-system functioning (thinking) is emphasized. In contrast, the functioning of the peripheral nervous system is emphasized in the conditioning process. This means simply that the individual's behavior and the environmental reaction to this behavior is what causes learning. A child who touches a stove and is burned learns that stoves can cause injury. However, a child who opens a door and finds candy will have the behavior of door-opening strengthened.

To repeat, people learn because of the environmental feedback which they receive. Simply put, behavior which is rewarded will be strengthened. Behavior which has received aversive feedback will be suppressed or inhibited. According to this point of view, central processes are relatively unimportant in the overall acquisition of new behaviors.

Emotions An angry person strikes another. A baseball player, ecstatic over a victory, leaps onto the back of a teammate. A mother upset because her child has been injured cries openly. A small child cringes in fear of a large dog. All of these are examples of how emotion has some effect upon the way we behave. Of course, emotions are not always this obvious and at times we even strive to cover up our feelings. This is particularly true of men who have been taught that it is not manly to cry or even to show sympathy or other emotions. Certain adolescent groups may also try to be "cool" in situations which would normally be reacted to with an emotional response. The human animal is capable of a wide range of emotions; joy, anger, jealousy, happiness, hatred, sorrow, etc. Indeed, some people claim that it is these emotions that distinguish human beings from lower animals. An emotion may be defined as ". . . a feeling or state of arousal that stirs an organism to observable action or to internal change."[2] According to this definition, not all emotions lead an individual to act, but there are either physiological or psychological changes which occur which may not be directly observable.

At the outset several instances of observable behavior resulting from various emotions were mentioned. There are other less subtle examples that could be given. You, as a student, may be reading this book for fear of flunking a course. You may be bored by certain sections of the book which causes you not to read them carefully. On the other hand, you may be excited by some sections which in turn stimulates you to read additional material. An emotion which might not be readily observable would be the times when you become disgusted with the book and course but continue on in your reading and class assignments for fear you will fail if you do not.

Emotions develop as the result of maturation and learning. Some psychologists believe that the child is born with a basic set of emotions such as fear, disgust, and anger, and that as the child matures these manifest themselves in various ways. Others believe that most emotions are learned directly from the people around them. Although there is some disagreement about the genesis of emotions, there is considerable agreement that the means by which they are expressed are to a very large extent culturally determined. In some societies men cry freely whenever they feel sorrow. In ours, this is not always the case. In other cultures the expression of fear is frowned upon, although there can be little doubt that fear is experienced.

In summary, emotions are instrumental in human functioning and they do, to a large extent, enrich that functioning. A person would be a colorless being without emotion.

Personality How many times have you heard the statement, "That person sure has a bad personality." This reference is, of course, not to the personality as the psychologist defines it, but rather to the overt manifestations of the personality. The word *personality* apparently stems from the Greek word "persona" which means mask. This lay definition of personality would indicate that only the behavior which occurs makes up the personality. Few psychologists or other social scientists would agree with this idea.

The personality is generally viewed as the consisting pattern of characteristics, traits, or attributes which persist over a period of time. The organization of the personality is dynamic, which means that it tends to change, but perhaps consistency or stability are the primary characteristics of the normal personality. People whose personality varies widely and frequently are usually viewed as abnormal, at least to some degree, in our society.

Emotions such as anger, fear, and anxiety produce bodily changes. One change commonly measured by psychologists in experiments on learning and personality is the galvanic skin response (GSR). The galvanometer records the change in the electrical resistance of the skin that can be measured by attaching a resistance meter or voltmeter to the skin. In strong emotional excitement, the increase in the secretion of the sweat glands ("nervous perspiration") is accompanied by a drop in the electrical resistance of the skin. *(Marcia Weinstein)*

Most of us have experienced mood shifts in relatively short periods of time. We may have been elated that we won the game from our arch-rival, but when our plans for after the game went awry we felt deflated and let down. This kind of reaction to situational variables is typical and normal. However, the abnormal individual may go from extreme euphoria to the depths of despair without any changes in his environmental circumstances.

Psychologists are interested in ascertaining the determinants of personality. As we shall see in the chapters which follow, there are theoretical explanations of why personality develops as it does. There are also some more generalized explanations. We know, for example, that parents and their techniques for rearing children have a tremendous impact upon the personality of the child. Some psychologists believe that the early-childhood environment is the chief variable in shaping personality. We know also that the culture in which we live has a tremendous impact upon the personality. A recently discovered Stone Age tribe in the Philippines illustrates this graphically. In this culture there is no aggressive behavior. People do not argue or fight. Disputes do not arise because of the totally unselfish attitudes of the members of the culture. One need only contrast that with our own situation to see the impact that culture makes upon the personality.

The family and the culture are but two of the determinants of personality. Sex roles, reference groups, socioeconomic level, and traumatic experiences may have an impact upon personality. In the past, the description of the ideal female personality might have included words and phrases like submissive, dependent, and unable to make decisions. To describe the male role, words and phrases just the opposite of these would be used: dominant, independent, and decision maker. These stereotypical ideals played a great part in the development of male and female personalities. Today these ideals are changing with the new women's-consciousness movement. Essentially the thrust of this movement is to establish a new place of women in our society which is equivalent to that of men. As a part of this movement a new ideal role for women is being established and thus a new ideal personality. It will undoubtedly take one or two generations before this ideal emerges totally, but there can be little doubt that the woman of the future will have shed her submissive, dependent role.

There is some evidence that socioeconomic level has some impact upon personality development, but the evidence is conflicting. The black from the South was often stereotypically viewed as being passive in nature. However, behind Martin Luther King many of these passive individuals marched in places like Selma and Birmingham to communicate in no uncertain terms that blacks had rights which were expected to be met. Families from lower socioeconomic classes do have different child-rearing techniques which are characterized by more punishment.

They also have different expectations of their children than do their middle-class counterparts in the area of school performance, aggressive activities (fighting), and accepting responsibility at an early age. These expectations lead to varying personality types, but it is difficult to stereotype socioeconomic classes regarding personality.

Traumatic experiences, particularly in early childhood, have long been viewed as having an impact upon personality development. In a classic case, a young girl was forced to kiss her dead grandmother goodbye, which was the custom in her culture. Apparently as a direct result of this experience, the child developed three distinct personality patterns. This case was popularized during the sixties in a movie entitled *The Three Faces of Eve.* Traumatic experiences such as the loss of a parent or loved one, being molested, being subjected to severe physical punishment, or exposure to extreme psychological stress have also been linked to personality problems. Abnormal personality development will be discussed more fully in the next section.

Finally, there are a number of factors which may have an impact upon the personality, some of which have been discussed here. Perhaps the safest thing to say at this point is that psychologists do not understand fully how and why personality develops. Continuing research will hopefully provide answers in this area.

Abnormal behavior Interest in abnormal behavior is not a new preoccupation. Apparently Stone Age people chipped away holes in the skull of the individual to allow demons that occupied the skull to escape. The idea that demons possessed the person who was functioning abnormally persisted even in some enlightened cultures until nearly the twentieth century. More primitive cultures still subscribe to the demonological explanation of abnormal behavior.

The Greeks developed a more enlightened point of view about the abnormal individual and their ideas carried over into Arabic culture. In these societies the mentally ill escaped the inhuman treatment which emotionally disturbed individuals had to endure in other areas. It was not uncommon for abnormal persons to have their heads cut open, to be branded with red-hot pokers, or to be killed, often by incineration. For the most part, these acts were designed to free the individual from the demons which possessed one or to protect other members of the society from the individual.

In modern society we have come to understand that the abnormal personality develops because of psychological or physical reasons or both. With this understanding, modern psychologists and psychiatrists have developed a variety of means for the treatment of and cure of mental illness. However, the recognition that emotional illness has causes which can be treated and that the mentally disturbed individual can be restored to normal functioning has not totally solved the problem.

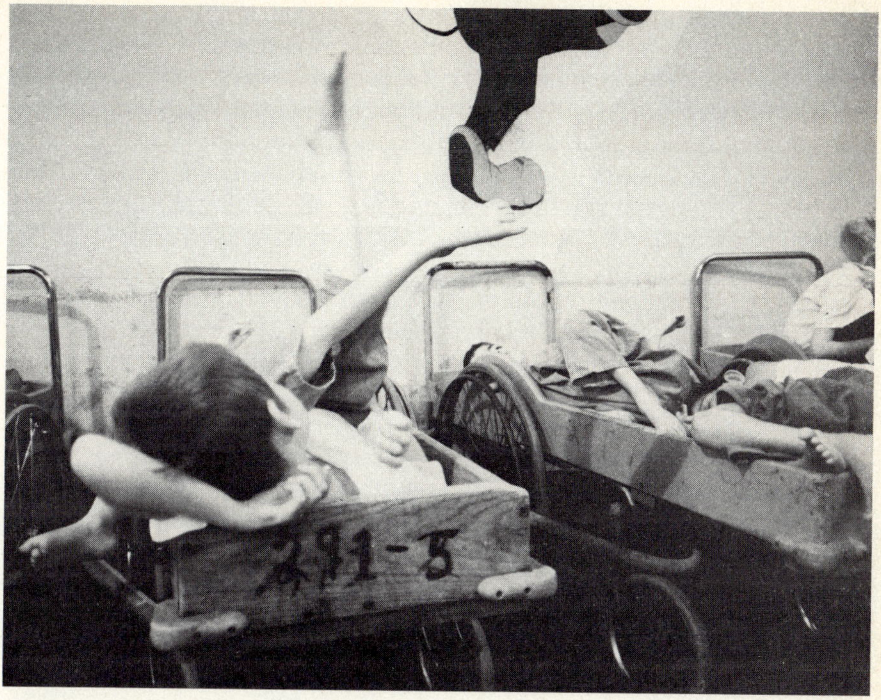

Outmoded institutions such as this one for emotionally disturbed children will improve as society becomes more insistent about providing better care and treatment for the mentally ill. *(Willowbrook Development Center)*

Even in our enlightened society people are still fearful of people who have been mentally ill. This is illustrated by the fact that some companies will not hire people who have had emotional problems. It was also illustrated graphically in the 1972 presidential race when George McGovern dropped Thomas Eagleton as his vice-presidential running mate when it was revealed that he had been treated for mental illness. Needless to say, we are making studies in this area and hopefully members of society will accept the person who has been cured of mental illness in the same manner that they now accept the person who has recovered from a physical illness.

Abnormal behavior can be generally classified into two broad categories—neuroses and psychoses. The neuroses which will be discussed first here are generally less disabling than the psychoses since the neurotic can very often continue to function in everyday life. It can be stated with great certainty that most of us as human beings suffer in some degree from neuroses and some people have gone so far as to suggest that it is our neuroses that make up an important part of our humanness.

A *neurosis* can be defined as a disorder in which some type of anxiety is present. However, the individual can continue to function because the disorder is not likely to become violent and maintains some perspective regarding the reality of the events which occur in one's life. Unlike the psychotic, the neurotic does not suffer from delusion or hallucinations. Neurotics are characterized by feelings of inadequacy, anxiety and fearfulness, irritability, the inability to learn from their experiences, general unhappiness, and in some instances certain types of symptoms such as excessive sweating, headaches, or a variety of other aches.

Neurosis has been classified into at least seven categories.[2] These are: (1) anxiety reaction; (2) asthenic reaction; (3) conversion reaction; (4) dissociative reaction; (5) phobic reaction; (6) obsessive compulsive reaction; and (7) neurotic depressive reaction. Each of these will be discussed briefly at this time.

A person suffering from *anxiety reaction* represents about 30 to 40 percent of all neurotic types. Generally this person is uneasy, irritable, and may be described as tense or nervous. One may become nauseous, have heart palpitations, suffer from dizziness, may sweat profusely for no apparent reason, and may at times have trouble getting one's breath. The neurotic who is having an anxiety reaction is often partially or totally immobilized by the inability to make decisions and by constant worrying about one's mistakes—real or imagined. Although persons suffering from this type of neurosis may at times appear quite normal, they are generally tense even during these periods.

Asthenic reaction, more commonly referred to as neurasthenia, is much less common than anxiety reaction. The major symptoms of this reaction is that the individual suffers from mental and physical fatigue. One may spend a great deal of one's time sleeping or resting, but these have little or no impact upon one's fatigue. *Conversion reaction* is another of the less common neurotic reactions, but its symptoms have been popularized by movies and television. In conversion reaction or hysteria, the individual develops a physical symptom without an organic cause. The symptoms range from blindness, deafness, and loss of touch to loss of the use of a limb and mutism or the inability to talk. It should be pointed out that the symptoms are usually quite real and the individual generally reacts in the same manner that one would if one had lost the use of an arm or had suddenly been struck blind.

Amnesia, the partial or total inability to recall past experience, is the major symptom of dissociative reactions. Sleepwalking or somnambulism is another symptom, or perhaps more correctly, type of dissociative reaction. So is the development of multiple personalities, although this condition is typically associated with schizophrenia, a psychotic reaction.

Phobic reactions or unrealistic fears occur most frequently among young adults and particularly among young women. These irrational fears are intense and severe, but these intense fears are not the only symptoms experienced by this group. They generally experience headaches, back pain, dizzy spells, and are concerned about going "off the deep end." Some common phobias follow:

acrophobia—fear of high places
agoraphobia—fear of open places
algophobia—fear of pain
claustrophobia—fear of closed places
hematophobia—fear of blood
monophobia—fear of being alone
nyctaphobia—fear of darkness
ochlophobia—fear of crowds
pathophobia—fear of disease
syphilophobia—fear of syphilis
zoophobia—fear of animals or a particular animal

It should be noted that most people have fears in some or all of these areas. However, the intensity of the fear is what makes the phobic person unique.

Another very large group of neurotics are those suffering from an *obsessive compulsive reaction*. Have you ever known persons who had to have all hangers pointing in the same direction in the closet, or all drawers perfectly organized? These people are to a degree compulsive in their nature. An obsessive person has certain recurring thoughts but may not carry these thoughts into action. Individuals may have obsessive thoughts about harming themselves or others or simply wishing that something would occur. Obsessive-compulsive thoughts may be carried into action, however. The compulsive person may rise from bed to put the towels in order, or the person obsessed with the idea of being a success may work toward that end.

The *neurotic depressive* is dejected and discouraged and typically unhappy. This group, which makes up large parts of the neurotic population, is prone to suicide and often requires hospitalization. They can function in their day-to-day activities but their despair makes it somewhat difficult. At times this despair and discouragement is verbalized in the form of "nobody cares about me" or "what's the use—I'm no good anyway." More generally the depressed person just becomes less effective and more withdrawn, however.

Psychoses may be the result of psychological stress or certain physical problems or an interaction of the two. Those psychoses which are the result of psychological reactions are called *functional psychoses* and those resulting from physical factors are called *organic psychoses*. Psychologists are primarily concerned with the functional psychoses, which can be subdivided into schizophrenic reactions, paranoid reactions, affective reactions, and involutional psychotic reactions. It has been estimated that considerably more than 1 million persons suffer from psychotic reactions in the United States. Many are treated in custodial institutions generally referred to as mental institutions. Others are treated as out-patients by professional psychologists and psychiatrists who practice in mental-health clinics or in private practice. Those psychotics treated in out-patient clinics are able to function at some level and are judged not to be harmful to themselves or others. It should be noted that over 80 percent of the persons treated for psychoses are later discharged either fully recovered or improved. This, of course, means that one-fifth of the persons suffering from psychoses do not improve. These chronically ill patients are the object of considerable investigation.

About one-quarter of the people who develop a psychosis are schizophrenic. There are various subtypes of schizophrenics ranging from the simple type (which is most common among younger people), to the most common type (paranoid schizophrenic). Most are characterized by certain distinct symptoms. Generally, schizophrenics suffer from delusions and hallucinations. *Delusions* are false beliefs which are defended against all logical attacks. Delusional systems may be developed about a person's sin or guilt, about an imagined illness, about persecution from others, or there may be delusions of grandeur. In *hallucinations* the individual hears, sees, smells, tastes, or feels things that have no basis in fact. It is not uncommon for a schizophrenic to hear voices since auditory hallucinations are the most common.

Other symptoms of the schizophrenic are unsociability, lack of

Since hallucinations resemble dream states that occur during sleep, many experiments study the physiology of sleep in schizophrenics. Here a researcher monitors the electric equipment used to record the electrical signals from the eyes and brain of a woman during such an experiment. *(Marcia Weinstein)*

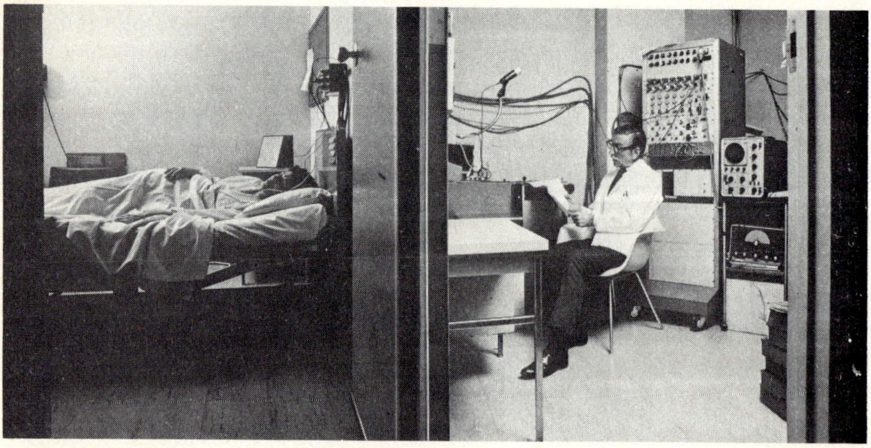

concern for appearance or personal hygiene, emotional apathy, and a host of others. Some of the symptomology of schizophrenics is bizarre. For example, the catatonic schizophrenic may sit rigidly in a single position for days.

In *paranoid reactions*, the person has an exaggerated feeling of being threatened, spied upon, cheated on by one's mate, persecuted, and so forth. Paranoids frequently develop delusions of grandeur. It is not uncommon for persons suffering from paranoid reactions to believe that they are God, Christ, or some important historical figure such as the President of the United States. It has been speculated that some of the major figures in history, such as Adolf Hitler, have been paranoids.

In discussing neuroses the category neurotic depressive reaction was discussed. Persons suffering from affective psychotic reactions may have similar symptoms, particularly those suffering from psychotic depressive reactions. However, the psychotic depressive is unable to function outside of an institution in most instances and suffers from delusions and hallucinations. Another subtype of the affective psychotic reaction is the manic-depressive. These individuals in a manic state may have boundless energy. They may stay up for days, may have sexual intercourse repeatedly, and may have what appears to be near superhuman strength and prowess. The manic-depressive may go from this state of extreme activity to one of total depression and self-doubt. Often at this time this person becomes suicidal.

Involutional psychotics are similar in symptomology to those suffering from a manic-depressive reaction. Depression is the overriding characteristic, but there are periods of agitation among persons suffering from this illness. They are extremely dangerous to themselves and are at times a threat to the well-being of others.

Causes of abnormality The speculation about the causes of abnormal functioning are as diverse as the types of illnesses themselves. Most psychologists agree, however, that no one factor can be related directly to the development of neurotic and psychotic reactions. Most hypotheses about the development of abnormal behavior list at least four potential causes. These are genetic or inherited factors, immediate environmental causes such as psychological stress, cultural factors such as child-rearing techniques and cultural expectation, and organic factors such as diseases which are not related to inherited traits. These may be further subdivided so that at least a dozen potential explanations for abnormal could be derived.

Treatment of mental illness The most typical approach to treating mental illness is the talking cure—psychotherapy. Psychotherapy is conducted by a psychologist or psychiatrist and includes one or more clients or patients who are suffering from some form of mental illness. The goal of psychotherapy is to assist the client to get rid of emotional problems. The exact nature of the process varies from therapist to therapist as will be illustrated in the two chapters to follow.

Several adjuncts to psychotherapy are utilized. Among the most common is the use of chemotherapy or drugs. Tranquilizers of various types may be used to lower the anxiety level of certain patients. Mild stimulants may also be utilized to help some patients overcome their severe depression.

Shock therapy, once a fairly common treatment for psychotics, is now nearly totally restricted to use with severely depressed patients who have not responded to drugs.

Another device which has received much publicity but only little use is *psychosurgery*. Prefrontal lobotomies, which involve the removal of a predetermined amount of nerve tissue from the frontal lobes of the brain, have not met with much enthusiasm because of the postsurgical results. Patients typically have reduced intellectual levels and are frequently left with childlike personalities which often do not mature. For the most part, chemotherapy has replaced psychosurgery as a means of dealing with the severely emotionally disabled, the group for which the technique was originally developed.

Normal behavior In this section, normal functioning will be discussed. It should be stated at the outset that most of us are normal and by that is simply meant that we are able to cope with our daily problems without suffering undue stress or anxiety. However, as was the case with abnormality, there are degrees of normal functioning. Most of the effort in this section will be devoted to what is called the fully functioning or self-actualizing person. The reader should not become upset if one does not recognize oneself as a fully functioning person, for few of us are. Psychologists have estimated that only about 5 to 10 percent of our population reaches the level of personal functioning that will be described in the paragraphs that follow.

Abraham Maslow[3] spent much of his career researching and writing about normal individuals. From his works we can derive many aspects of the so-called normal individual.

In looking at fully functioning or normal individuals, it is probably most important to look at how they view themselves. The people who operate at the highest level of their personal potential accept themselves for what they are. They are aware of their own strengths and weaknesses and readily admit to both. A homely boy would recognize his physical characteristics, but would also realize that he had skills above and beyond those of his peers. He would not dwell on either his strengths or his weaknesses, but merely accept them. Neither would he try to pretend that he was something that he is not, for self-acceptance implies that the individual is free from the phony quality often observed in persons in our society.

Another important key to normalcy can be found in the way individuals treat each other. Normal people, or *self-actualizing* people as Maslow called them, accept other people in the same manner that they accept themselves. They tend less to evaluate the people they come into contact with, and more to appreciate them for what they are. Fully functioning people are relatively free from stereotypical thinking, and therefore a Chicano is not a Spanish American with certain characteristics, but an individual who has certain characteristics that make one a unique individual for those people. For the normal person, each personal encounter is a new experience which is to be relished and enjoyed.

Self-actualizing people are able to form intimate relationships with individuals. These relationships tend to be deeply emotional and profound experiences for these people. Their love relationships are characterized by a deep sense of sharing and are relatively void of personal manipulation and attempts at self-gratification. The ability to love deeply and without fear may be the greatest asset of fully functioning persons. As a result, their marriages and relationships with children are more enduring, as are their friendships.

There is another important aspect of this individual that has been labeled variously as normal, fully functioning, and self-actualizing, that might be surprising in light of the foregoing. These people tend to be autonomous and independent in their functioning. They also may appear aloof and most have a need for privacy. While these persons are capable of giving and sharing in the best sense of those words, they also are capable of functioning apart from the group. Because of their self-acceptance, people are not needed to provide constant reminders of self-worth, and independent action can be embarked upon. However, because of this characteristic, the relationships engaged in are done so for mutual benefit, not the benefit of an individual.

Normal people are realistically oriented. They are able to size up a situation and derive the salient points from it. The authors are reminded of an individual who saw a pot of gold at the end of every business deal. As a consequence, the person continuously became involved in speculative ventures, most of which resulted in failure. That person lacked that basic ability to make judgments about the reality of a situation.

Most of us confuse means with ends from time to time. The acquisition of a job really is a means to an end of economic independence, status, and other rewards. The fully functioning person tends to establish goals and to separate means from goals.

A sense of humor has long been viewed as an indicator of normal functioning. One is struck with the lack of this characteristic when contact with mentally ill individuals is made. However, a sense of humor may be cynical or hostile. Most of us are familiar with the practical joker who thinks nothing of making others the butt of pranks. The fully functioning individual tends to be an individual whose sense of humor is more philosophical. The comic strip *Peanuts* is illustrative of a philosophical approach to humor.

There are a variety of other characteristics of the self-actualizing people. They tend to identify with mankind; most have profound spiritual experiences although not necessarily of a religious nature; they tend to focus upon the problem at hand, rather than themselves in relationship to the problem; and they tend to be democratic in their attitudes and values. These and other characteristics make individuals more human and enable them to be contributors to our society.

As was stated at the outset, only a few people reach the so called self-actualized state. The current boom in books that focus upon personal development and the interest in introspective approaches to self-development such as transcendentalism and yoga are indicators that persons are attempting to help themselves function at a higher level. Many persons who would be classified by all who know them as well-adjusted have entered into counseling or therapy of some type to assist them to learn better means of coping. These trends appear likely to continue and accelerate.

Aging and death In the decade of the seventies, the population of the United States will start to get older. This is in contrast to the sixties when the mean age decreased steadily. The present trend amplifies the need to study the psychological aspects of aging. We need to know, for example, how old age affects mental health, the psychological impact of retirement, and the result of losing friends to determine means by which the psychological stress associated with these problems can be alleviated.

Psychologists are also increasingly aware of the need to study the psychology of dying. Kubler-Ross[4] points out that we have to a great extent ignored the process of dying because to recognize it means that we have to deal with our own mortality. However, when we ignore dying we make it a lonely, frustrating experience. Because of modern medical practice which may keep a dying patient alive for months or years, we increasingly need to examine the psychological conditions of the dying and the people around them.

There is also a need to look at the psychological correlates of long life. Psychologists believe that factors such as a good, successful job, happy interpersonal relationships, and a variety of other factors contribute to longevity. Most of us have known people who, after the loss of a loved one or retirement from a job, seemed to capitulate in some manner and died soon after. Psychologists are trying to understand more fully what happens in this process.

ISSUES IN PSYCHOLOGY

That psychology is not a monolithic science in which all psychologists agree on the issues has perhaps become obvious already. In this section some of the areas of disagreement will be more fully discussed. It has already been pointed out that psychologists disagree about the nature of people and along certain theoretical grounds. However, there are certain other more mundane areas of disagreement which will be detailed here.

What are acceptable data? This may seem like an absurd question to the lay person, but to the professional psychologist it is a very serious issue. As a group, psychologists must collect data to test their theories and substantiate their hypotheses about human functioning. Some psychologists accept everything from the reactions to the Rorschach inkblot test, autobiographies, and verbal self-reports to objective, observable behavior as data. Others believe that the only source of data that should be utilized is observable data objectively collected under experimental conditions. These two positions represent one of the major issues in psychology.

Central versus peripheral processes Is a person's brain the center of one's functioning? Is this nerve center the cause of one's thoughts, emotions, and problem solving? Or does the human animal react to environmental stimuli and the brain serves only as a clearing house for the stimuli which comes in through the senses? This question has raged since psychology began to form as a science and will in all likelihood continue.

Nature versus nurture Of all the issues in psychology perhaps none have been so hotly contested as the nature-nurture debate. Although this debate could be applied to personality development, or the evolution of abnormal behavior, the development of intelligence has been selected to demonstrate how two sides can form on an issue such as this.

Intelligence as a case-in-point The nature-nurture conflict dates back to at least Plato's time in early Greece. Plato believed that human characteristics are primarily inherited and thus put himself firmly on the nature side of the argument.

Watson and many other psychologists from the behavioral school of change took a stand quite opposite to that of Plato and other early philosophers. Watson in particular contended that animals and human beings do not inherit instincts, intelligence, or other innate abilities of any type. Perhaps Watson's most famous statement regarding the importance of nurture (environment) follows:

> Give me a dozen healthy infants well formed, and my own specified world to bring them up in, and I'll guarantee to take any one at random and train him to become any type of specialist I select—doctor, lawyer, artist, merchant-chief, and—yes—even beggar-man-thief, regardless of his talents, tendencies, abilities, vocations, and race of ancestors.[5]

This statement and others like it were undoubtedly the beginning of the modern nature-nurture debate—a debate which is raging more heavily in the seventies than probably at any time since the early 1900s.

Of late, the group which believes that inherited material is primarily responsible for humans' abilities has taken the offensive. The first shot was fired by Arthur R. Jensen[6] in 1969, in an article entitled "How Much Can We Boost IQ and Scholastic Achievement?" In this presentation, Jensen makes several points. First, he argues that the source of abilities such as *intelligence* should be opened to scientific inquiry and studied in much the same manner as are other human traits. Few social scientists would disagree with this contention although some would debate the point that this is really a reasonable question because of our present scientific limitations. The second point made by Jensen is that compensatory education programs designed to raise IQ and scholastic achievement have largely failed. Again, the data is on Jensen's side. Headstart programs for preschoolers and follow-through programs for the first three grades have been able to raise IQ and achievement scores for a short time, but these have ultimately regressed to a point commensurate or near their early levels. Jensen's third point has drawn widespread criticism, however, Jensen points that the reason for the failure of compensatory education, particularly among blacks, is that they are genetically inferior, at least with regard to intelligence.

The basis for Jensen's argument seems to rest on two sources of data. The first of these was the so-called Coleman Report,[7] and other reviews of the literature (Shuey[8]) which indicate that black Americans test 15 points below white population on IQ tests and one standard deviation below on scholastic achievement tests. These tests seem to show that the average IQ of black Americans is 90 and white Americans 100.

The second source of Jensen's argument appears to be studies which have looked at the intelligence level of identical twins reared apart. Identical twins are *monozygotic*, that is, they are the result of a split in a single egg and thus have the same genetic material. Thus, when identical twins are reared apart we supposedly have a true test of the environmental hypothesis. The findings of this research show that, in fact, the relationships between the IQs of monozygotic twins reared apart is very similar to those of the IQ of twins reared in the same home with the correlations of the two groups being .75 and .87 respectively.

Jensen[9] concludes from his research and by examining and analyzing the research of others that inherited traits account for 80 percent of the resulting IQ, and correspondingly, only 20 percent of intelligence can be accounted for by environment. He is joined in this view by William Shockley,[10] a Nobel Prize winner in physics for his invention of the transistor. Dr. Jensen has use of convincing mathematical deviations to support his position.

Arthur Jensen (a noted educator) and William Shockley (a Nobel Prize winner in physics) both have impressive academic credentials; both have declared that intelligence is determined primarily by inherited characteristics; both have suggested that the gene pool for blacks may well be inferior to that of whites. These positions have brought forth a storm of protests. The most cogent of these will be reviewed here.

Gage[11,12] has perhaps best summarized the rebuttals to Jensen and Shockley and others who have continued to claim that IQ is determined to a high degree by hereditary factors. The first point of examination must be the "naturists'" view that 80 percent of intelligence is inherited. The argument put forth by Gage, and rightly so, is that the scores which have demonstrated that the IQ of blacks is approximately 15 prints below that of whites have only demonstrated that this is true under very specific conditions. It is a well-known fact that blacks have been discriminated against systematically in this country and in other predominately white countries for more than a century. What our tests are measuring, according to Gage, may well be the impact of our environment upon inherited traits. This would not refute the 80 percent figure; neither would it deny the probability that given different circumstances the IQ might be raised.

Secondly, Gage attacked the very cornerstone of the "naturists'" position—the reliance upon the research conducted with monozygotic twins. He points out that when twins are placed in different homes an attempt is made to place them in similar environments, and in fact, this is often the case. However, when identical twins are placed in environments which are sharply different, the correlation between their IQs drop considerably. Gage further contends that it is doubtful that any of the literature dealing with identical twins deals with children placed in environmental circumstances which are as markedly different as those which exist between two random populations, one black and one white. Therefore, even though the research conducted with identical twins is indicative of the influence of inherited traits, it cannot be assumed that it is directly related to differences which occur in black and white IQs.

Another point was made by Hudson[13] which is germane not only to the nature-nurture debate about the heritability of IQ, but also to other debates within the social sciences. In making his point, Hudson poses what he calls his "Law of Selective Attention to Data." His law follows:

1. That psychology is relevant inasmuch as it bears on ideology; bears, that is to say, on the general assumptions about life that direct man's actions.
2. That the greater the relevance of research to ideology, the greater the tendency of the psychologist to pay selective attention to his data. Further:
3. The greater the intensity of his own involvement, the more vigorously will the psychologist appeal to external authority; to the authority of *Science*, or on the other hand, to humane virtues such as "democracy." And:
4. That the greater will be his tendency to adopt an extreme position, either as very "hard" or as very "soft." The law goes on to assert:
5. That the involvement of psychology in ideological issues will increase at times of impending political crises in the world at large. Indeed, such an increase may not only reflect such tension, but contribute to it. And finally . . .
6. That a psychology is not both ideologically relevant and as dispassionate as possible unless the psychologist's own involvement is made explicit. His presuppositions must be included as a part of the intellectual and social process he hopes to explain.

Hudson's point is simply that for the social scientist, personal biases may direct the selection of data in order to provide the point. Without a knowledge of these biases it is impossible to understand fully the points which are being made. One other factor should be noted here. By the process of selecting data which fits a bias or presupposition, the social scientist can "usually" prove the point or at least justify its existence.

Since it is likely that both those who favor the environmental hypothesis and those who lean toward heritability of traits have selectively attended to data, the argument will continue. Probably the only point upon which both sides would agree is that genetic make-up contributes to a wide variety of human characteristics and that environment to some measure serves as a device to temper these characteristics. Beyond this point little agreement seems possible.

SUMMARY

In this chapter the general field of psychology has been examined. As was the case with sociology, psychology is a diverse discipline with a variety of specializations. However, most psychologists have a common educational core on which a specific field of study is built.

Psychology tends to focus upon the individual as the basis for its theorizing and research. As we shall see in Chapters 6 and 7, little attention is given to collective behavior although one group, social psychologists, is interested primarily in the functioning of groups.

Psychologists disagree on many aspects of human functioning. Issues such as the true source of data, the importance of the brain in human functioning, and the contributions of instincts to behavior are but a few of the areas of disagreement among psychologists. These disagreements have stimulated not only a great deal of debate, as was illustrated by the furor over Jensen's stand on intelligence, but voluminous research studies. These disagreements will be further illustrated in the chapters which follow in this section.

REVIEW QUESTIONS

1. What is psychology?
2. What are the different types of psychologists?
3. Of the varying methods utilized by psychologists, which holds the most promise of illuminating the issues? Why?
4. What is your philosophical view of people? Is functioning determined by forces which they cannot control or do they function autonomously?
5. In your opinion, why have psychologists focused on abnormal behavior?
6. Do you know any self-actualized people? Describe them.
7. What is your position on the inheritance of intelligence? Defend it.
8. It was stated in this chapter that normal functioning means being able to cope with day-to-day problems. Do you agree with this definition? Why or why not?
9. What are the major categories of mental illness? Differentiate among them.

CHAPTER SIX
HUMAN FUNCTIONING: AN INTRAPSYCHIC VIEW

IDEAS AND CONCEPTS

life style
an individual's personal perceptions of the world and the overt manifestations of those perceptions

pleasure principle
a system of behavior whereby self-gratification is the basic rule of operation

reality principle
dealing with the world as it is by recognizing consequences of behavior for self and others

self-actualization
the ability of an individual to transcend environment

transference
a phenomenon in psychoanalytic therapy where the patient attaches emotions for other people to the therapist

Intrapsychic and behavioral ideas There is a ghost in the machine, at least according to the psychologists who hold an *intrapsychic view* of man. Simply defined, an intrapsychic view of man is one that holds that man is more than his observable behavior, more than the gestalt. Man is, in effect, greater than the sum of his parts.

In the chapter which follows, a behavioral view of people will be discussed. The position taken by this group is simply that man can best be understood through objective observation of his overt behavior. The intrapsychic psychologists believe that man must be understood, at least in part, by examining his own view of himself or his internal frame of reference. For this reason, the intrapsychic view of man is necessarily subjective since the social scientist attempts to infer the genesis of behavior through self-report and other devices designed to measure internal personality structures. Because of this subjective nature, intrapsychic psychology tends to be less scientific than the objective, behavioral approaches. Indeed, some branches of the intrapsychic school, such as the *existentialists*, reject empirical research as a valid tool for exploring human behavior because research requires the grouping of people and that in itself is deemed inappropriate since according to some, man must be understood as an individual—not as a part of a group. For the most part, however, the intrapsychic group has pursued research utilizing the scientific method as a means of proving or disproving their theories about people's behavior.

Tips to the student During your perusal of this chapter, several questions should be kept in mind. Perhaps most important to the reader will be the question regarding the personal importance of the approach being presented. Specifically, can the ideas being presented in each of the three approaches help me deal with my own life situation? Can I, if I absorb the facts being presented, deal more effectively with myself, my friends, my parents, and the other people in my life? Another important question is simply, which ideas are best? The authors have attempted to help you deal with this problem, but ultimately you must draw these conclusions for yourself. One final question that should be entertained is simply how different are the ideas of Freud, Adler, Rogers, and others? This is a question which has bothered many students and professors. You will find some distinct similarities among the ideas presented, and some marked differences. From the start of your reading, points of agreement and disagreement should be compared and contrasted.

A myriad of theories There are literally dozens of intrapsychic theories of human behavior which are nearly as diverse as are the two major schools, intrapsychic and behavioristic. Attempts have been made to classify these theories in various ways, all of which have had major shortcomings. Since space is limited, an attempt will be made to present three major intrapsychic explanations of human functioning. These are chosen because they are hopefully representative of the diversity which exists, because they represent major movements in psychology, and because they present the student with a wide variety of potentially useful information about human behavior.

PSYCHOANALYTIC THEORY

Introduction Sigmund Freud, perhaps the best-known psychological theoretician, founded the *psychoanalytic* movement at the turn of the twentieth century. Freud was trained as a physician in Vienna, graduating from medical school in 1881. Freud intended to become a scientist, but he found limited opportunities for advancement for a Jew in the scientific area and finally entered private practice. During medical school Freud had developed an interest in neurological disorders and was naturally attracted to disorders of the mind.

When Freud entered medical practice he associated himself with Dr. Josef Breuer, another Viennese physician, who had developed a method of dealing with neurotic disorders that involved "talking out" or catharsis. Freud soon found himself dealing with various mental disorders. In 1885, Freud studied for a year with Jean Charcot, a famous French psychiatrist who had developed a hypnotic technique for dealing with mental disorders. After a year of study, Freud returned to Vienna and reassociated himself with Breuer and practiced both the hypnotic technique (which he had learned from Charcot) and the carthartic method, which Breuer had developed. As time passed, Freud became less involved with hypnotic approaches and started to rely upon a form of the carthartic technique known as *free association,* which he developed.

Freud and Breuer worked together until two major issues drove them apart. Of these, the sexual origin of abnormal behavior was perhaps the point of greatest disagreement. Freud felt that sexual conflicts were the basis of all neuroses. This was a position which was to remain as a cornerstone of his approach to psychoanalysis throughout his life. Breuer rejected this idea, however. Breuer also rejected the therapeutic procedure which Freud was creating because of the development of *transference.* When transference occurs the patient develops a deep affection for the therapist or becomes very hostile and tends to reject the therapist. Freud saw this as the natural outgrowth of the sexual conflicts which the patient was experiencing, while Breuer disagreed. As a result of these disagreements, Breuer and Freud separated.

This background about the beginning of psychoanalytic theory has been provided for one major reason. As the reader has perhaps realized by this time, Freud's theories grow not out of the scientific laboratory, but out of his day-to-day practice as a psychiatrist. His theory evolved not so much out of the logical contrivance of an explanation of human behavior, but as a description of human behavior as one man came to see it. This one man, however, became an extremely influential theoretician.

Freud's theory Freud postulated what may be viewed as a biological theory of human development. Freud's approach is biological because he sees the individual personality evolving out of a mass of instincts and drives which are present at birth. The instincts according to Freud can be classified into two rough categories: life and death. Hunger, thirst, and sex are life instincts, and death instincts, while less well-defined, are present and can be viewed essentially as an unconscious wish to die. These instincts, along with the other psychological variables which the individual is, both combine to form the id, the basic portion of human personality.

Pleasure principle The id operates on the *pleasure principle*; that is, the human organism, if it operated solely on the basis of the *id*, would fulfill its desires without consideration of others. The young child is a good example of this. Whenever a baby is hungry he screams for relief from his hunger state, and similarly whenever the child becomes uncomfortable because of a wet diaper he demands that he be relieved from this state without concern for others.

Reality principle The id is the source of two other personality structures. The *ego* differentiates itself from the id whenever the developing child begins to communicate with other persons in his environment. The ego, quite differently from the id, operates on the basis of the *reality principle*. Whereas the child may cry for food without consideration of the circumstance, the reality principle dictates that the person form a plan based upon realistic thought and attempts to carry out the plan based on the circumstance present at the time. The ego is viewed as the executive of the personality since it governs thought processes.

The last personality structure to evolve is the *superego*. The superego can best be conceived as the conscience of the individual since it is in fact the development of a value system, a means of judging right from wrong. According to Freud, this value system is an internalization of societal mores as interpreted to the child by his parents. The major function of the ego is to control the impulses of the id, which are hedonistic. The id, of course, has as its primary goal self-satisfaction. The superego attempts to alter this in terms of making the individual less self-centered and more oriented toward others.

Parts of the personality Freud believed that all personality structures were formed by about age six with the superego being developed last. Freud[1] (1933) himself illustrated his structured approach to personality in the following manner.

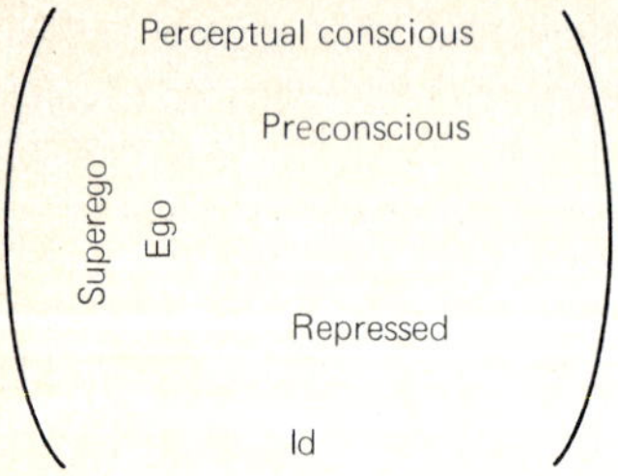

Figure 6-1 Freud's view of personality

As can be seen from the illustration in Figure 6-1, the personality resembles an iceberg with much of it submerged or unconscious. The preconscious contains material which is readily available to the individual, while the perceptual conscious is, of course, that material which an individual utilizes on a moment-to-moment basis. It should be emphasized that the material in the unconscious, including that which is repressed, is not available to the individual under normal circumstances. Repressed material is ideas, impulses, or instincts which have entered consciousness. Some people may have, for example, become so enraged with their mothers that they thought of murder (instinctual drive from id) and this so threatened their egos (ego unable to handle within the context of a real situation) that the thought was repressed. As we shall see, this is only one of the means that the ego has of protecting itself.

Stages of development Freud believed that the key to personality development was a series of stages which he labeled as *oral, anal,* and *phallic* stages. In each of these stages children receive their basic sexual gratification from certain *erogeneous zones* of the body. These stages were labeled as pregenital stages by Freud and occur during the first five to six years of life.

Oral stage During the oral stage the mouth is the primary source of gratification or pleasure for the individual. For very young children, this pleasure is, of course, gained from sucking, whether at the mother's breast or the bottle which is offered to them. This is, of course, a very dependent stage for children since they are necessarily fed and protected; and according to Freud these feelings of dependency are aroused throughout one's life whenever threatening circumstances arise. This is also the first time that a child's food is taken away, and it senses its inability to do anything about the situation.

Anal stage The anal stage, of course, has to do with the expulsion of wastes from the body, and during this stage children derive their primary pleasure from this activity. It is during the anal stage that children have their first experience with controlling the impulses of the id. Up to this time they have primarily followed their instincts and sought relief from the tension of the body. Now children are taught by parents through toilet training that they must not follow their impulses, but must deal with them. Because of the importance of this process, the anal stage is a crucial one in the overall development of the individual.

Phallic stage Usually when children are about four years of age the focus of their gratification shifts to the phallic region. Male children may have erections. Both boys and girls derive pleasure from fondling themselves (masturbation), and sex play among children may be common. Freud called this stage the phallic stage to differentiate it from genital development, which can result in mating and reproduction.

Freud made much of the differentiation which occurs between the sexes during the phallic stage. He believed that the penis was valued by both sexes and that when the female child discovers that no penis exists, a circumstance known as penis envy develops. Once this realization occurs the little girl begins to pursue the ". . . passive aims of the vagina in the development of normal femininity."[1] This idea understandably infuriates many women in today's modern society.

During the phallic stage the unconscious sexual drive causes boys to fall in love with their mothers and see their fathers as rivals. This Freud labeled the *Oedipus complex*, after the Greek tragedy in which the rejected son (Oedipus) murdered his father and married his mother. The female counterpart of the Oedipus complex is the *Electra complex*. Later this entire series of feelings and thoughts are repressed because children sense the disapproval of society and begin to both love and fear their fathers. At times this fear is manifested in a castration complex, or the direct fear that the father will cut off the boy's penis.

Later stages After children leave the phallic period, they enter what Freud called a latency period. During this time the sexual impulses from the id supposedly subside and do not reappear again until the genital period which begins with the onset of puberty. At this time, many of the pregenital conflicts will arise and remain throughout the individual's life.

Development of ego and superego For the past several pages the various stages of personality development have been presented. The reader may be asking at this point, "But what have these to do with the ego and superego, the major personality structures which Freud postulated?" The stages and the development of the various personality structures are inextricably linked and at this time these will be related.

The ego is, of course, the first structure to develop because of its function in dealing with the reality of the outside world. The development of a healthy ego, that is, one that enables the individual to deal with the factors which arise in the environment, is dependent upon a set of different circumstances at each level. Erikson,[2] a contemporary psycho-

TABLE 6-1 CONDITIONS WHICH LEAD TO HEALTHY EGO DEVELOPMENT

Stage	Positive Condition	Antithesis of Positive Condition
Oral	Trust—a basic trusting relationship between child and mother or father figures.	Mistrust—uncertainty in the child's environment.
Anal	Autonomy—child given opportunity to explore, develop at its own rate.	Shame, doubt, child ridiculed; expulsion portrayed as "dirty"; undesirable.
Phallic	Initiative—individual allowed to explore, given valid explanations.	Guilt, sexual contact portrayed as unacceptable activities.

analyst, has provided a description of conditions at the various stages of development which will lead to a healthy ego development. These have been paraphrased in Table 6-1.

It should be noted in examining Table 6-1 that the process is a developmental one and that retardation in the oral stage, for example, will retard development in all other stages. It should also be noted that a new ingredient is necessary for the development of the ego at each level. In fact, Erickson extends these levels through adulthood in order to demonstrate the developmental aspects of psychoanalytic theory.

Defense mechanisms One other major topic regarding the ego and its functioning should be inserted at this time: *defense mechanisms*. Since the ego is the executive of the personality, it is important that it be able to function at all times. For this reason, it must be able to control the unacceptable impulses which the id emits without becoming engaged in a constant struggle, for the reality of the everyday world demands the efforts and energies of the ego. The ego must be able to defend itself against the impulses of the id and in this regard a series of defense mechanisms are developed. It should be noted that defense mechanisms are normal means by which the ego handles the id, and that they only become abnormal when the ego has to overly rely upon them to the extent that these mechanisms become a primary means of functioning.

Repression is, of course, the most basic defense mechanism and is, as it formerly has been defined, the dismissal of material from consciousness. Repression has been illustrated earlier in the chapter and will not be reillustrated at this time. However, the mechanics of repression will be presented here. The reader may be asking, "Why does repression occur?" It occurs quite simply because the ego, which operates on the reality principle, recognizes that to satisfy the impulses of the id would be painful rather than gratifying. For example, the id might demand immediate gratification of a hunger drive, but the ego, recognizing that this would result in a stomach ache, postpones the pleasure. This is, in effect, why the other defense mechanisms are utilized by the ego—to protect itself against pain.

Reaction formation is another commonly used defense mechanism. Reaction formation could be an overreaction to an impulse. It is in Munroe's words, ". . . the exaggeration of the opposite tendencies."[3] A young girl who finds caressing her body pleasurable may steadfastly be against any kind of sexual contact or even literature that suggests pornographic content. A young boy who has impulses about violence may become the "super peacenik" on the college campus. Not out of character, these "peaceful people" may end up leading a college riot that calls for burning, bombing, and other types of violence. In these instances the impulses of the id overwhelm the ego and superego.

Projection is still another form of a defense mechanism. Projection is placing the source of anxiety upon the outside world rather than recognizing that it stems from one's own impulses. The young child who says of its new baby brother, "He doesn't like me," is denying her own impulses of dislike and displacing or projecting them onto her brother. Young adults may be projecting when they indicate that blacks really have a deep-seated hatred for whites instead of recognizing their own personal prejudices. Anxiety arising from this type of explanation is easier for the ego to handle.

Rationalization is such a commonly used term that most of us are familiar with it. It means to substitute one explanation (not real) for the real explanation for our behavior. Essentially the new interpretation makes our behavior seem rational or reasonable. An individual may offer excuses for one's behavior—a kind of "That's not typical of me." The college student who indicates that her low marks are the result of unfair testing practices may be rationalizing. So may the adult who has a love affair with his neighbor's wife and blames it on his wife's sleeping habits.

Regression: One last defense mechanism will be presented here although at least a dozen could be cited. Regression is the tendency to return to an earlier stage of development when confronted with impulses or situations that create overwhelming anxiety. A child may regress to bed wetting or thumb sucking when faced with the loss of a friend or pet. Adults have been known to regress to extremely childlike states whenever traumatic circumstances arose such as the death of a spouse or a loved one. Most individuals have experienced regression of some sort.

In summary, it should be recalled that defense mechanisms are a normal means of handling stimuli which may overwhelm the ego. It should also be remembered that they distort reality so that frequent

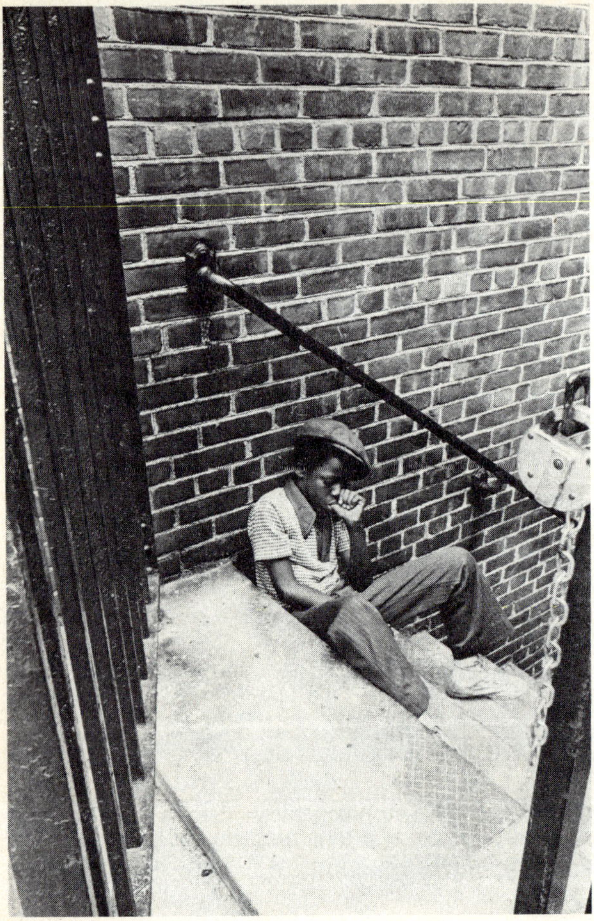

Psychological evidence indicates that infants who suffer from parental neglect and inadequate care and love will show a wide variety of serious emotional problems. This dejected-looking adolescent probably has unfulfilled needs or unresolved conflicts and resorts to the defense mechanism of thumb-sucking retained from infancy. *(Marcia Weinstein)*

usage of defense mechanisms indicate that the ego is dysfunctional. Last, defense mechanisms operate unconsciously so that individuals are not aware that they are in fact utilizing defense mechanisms.

The superego develops primarily as a result of the resolution of the Oedipus or Electra complex. The child typically resolves his conflict with his father by incorporating his view of his parents' attitudes as his own.[4] Thus, if the parent has portrayed strong, negative feelings about sexual matters and rejected the child for his sexual activities the child may incorporate these same feelings about sex and may become very self-critical at the same time if this is the way he viewed his parents' actions.

Explaining human behavior But what does all this have to do with how people behave? How can we use the rather picturesque terms and complicated concepts to explain why human beings act as they do? This is, of course, the most complicated part of any theory, particularly one as complex as psychoanalytic theory. Normal behavior is perhaps the easiest to explain, although psychoanalytic theory evolved primarily as a means of explaining abnormal behavior. Normal behavior occurs whenever there is a balance between the id, the ego, and the superego, when none of the triad dominates. Normal behavior occurs whenever the ego and superego are able to control the impulses of the id, not by the use of defense mechanisms, but by rationally recognizing the impulses, putting them into the perspective of reality, and acting appropriately. The id is dominant whenever the individual acts impulsively without regard to environmental circumstances, or without regard for the impact of the behavior upon other individuals. Stated differently, when the id dominates the personality the individual may find himself in situations which inflict personal and psychological pain upon self or others.

In the absence of the superego, the ego is unable to function properly, thus enabling the id to dominate. An individual of this type may perform acts against others or against society and is generally regarded as a *sociopathic personality*. Whenever the superego is dominant quite a different situation may exist. The individual may be overly self-righteous, or, particularly if the ego is not well developed, may be overly hard on himself. He may, for example, continuously second guess his actions, always feeling that what he has done is not good enough. In short, he may set unduly high standards for himself or for his friends.

The normally functioning individual is most of all able to learn from experiences. Since the ego operates on the reality principle it ingests data from even the most disasterous of experiences and makes appropriate alterations in future actions. The individual who continues to perform in what appears to be an irrational way without changing his actions is functioning abnormally.

Changing behavior Freud worked throughout his lifetime on a method of changing behavior. He called the total approach psychoanalysis. The basic premise of psychoanalysis is that in order for behavior to change there must be an "uncovering" of the problem. According to Freud, the basis for all personality development occurs during the first five or six years. Thus, the aim of traditional psychoanalysis is to discover that time in the child's life when the development of the personality was stymied. One can imagine that this would be extremely difficult for a forty-year-old adult and indeed classical psychoanalysis sometimes takes as many as four to six years.

At the outset some of the techniques of psychoanalysis were mentioned. These techniques will be discussed briefly at this point. Free association is the basic technique of psychoanalysis and is based upon Breuer's talking out or carthartic method. However, Freud did not believe that just talking about problems was enough and he had people free associate or talk about anything that came to their mind because he felt that this was a way to get to unconscious material. In free association, the patient is told to talk about anything that comes to mind regardless how trivial.

Another source of information about the unconscious is dream analysis and is a technique utilized by most analysts. Dreams may represent wishes such as the wish to die, may be symbolic and be indicative of experiences of people in life, but always they represent a part of the unconscious, according to Freud. The skilled analyst can determine this meaning by examining the dream within the context of what is known about the individual, and once this interpretation is made it is given back to the individual in the form of an interpretation.

For example, Freud[5] reported that one of his patients, a young girl, dreamed that she saw her sister's infant son dead in his coffin, but in her dream felt no distress. Freud's interpretation was that the dream was merely the manifestations of a wish to see the man whom she loved. In another instance, Freud indicated that a patient of his reported the following dream (paraphrased).

Dream: I was in bed and a man who was known to me entered the room. I tried to turn on the light repeatedly but was unable to do so. My wife got out of bed and attempted to assist me but to no avail. Since she was dressed in a negligee she became embarrassed and returned to bed. This entire occurrence was so funny that I began to laugh, and laughed until I awakened.

Freud's Interpretation: The gentleman known to him was death and the laughter was actually a substitution for crying which would accompany death. The light referred to the light of life which he could not turn on. Freud reports that the gloomy dream may have been brought on by attempts at copulation which his wife had tried to encourage by dressing in a negligee.

These two brief interpretations probably leave the reader somewhat mystified as to how Freud drew his conclusions. The point to be made is that dream interpretation must be analysized with a knowledge of the individual's situation and for the Freudians can best be accomplished within the context of psychoanalysis.

Transference has already been defined as the emotional attachment the patient develops for the analyst. *Countertransference*, another phenomenon of analysis, is the emotional involvements which the analyst develops for the patient. This phenomenon must be controlled throughout analysis or the likelihood of success is drastically reduced. So that the psychoanalyst will become aware of the nature of his own unconscious the analyst must undergo extensive psychoanalysis. As a result of self analysis, analysts become more closely attuned to their own reactions and will be better able to understand what is going on in the therapy sessions and thus control it.

During the course of analysis the patient, because of dream interpretation, free association and other techniques, develops a transference relationship with the psychoanalyst. The relationship, according to the theory, in great measure resembles that which resulted in the impairment of his personality development. With the analyst directing the experiences and helping the individual relive the situations which caused problems, the individual is able to "work through" the difficulty with the analyst. This "reliving process" enables the patient to continue his personality development from the point of origination and reorient his behavior. It should be noted that it is not necessary that the individual remember specific situations which resulted in personality disorder, only that he relive the emotional experience with the therapist.

APPLICATIONS OF PSYCHOANALYTIC THEORY

Child rearing Because early childhood is the most important period of development for the individual according to psychoanalytic theorists, most of their focus has been upon this process. Some people have interpreted Freudian theory as being a mandate for so-called "permissive" child-rearing techniques because traumatic experiences—such as inflicting corporal punishment during the critical developmental stage—might result in fixation in that stage. Indeed, most Freudians believe that a trusting, accepting relationship between the parents and the child is necessary for his personal development, but none would suggest that the child be allowed to tyrannize the household or be allowed to do completely as he chooses.

Freudians believe that in infancy a relaxed atmosphere is necessary at feeding time since disruption at this stage may have negative consequences at a later time. The child who is interrupted frequently may become an oral aggressive type. These people want what others want since they have no internal value system. They desire certain automobiles because others desire it and a house for the same reason. Their personality type is exploitive—they are, to use a trite phrase, "on the take." Similarly, an accepting attitude about toilet training is essential since the child who is hurried and rushed may become anally retentive. In adulthood this is the possessor—the hoarder. These individuals want things, including people, and want them in their places, since they are generally very orderly people. Other and numerous examples could be given whenever the child is retarded in some stage of his overall personality development. It should suffice to say that early child-rearing approaches are crucial for the developing child.

Although later childhood (after six) received very little attention from Freud, some of the modern Freudians (such as Erikson) have emphasized that the latency period and adolescence are important developmental stages. For the most part, warmth, acceptance, recognition of the child's dignity and integrity, and freedom from extraordinary threat and experiences have been the cornerstone of their recommendations to parents.

Education Psychoanalytic approaches have made little impact upon education with the exception of some notable exceptions in the area of preschool education. In these instances, free, unrestricted play, freedom from threat and trauma, and warm accepting relationships have been recommended. For the most part, the peculiarities in the nature of Freudian theory have precluded its use in education.

Business Like education, business has not been greatly influenced by psychoanalytic theory. There have been a few approaches to subliminal advertisement which seemed to be psychoanalytically based because they were designed to appeal to the unconscious of the individual. These advertisements were flashed on the television screen at such rates of speed that they were not consciously recognized. Some advertisements also attempt to exploit sexual anxieties and fantasies. Advertisements for breath fresheners play upon sexual anxieties, and many advertisements hint that sexual rewards will follow if you just use their products.

Status of psychoanalytic ideas Freud was a physician and because of this many psychoanalytic theorists and practitioners traditionally have been medical doctors. It is now possible for an individual with an academic background in a psychological area to learn psychoanalysis, however. But, because the psychoanalytic theory was developed primarily by one man and because the medical profession has been the primary group which has utilized psychoanalytic theory, the influence of the approach is on the decline. There are still many psychoanalytic practitioners in private practice, mental health clinics, and mental hospitals.

There are, of course, other reasons why psychoanalytic theory is declining in influence. One of the major causes is that it is not a theory which lends itself well to research, because terms like id, Oedipus complex, and anal stage are hard to define and would be even more difficult to research. Further, advocates of psychoanalytic theory have to a great extent derided the importance of research because they believe the best way to extend the theory is through the means employed by Freud to develop the theory—observation.

Freudian theory has great historical significance because it was the first theory of psychology to be fully developed, and as we shall see in the next chapter, many other intrapsychic schools of thought still joust with Freudian ideas. Finally, the student in the social sciences would hardly be considered a student without some knowledge of Sigmund Freud and his ideas.

PSYCHOSOCIAL PSYCHOLOGISTS*

Freud developed what can be termed a truly psychological explanation of behavior because he believed that social variables were of very little importance in the development of the individual. Basically, for Freud, the individual was the result of the urgings of instincts which were centered in the id, and the environment tempered these instincts, but never really altered them. Many psychologists of Freud's time and since have disagreed with this position and many explanations of human functioning which are in large part reactions to Freud's theories have evolved. In this section some of these ideas will be discussed.

How ideas developed Many psychologists were attracted to Vienna during the early 1900s. Most, like Carl Jung and Alfred Adler, came with their own ideas about the development of the human organism. Many of these people stayed in Vienna only a relatively short time because their ideas soon came into conflict with those of Freud. Although there is some disagreement about Freud's toleration of other ideas, it seems that he could best be described as nontolerant.

The issue that separated Freud from many other psychologists was his insistence upon *causality*, that is, behavior is determined by the past. Both Jung and Adler believed that the concept of teleology must be added to the concept of causality if we are to fully understand human functioning. To these men, present behavior is the result of both past experiences and future goals (teleology). Additionally, many of those people who came into contact with Freud could not accept his idea that sexual drives formed the basis for the energy that motivated the personality.

Ideas of Carl Jung Carl Jung developed what is perhaps the most complex explanation of human functioning and a few of his main contributions will be touched upon here. Alfred Adler was the forerunner of the modern social psychological explanation of human behavior, and will be discussed in more detail.

Jung[6] believed that people inherit what he saw as a vast number of memory traces from their ancestral past which includes not only their human, but their prehuman history. These memory traces are the foundation for the personality and although Jung called them by many names, *archetype* is the most frequently used label. Among the numer-

* My deepest thanks go to Manford A. Sonstegard for his thoughtful review of this section.

ous inherited archetypes are animal, death, birth, rebirth, God, the child, the hero, mother, the demon, the anima and animus, and the shadow.

The feminine archetype in man is called the anima. This inherited archetype gives man an instinctual picture of woman which is altered by his actual experiences with women. The animus is the masculine archetype in women and functions in the same manner.

Jung believed that these archetypes served a valuable purpose in the development of men and women. For him, certain rather abstract ideas developed easily because of people's ancestory. The conception of God comes about not solely because of our present experiences, but because of our ancestral heritage. Similarly, our conception of the devil, dangerous animals, children, and rebirth are facilitated by our inherited memory traces.

According to Jung, all our ancestral archetypes are stored in what is termed a *collective unconscious*. This idea is the most provocative aspect of Jung's writings about human functioning. Many of his other ideas are similar to those of other psychologists and, thus, acceptance or rejection of his ideas must ultimately rest on the position taken regarding the inheritance of archetypes.

Ideas of Alfred Adler Alfred Adler, like Freud, was Austrian-born and like Freud graduated from medical school; in fact, both graduated from the same medical school only fourteen years apart. Adler was invited to join the Vienna Psychoanalytic Society after he defended Freud's theory in a Viennese newspaper. Adler later said that even at the time he defended Freud he was defending his right to take a stand and not his views. However, Adler joined the psychoanalytic group and pursued his own investigations of the personality. It was these investigations which resulted in Adler's differences of opinion with Freud and these in turn resulted in Adler being asked to leave the society.

Behavior as purposive Essential to all psychosocial explanations of human functioning is the idea that behavior is purposive. For the most part the goals or purpose of behavior are not known to the individual and can therefore be viewed as unconscious. These goals are developed during the child's first few years, according to Adler, and like Freud, he considered the first six years of the child's life to be crucial in its development. However, with the emphasis upon the early years as important developmentally, the similarity between Freud and Adler ended.

Adler believed that the basic motivating forces of the personality are feelings of inferiority and strivings to overcome these feelings. The feelings of inferiority develop primarily because the child is born small and helpless and must, by necessity, be dependent upon the larger adults and children around him. The drive to overcome inferiority or to achieve superiority are tied up in what Adler believed is an overall striving for perfection. This striving for perfection is manifested in a *life-style* which is developed as a result of the child's early experiences.

The idea of life-style A life-style can be roughly equated to an individual's personal perceptions of the world and the overt manifestations of those perceptions. Adler believed that the child developed his own *private logic*, his own way of perceiving the world, and acted upon these perceptions. The precise value of the child's goals can be ascertained by observing and ascertaining his feelings about himself, according to Adler. Interestingly, the goals which are developed by most individuals are fictitious goals since they are aimed primarily at overcoming the feelings of inferiority and not at furthering the situation of mankind.

Rudolf Dreikurs,[7] a contemporary Adlerian, developed Adler's approach even further. He believed that the fictitious goals of children under age twelve could be classified into four areas: attention, power, revenge, and withdrawal.

The child whose fictitious goal was attention was fairly easy to identify, according to Dreikurs. He could be recognized by his efforts to get the attention of adults and children, either through his antics or by other means. This child, when told to stop, would do so, at least for a short period of time. The child whose fictitious goal is power can be recognized because of his impact upon other people. The child who pursues his behavior until he angers or upsets others can be said to be seeking power as a means of overcoming his feelings of inferiority. Revenge is perhaps an obvious goal since its overt manifestations are acts against other people. The child who tries to "get back" at others is obviously a revengeful child. The child who has been completely defeated by his environment withdraws. The discouraged child does not enter into relationships with others and does not pursue human relationships.

When the individual reaches adulthood fictitious goals are not so easy to ascertain and must be done via a complicated process known as a life-style analysis.

To this point we have been discussing fictitious goals, goals which have as their purpose overcoming inferiority. These are, of course, abnormal goals and the reader may be asking, "What about normal children and adults?" How can these be identified? The opposite of striving for superiority or selfish goals is the individual who has social interest. Adler believed that a person is a social being and ultimately must learn to live in social groups. The individual who has achieved a high state of social interest is one who places the goals and welfare of the group to which the person belongs ahead of personal goals and welfare. To produce individuals who have high social interest should be the goal of all societal institutions, according to Adler.

Life-style development The family, of course, is the basic source of the individual's view of the world and the basic source of fictitious goals. Adler believed that the *family constellation*, or the number of parents and children and their relationship to each other, had much to do with the development of the life-style. Similarly, birth order and the child's interpretation of his place are viewed as having great significance for the individual. Oldest children are more likely to be serious, authoritarian, and responsible while youngest children are likely to have quite different traits.

The actions of parents toward children received great attention from Adler. He did not believe in corporal punishment since he felt that to modify behavior one had to change the perception which was the root of that behavior. In this same vein, Adler did not believe that parents should be authoritarian in their dealings with children since domination by the parents could only heighten the feelings of inferiority, thus contributing to the fictitious goals. Adler advocated that the family operate democratically with children sharing equally in decision-making responsibility.

Although Adler believed that a basic life-style was formulated by age six, he also believed that the life-style could be changed in a variety

Some of the most important factors which shape personality are found in the multipurpose institution—the family. The structure of the family determines many of the influences brought to bear on the child during the socialization process. *(Susan Yluisaker)*

of ways. He once wrote that a close human relationship could be instrumental in changing fictitious goals. Because of Adler's belief, he stressed the importance of the school in the fostering of the personality. Throughout his career he worked with teachers and attempted to develop in them skills in dealing with children. This is an attribute which is carried on by most contemporary Adlerians.

Although Adler believed that there were a variety of social, psychological, and environmental factors which could lead to the development of faulty life-style, three important factors stood out in this area. These factors are organic or mental deficiencies, pampering or overindulgence in childhood, and neglect in childhood. According to Adler, these conditions, if severe enough, could lead to a life-style which would totally cripple the individual so far as the ability to function in society is concerned.

Physical disability is very instrumental in the formation of a life-style. The physical disability, if it is severe enough, can lead to such severe feelings of inferiority that the individual becomes withdrawn and unable to function. Most of us have known people who either because of chronic illness or physical disability become totally discouraged. These people may not be totally mentally incompetent in the sense of being psychotic, but they may be at the mercy of their environment. The physically handicapped person who begs on the streets and endures the verbal and physical abuse of other people is such an individual.

Conversely, an individual may compensate for weakness to the extent that one is more highly successful than would normally be expected. Napoleon, a very short individual, became a great general. Demosthenes, the great Greek orator, lisped and stuttered as a boy. Franklin D. Roosevelt overcame a crippling attack of polio to become a great president, and Theodore Roosevelt overcame a delicate childhood to lead the great Rough Riders. Many other examples could be cited.

According to Adlerian theory, mental impairment in the form of mental retardation is much more difficult to compensate for than is a physical disability. The result is greater feelings of inferiority and a greater incidence of problems in day to day living.

Pampering a child was to Adler one of the most serious mistakes a parent could make. Pampering, to Adler, was giving in to the child, letting it have all the things it desired and wished for. When the parent gives in to the child, the parent is—according to Adler—robbing the child of the opportunity to solve his own problems and thus gain the superiority he needs to deal with problems realistically. By consistently taking away opportunities for the child to gain superiority, the parent in effect creates an individual who is of no value to himself or to society. The pampered dhild grows up to be a demanding adult and according to Adler is a potentially dangerous individual. The adult with this life-style expects that his whims will be satisfied, and if they are not, may resort to violence because he believes that the individual or society should fulfill his demands upon request. This type of individual may also turn to such crimes as shoplifting and explain his actions by indicating that the stores are obligated to him because of other purchases for which he was overcharged.

Child neglect has equally serious consequences for the developing child. Adler advocated that parents should serve as a good model for their child. When a child is neglected, he has only his own thoughts and ideas from which to gain success. Because the individual cannot in himself generate the ideas, behaviors, etc., necessary to overcome his problem he is likely to give up in despair. It is also possible for an individual to have models which do not give the basis which is needed to attain success in life. Although this is a type of sociological neglect[8] which can occur among the very poor or under other circumstances, the results are identical for the individual.

Other types of life-styles grow out of less dramatic conditions than those described in the foregoing paragraphs. An adult may become a "driver" because of an inability to cope with a younger, competitive sibling. A driver may be orderly and domineering, and is most likely task-oriented and may appear to others to be an overachiever. Similarly, girls or boys may develop a "center of the universe life-style" which demands that all events focus on them because they were showered with attention as a child. Other individuals may become highly cooperative, helpful people because of their early childhood experiences.

Changing the personality It has already been mentioned that Adler believed that the individual might change personality because of a relationship with another individual. Thus, Adler recognized that interpersonal situations might contribute to personality change. Adler sought to make this change more systematic by helping teachers, parents, and other lay people to develop therapeutic community where everyone would be involved in helping others to develop personality traits. However, since Adler was a practicing psychiatrist he also developed an approach to psychotherapy. Adler's approach consisted of four phases: relationship, exploration, disclosure, and redirection.

Relationship This step involves the establishment of open communication and trust between the therapist and the client being treated.

Exploration The first phase of the process of changing personality requires that the therapist determine the nature of the individual's life-style. In order to do this, Adler worked out a scheme based upon the family constellation, early childhood recollections, the analysis of dreams, and other approaches. Of these, perhaps the family constellation and particularly birth order and early recollections are of great importance.

Early recollections are requested from the individual during the therapy sessions. To Adler, it did not matter whether these were memories of personal experiences or the reports of experiences that the child has had from his parents. They still reflect the way the individual views his world. Some examples of early recollections follow along with their interpretation.

Recollection: I remember during my early childhood it had not snowed during the winter. We (brother and sisters) hit upon the idea of riding our sled down the stairs of our apartment building. I remember pulling the sled to the top of the stairs while my brother pushed.

Interpretation: Cooperative efforts with boys are rewarding.

Recollection: I had planned to go to the Fourth of July celebration with my parents and was quite excited by the prospect. At the last moment my father decided not to go.

Interpretation: Men may disappoint me.

Usually the therapist will try to get several early recollections and make an interpretation of them based upon a common theme which runs through them. This, along with other data, will form the basis for his conclusions about the life-style of the individual.

Disclosure It was stated at the outset that Adler had an indeterministic view of the nature of humanity. He believed that people had the ability to change and to shape their own destiny regardless of antecedent conditions in their lives. He viewed the therapist more as an enabler than an authority figure. Disclosure, or telling the individual what the therapist believed the life-style to be, had the purpose of informing the individual of his fictional goals, thus enabling him to make corrective changes in his life.

The disclosure of the life-style is always presented tentatively to the client because the possibility exists that the therapist is wrong. However, Adler believed that very often the therapist would get a confirmation of his interpretation via a recognition reflex. A recognition reflex may range from a slight smile to a startled facial expression, but to the Adlerian therapist, it is the confirmation needed to verify the interpretation of the life-style. It should be stressed, however, that recognition reflexes are not always forthcoming from the individual.

Redirection There is one basic ingredient to Adler's redirection whether it be for the psychiatrists or for the patient attempting to help a discouraged child gain feelings of superiority. *Encouragement* is essentially the act of communication to the individual that he has worth as a person outside of his acts and demonstrating a faith of belief in the individual. The individual is praised for his efforts, not for achievements. The entire encouragement process focuses on the strengths and assets of the individual and attempts to capitalize upon them in order to provide successful experiences so that he can gain superiority.[9]

To Adlerians, encouragement is different from praise or positive reinforcement. Although they have not specified in concrete terms how it differs, the Adlerians believe that praise contributes to the inferiority feelings of the individual while encouragement does not.

Not unexpectedly, Adler encouraged individuals to have more social interest and to demonstrate this interest in their marriage, work, and in their community life.

IMPLICATIONS AND IMPACT OF ADLERIAN PSYCHOLOGY

For many years, Adlerians and Adlerian psychology were contained in enclaves in New York, Chicago and Los Angeles. In these cities, Adlerian Institutes were operated and a few persons trained in Adlerian technique were produced. However, the late sixties and early seventies evidenced a new interest in Adlerian methods in America. At this point in time, the movement continues to expand into departments of psychology and education, the mental health field, family-education centers, and public education. It seems unlikely that the apex of this current thrust will not be reached for some time.

One of the major reasons for the growth of the Adlerian movement is the willingness to become involved with persons outside of the psychiatric and psychological professions. The Adlerians have worked actively to assist parents, teachers, and lay persons to learn the theory, and in each instance they have a prescribed set of formulations to help the group with which they are working.

The family The family is, of course, important to the Adlerians because of its impact upon the life-style. It has already been mentioned that the Adlerians believe in a democratic family structure with children given equal privileges and responsibilities with adults. They believe that the family should be operated via a family council or family meeting where democratic decisions are made.

The Adlerians are opposed to the use of corporal punishment with children since they do not believe that punishment is effective. To take the place of punishment they recommend that natural consequences and logical consequences be utilized. Natural consequences, according to Dreikurs,[10] ". . . expresses a logical and immediate result of the transgression, not imposed on him by authority, but by the situation itself. . . ." The natural consequences of approaching a forbidden, hot stove is to be burned, although the Adlerians do not believe that children should be allowed to injure themselves. However, instead of punishing a child for not going to bed, an Adlerian would recommend that the child be allowed to stay up as late as it wishes but awakened at a regular hour, thus letting the natural fatigue be the agent that prompts the child that it needs to go to bed earlier.

Logical consequences grow directly out of the situation itself but are not necessarily the result of natural phenomenon. A child is late for a meal and he must miss that meal because of his tardiness. A rather drastic logical consequence was recommended by an Adlerian psychiatrist to a distraught mother whose teenage child failed to come in from dates and parties at a decent hour. He recommended that the door be locked and the child forced to stay out overnight.

Adlerians contend that parents are not prepared for the task of child rearing. In order to remedy the deficiencies they have started numerous family-study groups throughout the country in order to teach parents child-rearing techniques. These centers are growing and are well attended.

Education Literally thousands of teachers have to be taught the use of encouragement techniques and the application of logical and natural consequences in the classroom and more are being taught every day.

As in the family, Adlerians advocate a democratic classroom atmosphere. The contention is that only in a democratic atmosphere can the teacher be helpful to understanding and redirecting the child's mistaken goals. The family counterpart of the family council is the class discussion where class problems are discussed and handled by the class.

Teachers as *parental surrogates* are admonished not to use punishment, but rather to apply logical and natural consequences. A student who refuses to stay seated may have the chair removed and have to stand (logical consequence), or a student may be made to stay in after school to complete work unfinished during regular class hours (natural consequences).

Mental health Adlerians have not been highly influential in the area of mental health, primarily because much of this area has been traditionally controlled by Freudians and the two groups have literally been at odds since the Freud-Adler split in 1911. It is safe to say, however, that the Adlerians will become increasingly more influential in this area, especially in the areas of family counseling, child counseling, and school counseling. It is difficult to predict what impact the Adlerians will make on the treatment of the mentally ill, but their influence in that area seems destined to increase.

Business, industry, and corrections Some businesses are now acting to give workers more control over their own schedules and working conditions. One business in Cincinnati, Ohio, has completely adopted Adlerian principles by allowing workers to participate directly in the decision-making process.

Assessment of the Adlerian movement The Adlerians have a great many factors which will continue to fuel the movement. First, they have a philosophy which appeals to most Americans. Whether true or not, Americans like to think of people as being able to transcend their environment and exercise their free will to make decisions for their own enhancement. Second, the Adlerians advocate democracy in the family and the school. Although both institutions have traditionally been autocratic, democracy is a popular concept in our society and is firmly rooted in our traditions. Third, the Adlerians are willing to go beyond the establishment—academic psychology, and psychiatry—to develop a following. This has resulted in a large following, and among lay people one cannot help but wonder how long psychology and psychiatry will hold out against popular opinion.

There are, of course, negative factors which will retard the growth of Adlerian psychology. One of these is the lack of empirical data to support the assumptions of the approach. Although lay people may accept the approaches that the Adlerian recommends without question, the hard core of social scientists still require that a theory and its techniques be researched. It should be said in defense of some Adlerians that they are sensitive to this criticism and research regarding the Adlerian approach is being conducted on a limited basis.

Not only is there a lack of data about the theory, but some have argued that the theoretical formulations are poorly constructed. Adler was somewhat like Freud in his failure to define and operationalize his terms. In fact, Adler was more of a practitioner than a theoretician and terms like life-style and social interest were for him more things he observed in his practice than terms to be defined and researched. This lack of rigor in defining terms has been one barrier to acceptance of Adler's ideas. Can you identify others?

Finally, it remains to be seen whether academic psychologists will accept Adlerian approaches. It has been stated earlier that acceptance by psychologists is increasing and this is true, but the acceptance is somewhat slow. In the final analysis this acceptance or lack of it may determine the fate of Adlerian theory and practice.

Summary In summary, Alfred Adler created a theory which was unlike Freud's in many respects. Adler, unlike Freud, did not receive immediate recognition. At this time, it would appear that Adler's basic ideas have wider support than those of Freud, but this remains to be seen. It can be said, however, that Adler's focus upon the holistic concept of personality and his view that behavior is purposive are concepts which have already been incorporated into much contemporary psychological thought.

HUMANISTIC PSYCHOLOGY

In the foregoing sections of this chapter, explanations of human functioning advanced by Sigmund Freud and Alfred Adler were presented. In Freud's view the unconscious was an important part of his explanation of the functioning of the human animal. In this section, an explanation of human behavior will be presented that places major emphasis upon the role of consciousness in behavior. Additionally, the *phenomenological-existential* approach tends to emphasize the positive nature of people where Freud stressed the negative and Adler viewed many as striving to overcome their deficiencies. This third force in psychology has drawn heavily upon the work of Kurt Lewin, Gordon Allport, Abraham Maslow, Donald Snygg, Arthur Combs and many others. Space will permit only a very limited presentation of the many and varied ideas found in this school of psychological thinking.

Subjectivity of approaches Some psychologists accept observable behavior as the only true source of data about individuals. Others, such as Freud, rely upon material extracted from the unconscious as the important facts about the individual. The phenomenologists accept feelings, thoughts, behavior, and other subjective data as legitimate sources of information about the individual. Carl Rogers,[11] a leading contemporary spokesman for the phenomenological stream of thought, indicated that there are three ways of knowing. He has defined them as follows:

1. Subjective knowing. This is a knowing from within one's self. I know I love, I hate, I feel.
2. Objective knowing. This is based upon hypotheses which are externally observable.
3. Interpersonal knowing. This is the "knowing" about the feelings of others. I know you are disappointed. I know you are excited. I know these things because we are human beings and I can sense these things in you.

These sources of knowledge are, of course, quite different from those accepted by most other psychologists. The acceptance of these sources along with many other factors make the phenomenological school of thought attractive to many people who believe that people have characteristics which are uniquely individual.

Philosophical premises Phenomenologists are indeterministic in their philosophy. They believe that people are able to transcend their environment and their biological drive states and operate in the human sphere. As we shall see, people do not always act rationally, and at times they may appear to be affected by various factors. However, the important factor is that they are able to overcome determining factors by exercising their will, although they may not always do so.

According to the phenomenologists, people have one basic life striving—self-actualization or becoming. Self-actualization cannot be defined precisely since from a phenomenal point of view the perceptions of each person differ. This striving for fulfillment is related to attaining self-esteem and the personal esteem of others, however. This goal of self-actualization or the pursuit of self-esteem is the unifying drive in personality, and it is this force that causes the individual to overcome environment and internal biological drives. It is this striving for self-actualization that gives the individual human qualities.

How the personality develops When an individual is born he comes into a world which is uniquely his own, his *phenomenal field.* Very early in the child's life this perceptual field is completely undifferentiated, and none of the objects in the child's environment have any special meaning.

Early family experiences are of great importance in the formation of personality. Affection and attention are essential to the personal development of the child. However, when parental affection gives way to overindulgence, the results can lead to personal qualities or patterns of behavior which retard self-actualization. *(Charles Gatewood)*

However, the child very quickly begins to differentiate factors within his perceptual field. Perhaps the first item to be recognized is his mother's breast or his bottle. These items are probably followed by the child's parents, his crib, items in his crib, and so forth. As the child matures and experiences more and more, items become differentiated.

Emergence of self As the child grows and starts to interact with other persons he begins to develop perceptions about himself. These perceptions may be rather vague in the beginning but are sharpened as the individual matures. Essentially these perceptions take the form of "this is me" or "this is not me." At the time this process begins, the individual has started to form a self-concept which may be defined as all the feelings, thoughts, perceptions, attitudes, etc. that the individual has about himself. The development of the self-concept continues throughout the individual's life until he literally has hundreds of things which he believes about himself.

The *self* is the only personality structure hypothesized by the phenomenologists, but it plays a tremendous role in governing the person. From the time the self-concept is formed, the efforts of the organism are aimed at maintaining, enhancing, or as we have stated earlier, actualizing or fulfilling the self. Because of this a very simple principle of the organism—the individual—will not do anything that will make it look bad to itself. The impact of this statement will be more significant as we explore the individual person's functioning.

The individual operates in his environment on the basis of his perceptions about his environment. Because every individual is the product of a different set of experiences his perception of a situation is different from that of any other person. Two students reading this book are unique because of their experiences. One may be taking the class because it is a requirement in a major, but he has little interest in the social sciences. Thus, the student reads the book not because of an interest in the social sciences but so that a test can be passed and what seems like a meaningless hurdle can be overcome. A second student who eventually hopes to become a social scientist may also want to pass the test. But the second student, because he perceives himself as a potential social scientist, is intrigued by some of the ideas and stimulated to do additional readings. Both students are functioning upon their own perceptions of their own phenomenological field as they see it now. The important point to be made here is that the interest is the result of experience but the behavior is the result of feelings, attitudes, and thoughts related to the present situation.

Perceptions and feelings about the individual environment and one's personal relationship to it are thus the determiners of behavior. According to Combs and Snygg,[12] "There are at least seven factors which may influence perceptions, with the self-concept being the most important of these variables. The seven variables are:

1. The physical organism
2. Time
3. Opportunity
4. Need
5. Goals and values
6. Self-concept
7. Restriction of the phenomenal field

The physical nature of the human animal of course limits its perceptions. A blind person would have different perceptions from those of a sighted person because of reliance upon other senses for experiencing. Time and opportunity are also obvious factors in perception. Time is an important factor in numbers and types of factors since a young child may not have lived long enough to have perceived a wide variety of situations and thus may be naive about much of the world. Time may be a factor in distorting perceptions, too, since experiences early in our lives may be altered by our experiences and the mere forgetting of some of our experiences. An individual may have lived for a long period of time, but not had the opportunity to perceive or experience a wide variety of things. A black man who has been discriminated against by the whites in his neighborhood will be suspicious of whites who are attempting to function in a nondiscriminatory manner because of not having had the opportunity to experience a relationship with a white person other than one which was aimed at exploitation.

Although the other four variables presented by Combs and Snygg could be discussed separately, the phenomenal self or the self-concept is the major psychological variable which determines perceptions, even perceptions of so-called psychological needs, goals and values.

In order to understand the nature of the self-concept and its functioning more fully, the concepts of positive and negative have to be introduced. An individual who has had positive experiences in early and middle childhood, and has had these continued throughout its life, will undoubtedly have developed a positive self-concept. Conversely, the child who was rejected in the home, inadequate in school, and unsuccessful as a young adult will develop a negative or inadequate self-concept. The result of a positive and negative self-concept will be adequate and inadequate functioning, as we shall see. There are naturally degrees of adequacy and inadequacy.

Events in the individual's phenomenal field are perceived and interpreted in the light of the self-concept. The person with the negative self-concept may deny certain experiences as being reality. A 225-pound college football player who cannot make the freshmen team because of a three-second slowness in running 40 yards may deny the failure by saying things like, "The coaches didn't like me, it was all political," or "I was cut because I was the wrong color (black or white)." A beautiful girl with a negative self-concept may deny that she is beautiful or an intelligent boy may regard himself as stupid. All these denials take place in spite of the presence of objective evidence which can be presented to demonstrate the reality of the situation.

Not only will an individual deny what seems to be objectively true, but his behavior will carry out the theme. The football player may transfer to another school, and even given failure there, will tend to deny that experience. The beautiful girl will wonder why boys are interested in her, surround herself with homely friends like "herself" and be very unsure about her relationship in general. The intelligent boy may go through life expecting failure to befall him because of his stupidity and not attempt many tasks which he could successfully complete because of his negative feelings about himself.

The person with a positive self-concept will operate quite differently, being more able to accept failure and act upon it in a constructive manner. A football player who fails a major university because of slowness may enroll at a smaller school because football players of his speed and caliber can participate. Persons with positive self-concepts are better able to interpret the feelings and meanings of others and thus have more satisfactory interpersonal relationships. These people are risk-takers because the experiencing of failure is not a crushing personal blow. Persons with positive self-concepts make decisions more easily and function on a higher level than those with poor self-concepts. Perhaps most importantly, these people have a high degree of *empathy* for others, that is, they are able to understand and accept the inner world of other people.

How self-concepts develop and change What conditions produce individuals who act defensively? Or conversely, "How are adequate personalities formed? Unlike Freud or Adler, the phenomenologists do not place sole emphasis upon early childhood. Rather, they see the organism as one which is continuously unfolding, growing, actualizing. The phenomenologists do view early childhood years as important since the self-concept starts to form before age one. It forms in these early years as a result of feedback regarding adequacy from parents, siblings, and other esteemed individuals. Early feedback becomes internalized and these perceptions begin to govern the way the individual functions.

The self-concepts may change at any time as the result of human relationships which have certain characteristics. The phenomenologists believe that it is an inborn characteristic of the organism that it has the power to correct its deficiencies, and whenever another human being is willing to accept a person with a negative self-concept and communicate acceptance to that person, the person can let down personal defenses, look introspectively, and start to alter self-perceptions. The important aspect of this process is the quality of the human relationship for it is this quality that leads to change.

Personality change is not restricted to the therapist's office for the

Since individual problems and difficulties often stem from interpersonal relationships, the group serves as a therapeutic unit through which the individual may be reeducated in the techniques of social adjustment. *(Charles Gatewood)*

phenomenologists. In their view, lay people and everyday relationships have as much potential for change as do therapists who hold Ph.D.'s or M.D.'s. One outgrowth of this belief has been the encounter-group movement. These groups, also called sensitivity groups or T-groups, have assumed that small groups (8 to 10) of people meeting together in a warm relationship can lead to meaningful personal growth. While the movement has been bastardized by movies and the popular press which depicts these groups as little more than sex orgies, and by some psychologists and lay people who have utilized the groups for personal gain, the underlying assumption and belief in their potential has not changed.

Phenomenologists have seen all types of human relationships as having potential for fostering human growth. An individual may alter self-concept as the result of a close marital relationship, or as the result of a satisfactory experience with a teacher or clergy member. In short, all people have as their potential the ability to help others.

There are, of course, counselors, psychologists, and psychiatrists who practice relationship-based approaches to personality reorientation. Carl Rogers[13] first spelled out this approach in the early fifties, and while there have been some major changes in the approach, the importance of the relationship remains. Essentially, Rogers believes that if the therapist can establish a relationship in which the individual's differences can be accepted and can communicate the acceptance of the differences, the individual is enabled to muster innate forces and the therapist fosters positive growth. It should perhaps be pointed out that acceptance does not mean agreement with rather it means that the therapist, parent, or teacher, recognizes the individual's right to be different.

Impact of phenomenology Phenomenology and behaviorism are the two most pervasive schools of psychology in the United States. Phenomenology has been widely accepted because its philosophy fits nicely into the traditional optimistic view of human personality. It has also been accepted widely because of its simplicity and because of its "humanistic" view of man. The impact of this humanistic approach to explaining human functioning has been considerable.

Education Today in American education there is a ground-swell movement to humanize the educational process. This movement stems from many legitimate criticisms when shown that elementary and secondary schools have treated students with less than human concern. At the center of the present movement is the phenomenological view of man and psychologists such as Carl Rogers. The entire thrust of the current movement is to teach teachers how to relate to their students and to establish a warm, accepting atmosphere in the classroom. Literally hundreds of teacher education institutions and school systems are stressing some form of this approach so it is safe to say that the impact of phenomenology is and will be considerable.

Mental health Many counselors, psychiatrists and clergymen have been educated to function as relationship counselor and therapist. While the exact impact of this movement cannot be accurately assessed, it must be viewed as considerable. Contemporary advocates of relationship-based approaches such as Charles B. Truax and Robert Carkhuff have attempted, and according to their reports, have been successful in training lay therapists who can render assistance to individuals. The encounter group movement also continues on a large scale at this writing. Relationship approaches are and can be expected to be at the forefront of the mental health movement.

Business and industry Psychological consultants of various types have utilized relationship-based approaches in business and industry. The area where these approaches have been most greatly utilized in the industrial setting is in the training of managers. Hundreds and probably thousands of seminars have been held to teach prospective managers to perceive and communicate perceptions to their colleagues. Additionally, countless numbers of managers have been placed in sensitivity groups in hopes of producing a more effective human being and manager. These and other approaches based upon phenomenological psychology make it clear that the business establishment has been affected by this approach.

The family During the last few years, humanistic psychologists have attempted to adapt methods by which their ideas can be taught to parents. Haim Ginott's *Between Parent and Child* and Ira Gordon's *Parent Effectiveness Training Programs* are both very successful attempts in this direction. As a result of Ginott's and Gordon's work, the influence of humanistic psychology upon the family is undoubtedly at its zenith.

Assessment of status of phenomenology From the foregoing account it should be obvious that phenomenology is alive and well in America. It should perhaps be pointed out that the major interest in phenomenology is centered in this country whereas other schools of thought have attracted more of an international following. However, phenomenology is well entrenched and well accepted in academic psychology, in education, in the mental health movement, and among lay people. It is doubtful if this school of thought has reached its apex, and it will in all likelihood become even more influential in the next decade.

Phenomenology can credit its status to two or three variables. First, many members of the school have not rejected empiricism as a means of studying the personality. Phenomenologists have produced research data on a scale second only to the behaviorists. Second, the movement has a number of vocal and articulate leaders of which Carl Rogers is probably the best known. These leaders have been willing to debate their positions with advocates of other positions, thus making the phenomenological viewpoint well known. Last, the simplicity of the model makes it attractive to many. It seems that these same forces will continue to give the movement impetus.

SUMMARY

In this chapter, three intrapsychic views of human functioning have been presented. These were psychoanalytic ideas or essentially the ideas of Sigmund Freud, the psychosocial ideas of Alfred Adler, and so-called humanistic explanations of human functioning.

Freud believed that the basic energy for man's behavior comes from sexual instincts. The id is the part of the personality that contains these basic drives. The ego develops partially to deal with the impulses from the id and partially to deal with the real world. The superego or conscience is the last personality structure to develop and is that part of the personality which deals with morality.

Freud's work in Vienna attracted many prominent psychologists among which was Alfred Adler. However, they soon parted because of their disagreement over the importance of the sexual drive and because Adler believed that behavior had to be understood in terms of the goals of the individual rather than in terms of the individual's history. Adler, like Freud, believed that personality is developed in early childhood and that the personality results in a certain life-style. Central to Adler's ideas was the concept that some goals of behavior were out of awareness and these often resulted in faulty behavior.

To speak of a humanistic explanation of psychology may seem strange to the reader. However, this group was so named because of their emphasis upon the unique, human qualities of the individual, and because of their belief in the basic potential of man. Perhaps the most important aspect of the humanist position is the idea that a self-concept develops as a result of the developing child's interaction with people. It is this self-perception that dictates its behavior.

These three explanations of human functioning were chosen from among dozens. The thoughtful student will want to seek out others as a means of enhancing his own knowledge of psychology.

REVIEW QUESTIONS

1. Can you construct a better model of personality than Freud did? Specifically, what do you think of the idea that the personality is made up of a series of component parts that function somewhat individually? Why or why not?
2. Have you known people who seemed to have an overdeveloped superego? Describe them.
3. React to Freud's ideas of infant sexuality.
4. Both Freud and Adler believed that personality developed in early childhood. Do you agree? Support your position.
5. Have you ever observed a person use a defense mechanism? Which ones? Have you ever used any of them yourself?
6. What is your personal assessment of Freud's ideas?
7. Compare and contrast Freud and Adler. How much alike and how different are they?
8. React to Jung's ideas about archetypes and the collective unconscious.
9. Research has demonstrated that birth order can make a difference. Do an informal study of first, second, and last borns. Are there differences in the way they behave?
10. What do you think of Adler's ideas on pampering, child neglect, and disabilities on personality development?
11. How does the humanistic idea of self-concept development compare to the ideas of Freud and Adler?
12. Have you ever known anyone who seemed able to do a chore but

was unsure of his or her ability? Could the idea of poor self-concept explain his or her behavior?

13. Of the three explanations of human functioning presented, which one relies the most upon intellect? Emotions?
14. If you were going to become a psychologist, which explanation would you choose as a guide to your actions? Why?

CHAPTER SEVEN
HUMAN FUNCTIONING: A BEHAVIORAL VIEW

IDEAS AND CONCEPTS

discrimination
the process by which relationships that have come about through generalization are broken down into smaller units.

generalization
the act of applying learned patterns of behavior to new situation.

modeling
the act of imitating the behavior of another.

positive stimuli
reward or reinforcement

shaping
the developing of complex behavior from small units of behavior

In Chapter 6 three general explanations of human functioning were surveyed. While these were divergent points of view, they had one factor in common: People's personality development and subsequent behavior is the result of certain internal or intrapsychic phenomena. In this chapter, a different view will be examined, that is, the view that people are products of their environment.

During the reading of this chapter the students should attempt to clarify their positions on the phenomena discussed. The reference point for this discussion should be first, their own beliefs about how humanity functions and second, the positions presented in Chapter 6. You, the reader, may be left with one question: "How can I decide which explanation is best?" Ultimately, that decision will be based upon your own philosophy, and hopefully, the data that you derive from this and other readings.

Another question may be, "What difference does it make?" The answer is simple—a great deal. Throughout your life you will be exposed to the various approaches to psychology. If you have children you may want to join a group to learn how to rear your children more effectively. Undoubtedly, any teacher or leader will have a bias regarding a particular approach to explaining human behavior, as will school administrators and teachers where your children attend school. As we have seen, businesses also employ psychologists to develop better work situations, so ultimately you will be exposed to different "psychologies" at work. To be an intelligent consumer of psychology, it is incumbent upon you to learn and make decisions about the relative worth of various ideas.

Psychologists have as their primary goal the understanding and prediction of human behavior. One group, the *behaviorists*, has asserted that the scientific method is useful in this process and has sought to apply natural-science principles to the study and understanding of human behavior. The other group of psychologists, which we shall call the intrapsychic group, contends that the scientific method is inappropriate in studying human behavior because of man's special qualities. These so-called special qualities are usually of two types. One of these involves cognition or thought processes; the other, will or the ability to transcend or go beyond the factors confronting him and succeed.

Is man a problem-solving-being who relies only upon his intellect for solving life's problems? The behaviorists say no. According to this group, man's so-called problem-solving ability rests simply upon his experiences. What humanity does, according to the behaviorist, is to react to elements in situations which confront it in a manner which was successful in the past under similar conditions. Its ability to react in an appropriate manner stems from having similar past experiences. Most of us can remember, for example, our first confrontation with a formal place-setting at our first formal dinner. When confronted with three forks to the left and three spoons to the right, how did we react? Did thought processes take over, and reason and logic dictate which fork was to be used? Or did we react to the situation on the basis of our past experiences because of the common elements which existed? The behaviorist would opt for the latter explanation.

The concept of free will also comes into the argument between the behaviorists and some intrapsychic groups. Psychologists who theorize that humanity operates on the basis of internal processes and mechanisms indicate that man has the unique ability of transcending his environment, of rising above it, and of achieving personal goals. In short, humanity has the ability, if it chooses, to disregard environmental circumstances. That is, of course, traditional American "boot strap" philosophy which contends that humanity is solely responsible for its action. For example, a statement often heard about welfare recipients is, "They wouldn't have to take welfare if they weren't so lazy." Inherent in this idea is that the person or welfare recipient could get a job, could solve the family problem, could get out of the ghetto by exertion of free will.

Behaviorists make no assumption of free will. Rather, their contention is that humanity is indeed a reactive being, a product of environmental circumstances. Further, if the government, schools, psychologists, and others who try to improve the human conditions are to succeed, according to the environmentalists, they must alter humanity's circumstances—they must change its environment.

It perhaps goes without saying that the behavioral point of view has not been a highly popular view with the public at large, because it strikes at popular philosophy. The methods and ideology of behavioralism have been attacked by congressmen, and in 1971, then Vice-President Agnew spoke derisively of this approach to explaining human behavior. However, many psychologists who have viewed the outcomes of teaching, psychotherapy, counseling, and other approaches to altering human behavior using the principles of behavior modification (behaviorism) have become convinced that the approach has great merit. Indeed, as we shall see, some have even suggested that our entire society be managed using the principles of behaviorism.

ROOTS OF BEHAVIORISM

Behaviorism is firmly rooted in the scientific psychologies which began during the late nineteenth century in psychological laboratories in Europe and America. According to Heidbreder,[1] psychological historian, John Broadus Watson must be credited with founding the school of behaviorism. As we shall see, other psychologists have overshadowed Watson in their contribution to the behaviorist movement, but perhaps no other psychologist has done more to shape the philosophy and methodology of the movement.

Watson began his formal work at a time when cognitive, intrapsychic approaches held sway in American psychology. From the outset, Watson vehemently opposed these approaches, primarily because they smacked of the antiscientific and because of their emphasis upon internal, nonobservable processes. At the outset, Watson asserted that observable behavior was the only data about animals or human beings which was admissible as evidence about their functioning. This idea was, of course, the fundamental basis for the label behaviorism. Further, Watson contended that the scientific method must be utilized to determine the causes of behavior. This was in direct opposition to the technique of introspection or self-study which pervaded the other schools of psychology popular at that time. According to Watson, subjective self-study had to be discarded in favor of objective observation of behavior. The use of the scientific method, the focus upon behavior, and emphasis upon objectivity are concepts developed in the early 1900s which still characterize behaviorism.

If J. B. Watson set the stage for modern behaviorism, it must be noted that a Russian psychologist, Ivan Petrovich Pavlov, provided the process which serves as the cornerstone for modern behaviorism.[2] The conditioned reflex or conditioned response was discovered by Pavlov in his experimentations with dogs. He found that he could elicit an involuntary response such as salivation by the use of a device such as a bell if the bell had been previously associated with the presentation of food. However, the process called respondent conditioning is not limited to dogs or other lower animals. Most of us have experienced the sensation of salivating on an occasion when we were hungry and by chance saw a roadside sign with the word FOOD emblazoned upon it. Respondent conditioning is illustrated in Figure 7-1.

Simply put, respondent conditioning can be described as pairing a neutral stimulus with an eliciting stimulus until the neutral stimulus becomes an elicitor. Pavlov's primary contribution in the discovery of this process was to give behaviorists a means of investigating behavior, as well as a rationale for the existence of behavior.[3]

As has perhaps already been inferred by the reader, early behaviorism was an animal psychology. Behaviorists have been disdainfully

Figure 7-1 The respondent process.

Food ——————→ Salivation Results
Food plus bell ——————→ Salivation
Repeat step 2 a number of times
Bell only ——————→ Salivation

called rat psychologists because of their reliance upon the white laboratory rat for much of their research. Not until the last twenty-five years has experimentation with human beings been a common practice. The critics of behaviorism have pointed to this early research with rats and made the point that principles developed using rats and dogs could not necessarily be assumed to work with human beings. The basis for this argument is, of course, a belief in what has been characterized as people's special qualities. As we shall see, behavior principles have been very successful in altering and developing human behavior.

Development of human behavior Before any meaningful discussion of the manner in which human beings develop behavior patterns, the student must acquire the vocabulary of the behaviorist. Although it is not unique among behaviorists, they have their own way of describing and labeling the processes which affect human behavior. Some of these terms have already been introduced in the foregoing discussion and are included at this point only for clarification.

Types of behavior Respondent conditioning has already been presented and discussed. The process is primarily associated with involuntary behavior such as salivation, dilation of the pupil of the eye, and other biological functions. However, only a small percent of human behavior can be directly associated with biological states or drives, at least according to some behavioral thinking. B. F. Skinner[4] proposed a theory of operant conditioning which held that most behavior is not attached to a specific stimulus. According to Skinner, behavior is emitted, and since it is this type of behavior with which the individual "operates" in his environment, this class of behavior is known as operant behavior.

There are dozens of examples of operant behavior which could be listed at this point. Behavior such as that used in making friends is operant behavior. This might include speech patterns, smiling, sharing behavior, etc. Behavior which enables a person to get along in school also falls into the operant class. Behavior such as the young child holding up his hand to recite, study habits learned as a college freshman, are operant in nature. In the acquisition of behavior we are primarily concerned about operant behavior.

Conditioning Conditioning is the basic process by which behavior is acquired. We have already looked at the process of respondent conditioning. However, just as there are two types of behavior, operant and respondent, there are two types of conditioning processes. *Operant conditioning* is the process by which operant behavior is strengthened or weakened as a result of environmental consequences. These environmental consequences are classified as either *positive*, *neutral*, or *negative stimuli*.

Positive stimuli are usually referred to as positive reinforcers since their effect upon a behavior is to strengthen it. Technically, a positive reinforcer is a stimulus which when presented after a response increases the probability of that response occurring under similar circumstances in the future. This can be illustrated in a number of real-life situations. When a small child picks up her toys, her mother is likely to compliment her for doing so, thus strengthening the response of cleaning up her room. A junior high school student receives a citation for performance of duties as a junior police officer. The result should be an increased chance that the student will continue to perform in a similar manner. A college student asks a girl whom he has admired from afar for a date, and she accepts. His behavior in requesting dates from girls should be strengthened.

Positive reinforcers are of two types. One is the so-called *primary reinforcer*, which is related to biological states of the organism and is supposedly reinforcing for everyone. Food, water and sexual contact are primary reinforcers. *Secondary reinforcers* are materials or events which have acquired the properties of reinforcers. Money is perhaps the best example of a secondary reinforcer. A smile, praise, eye contact, or a pat on the shoulder may serve as a *social reinforcer*, which is a class of secondary reinforcers.

Food is a positive, primary reinforcer that satisfys hunger, one of the most basic of human needs. *(Editorial Photocolor Archives, Inc.)*

The question which often arises is how does a secondary reinforcer acquire its reinforcing property? Some obviously acquire this property because of their association with primary reinforcers. Money will, of course, furnish shelter, purchase food, and provide other types of reinforcers. However, what about social reinforcers? How do people become influential in the lives of others? Skinner has discussed this problem and put forth at least one possible explanation. He said:

> The attention of people is reinforcing because it is a necessary condition for other reinforcements from them. In general, only people who are attending to us reinforce our behavior. The attention of someone who is particularly likely to supply reinforcement—a parent, a teacher, or a loved one—is an especially good generalized reinforcer and sets up especially strong attention getting behavior.[5]

In summary then, it seems that people who listen and look at other people may become reinforcers in those peoples' lives.

Finally, some acts have inherent reinforcing properties. Put somewhat differently, there are times when doing a task and realizing that it is done well or reading a book and deriving satisfaction from the knowledge gained from it are reinforcing. Curiosity, novelty, pride in achievement, and gaining in knowledge all contribute to *intrinsic positive reinforcement.*

A neutral stimuli is when nothing occurs and although this may appear to be inconsequential to the casual observer, neutral stimuli have a considerable impact upon human behavior. If a behavioral response is not followed by a positive stimuli, the response will eventually extinguish. To put extinction into a practical context, we might again think of the problem of child rearing. Most of us have viewed children having temper tantrums. In some instances, adults rush in and give attention to the child (positive stimuli); in other circumstances, the parents or adults present ignore the child (neutral stimuli). In the former situation the response is being strengthened, and in the latter—if the parents continue to ignore the child—extinction of the response will occur.

The exact nature of the impact of negative or *aversive stimuli* is not fully understood. Aversive stimuli, such as threats, physical punishment, and nagging have been used repeatedly as means of changing human behavior. By and large, it is felt that their use for this purpose has been largely unsuccessful. Psychologists also believe that in some instances the use of punishment has had numerous bad effects, in addition to not achieving the desired effects.

What is the goal of applying an aversive stimuli after a behavior has occurred? Generally, the person applying the punishment intends to suppress the response and hopefully eliminate it from the person's behavioral repertoire of responses. It is known that punishment will suppress a response, but it is generally believed that aversive stimuli do little to hasten the extinction process. Extinction seems to come as a result of ignoring the response. Further, punishment may suppress responses which were not intended to be suppressed. The teacher who administers a hard spanking to a student because that child was out of his seat may also suppress other types of desirable activities such as participation in games. An overzealous judge may overreact to an incidence of shoplifting by handing out harsh penalties, but may at the same time effectively teach students to avoid the law whenever they need assistance. Avoidance of the punishing agent is also an undesirable side effect of punishment.

It cannot be said with complete certainty that punishment is bad. At times it is necessary to suppress certain types of responses before others can be developed. If punishment is used judiciously and in concert with positive approaches, it can be helpful in promoting certain types of behavior.

Positive reinforcement is, of course, the presentation of a positive reinforcer after a response thereby strengthening that response. *Negative reinforcement* is quite different, however. Negative reinforcement is the removal of aversive stimuli, thus increasing the probability of a particular response occurring under similar circumstances in the future. If a person's shoes pinch his feet and removing the shoes reduces the pain, negative reinforcement has occurred. It has also occurred whenever a small child hits another child for teasing him if that act stops the teasing. Under similar circumstances in the future, the person is likely to remove the shoes, and the small child is likely to strike out.

Conditioning is the basic means by which behavior is acquired. It is the behaviorist's explanation for this process and is peculiar to them. Without a thorough understanding of the steps in this process, it will be impossible to understand the remainder of this chapter. Thus, students should make absolutely certain that they have the principles in mind before proceeding.

Shaping *Shaping* is the procedure by which complex behaviors are developed from small units of behavior which at times seem unrelated to the behavior desired. B. F. Skinner taught pigeons in his laboratory to play ping-pong using shaping techniques. He also taught them to dance in clockwise and counterclockwise motions. Shaping techniques have been utilized to reach children to read, schizophrenics to take care of themselves, and college professors to stand on one side of the room. In this latter case a group of students who were familiar with the principles of behavior modification successfully shaped this professor's behavior so that he stood on one side of the room and lectured. Prior to their efforts, he had paced up and down in front of the room. The students decided that they would listen intently and take notes when the professor went to a particular side of the room. Gradually, the professor spent more and more time on the side of the room where he received attention until finally he lectured totally from that side of the room.

In the case where Skinner taught his pigeons to dance, his procedure was simple. Whenever pigeons made a random move in a desired direction, a food pellet was dropped. This pellet, of course, acted as a positive reinforcer and increased the probability of that random motion occurring. Gradually, through a series of successive approximations, the pigeons danced in the desired direction.

Modeling When a girl observes another wearing her hair in a particular manner and fixes hers in a similar manner, *modeling* is taking place. Modeling is also occurring whenever a child hears his father swear and repeats the word. Modeling in its simplest sense is imitation.[6] Albert Bandura has asserted that the development of such complex behavior as language cannot be accounted for using the shaping paradigm. He believes, and his research has supported the idea, that much behavior is acquired through direct imitation. Of course, this behavior must receive environmental approval (positive reinforcement) before it becomes a regular part of the individual's behavioral patterns.

Schedules of reinforcement Behaviorists have discovered that not only is it mandatory that behavior be reinforced if it is to be strengthened or maintained, but when reinforcement is delivered, timing is also of considerable importance. It has been discovered that the closer in time the reinforcer can be delivered to the response, the greater the impact of the reinforcer. If, for example, a researcher was deciding whether to reinforce the mentally retarded children in his sample one minute or five minutes after the performance of an assigned task, the former would be the better decision. If he waits five minutes he may lose much of the effects of the reinforcement process.

The researcher has another decision to make. Should the reinforcer be delivered based upon the number of tasks the children perform, or should they be reinforced on the basis of time in the project? The former approach, that is, the one based upon the number of tasks, is called a *ratio schedule of reinforcement.* The ratio may be 1:1, in which case it is called continuous reinforcement. Factories which pay workers by the number of pieces they produce use a ratio schedule of reinforcement. Those that pay each month without regard to productivity use an interval schedule of reinforcement.

Whenever a husband, a wife, a teacher, or a parent is starting to shape behavior a continuous (1:1) schedule of reinforcement should be used. However, the best schedule of reinforcement which can be used to fix a behavior is called a variable ratio or *intermittent schedule of reinforcement.* An intermittent schedule approaches a random pattern. Most fishermen are probably on intermittent schedules of reinforcement. They may catch fish several times in a row and then be unsuccessful for an even longer period of time. After that, they may catch fish every second or third time they go until another cycle occurs. Behavior fixed using this type of schedule of reinforcement is extremely hard to extinguish.

Interval reinforcement is used whenever behavior patterns are erratic and the behavioral modifier wishes to make them more consistent. A parent who wishes to influence the punctuality of a child might use an interval schedule of reinforcement to accomplish this goal.

Generalization It would perhaps seem that in order to act appropriately an individual would need to have an extremely wide range of experiences. However, according to the principle of *generalization*, the individual reacts to the common elements in the situations. For example, a person may go from restaurant to restaurant and function effectively although the physical characteristics and types of service differ. Similarly, once a person has learned a set of behaviors which enable him to function in interpersonal relationships, these will usually generalize to other situations. There are, of course, times when the individual has not had a sufficient experiential background and will make a serious blunder.

Discrimination *Discrimination* is the process by which relationships that have come about through generalization are broken down into smaller units.[7] Unless an individual had the power to break down auditory and visual stimuli into units, it is likely that it would continue to respond in much the same way to auditory and visual stimuli. A horse and a cow might be responded to in exactly the same way unless discrimination takes place. The small child who calls every animal a "horsey" is generalizing but has not yet learned to discriminate.

In higher order human behavior, discrimination has an extremely important place. In order to function well, we must learn to discriminate among various types of merchandise, between genuine and "phony" people, and among a variety of visual and auditory cues. For example, we must learn to discriminate among the various road signs which are posted for our benefit and between the sounds of a car horn and police siren. The ability to discriminate allows us to learn to read and is important in the acquisition of all educational skills. Without the ability to discriminate, we would not be able to function in the world as we know it.

ABNORMAL BEHAVIOR

Up to this time the discussion has centered upon the principles which govern the acquisition of knowledge from a behavioral point of view. At this point a brief discussion of abnormality in human functioning will be presented. At the outset it should be noted that from a behavioral point of view abnormality is learned—learned in the same fashion and according to the same principles as is normal behavior. However, there are some peculiar situations which seem to give rise to abnormal behavior which deserve special scrutiny.

Before a specific discussion of how the individual learns abnormal behavior is pursued, one matter of general concern should perhaps be perused. This is the matter of what constitutes abnormal behavior. There have been a variety of approaches to answering this question, but none have been totally satisfactory. Perhaps the simplest approach to defining abnormality is to take a societal point of view: that is, anything not acceptable by society must be considered abnormal. One case in point might be homosexuality. Homosexuality has been viewed as abnormal by many cultures for centuries. However, of late, there has been a tendency to redefine homosexuality as something which is a matter of conscience rather than an abnormal state. When states, such as California, and entire countries, such as England, legalize homosexuality, as is the case, then the first steps toward redefining homosexuality have occurred even though homosexuals are still viewed with fear and disgust by many members of society.

The basis for the definition of abnormality probably stems from society's desire to protect itself. As abnormal behavior has been better understood by society at large, different approaches to the abnormal individual have been taken. It is likely that the definition of abnormality will continue to change as our society advances.

Causes of abnormal behavior Watson was perhaps the first to illustrate that simple respondent conditioning could be used to induce abnormal behavior.[8] In his often cited case of Albert, Watson took an eleven month old boy who was not afraid of animals and placed him before a cage containing a white rat. When the boy reached for the rat, Watson would strike a steel bar with a hammer which produced fear in the infant. After this experience had been repeated a number of times, the boy would become greatly disturbed at the sight of the rat. Further, the boy was fearful of other furry animals, illustrating the generalization concept.

Operant conditioning has also been demonstrated to contribute to certain types of abnormal behavior. One type of disorder among schizophrenic children involves self-injurious behavior. In these cases children may repeatedly hit themselves in the face, may bang their heads against walls or sharp objects, and may even tear out bits of their own flesh.[9] Lovaas[10] and his associates at UCLA have demonstrated repeatedly that attention, physical affection, and other types of social reinforcement increase the incidence of this type of behavior. They have also demonstrated that withdrawal of social reinforcers reduces the incidence of this type of behavior.

Both the experiment by Watson and the observations by Lovaas suggest that conditioning contributes to abnormal behavior which in turn tends to support the contention of the behavioralist that abnormal behavior is learned.

Severe punishment may also be a contributor to the development of abnormal behavior. This may occur in at least two ways. First, just as was the case in Watson's experiment with Albert, punishment may result in conditioned emotionality. For example, as Skinner[11] points out, a child who is punished for sexual behavior in childhood may be prevented from completing the sexual act in adulthood because of fear or anxiety associated with the act which has resulted from punishment. What in fact occurs in this situation is that the circumstance in which the act was punished gives rise to the emotion thus thwarting the individual. In the sexual area, this may result in frigidity or impotency. It may also result in irrational fears (phobias) or other types of avoidance behavior. The child punished at bedtime may become literally terrified of the dark since darkness is associated with bedtime.

One peculiar characteristic of the process which is being described here is that if this is done repeatedly, particularly in the absence of positive reinforcement, the result may be discouragement and withdrawal. Complete withdrawal is, of course, the most severe form of abnormal behavior, and according to some mental health experts, the most difficult to deal with.

Modeling is also a source of learning maladaptive or abnormal behavior. There is little doubt that such behavior as lying, stealing, and other antisocial acts can be effectively taught by parents or peers. There is good reason to suspect that more serious conditions such as complete inability to function may also be modeled by parents and others. We do know that families in which emotional illness has been prevalent are more likely to produce individuals who display maladaptive behavior. For some time this was credited to an inherited predisposition for mental illness. Although few would deny the possibility that predisposing factors may lead to mental illness, increasingly psychologists—particularly behavioral psychologists—are looking to the learned experiences as the source of emotional problems. In the examples in the foregoing paragraph, the child was afraid of the dark simply because it had been punished in a situation which was associated with darkness, and the adult could not complete the sexual act because of having been punished as a child for engaging in similar activities. However, through the process of generalization, emotions may be attached to situations quite unrelated to the particular situation in which the original punishment took place. Acrophobia, for example, is a fear of high places. It is extremely doubtful that many persons acquired this extraordinary fear because they were punished on a firetower or a skyscraper. Abnormal behavior may also occur because severe punishment generalizes beyond the punished act and suppresses or extinguishes a series of related behavior. A child who attempts to complete a task such as putting the dishes away may break the dishes. If it is punished for this act, other striving behavior may be suppressed.

Modeling may also contribute to the development of abnormal behavior in another way. In the foregoing examples, the parents or peers modeling the behavior were demonstrating maladaptive behavior. Parents and others who influence behavior may contribute to maladaptive behavior in the form of discouragement or personal confusion by positively reinforcing one type of behavior and modeling the opposite type. A parent may tell the children that dishonesty is wrong and reward them for honest behavior such as returning items lost by others. The problem arises whenever the child observes the parent keeping a five dollar bill which has been given to the father by mistake, or cheating in some type of business deal.

Abnormal behavior may be acquired in a number of ways. Punishment which results in emotional conditioning or the suppression of certain positive behaviors may be a contributing force. So may modeling and other interactions. The important point to remember about maladaptive behavior is that it is learned and maintained in the same manner as so-called adaptive or normal behavior. Perhaps most importantly, in order for maladaptive behavior to be retained as a part of the individual's behavioral repertoire, it must find environmental reinforcement.

APPLICATION OF BEHAVIORISM

As the reader would expect, behavior principles have been applied to all phases of life in this country and in other countries as well. In Russia, for example, the Pavlovian form of respondent conditioning serves as the primary basis for societal planning. Although it seems doubtful that behavioral psychology will ever form the basis for societal planning in this country, the idea has been proposed. Some of the major applications of behavioral psychology will be explored here.

Child rearing Many examples which have involved child-rearing practices have been included in the first of these chapters, and it is perhaps obvious to the reader that behaviorism has many implications for the parent or would-be parent. Some of the major ones will be presented and discussed.

The generation gap has been an often discussed problem which purportedly exists in our society. Roughly defined, the *generation gap* is the inability of members of different generations (often parents and offspring) to communicate about matters which are important to both. The reason often given for the "gap" is the differing interests between the

Conflict between parent and child can lead to lack of communication and the so-called generation gap. The revolt of youth against the standards of their elders is, of course, an age-old phenomenon. *(Marcia Weinstein)*

two age groups. To the behaviorist, a generation gap might be defined as the time at which the behavior of one group stops being contingent upon that of another. Put more simply, whenever parents stop being influential in the lives of their children, a generation gap could be said to exist.

The important issue is not whether a generation gap exists, since that seems to be a fact. Rather, the question which arises is why the void develops and parents cease to be influential in the lives of their children. The answer to this lies in what makes a parent a secondary reinforcer. Initially, the parent is associated with providing biological reinforcers and, therefore, assumes reinforcing potential. As the association is weakened, the parent must find other means of maintaining status. This must come primarily through attending behavior, that is, listening and looking at the child. For many parents this second step of attending to the child is not completed, and the parents' influence is weakened.

It is not being suggested that problems would never arise between parents and children if only the parents would attend to the child. Children are exposed to literally hundreds of contingencies almost from the moment they are born, and these influence the child's behavior. Parents can remain as a part of the child's contingency system by maintaining their attending behavior, however.

Parents should also formulate goals for their children and follow through consistently in the achievement of those goals. We have already seen that reinforcement of one set of behaviors and modeling the opposite type can lead to abnormal behavior or at least a dysfunctioning because of the resultant confusion. This generally occurs because the parent has not set goals. Children act primarily as their parents do. This has been verified in so-called "hippie communes" where young parents are supposedly reacting to the manner in which their parents reared them. Reinforcement and modeling practices must be consistent if parental goals are to be attained.

Needless to say, physical punishment would not be an acceptable child-rearing practice. If administered at all, punishment would consist of withdrawing expected reinforcers. However, the major emphasis would be upon developing behavior by using positive approaches.

Finally, parents would need to become more scientific in their child-rearing habits. The basis for this "scientificism" would be systematic observation of behavior and the application of the scientific method. This would be necessary since the behaviorist does not assume that all children react in the same manner to reinforcers. What is reinforcing to one child in a family might not be rewarding to another. Thus parents would need to observe the impact of various reinforcers upon the child and systematically determine those contingencies which would bring about the desired behavior.

Teaching Teaching, as it presently exists, is largely an unscientific enterprise which fails to take advantage of the principles of learning available to members of the profession. Behaviorism is viewed with a great deal of suspicion by many teachers because of the attempts of some behaviorists to introduce teaching machines. This concept, of course, threatened teachers for they feared that they might be replaced in a blaze of technology. Although teaching machines are still being used in many places, they do not seem likely to replace teachers. Rather, their role seems to be in supplementing the teacher's efforts. "A teaching machine is simply any device which arranges contingencies."[12] Many machines utilized in teaching do not fulfill this requirement. Television is an example of a widely used device which does not. Typical teaching machines provide material to students in some predetermined manner, allow the student to learn the material, and reward the student for doing so. In the event the student does not learn the material, he is "punished" in that he must restart the learning sequence. Teaching machines can be utilized to individualize instruction, but it should stressed that machines do no better than the classroom teacher.[13] However, to the behaviorist—and perhaps ultimately to others, the fact that a machine can do well as a regular teacher may be indicative of the importance of the utility of machines.

Behavioral principles are also being applied widely in the development of classroom-management strategies. The hickory rod has given way to new systems and contingency management. Disruptive classroom behavior has been significantly reduced, and at times the indirect benefit has been increased learning of subject matter.

The specific techniques of classroom management are easily derived from behavioral theory. The child who seeks the teacher's attention through snapping his fingers is ignored, thus extinguishing the response. In a more sophisticated example of the use of withdrawal of rewards, high school students are systematically excluded from classes. In these systems, disruptive teenagers are taken from classes and placed in detention areas where they can receive no attention (reinforcement). These detention areas are often not so affectionately referred to as the "hole," but the technique has been successful as a means of changing behavior. Positive approaches have also been used to shape desired behavior successfully.

Teachers of the mentally retarded have used behavior modification techniques to great advantage. Tremendous strides have been made in teaching students functional knowledge, that is, knowledge that can be utilized, and in developing appropriate behavior.

Business To a very great extent business has always used a systematic form of behavioral engineering, although unknowingly in some instances. Perhaps the most basic application of behaviorism in industry is paying (reinforcing) the worker for what the worker does. In order to enhance this effect, some businesses and industries use incentive systems such as prizes or cash bonuses for extra effort. It is difficult to consult any form of mass media today without discovering that some industry is giving its employees a bonus for serving or producing at a higher level.

Industries have also used tokens such as posting safety records or honoring the employee with the best service record. In some instances these reward systems become more tangible when cash bonuses are presented or promotions received as a result of the action.

Business has also made numerous attempts to modify habits of consumers by using behavioral techniques. Rewards (such as automobiles) are made contingent upon certain behavior such as buying gasoline at a certain service station. The intent of the campaign is to establish a habit pattern which will hopefully be rewarded not by the winning of a car, which is a remote possibility, but by the service-station attendant in the performance of duties.

Advertising is also utilized successfully by industry to change behavior. Approaches utilized vary, and only a few will be discussed here. One common technique is to refund a part or all of the money which a consumer has paid for a product after use of the product. This, of course, reinforces the process of buying and using the particular product. Another technique employed is to use modeling and vicarious reinforcement. An advertisement of this type characterizes many current approaches to commercials. Frequently, a typical-looking boy or girl (the model) will be in distress, utilize a product as a result of a recommendation, and end up with a boy or girlfriend (reward) and often with the admiration of his or her peers (reward). This type of vicarious reinforcement procedure has been found to be effective in many situations, and business now uses it to sell its products to the general public.

Psychotherapy Behavior therapy has been successful. Even some of its most severe critics admit that behavior therapy has been able to assist people with problems.[14] Eysenck,[15] perhaps the world's leading behavioral therapist has indicated that behavior therapy is more successful than some of the traditional forms of psychotherapy. Since Eysenck's original statement in 1952, the evidence has become even more compelling that his statements have merit. The issue today is probably more in the realm of why behavior therapy works.

Behavior therapy is the application of behavioral principles in the treatment of persons having behavioral deficits and disorders (abnormal behavior). The behavior therapist, assumes that these principles will enable the individual to learn behavior which will enable him to function in a manner more satisfactory to himself and to society.

One of the most controversial techniques developed by behavior therapist is called aversive conditioning. This approach is utilized in the treatment of such disorders as homosexuality, drug addiction, alcoholism, head-banging, and autism.

One special case of aversive conditioning has been developed by Lovaas and his associates in treating autistic children.[16] Autistic children are characterized by withdrawal but exhibit "fits of behavior" when approached. Before behavior therapy, the prognosis for this group was extremely poor. Dr. Ivan Lovaas developed an approach which is applied in the following manner. The therapist approaches the child, and if the characteristic behavior patterns surface, he slaps the child soundly on the thigh or the face. The therapist may also yell at the child. After that, the therapist stands squarely in the child's line of sight and models the behavior which he wishes the child to exhibit.

Typically, the thought of slapping "sick" children is repulsive to most people. The behavior therapist's view is that the slapping and the resultant progress are more humane than allowing the child to remain in his withdrawn state indefinitely.

In the treatment of homosexuals, aversive conditioning is used somewhat differently. Typically, homosexuals are shown pictures of individuals of the same sex in various states of undress. Under normal conditions these pictures would be sexually stimulating, but when in therapy the pictures are paired with aversive stimuli such as shock. The goal is, of course, to pair homosexual activity with incompatible emotional response, thus eliminating the response.

Another technique developed by behavior therapists is called desensitization. The rationale behind desensitization is that if an individual is exposed to anxiety-producing situations in small degrees, he will eventually be able to master the situation. A behavior therapist might expose a person suffering from claustrophobia (a fear of closed places) to closed, tight places a little at a time or gradually bring an adult with an irrational fear of furry animals closer to animals until one is finally touched. Techniques based upon the desensitization concept have also been used to treat frigidity and impotence.

Many other techniques have been utilized to treat persons with maladaptive behavior patterns. Shaping techniques, modeling approaches, and many other methods have been derived from behavioral principles.

DESIGN OF UTOPIAN SOCIETIES

In 1948, B. F. Skinner published his now famous novel, *Walden Two*.[17] In this publication, Skinner discusses the application of behaviorism in the establishment of a community which would have no discontent, no crime, and no unrest. Also, the citizens in *Walden Two* had no voice in the organization and government of the community. The complete control of the settlement was in the hands of a group known as the planners, and the overall scheme was administered by a group known as the managers. According to Skinner, the people would have no reason to be involved or even want to be involved since they were receiving rewards (reinforcers) for their activities. Not only was *Walden Two* apparently antidemocratic, but it struck at what behaviorists believe is the myth of human existence: his autonomous functioning. This position was summed up in one sentence. "We can make men adequate for group living—to the satisfaction of everybody." This quite naturally raised a furor among lay people and psychologists.

Again in 1953, Skinner raised the issue of designing a culture.[18] He pointed out many factors are apparently important in the overall development of cultures and that even accidents bring forces to bear which shape the destinies of groups. He raises two questions in his 1953 essay. Why should culture be left so largely to accident? And, is it not possible to change the social environment deliberately so that the human product will meet more acceptable specifications? Skinner goes on to elaborate that when he is referring to designing culture he means the introduction of practices which will result in certain desirable outcomes. Skinner believes that one factor which should perhaps lead us into the design of culture is the survival of that culture. Although he admits that determining those factors which may or may not lead to the survival of a species may be difficult, careful study may at least provide some answers.

In 1971, Skinner made his latest pronouncements about the need for designing culture. In *Beyond Freedom and Dignity*[19] Skinner asserts that the traditional concepts of freedom and dignity are actually violated by those who espouse their virtues. People's freedom or liberty to do as they please is at stake, according to Skinner. In this country, at least, people have learned that they should resist those who attempt to control them aversively, but we have not taught people to deal effectively with techniques of control which are positive in nature. For example, another person may control us by positively reinforcing our action, and in fact, governments, churches, and certain other societal agencies do just that.

Skinner indicates that most lay people and psychologists attribute human dignity to the fact that people are autonomous or internally controlled. Any idea which suggests that external conditions control human behavior threaten that dignity. People actually reinforce the actions of others which are apparently free from external control. People in our society who work for obvious reward are viewed with suspicion.

Freedom and dignity are both threatened by punishment since people cannot be truly free if they are under threat or appear to act autonomously if stress is placed upon them to act. According to Skinner, we are often neither free nor dignified because of threat. Alternatives to threat have, of course, been devised, but positive reinforcement is the only real alternative that is workable.

Finally, Skinner comes back to the theme which he began in 1953. The design of culture is not only important but necessary if we are to consider survival of the culture. He believes that present approaches to designing cultures are not adequate and suggests that it is necessary to embark upon a path which will insure the survival of our culture. Planning, Skinner believes, can do just that.

The question of the controller and the controllee is also considered by Skinner in his latest work. Perhaps not so strangely, his explanation of a method to control the controller or counter-control is similar to that which he employed in *Walden Two*. In *Walden Two* the planner was also a worker and was therefore under the influence of the contingencies which were established for the other members of the community. Skinner's argument is that a culture designer who must live in the self-built culture will necessarily be more careful in planning.

Skinner's various discourses about planning a Utopian society have raised the horrors of Orwell's *1984*, where societies are taken over and managed, primarily through aversive means, to the benefit of the government. This is obviously not Skinner's intent since he repeatedly holds that punishment cannot be an effective means of controlling the behavior of people. Skinner may have two purposes in mind. One is to prod our society to think about its consequences for its members and to start some planning that will vary this impact in a positive direction. The other is to set up a plan which he believes will ultimately be adopted and utilized in designing culture. It seems unlikely that Skinner, the scientist, would be so naive as to think the simple formulation which he has put forth would serve such a grand purpose.

ETHICS AND BEHAVIORISM

Many people have raised the question of whether or not it is ethical for one person to knowingly control and manipulate the behavior of another either with or without consent. One answer to this question from behaviorists is simply that control of behavior is and has been the aim of governments, educational institutions, and parents for centuries. Behaviorism only provides the basis for achieving this long sought control and should therefore be utilized. Another only slightly different argument is that the individual is controlled and manipulated anyway, and therefore, contingencies should be managed in a manner that will be beneficial to the individual being controlled. These opinions represent one school of thought in behaviorism.

Eysenck seems to take a different tack regarding the matter of control when he makes the following statement:

> We would never try to treat a homosexual who was happy and contented with his sexual orientation simply because society disliked homosexuality; but we would treat him if he willingly came and asked for treatment, even though his wish for treatment might have been due to social pressure which he was unable to resist.[20]

Eysenck seems to be suggesting that the principles of behaviorism should be applied using the individual, rather than society, as the reference point. He does not seem to view his role as developing behavior in all people which will meet acceptable societal norms.

It cannot be denied that many behaviorists, and B. F. Skinner in particular, have given considerable thought to the idea of developing contingencies which will produce certain prescribed behaviors. In his book, *Science and Human Behavior*[21], Skinner ponders the basis for the ethics of controlling the behavior of groups of people along prescribed lines. He suggests that there may be an ethical basis for this type of action if we consider such factors as "the greatest good for the greatest number", or "increasing the sum total of human happiness". Even in his conjecture in 1953,[22] Skinner seems less than certain that the ethical basis for group control can be found. In his 1971 work (*Beyond Freedom and Dignity*) Skinner seems to have resolved his earlier conflict and takes the stand that indeed increasing happiness or creating the greatest good for the largest number of people and ensuring the survival of a culture are sufficient reasons to make control of group behavior ethical.

It seems likely that the issue of controlling or engineering human behavior will continue both within behaviorism and among social scientists outside of the behavioristic school. The crux of the issue revolves around one point, however. Do people determine their own destiny or are they reactive beings who are a product of their environment?

CRITICISMS OF BEHAVIORISM

At the beginning of this chapter it was stated that behaviorism is a controversial, often criticized, school of psychology. At this point considerations will be given to the criticisms of other psychologists. It is assumed that these criticisms have more validity than those levied by the lay public (no matter how well-meaning they may appear.)

1. Behaviorists oversimplify human behavior. The charge is often made that behaviorists deal with segments of behavior, or that their primary thrust has been with children, retardates, and others who are not fully functioning individuals. This is true because the behavioral explanation of behavior does not lend itself to explanation of complex behavioral patterns and thus would be less useful in assisting those who are more completely developed.

   It is also frequently charged that behaviorists tend to overlook much that is important about human behavior because of their rather simplistic view of human functioning. For example, in psychotherapy the interaction (relationship) between the therapist and patient may be more important than the systematic desensitization which takes place. Similarly, processes such as cognition may be occurring which account for learning new habits according to critics.

   These oversimplifications are the result of strict applications of the scientific method to the study of human behavior, according to the critics. The behaviorist agrees that the danger of oversimplification and thus overlooking important variables exists. However, the rationale for use of the scientific principle to explore human phenomena is simply to increase the understanding of behavior—not to make it more complex, according to behaviorists.[23] Further, the behaviorists think the wisest course is to continue to take this simplified view until science provides data upon which the behaviorist can systematically alter his approaches. This data would, of course, be related to human behavior.
2. Behaviorism is nonscientific. The scientific method calls for certain conditions. There must be a clearly stated problem or hypothesis.

There must also be conditions established which will ascertain that the results of the experiment will be attributable to the conditions being studied and not to some extraneous factors. A biologist might, for example, want to determine the impact of aspirin. In order to make certain that no psychological effect reduced the symptom which was being studied, one might set up a placebo group and give this group sugar but tell them that they were taking aspirin. The researcher could then observe whether or not similar results occurred in the group taking aspirins and sugar pills and determine whether or not the results obtained were truly the result of the aspirin.

It has often been charged that many of the experiments conducted using human subjects have not been adequately controlled for extraneous factors. The most common deficiency pointed to by critics has been the lack of control groups. Most behaviorists acknowledge this deficiency, but point to a considerable number of these studies which far surpass those conducted by other fields of psychology.

Another criticism often made of the scientific basis of behavioral theory is that many of the laws were derived from research with animals and are therefore not generalizable to human beings. (This is, of course, a part of the charge of oversimplification discussed earlier.) The rejoinder to this is that many of these laws have already been demonstrated to have utility with people and that the behavioral scientists will continue to study the application of all behavioral laws to people.

3. Definition of abnormality. Many far-ranging criticisms of the behaviorist approach to defining abnormality have been put forth. Not only has there been a criticism of the position that neuroses and psychoses can be understood in terms of their symptoms, but objections to the position of defining abnormality in terms of social norms have also been raised. Of course, the critics of the symptoms approach are asking questions similar to those discussed throughout this chapter, specifically, "Are there internal forces which account for abnormality?"

The major reservation about defining abnormal behavior in terms of social norms seems to be that this position devises the importance of idiosyncratic behavior such as that often demonstrated by artists. Also at the root of the resistance to this definition appears to be a fear that if society adopted this approach, deviations from societal norms would not be tolerated. This could, of course, lead to situations which existed in Germany in the early thirties when a strong central government under Adolf Hitler set a norm which was adopted by German society and led to the mass murder of millions of Jews.

The behaviorist would rebut that there is really no other sound way to define abnormality since there must be a reference point. However, the behaviorist would not agree that forcing social conformity is necessary. Rather, the basis for forcing conformity would be if individuals posed direct threats to other members of society (e.g., potential killers) or they themselves wished to change their behavior. The position taken is that conformity is not necessary for the survival of a society and that in fact all societies demand that its members adhere to certain societal norms.

4. Behaviorists as a "controller" of the behavior of others. The ethical problems of control have already been discussed and will not be repeated here. However, it should suffice to say that many psychologists protest the inherent ideas in many of the writings of behaviorists that suggest the control of the behavior of other human beings.

   One question which is sometimes raised about the matter of control is "How can the behaviorist assume that one can know what is best for other people?" The basis for this argument is as follows. Since the behaviorist is a product of environmental contingencies which have produced certain behaviors or patterns of behavior, how can we assume that these are better than those produced by other environmental contingencies and manifested in other people? The behaviorist would answer this query by referring to the fact that people can solve problems and draw conclusions from these solutions. Certainly the approach to problem solving will be determined by the environment, and the conclusions drawn will also be environmentally determined. However, some environments are more capable of producing good problem solvers than others. These environments should be identified and utilized if it is society's goal that people be good problem solvers.

5. Principles of behaviorism: There abound in the psychological literature many articles and books which take issue with even those principles which have supposedly been proven via animal research. At this point in time the numbers of these articles dictate that they not be enumerated in detail. The student of the social sciences should be aware, however, that the possibility exists that behaviorism as it exists today may be drastically altered by future research.

Status of behaviorism Behaviorism is probably the most influential school of psychology in America today. This is not to say that most psychologists subscribe to behavioral theory, or that it has the greatest public support, for neither of these cases is true. It is, however, the most influential in terms of affecting the lives of American people. Large numbers of schools, businesses, correctional institutions, etc., have embraced behavioral principles and are applying them in varying degrees. It seems likely that before the apex of behaviorism is reached more and more lives will be affected.

SUMMARY

Behavioral psychology has been reviewed in this chapter. As we have seen, behaviorists believe that environmental consequences determine the behavior of an individual. Specifically, behavior which is reinforced is strengthened, and that behavior which is not responded to is gradually extinguished. The full impact of negative or aversive reaction to behavior is not fully understood, but generally it is believed that the result is repression of the behavior.

Behavioral principles are widely applied in our society in child rearing, education, and business. Advocates of these principles, such as B. F. Skinner, have proposed that they be utilized for designing a Utopian society. Opponents of this idea have decried Skinner's Utopia because the planning requires that goals be established for people. They believe this flies in the face of democratic ideals.

Behaviorism now occupies stage center in American psychology, but is challenged from all sides by more humanistic approaches. There can be little doubt that many specific behavioral concepts have utility in areas such as education and psychotherapy, but few would hold that they represent the final answer. Indeed, the behaviorists themselves are seeking new links with other ideas, and their own research may provide more inclusive answers to why people behave as they do.

REVIEW QUESTIONS

1. What is your reaction to the philosophy of behaviorism? Specifically, are people controlled by their environment? Defend your position.
2. Differentiate operant from respondent conditioning.
3. What are the different types of reinforcers? Which of these have an impact upon you? Specifically, are there things which you respond to?
4. Does corporal punishment work? Defend your answer using behavioral principles.
5. Describe the shaping process. Contrast shaping and modeling.
6. What are the types of schedules of reinforcement? Why is the idea of schedule of reinforcement important?
7. What is your reaction to defining abnormal behavior in terms of a societal norm? Give several examples of how this has occurred in our society.
8. In light of some of our discussion in the sociology section, what is your reaction to the modeling theory of abnormal behavior?
9. Should parents formulate goals for their children? How far should these goals be carried?

10. What is your reaction to Skinner's Utopia? Would you like to be a part of this type of society? Why or why not?
11. Do you agree with Skinner's ideas about freedom and dignity?
12. Is it ethical to control human behavior? Do you agree with Eysenck on this matter or would you prefer Skinner's position? Why?
13. What are your responses to the criticisms of behaviorism?

10·47
27

PART THREE
ECONOMICS

The link between economics and the other social sciences results from the effects that the methods used by groups of people to produce and distribute scarce goods and services have on other aspects of societal organization and the behavior of the people. Alfred Marshall (1843–1924), an economist instrumental in shaping modern economic theory, described economics as the study of

> . . . that part of individual and social action which is most closely connected with the attainment and with the use of the material requisites of well being. Thus it is on the one side a study of wealth; and on the other, and more important side, a part of the study of man.

The subject matter of economics is especially important to the study of those aspects of society which are the concern of sociologists and anthropologists. This relation becomes obvious when we look at the stated goals of sociology and anthropology. The long-run aim of sociology is "to discover the basic structure of human society, to identify the main forces that hold groups together or weaken them, and to learn the conditions that transform social life."[1] It would be impossible to pursue such a goal without careful consideration of the way a group attains and uses the material requisites of well-being. How can one hope to understand the interaction between the members of a group or between groups or between nations without fully understanding the economic forces involved? How, for example is the United States' relationship with Israel and the Arab nations of the Middle East influenced by our dependence on the oil controlled by the Arab nations? To what extent does one's income determine the groups with which one associates and the nature of one's relationship with the other members of groups of which one is a member? A listing of such questions could continue for pages.

The theme which underlies anthropological research can be described as "the search for a set of principles which governs man's physical and cultural development."[2] Such development must necessarily involve the techniques people use to produce and distribute scarce goods and services.

Behavior, the major interest of psychologists, is certainly closely linked to the economic well-being of individuals and groups. Close links have been found between poverty and psychological problems. Superiority-inferiority positions are closely related to economic advantage and disadvantage. It is common in the United States to measure individuals' worth by the size of their incomes. People with large incomes are held in high esteem by society, and those who fail economically are often condemned. The equating of financial success with personal worth must be included in any explanation of people's behavior.

Rationalization, a psychological adjustment mechanism, has been and continues to be used as a way of justifying economic exploitation.

Have you ever heard any of the following rationalizations? The blacks brought to the United States as slaves were better off than those left in Africa. The activities of United States businesses in foreign countries help those countries more than they help the United States businesses involved. Men need higher incomes than women because they have to support families.

It is interesting to note that much of modern economic theory is developed from assumptions about the people's behavior. One of the most important of these is the assumption that individuals maximize utility. Utility is a term used by economists which means satisfaction or, more literally, happiness. Tibor Scitovsky, a noted economist, argues that there is a need for more interaction between economists and psychologists so that such behavioral assumptions about people can be tested to determine whether or not they are consistent with what psychologists have been able to learn about people's behavior.

What can one conclude from this discussion? The most obvious conclusion seems to be that the skills and knowledge of social scientists from all the areas of specialization are needed if we wish to fully understand people and their organization.

FOR FURTHER READING

Those readers who would like to explore economics in more depth than is provided by the brief survey in these chapters will find *Economics* by Campbell McConnell (McGraw-Hill, 1972) and *Economics* by Paul Samuelson (McGraw-Hill, 1973) useful sources. A shorter introductory source for beginners in economics is provided by *Survey of Economic Principles* by Gary Brown (Richard D. Irwin, 1972). The McConnell and Samuelson texts are designed for a two-semester introductory economics course, and the Brown text is designed for a one-semester course. All these books combine a survey of modern economic theory with discussions of contemporary economic issues and policy. If the reader is more interested in the historical development of economics, *The Worldly Philosophers* by Robert Heilbroner (Simon & Schuster, 1972) will be useful. This book is well written and provides interesting insights into the personal and professional lives of the major economists who have contributed to the development of the discipline.

There are numerous good readings books available which deal with contemporary economic issues. Two of the more popular ones are *Economics: Mainstream Readings* by David Mermelstein (Random House, 1973) and *Current Economic Problems* by Royall Brandis and Steven Cox (Richard D. Irwin, 1972). The Mermelstein book is billed as a "radical" book of readings. Do not be surprised if it does not seem especially radical to you.

A book which is fun to read is *Walden II* by B. F. Skinner (Macmillan, 1962). In this fiction book Skinner, a psychologist, reveals what he believes to be a utopian society. It is interesting to read about the type of economy Skinner envisions for the best of all possible worlds. You will also find it interesting to analyze the social and political organization of Walden II, the name Skinner gives his utopia. *Walden II* also provides interesting insights into the extent to which the leading behavioral psychologist thinks human behavior can be controlled.

GLOSSARY

absolute poverty inability to secure the basic necessities

capital previously produced economic goods which are used in the production process

collective good a good which cannot be consumed by the individual alone and must be consumed by the group as a whole

democratic political system one in which the government derives its authority from the people it governs through an elective process

economic efficiency when the economy produces the maximum amount possible of the combination of goods and services which it is producing

economic good or service any good or service which is scarce enough that someone is willing to pay for it

economic growth an increase in the potential output of the economy

economic market a well-defined geographic area within which buyers and sellers negotiate the exchange of a well-defined good or service

economic profit a return to a factor of production which is greater than that needed to keep it in its present employment

financial flow a flow of economic activity that involves money or monetary claims

firm an economic unit that performs the production function of the economy. The three legal types of firm are the proprietorship, the partnership, and the corporation

franchise a situation in which the owner of a business operates it under the name of a national or regional corporation

limited liability the situation in which the owners of a corporation are responsible for the liabilities of the business only to the extent of the value of the corporation; that is, their personal wealth may not be demanded to settle claims against the corporation they own

market economy an economy in which economic decisions

are made by the interaction of buyers and sellers in the market

military-industrial complex a coalition of leaders of the military and the heads of businesses who supply the military for the purpose of influencing economic decisions

mixed economy an economy characterized by two or more of the kinds of decision making found in pure types of economies

money a mechanism through which economic value is exchanged

monopolistic competition a market situation in which producers are able to get consumers to differentiate among similar or even identical products

monopoly a market in which there is only one producer

natural monopoly a production situation in which having more than one firm producing would involve economic waste

natural resources those productive resources which exist as a part of the state of nature

oligopoly a market situation in which there are only a few producers

opportunity cost the value of something which must be given up or forgone in order to get something else

planned economy an economy in which economic decisions are made by a central authority

power of eminent domain the power of government to force people to sell property when it is needed for public use

production possibilities curve a graphic representation of all the possible combinations of goods and services that an economy is capable of producing at a given time

pure competition an economic market in which: (*a*) there are many buyers and sellers, (*b*) there is a standardized product, (*c*) all market participants have all the relevant information which will enable them to participate on an equal basis, and (*d*) there is easy entry into and exit from the market.

real flow a flow of economic activity that involves goods and services

relative poverty a state in which a family is able to purchase the essentials, but not able to purchase as much as other families

scarcity demand for a greater quantity of a good or service than is available at a zero price

state of technology the techniques that are being used or could be used in the production of economic goods and services

subsidy income given to a person or group to support and/or encourage activities that are deemed beneficial

subsistence economy an

economy characterized by the absence of markets and in which the individual economic unit independently makes all economic decisions relevant to it

transfer payment a situation in which government transfers part of its revenue to businesses or individuals, as opposed to purchasing goods and services and supplying these to the people

utility the satisfaction one gains from the consumption of a good or service

SOMETHING TO THINK ABOUT

Why do we have an energy crisis in the United States?

Should government be allowed to regulate private businesses?

Is the United States economy performing satisfactorily?

What is "private enterprise"?

Who benefits from government involvement in the economy?

Can government make "good" economic decisions?

Does the existence of a large public debt imply that government is "living beyond its means"?

Do businesses exploit their employees?

Does competition exist in the United States economy?

Why are there poor people in a country as prosperous as the United States?

CHAPTER EIGHT
THE ECONOMIC SYSTEM AND ITS FUNCTION

IDEAS AND CONCEPTS

barter
an exchange of goods or services for goods or services

economic good or service
any good or service for which wants (demand) exceed quantity available (supply)

labor
the human input in the production process

price
the mechanism usually used to ration a scarce commodity among those who desire it

utility
the satisfaction an individual receives from the use of his resources

The economic problem is the existence of scarcity. Scarcity implies that it is impossible to satisfy everyone's wants. Scarcity and wants are very closely related. Goods and services are only scarce when there is a desire for a larger quantity of them than is available. Any good or service for which wants (demand) exceed quantity available (supply) is considered an economic good or service, and people are willing to pay for such a good or service. The price of a commodity is the mechanism usually used to ration a scarce commodity among those who desire it.

Economic goods are not the only ones which have "value." For example, if you were given a choice of going without air (a free good) for an hour, or without gold (an economic good) for the rest of your life, you would have no difficulty making a choice. Air is not considered an economic good today because it is not scarce—but then land was frequently conisdered a free good in North America 200 years ago. At that time most of the people in North America did not foresee a situation in which there would not be enough land to go around, and land was frequently free for the taking or available for a nominal price. With respect to land, the people 200 years ago were correct, if one considers their lifetime as the relevant time period.

Economists often treat wants as exogenous, that is, they are determined by factors outside the study of economics. By taking this approach economists do not have to attempt to explain how wants are created or to evaluate the merits of different wants. Many wants are derived from needs for survival—food, clothing, shelter, etc. The society in which an individual lives influences the way these biological needs are manifested. Much of the demand for economic goods and services which do not fill biological needs is determined by cultural factors that are peculiar to a specific society. Demand may also be created by the forces associated with the operation of the economy. For example, there are certain needs, such as for education and transportation, which must be met if an individual is to be able to function effectively within the economic system. These needs vary from one economic system to another. In addition, much of the demands for goods and services in the American economy is advertising-induced.

Economists are frequently criticized for their failure to differentiate the source of "wants" for goods and services. The critics argue that the source of wants has social implications which must be considered before the functioning of an economic system can be understood and evaluated. For instance, it is often argued that an economy which diverts part of its productive resources to producing frivolous items for some members of society before fulfilling the biologically determined wants of the total population is not functioning "successfully," no matter how large the total output. Most economists avoid this type of issue by asserting that since the formation of wants is beyond the scope of economic analysis, the economists should treat the wants of society as if all wants were equal.*

ECONOMICS DEFINED

Economics can be defined as the study of how people through their institutions utilize their scarce resources of capital, natural resources, and labor to satisfy their material needs. Capital, natural resources, and labor are called the *factors of production*. Captial refers to goods produced in the past that are available for use in the production process at present. The United States has accumulated a large stock of capital.

Natural resources are those elements which exist as a natural part of man's physical environment that are used in the production process. The United States has been fortunate to be endowed with large stores of natural resources located within our political boundaries. We have also been able to gain access to many natural resources outside our political boundaries through foreign trade. What natural resources can be utilized in the production process is determined by the state of technology. Technology refers to the application of scientific knowledge to the production process. Thus, elements in the physical environment which may be considered useless or even a nuisance in one time period can become valuable factors in the production process as a result of advances in technology.

Labor is the human input in the production process. Because labor is human it presents some special problems. In addition to being inputs in the production process, workers are the recipients of the output of the production process. In fact, the whole operation of the economy is supposed to help improve people's well-being. Why else have an economy? Labor is different from the other factors of production because the fact that it is human means that it possesses certain rights. This has been true since slavery was abolished. In the United States many of the rights of labor have been incorporated into law. For example, there are laws which regulate the length of the work day, working conditions, use of child labor, and many other factors in order to protect workers.

THE ECONOMIC SYSTEM

The economic system is made up of all those interdependent variables which interact to determine what gets produced, how it gets produced, who receives the goods and services after they are produced, and what is done to ensure a continual and growing stream of production. The

*There is a growing minority of "radical economists today who strongly object to this approach. They are trying to get the profession to incorporate want formation and differentiation of wants into contemporary economic analysis.

Unwholesome working conditions, long hours, and women and child labor characterized the sweat shop of the nineteenth century. The effect on the worker was dehumanizing, but the newly arrived immigrant had few other chances for employment. (*Culver Pictures*)

economic system interacts with the other systems that make up the social order. Its operation is influenced by the operation of the other systems, and it also influences their operation.

The concept of an economic system is rather abstract. However, it is really nothing more than the interaction of institutions and people in some organized fashion. Some of the economic agents exist solely to facilitate the operation of the economy, and others perform some economic functions but are also involved in performing crucial functions that are not primarily economic. The monetary system that we have developed in the United States is an example of an agent whose existence is entirely a response to economic needs. Government is an example of an agent that performs vital economic functions but whose existence stems from reasons that are not primarily economic.

Functions of an economic system All economies perform certain basic functions. These functions are the same for a simple economy as for a complex economy, and they are the same in the United States as in the Soviet Union. These functions are:

1. Determining the composition of output
2. Allocating the productive resources
3. Distributing the output
4. Providing for economic growth
5. Providing flexibility in the short run

Later in this chapter we shall develop a system for classifying economies based on the decision-making process as related to these basic functions.

Determining the composition of output This refers to selecting the actual bundle or combination of goods and services to produce out of all

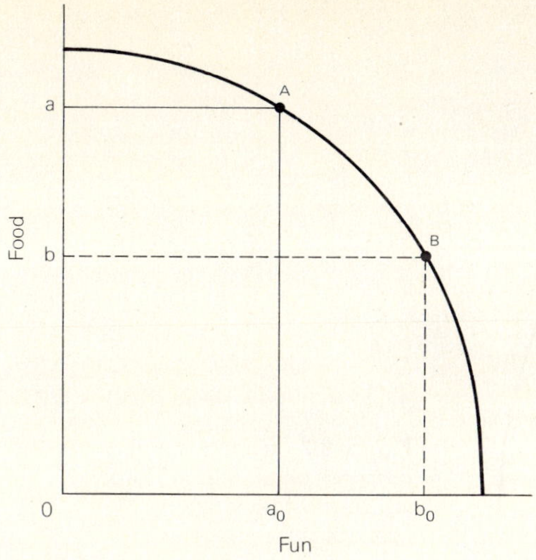

Figure 8-1 The production possibilities curve (ppc). The ppc is a graphic representation of all the possible combinations of goods and services the economy is capable of producing.

the possible bundles that an economy is capable of producing. The potential combinations of goods and services that an economy is capable of producing are technically determined. By this we mean that they are determined by the availability of the factors of production and the state of technology.

Economists frequently use a model to represent this relationship between the potential technical solutions and the economic decision as to which actual bundle to produce. This model is called the production possibilities curve (ppc). The model is developed by assuming that the economy produces only two goods. We shall call these two goods food and fun. Since there are only two goods being produced, the maximum of one which the economy can produce for each given amount of the other can be represented on a two-dimensional graph. (Students sometimes refer to economics as the two-dimensional science because economists use two-dimensional graphs so much.) When the two-dimensional graph is used, food is put on one axis and fun on the other. In this context food represents those goods and services necessary for survival and fun all other goods. All the maximum possible combinations of food and fun which the economy can produce are located, and these points are then connected by a line which is called the production possibilities curve. The location of the ppc, therefore, reflects the upper limits placed on the potential production of an economy at a given time by the availability of the factors of production and the existing technology. Figure 8-1 shows a production possibilities curve.

The economy can also produce the bundle of goods and services represented by any point inside the ppc. If the economy produces the combinations of food and fun represented by point *A* it can produce $0a$ of food and $0a_0$ of fun. If the economy chooses to operate at point *B* on the

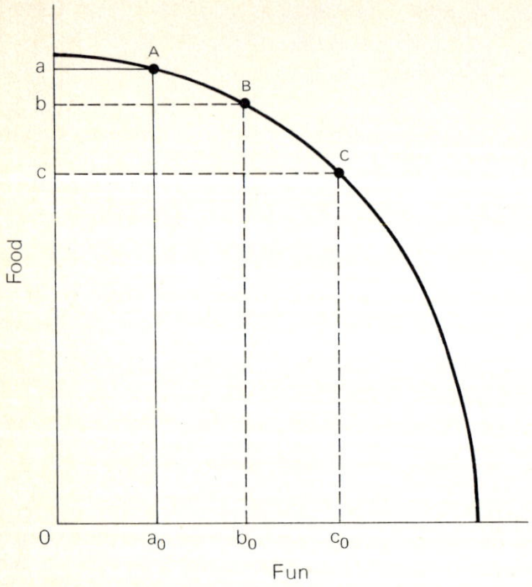

Figure 8-2 Changes in the composition of output. The food which must be foregone to produce fun represents the opportunity cost of the fun.

ppc it can produce $0b$ of food and $0b_0$ of fun. The ppc has the shape that it does because of the differences in the adaptability of the productive resources. It can be seen from Figure 8-2 that in order to increase the output of fun from $0a_0$ to $0b_0$ it is necessary to give up production of a quantity of food equal to ab, and to increase the output of fun from $0b_0$ to $0c_0$ requires foregoing production of bc of food. Thus as the output of one good is increased it is necessary to give up larger and larger quantities of other goods and services for each additional unit of the good produced. This is because the productive resources are not all equally adaptable to the production of all goods and services.

The production possibilities curve can be used to explain a very important concept. This is the concept of *opportunity cost.* The opportunity cost of producing any good or service is the amount of production of other goods and services that must be foregone in order to produce the good or service. In Figure 8-2 the opportunity cost of producing a_0b_0 of fun is ab of food. Therefore, if a_0b_0 of fun is more desirable to society than ab of food, the output represented by point *B* on the ppc is preferable to the output represented by point *A*. When determining whether an economy should produce something, it is not enough to ask whether or not the thing is good. It is necessary to determine whether the output in question is more desirable than the output which must be foregone to produce it.

The concept of opportunity cost is also very useful in explaining the behavior of individuals. Individuals, like economies, have scarce resources, and they attempt to utilize their resources in a manner which will enable them to achieve the greatest possible amount of satisfaction.

Economists usually refer to the satisfaction an individual receives from the use of his resources as *utility.* For example, one of the scarce resources that an individual has to allocate is his time. The opportunity cost of reading this book is the satisfaction which you could gain from the activity in which you would be engaged if you were not reading this book. However, explaining the maximization of satisfaction by an individual is complicated. One reason is that satisfaction is subjective, i.e., the amount of satisfaction gained from an act such as eating an apple differs from one individual to another. The time period involved is also an important consideration. There would be a different amount of satisfaction associated with eating a dozen apples in two days than with eating a dozen apples in a week. Thus, the length of the time period during which satisfaction is to be maximized is an important consideration. In addition, many people will engage in activities in one time period which result in less satisfaction in that time period than other activities in order to gain greater satisfaction in future periods. Another thing that complicates the study of the way individuals maximize satisfaction is the existence of uncertainty. When an individual does something it is frequently impossible to accurately determine in advance the amount of satisfaction that will be gained from the act. Nevertheless, much of economic analysis is devoted to the study of how the individual maximizes his satisfaction.

Allocating productive resources The second function which all economic systems must perform is the *allocation of the productive resources*, that is, labor, capital, and natural resources. This involves getting the most suitable combination of productive resources to pro-

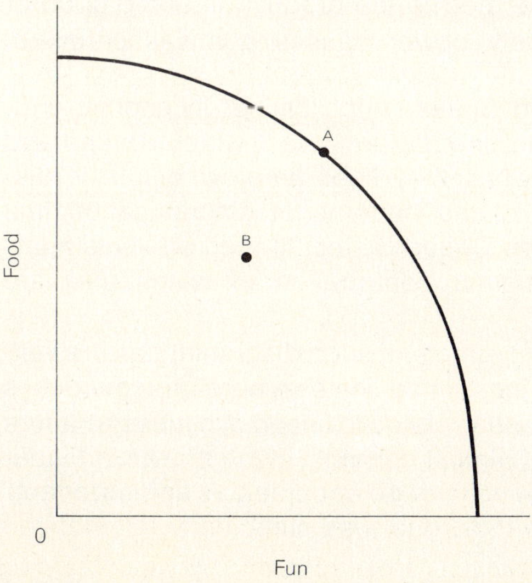

Figure 8-3 Any point in the interior of the ppc such as B represents economic inefficiency.

duce each of the goods and services in the desired bundle of goods and services. It is imperative that this function be carried out effectively if the economy is to produce the maximum amount possible of the bundle of goods and services produced. When resources are allocated properly, the economy produces one of the bundles of goods and services represented by a point on the production possibilities curve, and this means that economic efficiency has been achieved. If the economy produces any bundle of goods and services inside the production possibilities curve, it is operating inefficiently. Thus, in terms of Figure 8-3, point *A* is an efficient level of output and point *B* is inefficient.

An economy might end up at *B* because of unemployment within the economy, which is a form of inefficiency, or because improper allocation of the productive resources leads to waste, which prevents the economy from achieving its potential level of output.

Two major potential (and in many instances actual) causes of misallocation of productive resources in the United States are monopoly elements and patterns of discrimination which interfere with the free movement of productive resources from one place of employment to another. The monopoly elements include businesses and labor organizations. For example, labor unions frequently limit the number of workers in an occupation in order that their members may receive higher wages. This forces workers who would otherwise enter the restricted occupations to seek alternative employment which is less efficient from the standpoint of the operation of economy. Businesses with monopoly power can restrict the output of a good or service, which will drive the price up because of the contrived scarcity. The restriction of the output of the good or service implies that in the absence of monopoly power, more resources would have been allocated to the production of the good or services, so that such monopoly power causes a misallocation of resources.

Discrimination in the United States which causes economic inefficiency consists primarily of the unequal treatment which women and many minority groups receive when they seek employment. This discrimination is a manifestation of the patterns of discrimination that permeate the entire society in the United States. It often prevents many people from making the economic contribution of which they are capable.

The social and psychological effects of such discrimination are very important in a society such as the United States where an individual's social status and worth are so closely related to financial success. Failure to achieve financial success will almost certainly mean that an individual will have low social status and will not be accepted as an "important" person by the community. If an individual has sufficiently internalized the values of the community, this can keep that individual from developing the type of self-esteem needed to function successfully in a complicated and frequently confusing world. This leads to a vicious circle in which the operation of the economy reinforces and helps perpetuate other patterns of discrimination in society. Recent efforts by black leaders to raise the level of black consciousness and efforts by the leaders of the Women's Liberation movement to raise female consciousness are examples of efforts to break the patterns of discrimination which exist in the United States. In both cases much of the attention has been centered on persuading those involved that they are just as capable as the white males who control society and on achieving equal employment opportunity. The long-run success of any efforts to improve the status of any group in the United States will be dependent on that group's ability to achieve parity in the marketplace.

The medical profession is an example of an area in which a combination of monopoly control and discrimination has led to a great shortage of doctors. When asked why there are not more, doctors often contend that to increase the number of doctors you would have to decrease the quality of doctors because the medical schools currently are taking only the best-qualified applicants. If this is true, which is debatable, it would still be possible to nearly double the number of doctors by opening the profession to women and encouraging them to become doctors. In the Soviet Union and many European countries over half of the doctors are women.

There is also some improper allocation of productive resources because of a lack of good information. For example, individuals may not sell their labor in the place where they and the economy would gain the most benefit from it because they do not have enough information to locate the optimum source of employment. In an economy as large as that of the United States it is impossible to completely avoid some poor allocation of productive resources as a result of poor information.

The impact of poor information is not spread equally among all members of society. Howard Tuckman argues in *The Economics of the Rich*[1] that the education system, as it is constituted in the United States today, does not adequately prepare a student to make money, and this tends to work to the disadvantage of lower income groups. He contends that a large part of the information needed to succeed financially is acquired from the family and through one's associations with other people. As a result of this, the successful and the children of the sucessful tend to have better information, and this improves their ability to compete in labor markets in the United States. Thus, if better information on the operation of the economy is provided in the schools, it will tend to improve the efficiency of utilization of productive resources,

Poor children in the United States, the majority of whom live in urban slums and ghettos, do not have an equal opportunity for education, medical care, or decent housing. Their environment does not promise much for growing up with a sense of personal worth and dignity. *(Charles Gatewood, George W. Gardner)*

and at the same time tend to equalize the economic opportunities available to different segments of society.

Distributing the output From the individual's point of view, the most important function which an economy performs is the determination of the *distribution of the output of the economy, or income.* After all, what difference does it make how prosperous an economy is if "my" share is almost nothing? In the United States the two criteria most commonly used to evaluate the pattern of distribution of the output of the economy are: (1) the contribution which the individual makes to the operation of the economy, and (2) some consideration of social justice.

At one time the pattern of the distribution of goods and services was believed to reflect some divine will. In such a system there was no reason to question the fairness of the distribution of goods and services among the members of society. This view was later modified, and individuals were assumed to be totally responsible for determining their share of the output of the economy. It was assumed that an individual who worked hard and lived a clean life would be economically successful. The belief that those who were successful economically deserved it was incorporated into this new view. Of course, not to be successful was the fault of the individual. In an economy as complex and impersonal as that of the United States, it does not seem reasonable to assume that individuals have complete control of their economic fortunes. It seems more probable that success or failure is frequently determined by the way the system functions rather than by anything that an individual does or does not do. Nevertheless, there is a tendency in the United States to say that people who do not succeed have only themselves to blame. This seems like an irrational attitude in view of the evidence. Whether one fails or succeeds is also associated with the problems of unequal motivation and/or opportunity in education, which were discussed in an earlier chapter.

In order to understand the way income is distributed in the United States, it is necessary to realize that initially nearly all income accrues to the owners of the productive resources. Thus, an individual's share of the output of the economy is determined by his control of labor, capital, and natural resources. Everyone has labor to sell, but only part of the population gains income from the ownership of the other two factors of production. Therefore, any explanation of the pattern of income distribution in the United States would have to include consideration of how individuals gain control of capital and natural resources. It is also necessary to consider the way the individual is treated in the marketplace where productive resources are sold. This is especially important for labor due to the discrimination that exists against some sellers of labor. In addition, much of the recent evidence indicates that many of the income differentials in the United States are attributable to differences in investment in human capital, i.e., in education. Becker and Cheswick[2] have suggested that in order to have equal educational opportunity it would be necessary for everyone to have equal access to funds to finance education, and the cost of these funds would have to be the same for everyone. Since this is not the case, it seems probable that much of the inequality in income distribution in the United States is the result of unequal educational opportunities.

Lastly, no explanation of the distribution of income in the United States can ignore the effect of government regulation and intervention in the economy. For instance, the tax structure in the United States plays an important role in determining the final distribution of income. Income from all sources is not taxed at the same rate. A good example of this would be two individuals with incomes of $15,000, one from wages and the other as interest on municipal bonds. The individual whose income comes from municipal bonds pays no federal income tax because income from municipal bonds is exempt from federal income tax; whereas, the person whose income comes from wages might have to pay as much as $1,540 in federal income tax.

Providing for economic growth The fourth function of an economic system is *providing for economic growth.* Economic growth is defined as an increase in the potential output of the economy. In terms of the production possibilities curve, economic growth implies a shift outward of the ppc. Hence, economic growth would shift the ppc from I to II in Figure 8-4.

Economic growth has historically been considered one of the most important functions which the economic system performs. There have been two reasons for the emphasis put on economic growth. First, in a society with an expanding population it is essential that the output of the economy grow at least as fast as the population, or the per capita output, or output per individual decreases, which lowers the potential standard of living of the society. In order to raise the standard of living of a society, it is necessary for the output to increase at a more rapid rate than the population. The other reason that economic growth has been emphasized is that historically people have been subjected to poverty, and economic growth was the way to escape the repressing burden of poverty.

While economic growth still holds the potential for salvation for most of the countries of the world, many observers are questioning whether or not it is something which is good per se for the United States. There are an increasing number of people who believe that more emphasis should be put on population control and less on economic growth. The contention of this group is that a continuation of the past pattern of economic growth and an increasing population will destroy the environ-

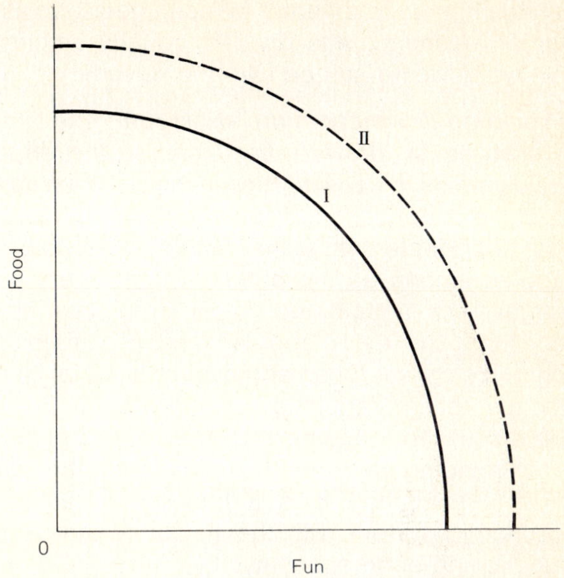

Figure 8-4 Outward shifts of the ppc reflects an increase in the potential output of the economy.

ment and that there will be a decline in the real standard of living as a result of the harmful external effects associated with unregulated economic and population growth.

A current economic issue which is directly related to the question of economic growth is the energy crisis. The energy demands associated with the growth of the United States economy (and that of the world) have expanded so rapidly that it is questionable whether or not the available supply of natural resources is adequate to meet current needs, and it is very unlikely that the supplies will be sufficient to support continued economic growth similar to past patterns. This issue will be discussed further in Chapter 9.

The current output of the United States is more than adequate to provide everyone in the country with an income well above the poverty level. In 1972, for example, the per capita output in the United States was approximately $5,500, which means that if output had been equally divided among all citizens, a family of four would have had claims to $22,000 of output. Since approximately 60 percent of the output of the United States economy consists of goods purchased by households in the marketplace for consumption, a family of four, after deduction for government (taxes) and investment in capital by business, could purchase $13,200 worth of goods and services. Thus, economic growth is not necessary to enable the United States to provide all its citizens with an income large enough to raise them above the poverty line. The situation is quite different for countries such as India. If the output of the Indian economy was divided equally among all the people of India, everyone would still be living in poverty.

Providing flexibility in the short run The final function of an economic system is to *provide flexibility in the short run,* that is, to make adjustments in consumption in the short run as dictated by the availability of the supply of goods and services. Suppose, for example, that there is a poor apple crop in the United States; how do you ration the available apples among all the potential consumers of apples? Or if there is a larger than anticipated apple crop, how do you get the people to consume the extra apples? The two major techniques used to synchronize consumption and available supply are the behavior of prices in the market and regulation by government. Both of these techniques shall be discussed in the next section.

Providing short-run flexibility is not the same type of function as the first four. Rather, it is a method or technique which provides the economic system with the flexibility that is essential to the long-run functioning of an economy.

Any evaluation of the performance of an economic system must include consideration of how all the functions are being conducted. Many people assume that the fact that the Unites States economy produces a large output is proof that it is operating efficiently. This is not necessarily so. In order to determine whether or not the economy is operating efficiently, it is necessary to determine (1) whether the bundle of goods and services is the most desirable of all potential bundles, (2) whether resources are being allocated in a way which will ensure the maximum possible production of the bundle being produced, (3) whether the pattern of distribution of the output of the economy is the most desirable pattern, and (4) whether or not the rate and pattern of economic growth are the optimum achievable. In other words, the economy is operating efficiently if and only if it performs all the functions in the best possible way. The evaluation of whether or not the economy *is* performing these functions in the best possible way involves the personal values of the individual doing the evaluating. Thus, two individuals with different sets of values would not rate the performance of the economy the same.

TYPES OF ECONOMIC SYSTEM

Economic systems are frequently classified according to the decision-making process which is involved in determining the way the basic economic functions will be performed. Economists divide economic systems into three categories: (1) subsistence or traditional, (2) market, and (3) planned.

Before discussing the types of economic systems, it is important to recognize that in all types of economies, economic decisions are influenced by the availability of the factors of production, the state of technology, and cultural factors. The availability of the factors of production determines the types of economic activities which will develop. For example, it is highly unlikely that Alaska will develop a large agricultural sector. However, many of the constraints which are imposed on an economy can be overcome through technological developments. The development of agriculture in California has been made possible by developments in technology that make it feasible to irrigate areas that were previously unsuitable for agriculture. Also, through research, varieties of crops have been developed which will grow in areas in which crops could not be grown before. Culture influences the way all the functions of the economic system are performed, and it is an especially important factor in determining the composition of output: e.g., it determines whether a company that produces headwear produces turbans, derbies, or some other type of headwear; it determines whether dogs are raised for pets or for food, etc.

Subsistence Economy A *subsistence* or *traditional* economy is one in which decisions are made by those affected by the decisions. The most commonly used example of a pure subsistence economy is Robinson Crusoe on his island. In this case the decision as to what to produce is made by Crusoe, and he decides how to best use the productive resources available to him to produce the output that he selects. He also decides how much of his resources should be devoted to producing things such as hoes, axes, etc., in order to enable him to increase the potential output in the future. Of course, there is no problem with distributing the output and adjusting consumption to the available supply, since Crusoe is the only one involved. However, the situation becomes a bit more complicated when Friday arrives on the island. The important feature of the situation is that all economic decisions are made directly by Crusoe without any type of intermediate mechanism or interference. In fact, larger self-contained economic units than that of the Crusoe example are classified as subsistence economies. It is somewhat misleading to classify an economic svstem as a subsistence economy because this seems to imply that the people are living at a subsistence level. This is not necessarily the case. The standard of living can vary greatly among subsistence economies.

Subsistence economies are characterized by the absence of economic specialization and hence trade. As economic specialization occurs within a society, it is necessary to develop techniques for economic exchange. Economic specialization causes interdependence of those participating in the economy. It also greatly increases the productivity of the economy. However, as an economy grows in size and complexity, it is necessary to develop a different technique for making economic decisions because it is no longer possible for everyone to be directly involved in making all the decisions that must be made. In fact, it is even impossible for all people to be directly involved in making the decisions that closely affect them.

Transition to money economy Back-to-nature subsistence farms and communes are currently appealing to some people in the United States. These people have rejected the life-style imposed by a modern industrial economy and seek to escape to the idyllic life-style commonly believed to be associated with a subsistence system. Consideration of the merits of one life-style over the other is beyond the scope of our discussion. It is important to note, however, that while a few people can choose to withdraw from industrial society, it is not an alternative available to everyone. If everyone attempted to withdraw to a subsistence type of existence, the result would be economic disaster for all involved. Those who advocate a return to nature for everyone are guilty of the "error of composition"; that is, they are falsely assuming that because some people have been successful in establishing a subsistence life-style, everyone could do so.

As specialization begins to develop in the economy, economic exchange is typically done through some system of *barter,* i.e., an exchange of goods or services for goods or services. However, such an exchange system can constrain the development of the economy. In response to the need for a technique to exchange economic value, *money* develops. Money is a mechanism through which economic value is exchanged. It is not productive in the sense that the factors of production are. Its primary purpose is to facilitate economic trade. In the United States we have developed a monetary system which enables an individual to exchange tightening bolts on an assembly line for hamburgers, shirts, movies, etc.

Functions of money In order for money to fulfill its primary purpose, there are four functions which it must perform. First, money serves as a *medium of exchange.* Without some commonly accepted medium of exchange for goods and services it would be necessary to rely on barter. Under a barter system it is necessary to find someone who has the thing you want and who is willing to take the thing you have to trade. However, when you have money, which is acceptable for all goods and services, it is only necessary to find someone who wants to purchase the thing you have for sale; then you can take the money and buy what you want from whomever you want. The other functions which money performs in an economy stem from the medium of exchange function. Money also serves as a *measure of value*; i.e., it is a unit of measure which is used to express the economic value of all the different goods and services which the economy produces. The use of money as a measure of value provides a standardized unit which makes it easy to compare the value of very diverse goods and services and to negotiate the terms of the exchange agreement. By comparison, suppose that the unit used to measure value was a horse. Is there such a thing as a standarized horse? The third function which money performs is being a *store of economic value*. Money is one of the alternative ways in which one can hold his wealth. Money also makes it easy for the individual to store the value of labor, which is important in an economy in which many products are produced by many individuals in multistage production processes and which produce a large quantity of services which involve no physical product. Finally, money serves as a *standard of deferred payment*. If you purchase a car on credit, the payment of the car is designated in terms of dollars, not in terms of some equivalent market value.

The effect of the monetary mechanism on the economy constitutes a large part of the subject matter of economics. Economists are interested in explaining the relationship between the operation of the real economy, i.e., that part which involves goods and services, and the monetary system. An inefficient monetary system can hamper the development and operation of the economy. In the United States we have developed a monetary system that has enabled us to overcome most of the constraints associated with a monetary system. In fact, we find that the efficiency of the operation of the real economy can be improved by manipulating the monetary system. Thus, it is possible for a highly developed monetary system to act as a stimulus to the operation of the real economy rather than a constraint. Of course, this assumes that once you have developed your monetary system, it will be properly managed.

Market economy One type of economy that has developed in response to the need for a decision-making process in a complex economy is the *market* economy. In the market economy economic decisions are made through the price mechanism. The price mechanism is the interaction of producers and consumers in the marketplace. In this type of decision-making process, all those who participate in the marketplace are involved in determining the way in which the basic economic functions will be carried out.

The market economy is not democratic in the sense that each person has an equal say in economic decisions. The influence an individual has on the operation of a market economy is determined by the amount of resources that that individual controls and the value of these resources to the operation of the economy. An individual who controls resources worth $100,000 a year will have a greater influence on the composition of output than the individual who controls resources worth $5,000. It is somewhat ironic that those who idealize a democratic political system because of the equality associated with it also idealize a market economic system which is almost certain to contain great economic inequality.

In the market economy the prices determined by the interaction of producers and consumers in the market provide the information and incentive necessary to keep the economy functioning. Adam Smith, in the eighteenth century, referred to the seemingly unguided operation of the market economy as being controlled by an "invisible hand." This invisible hand was prices.

There is a separate market for every good or service traded in the market economy. A market is defined as the geographical area within which buyers and sellers negotiate the exchange of a well-defined good or service. Thus, a market economy is a system of markets which interact; and it is through this interaction that the decisions related to the basic economic functions are made.

Within the system of markets in the market economy, individuals can sell their labor and use the income so acquired to purchase the things that they want. Of course, the amount of goods and services that they can purchase is limited by the amount of income that they receive from the sale of their labor. The value (price) of different labor services is determined by negotiations which take place in the market. The same is true for the prices of both goods and services available for consumption and the other factors of production, i.e., capital and natural resources. In an economy where capital and natural resources are privately owned, the owners of these factors of production have an additional income from their sale to go along with the income they receive from the sale of their own labor to use to purchase goods and services. It is important to recognize that the type of result which is achieved in the market economy is determined in large part by the way the market is organized and the starting point of the participants in the market; e.g., the more resources an individual entering a market controls, the more advantageous that individual's bargaining position. Economists have developed several models to describe the existing organization of markets in a market economy. However, the only type of market in which the operation of the price mechanism ensures efficient performance of the economy is one in which there is pure competition. There are four basic characteristics associated with a market operating under pure competition. First, there are many buyers and sellers in the market. No single buyer or seller is large enough to have significant influence on the way the market operates. The good or service which is traded in the market is standarized. This means that the product of all the sellers in the market is the same. Under pure competition all buyers and sellers in the market have all the relevant information they need to participate on an equal basis in the market. Finally, there must be easy entry into and exit from the market. This means that anyone who wants to is free to enter the market to buy or sell at any time, or to leave the market at any time.

Planned economy The other type of decision-making process that has developed in complex economies is the *planned* economy. In a planned economy the decisions as to the composition of output, distribution of income, etc., are made by some central planning agency and passed down to those responsible for carrying out the decisions. The techniques used by the central planners in a planned economy to ensure implementation of their decisions is dependent in large part on cultural influences and other organizational aspects of the society outside the economy. Different techniques would probably be used in a society with a totalitarian political system than in a society with a democratic political system. The key factor to note about the planned economy is that the people are not involved in making the basic economic decisions unless the central planning agency is responsive to the desires of the people. Thus, the danger inherent in the planned economy is that the way the economy performs the basic economic functions may be a reflection of the preferences of the planning agency rather than a reflection of the preferences of the people.

In a planned economy it is also necessary to develop a system of markets in which economic exchange can take place as the economy develops. In a planned economy the size of the individual markets and the types of activity that transpire in each is determined by a central planning body. The terms of the trade that result in an economic market are also determined by the central planning body. Hence, in a planned economy the results obtained are not determined by the operation of the markets but rather by the preferences of the planners. However, the operation of the markets is an important factor which influences the extent to which the decisions of the central planners are implemented.

Mixed economies The three types of economies discussed are pure types of economies, and in actual practice there are few if any pure types of economies in existence. These pure types are classification models which enable us to analyze the decision-making process in the existing economies. Most economies are mixed economies, i.e., some combination of at least two of the pure types of decision making is found in a single economy. Economies are frequently classified according to the type of economic decision making which dominates. The United States economy is usually classified as a market economy, and the economy of the Soviet Union is classifed as a planned economy.

It is usually assumed in the United States that the market economy treats all individuals fairly. In order for a market economy to be "fair" to all individuals, it is essential that everyone have equal access to the markets and that all people who have similar skills and/or products to sell in the market to be treated equally. One of the most valid criticisms of the operation of the system of markets in the market part of the United States economy is that not all individuals are treated equally. For example, women and some racial minorities do not receive as high a price for their labor as do white males with similar skills.

It is frequently assumed in the United States that even though there is discrimination and prejudice in aspects of society other than the economy, somehow the economy will provide individuals with an opportunity to overcome this discrimination and prejudice. Generally, the operation of the United States economy reflects the patterns of discrimination and prejudice which permeate the rest of society. There is a tendency for people to point to a woman or a member of a minority group who has succeeded within the existing system and to accept this as proof that the economy does not discriminate. The success of individuals does not prove that the system does not discriminate against some group of which they are members. It is frequently an indication that these individuals were able to overcome the discrimination and succeed in spite of the system.

In the industrial countries of the world the characteristics that are associated with a subsistence economy are almost nonexistent. Many of the economically less developed countries still have large subsistence sectors in their economies.

However, since most industrial economies have small subsistence sectors, it is possible to describe the economic decision-making process in these countries as some combination of market and planned. This can be done by locating the countries on a continuum with a pure planned economy on one end and a pure market economy on the other end. Figure 8-5 is such a continuum. Some countries have been selected and placed on the continuum.

In the United States, the government sector represents the planned part of the economy and the private sector the market part. The planned sector directly accounts for approximately 25 percent of the output of the United States economy. However, this percent does not accurately reflect the relative role of government in the United States economy. The

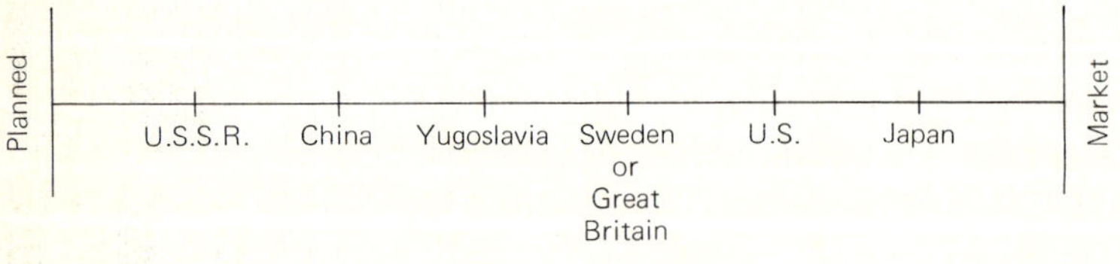

Figure 8-5 Classification of economic systems.

relationship between the public and private sectors of the United States economy is the topic of the next chapter.

UNITED STATES AND THE U.S.S.R.: SOME COMPARISONS

Most of the basic economic decisions in the United States are made through interaction in the marketplace, and in the U.S.S.R. most of them are made through a central planning agency. However, the difference is not as clear-cut as is often assumed.

Of the potential bundles of goods and services which the U.S.S.R. is capable of producing, the government planners select the one which is to be produced. In the United States the decision as to the composition of output is a joint decision involving both the public and private sectors. The percent of the output which consists of military, education, highways, etc., is determined by the government units which exist in the United States. The composition of the goods and services produced in the private sector of the United States is determined through operation of markets. However, the operation of many of these markets is regulated by government.

Resource allocation is quite different in the two economies. In the United States all the productive resources are allocated through the operation of the markets. With a few exceptions such as the military's drafting of men, the government competes with business in the marketplace in order to get the government output produced. There is a major difference in the government sector in the United States as compared to the U.S.S.R. In the United States the government does not have its own production facilities, but rather contracts with privately owned businesses to produce a large part of the goods and services that constitute the government sector. For example, the government does not have construction companies which build highways, so it relies on contracts with private companies to get highways built. The same thing applies to the military goods which government purchases. Also, since the government is democratically elected in the United States and not in the U.S.S.R., the method of selecting the economic decision makers is different.

There are many advantages to the type of arrangement developed in the United States, but there is a danger inherent in this type of arrangement that must be avoided. The military-industrial complex represents an example of this danger. The military-industrial complex is a coalition of the military leaders of the United States and the leaders of the businesses that supply the military for the purpose of influencing the decisions as to the mix of goods and services that our economy should produce. In 1972 the expenditures on military and related items accounted for about 6.8 percent of the output of the United States economy. There is an ever-present danger that because of the influence exerted by the military-industrial complex we will use more of our resources for military purposes than we really need to in order to ensure our national defense. This situation can occur as a result of the military's desire for increased power and prestige. The military leaders receive support from the industrial leaders that supply the military with goods and services because an expansion of the military represents increased profits, power, and prestige for the industrial leaders as well as for the military. This is a much more serious problem today than in the past because of a growing tendency for the businesses that supply the military with goods and services to recruit their leaders from the ranks of ex-military leaders. In 1970, the 100 largest defense contractors employed more than 2,000 retired generals, colonels, navy admirals, and captains. Their numbers tripled between 1960 and 1970. Hence, "civilian" businesses are apt to be even more sympathetic to the desires of the military. The problem that is associated with the military-industrial complex is potentially present in all situations in which private businesses are supplying government with goods and services. If we are to continue to operate the planned sector of the United States economy as in the past, it will be necessary to constantly be on guard against coalitions of those in government and those in the private sector who are supplying government for the purpose of exerting undue influence on those responsible for decision making in the planned sector.

The distribution of output is determined primarily by the government planners in the U.S.S.R., whereas in the United States it is influenced by both the government and the market mechanism. In the U.S.S.R. the income of the individual is determined by the wage that he receives from his labor. Since capital and natural resources are not privately owned, the people cannot receive an income as a result of their ownership. The exception to this that is frequently pointed to is the system whereby farm families are allowed to rent small plots of land for private use. These are usually from 1/2 to 2 acres in size. The farmers are permitted to sell what they produce on these small plots, and all the income they receive is theirs. In the United States an individual's income is determined by the amount received from the sale of the labor plus the amount received as a return on capital and/or natural resources owned. Government influences the distribution of income in the United States through the manipulation of the tax system, including both taxes collected and money returned to some people through subsidies, and through regulation of the economy. A major change which is likely to be made in the tax system in the near future is the inclusion of a guaranteed annual income. This would ensure everyone in the United States some minimum share of the output of the economy.

Something that is often misunderstood about the U.S.S.R. is the process by which workers select jobs[3]. Workers in the U.S.S.R. are free to choose the type and location of the job that they like just as in the United States. They are also free to decide how hard they work. The planners use money wages and fringe benefits as incentives to get workers to do what the planners want them to do. Thus, the motives and system of incentives that exist in the U.S.S.R. are basically the same as in the United States. The major difference is that the incentive system in the U.S.S.R. is designed to achieve an outcome which represents the preferences of the planners, and in the United States the incentive system is supposed to operate in such a way that the outcome achieved represents the preferences of the people. The Soviet planners have found that it is much easier to manipulate the people by manipulating the incentive system than by attempting to control them directly. As a corollary to the freedom in job selection, Soviet consumers are free to purchase whatever they want to with the income they earn. However, the government planners are the ones who determine the types of choices the consumers have in spending their income when they decide the composition of output.

Historically, economic growth has been considered one of the most important functions which the economy performs. Both the United States and the U.S.S.R. have had excellent success in achieving economic growth. In the U.S.S.R. the economic planners have devoted much of their effort and resources toward ensuring growth. This has been achieved by devoting a large part of their resources to the production of capital and to research which has led to improvement in technology. Both of these are key elements in economic growth. In the United States the government has played an important role in our successful economic growth. This has been done primarily by providing incentives to private businesses through tax benefits and subsidies in order to ensure that they do the types of things necessary to achieve economic growth. For example, the government provided large grants of land to the railroads in order to get them to develop our railroad system in the nineteenth century, and in 1967 the government directly financed $14.1 billion of the $23.7 billion spent on research and development in the United States. Also, there are special provisions in our tax structure which encourage private businesses to invest in capital. In fact, the Employment Act of 1946 officially made the federal government responsible for ensuring a satisfactory rate of employment and a satisfactory rate of economic growth. In both the United States and U.S.S.R. the government finances the educational system, which ensures that the economy will have a productive labor force. This is essential if a country is to have a successful program of economic growth.

A problem inherent in government's use of grants and subsidies to control the economy, as in the United States, is that there are limitless possibilities for corruption and abuse. This makes it necessary to continually scrutinize the administration of the numerous programs developed and the effects associated with them.

The major technique for handling shortages and surpluses in the short run in both the United States and the U.S.S.R. is prices. The prices of goods and services fluctuate in order to adjust the quantity which is demanded to the available supply. However, the fluctuation in prices in the U.S.S.R. is in response to actions of the planners, whereas in the United States the fluctuation is in response to forces in the marketplace. Direct rationing of goods and services has been used in both countries in emergency situations. The notable example in the United States was during World War II. The United States is currently attempting to determine how to handle the rationing problem associated with the energy crisis. Presently, a combination of allowing prices to rise and direct controls is being utilized in an effort to gain an optimal allocation of energy. As of the writing of this book, the government is in the process of deciding whether or not direct rationing should be used to allocate gasoline among consumers. The allocation problems associated with the energy crisis will be explored in Chapter 9.

Direct rationing programs tend to be unpopular and difficult to enforce, and so their use is restricted to emergency situations. They frequently lead to the development of black markets and present other problems of enforcement which tend to undermine the program and the authority of those in charge of administering the program. Thus, the Soviet planners have found it more effective to set the prices of goods and services so high that people are priced out of the market than to tell them that they can not purchase certain goods and/or services or that they can only purchase them in limited quantities. In this way they have been able to avoid the administrative problems associated with direct rationing.

In conclusion, it is not surprising that many people from the United States are astonished when they visit the U.S.S.R. to find that they can see very little difference between the daily operation of the Soviet economy and that of the United States or other Western nations. The workers in the Soviet Union seek employment in much the same manner as those in the United States, they receive wages from their jobs and spend the income received in stores located in shopping areas. The difference between the two lies in the invisible decision-making process which guides the operation of the economies and determines how the two economies shall perform the basic economic functions. Also, it is important to note that the most important difference between the United States and the U.S.S.R. is the difference in political freedom, not in economics, and the difference in political freedom is not immediately visible to the casual visitor.

PROBLEMS ASSOCIATED WITH CLASSIFYING ECONOMIES

When an economic system is classified as one type or another, people sometimes make certain assumptions about the general social organization of the society. For example, it is often assumed that a country that has a planned economy must have some type of totalitarian political system. This is not necessarily the case. It is possible to have a planned economy and a democratic political system. The confusion results in large part from a failure to realize that there are alternative ways that a society can develop to perform the various functions that need to be performed. The confusion is complicated because the systems developed by society to perform different functions frequently overlap, as is illustrated in Figure 8-6. For example, the decision as to the amount of productive resources that are to be devoted to the provision of military protection involves both political and economic considerations. In order to clearly understand the functioning of any particular system in a society's social organization, it is imperative to recognize its uniqueness, and at the same time to allow for the effects which result from its interaction with other systems.

There is a serious danger that people will start identifying "good" with one type of economic system and "evil" with another, and thereby lose the objectivity needed to evaluate the performance of any particular system. For example, many people are reluctant to undertake measures necessary to solve many of our social problems because they fear that these measures will somehow alter our economic system, which they consider good per se. The problem is even worse in some situations because there are some people who believe that the survival of our political system is dependent on the preservation of our economic system in its current form. It is quite possible that just the opposite is true; i.e., unless the functioning of our economic system is modified to solve some of our social problems, our economic system and political system may both fail to survive.

The provision of adequate medical care for everyone is an example of a situation which illustrates how the equating of certain types of activities with stereotyped political and economic systems has prevented many people from receiving a much-needed service. The mention of

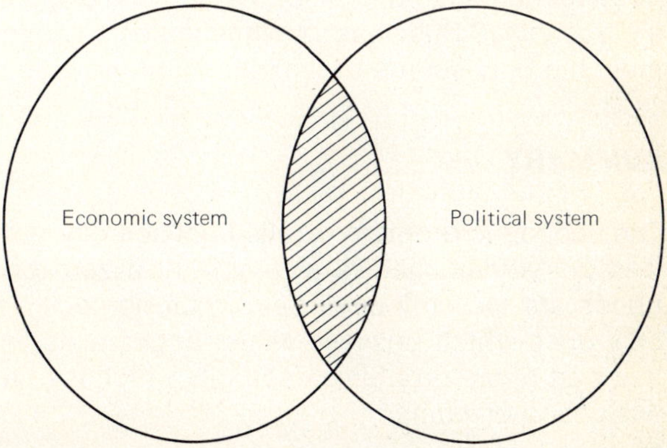

Figure 8-6 Overlap of social systems.

free medical care for those who cannot afford the current cost of such care usually evokes outcries of "socialism." This very thought is enough to convince most people that the idea of free medical care is bad. Thus, many people who might otherwise support programs to provide free medical care to those who cannot afford it back off because they do not want to destroy our economic and poltical systems.

THE RISE OF THE PLANNED SECTOR AND FREEDOM

The planned sector in the United States has greatly increased in size during the twentieth century. It has grown from approximately 2 percent at the beginning of the century to nearly 22 percent in 1972. This means that 22 percent of all the goods and services in the United States were produced by government. These goods and services included such things as education, the court system, highways, the military, and public recreational facilities. However, there are some people in the United States who view the increased participation of government in the economy as bad per se, and they contend that this participation has lessened individual freedom.

It is very debatable that the government's increased involvement in the economy has been associated with a decline in personal freedom. A strong argument can be made that the increased involvment of government in the economy has in fact increased individual freedom. In order to resolve this issue it would be necessary to select the time period in the past when there was supposedly more individual freedom and compare this time period with today. This would in turn entail defining individual freedom and establishing some system to measure it. This issue of the effect of increased participation of government in the economy on individual freedom is beyond the scope of this chapter. However, there are some questions that would have to be answered. To what extent is government's involvement in the economy to protect the freedom of the consumer equated with the restriction of individual freedom? Whose freedom has been diminished as a result of government's involvement in the economy? Business's? White males'? Women's? Blacks'? Is government the only source of limitations on individual freedom?

SUMMARY

The economic problem results from scarcity. An item is scarce if more of it is demanded than is available at a zero price. Although economic goods are the only ones people are forced to pay for, they are not the only ones which possess value. Economists typically do not deal with that part of the problem of scarcity which is related to the formation and evaluation of wants.

Economics is the study of how people through their institutions utilize the scarce resources of labor, capital, and natural resources to satisfy their material needs. Labor is the human input in the production process, and natural resources are those elements that exist in the state of nature which are used in production. Technology determines which natural elements can be used to produce goods and services.

The economic system is made up of all those variables which interact to perform the economic functions. The five basic economic functions are: (1) determining the composition of output, (2) allocating productive resources, (3) distributing the output, (4) providing for economic growth, and (5) providing flexibility in the short run. The economic system interacts with the other systems which constitute the social order. The organization and operation of the economic system influences the other systems which are a part of the social order and is influenced by their organization and operation.

Economists frequently classify economies as subsistence, market, or planned. The source of the decision making required to perform the five basic functions serves as the basis of this classification system. In all economies decisions are influenced by the availability of the factors of production, the state of technology, and cultural factors. In the subsistence economy those who are affected by the economic decisions are directly involved in making them. In a market economy the economic decisions related to the five basic economic functions are made through the interaction of buyers and sellers in the market. The decisions are made by a central planning agency in a planned economy. The three types of economies used in the above classification system are pure types. In the real world most economies are mixed economies, i.e., some combination of at least two of the pure types. In the industrial countries of the world the characteristics that are associated with the subsistence economy are nearly nonexistent.

As economies develop, it is necessary to develop a technique to exchange economic value. Money is the mechanism which usually develops to fill this need. Money is not productive in the sense that the factors of production are. Its primary purpose is to facilitate economic trade. Money must perform four functions if it is to fulfill its primary purpose. It must be a: (1) medium of exchange, (2) measure of value, (3) store of economic value, and (4) standard of deferred payment.

A comparison of the economies of the United States and U.S.S.R. reveals that people living in the two systems seem to function in much the same manner. The major difference between the two economies lies in the invisible decision-making process which determines how the basic economic functions shall be carried out.

There is frequently confusion associated with the classification of economic systems because the economic system overlaps with other systems which make up the social order, particularly with the political system. It is important to realize that one type of economic system does not necessarily imply a particular political system and vice versa.

The increase in the planned economic sector has been associated with a decline in personal freedom by many people in the United States. To determine whether or not this is true, it is necessary to define personal freedom and select a past period for comparison. It is also necessary to decide whose freedom we are talking about.

REVIEW QUESTIONS

1. What is the economic problem?
2. What determines whether or not a good is scarce?
3. Why has the treatment of "wants" by economists been criticized? Do you think it is valid to accept wants as given without considering their source? Why?
4. What are the factors of production? Define each.
5. What is an economic system?
6. What are the five functions of an economic system? Explain each. Evaluate the way the United States economy is performing each function.
7. What is a production possibilities curve?
8. Define opportunity cost and economic efficiency verbally and in terms of the production possibilities curve.
9. What are two factors which cause improper allocation of resources in the United States? Discuss each. Do you agree with the author's implicit assumption that the economic system is controlled by white males? Discuss.
10. Discuss the factors which influence the way goods and services are distributed in the United States.
11. Why is economic growth sometimes viewed differently in the United States than in the less-developed countries of the world? Should the United States continue to emphasize economic growth as a major economic goal? Why?
12. What factors should be considered when evaluating the performance of an economic system?
13. Discuss the three factors which influence economic decisions in all types of economies.
14. What are the three pure types of economies? Describe the way economic decisions are made in each.
15. What is a mixed economy?
16. What causes an economy to develop a monetary system?
17. List and briefly describe the four functions which money performs in an economy.
18. What are the characteristics of an economic market which operates under conditions of pure competition?

19. Are the markets in the United States "fair"? Explain.
20. Compare and discuss the United States and the U.S.S.R. on the basis of each of the following:
    a. Selection of the bundle of goods and services to produce
    b. Allocation of productive resources
    c. The government sector
    d. Distribution of output
    e. Ownership of capital and natural resources
    f. Selection of an occupation
    g. Economic growth
    h. Dealing with shortages and surpluses
    i. Role of prices
21. Discuss some of the potential problems associated with classifying economies.
22. Does it seem more rational to guarantee individuals political freedom than to guarantee them some degree of freedom from economic want? Discuss.
23. Has the growth of the planned sector in the United States tended to restrict individual freedom? Discuss.

CHAPTER NINE
THE UNITED STATES ECONOMY

IDEAS AND CONCEPTS

capital
facilities of a nation which produce consumer goods and services

consumer units
the families and individuals living by themselves in the United States

profit
the remainder from revenues after deduction of all expenses

stocks
negotiable securities representing part ownership of a corporation which the business distributes for fund-raising

tax
a monetary charge levied on people or property for the public good

For purposes of analysis, the domestic part of the American economy is frequently broken down into three sectors—the household, the firm, and the government. This classification is based on the type of activity performed by each sector. The household is the classification given to consuming units in the United States; firms perform the function of production in the United States economy; and government is involved in both consumption and production, as well as performing a supervisory function.

HOUSEHOLDS

Consumer units are the families and individuals living by themselves in the United States. There are over 53 million households and over 13.5 million individuals living alone. (The people living alone are persons fourteen years of age and over who are not living with any relatives. This does not include inmates of institutions.) Ultimately, the goal of all economic activity should be to serve these consuming units.

The output of the United States economy is not equally divided among the households. Table 9-1 shows the distribution of incomes among families in the United States in 1971.* It shows that a large percentage of the people in the United States were living in poverty in 1971 and still are, no matter how poverty is defined. The major difficulties involved in defining poverty are distinguishing between absolute and relative poverty and the changing purchasing power of the

TABLE 9-1 DISTRIBUTION OF INCOME AMONG FAMILIES IN THE UNITED STATES, 1971

Part A		Part B	
Income level by family	Percent of families in category	Family units	Percent of all aggregate income
Less than $3,000	8.3	Lowest fifth	5.5
$3,000–$4,999	10.2	Second fifth	11.9
$5,000–$6,999	11.2	Middle fifth	17.4
$7,000–$9,999	18.5	Fourth fifth	23.7
$10,000–$14,999	26.9	Highest fifth	41.6
$15,000 and over	24.8		

Source: *Statistical Abstract of the United States,* U.S. Government Printing Office, Washington, D.C., 1973.

* Part A of Table 9-1 shows the absolute and Part B the relative distribution of income among families in the United States.

dollar income of families. Absolute poverty refers to a family's ability to secure the basic necessities, whereas relative poverty is a comparative state in which a family is poor not because it is unable to purchase the essentials, but because it is not able to purchase as much as other families.

The households also supply the labor force. All the people in the population who are sixteen and over constitute the potential labor force. In 1970, out of a total United States population of 204.8 million, 85.9 million were in the labor force. When we subtract those who were in the military, we find that the civilian labor force was 82.7 million. In order to be considered a member of the labor force, a person must be employed in the market at least fifteen hours a week or be actively seeking work. This means that people engaged in incidental unpaid family work, those who engage exclusively in housework in their own homes, and those who are attending school are not considered members of the labor force.

FIRMS

Firms are classified according to the way they are legally organized. There are three basic types of firms in the United States: the *proprietorship,* the *partnership,* and the *corporation.*

Proprietorships Approximately 78 percent of the firms in the United States are proprietorships. Nearly one-third of these are farms. A proprietorship is the type of business in which the individual who owns the business supplies the resources to get the business started and to keep it functioning. The individual is legally responsible for the liabilities of the business. This means that anyone who has a claim against a proprietorship can force the owner of the business to use his personal wealth to settle the claim. Suppose, for example, that the proprietorship is a farm, and the farmer has purchased fertilizer on credit and has accumulated total liabilities greater than his or her assests. In this case, the person who has sold the farmer fertilizer on credit can lay claim to the farmer's personal property (such as house or car) to settle the debt. The corner drugstore that is owned and operated by the same person is another example of the proprietorship.

Partnerships The partnership is a type of firm much like the proprietorship, the major difference being that in the case of the partnership, two or more individuals jointly provide the resources necessary to start the business and keep it operating. The liability of the different owners of a partnership is determined by the nature of the partnership agreement. The types of agreement which can be drawn up vary from one state to another, but usually there is unlimited liability associated with a partnership. A common type of partnership is one with unlimited liability in which the division of this liability among the different partners is determined by the share of ownership. Another common type of partnership agreement is one in which one of the partners has unlimited liability for claims against the business, while all the other partners have limited amounts of liability as specified in the partnership agreement. In some states it is legal to draw up partnership agreements which limit the extent of the liability of all the partners, although most partnerships in the United States have some form of unlimited liability associated with them. In terms of numbers, partnerships are the least common type of business organization, representing only about 8 percent of the total firms in the United States in 1970.

Corporations The third type of firm is the corporation. While only about 14 percent of the firms in the United States are corporations, the corporate form of business organization is the dominant one. The reason can be seen from Table 9-2.

As can be seen from Table 9-2, 14 percent of the firms in the United States accounted for 84 percent of the business receipts in 1967. The concentration is even greater than these figures would indicate, however, because in 1970 less than half of the corporations accounted for most of the output of corporations.

Based on the figures in Table 9-2, the United States economy can be represented as an economy of small producers or an economy dominated by giant firms. A person who is trying to convince someone that the United States is the land of small businesses will probably point to the large number of proprietorships in the United States. On the other hand, someone who is describing the United States economy as one dominated by large firms will probably point to the fact that a relatively small number of firms account for most of the output. Both arguments have relevant points to make, and any accurate description of the United States economy should include both points. Policy measures that affect the businesses of the United States may have a different impact on the

TABLE 9-2 BUSINESSES (1970)

Types	Number	Percent of total	Percent of total business receipts
Proprietorships	9,400,000	78	11
Partnerships	936,000	8	5
Corporations	1,665,000	14	84
Totals	12,001,000	100	100

Source: *Statistical Abstract of the United States*, U.S. Government Printing Office, Washington, D.C., 1973.

Large-scale economic enterprises dominate the modern industrial society, but single proprietorships and partnerships remain the backbone of our free, competitive system. *((a) Exxon, (b) George W. Gardner)*

large firms than on the small ones, however, and economic policymakers should realize this. One should also be aware of the implications of having firms of differing sizes involved in the same economy.

Advantages of the corporation The growth of the importance of the corporation in the American economy can be traced to four advantages that are associated with this type of organization. The most important of these is that *the owners of a corporation have limited liability* as compared to the owners of a proprietorship and a partnership. The owners of a corporation can never lose more than the amount they put into the business. If a corporation goes broke and it has liabilities which it cannot meet, the creditors of the corporation cannot force the owners of the corporation to pay the debts out of their personal wealth or income. In the case of the partnership and proprietorship, however, all financial resources that the owners possess can be demanded to meet the obligations of the business.

A second advantage that the corporation has is its greater access to financial resources. The corporation can raise funds by selling stocks and bonds as well as by borrowing from financial institutions. Partnerships and proprietorships cannot sell stocks or bonds.

A third advantage of the corporation is that it has perpetuity of existence. If the owners of the corporation die or are disabled, the corporation continues to operate without the kind of disruption that is often associated with the death or disability of the owners of partnerships and proprietorships.

The fourth advantage of the corporation is that its stocks and bonds can easily be transferred from one person to another. This makes it possible for the individual owners of a corporation to sell their ownership without any disruption of the operation of the business. It also makes people willing to purchase shares that they would not otherwise be willing to purchase, since they can easily convert their wealth from stocks back to money.

Disadvantages of the corporation From the business point of view, there is only one major disadvantage connected with the corporation. The disadvantage results from the way the United States tax structure is designed. The corporation has to pay a tax on the profits that it makes before it pays anything to its owners, the stockholders. Then, when the stockholders receive dividends on their stocks, they have to pay personal income tax on this income. Thus, since the money paid to stockholders comes from the profits that the corporation earns, corporation profits are taxed twice—first when the corporation earns profits, and again when the corporation pays the profits left after corporate profit taxes to the owners of the corporation as dividends. Corporations are able to compensate for this in part by including corporate profit taxes as a cost of doing business, and they pass part of the cost on to those who purchase their product as a part of the price of the product. But this means that those who purchase the product end up paying part of the corporate tax in the form of higher prices. There is disagreement economists as to how much the corporation has to pay out of real profits. The experts in this field take quite opposite views.

For the economy and society in general, there are three disadvantages associated with the development of the large corporation in the United States. One of these is that *many corporations engage in nonbusiness activities,* such as supporting particular political candidates. A corporation is a legal entity that is created for the purpose of carrying out business activities. When it engages in nonbusiness activities, it is stepping beyond the scope of activities that it was created to conduct. A second disadvantage is that *the growth of giant corporations has led to a breakdown in the forces in the market economy that operate to ensure consumer choice.* That is, the development of giant corporations impedes the proper functioning of the price mechanism. The third problem associated with the giant corporation is *the development of irresponsibile, self-perpetuating management.* Because the ownership of the shares of most large corporations is so widespread, their stockholders frequently have little or no say in the selection of management. Thus, management is not responsible to the owners of the company. In fact, most people who purchase stocks today have no interest in *who* operates the business or *how* the business is operated, so long as the business is a success. Under most circumstances, dissatisfied stockholders sell their stock because they know that their chances of influencing the operation of the business are almost zero. It would probably be as easy for a dissatisfied citizen to get an appointment with the governor of the state as it would be for a dissatisfied stockholder of General Motors to get an appointment with the president of the corporation. There are various groups in the United States today who are attempting to make the management of large corporations more responsive to the stockholders and the public, but it is still too early to assess the impact of such efforts.

Franchises Franchises are variant forms of business organization which are important elements in the organization of the production sector of the United States economy. A person who wishes to understand the functioning of the production sector of our economy must consider it. *The franchise is a type of business in which an individual operates a business under the name of some larger company.* Most franchises are retail businesses. McDonald's, Kentucky Fried Chicken, and various service stations such as Shell are examples of franchise businesses. The reader should not confuse franchise businesses with stores such as Penney and Sears. In the franchise, the business is owned by the person who has the franchise. (Legally, this ownership can be in the form of a proprietorship, a partnership, or a corporation. Most franchise businesses are proprietorships.) In the case of nationwide stores such as Sears, however, the individual stores are owned by the national corporation, and the corporation selects people to manage its individual stores. The owner of the individual franchise business usually pays the national corporation for the privilege of being a part of the national or regional franchise network. The corporation that starts a franchise network frequently owns the physical facilities that the individual franchise business uses, and there is usually some type of formal or informal agreement to the effect that the corporation which started the franchise network will supply certain of the products that the franchise business sells. *The importance of the franchise relationship is that many of the activities that are associated with starting and operating a business are performed by the company that starts the franchise network rather than by the owner who operates the individual franchise business.* Examples are the location of the physical facilities and type of physical facilities to be used.

What we have been saying about franchises are generalizations, and it is possible to find exceptions, since there is no single organizational pattern that describes all franchises. The important thing, however, is to recognize that the influence of the corporations which start franchises extends into the operation of the individual proprietorships, partnerships, or corporations that operate the individual franchise units.

GOVERNMENT

The government sector consists of the activities carried on by government at all levels—federal, state, and local. The government sector of the economy has increased from approximately 2 percent in 1900 to about 22 percent in 1972.

Most of the activities of government in the United States economy fall into one of six categories. One of the major functions of government is that of "police officer." This involves national defense and maintenance of domestic conditions that make it possible for the United States economy to function smoothly. Second, the government provides such things as highways, education, etc. The third function performed by government is that of "regulator of the private economy." The regulation of the private sector is supposed to protect the consumer and ensure efficiency in the operation of the private sector. Examples of this are the functioning of the Pure Food and Drug Administration and the Truth-in-Lending law that went into effect in July 1969. Sometimes the regulated industries are able to get their friends on the regulatory commissions, and the regulated become the regulators. A fourth task of government is the "administration of the public domain." This involves the administration of all the wealth that is owned by the people of the United States collectively. It includes such things as public lands, public airways, rivers, and the oceans that surround much of the United States. Fifth, the federal government also has the responsibility to "insure a satisfactory rate of employment and a satisfactory rate of growth." This became an official responsibility of the federal government with passage of the Employment Act of 1946. The final function that government performs is that of "redistribution of income." This function is carried out primarily through the tax structure and various welfare and subsidy payments. Many groups, such as farmers, do not regard the subsidy payments they receive as a redistribution of income; nevertheless, they are. There is mounting pressure for the government to accept increased responsibility for correcting the inequities in the distribution of income created by the functioning of the United States economy.

FLOW OF ECONOMIC ACTIVITY

In reality there are two economic flows in the United States economy. One is a financial flow, that is, a monetary flow, and the other is a flow of goods and services. The flow of goods and services is often called the "real" flow by economists. In economic models, the monetary variables are called financial variables and the variables representing goods and services are called real variables. Frequently, confusion results from a failure to distinguish between these two types of variables. For example, all too often people think of the activity in the stock market as representing the behavior of the real variables within the economy. This may or may not be true. A decline in the value of stocks in the market does not necessarily mean that the value of any real variables has changed, that is, that firms have changed the rate at which they are producing goods and services. It may not even mean that the potential value of the real variables has changed.

Figure 9-1 is a very simplified representation of the flow of economic activity between households and firms in the United States. The inner flow in the diagram represents the flow of real economic activity, and the outer flow represents the flow of financial activity. The government sector is missing from Figure 9-1. Government can be introduced into any of the four parts of the flows. Government makes withdrawals from both monetary flows via taxation. There are various income taxes on the payments to the factors of production, and there are excise and sales taxes associated with payment for goods and services. The government uses these withdrawals to purchase goods and ser-

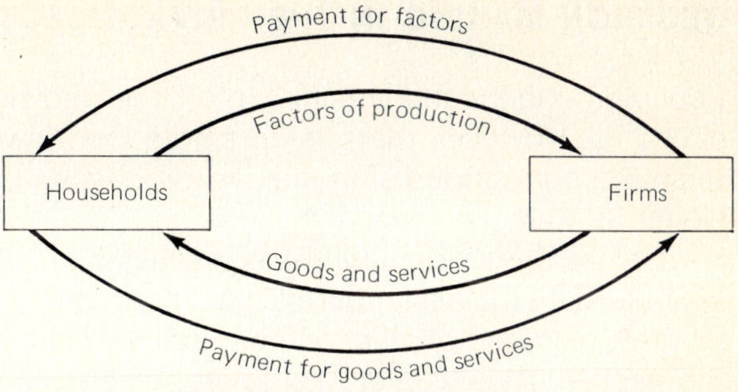

Figure 9-1 Flow of activity in an economy without a government sector.

vices, most of which are then given to households and/or firms without a charge, or perhaps for a nominal charge. Keep in mind that these goods and services are being paid for with withdrawals from the monetary flows. In terms of the flow of real economic activity, the government uses the purchasing power it has gained through taxation to purchase factors of production, and then it uses these to produce goods and services which flow to households and/or firms, such as education and highways. Thus, the decision as to which goods and services shall be produced is made by government, whether the government produces them directly or indirectly through private firms. The government also makes financial transfer payments to households and firms. Social security payments to households are an example of a transfer payment to households, and subsidies paid to farmers are an example of a transfer payment to businesses. Figure 9-2 shows the flow of economic activity in the United States with government introduced into the flow.

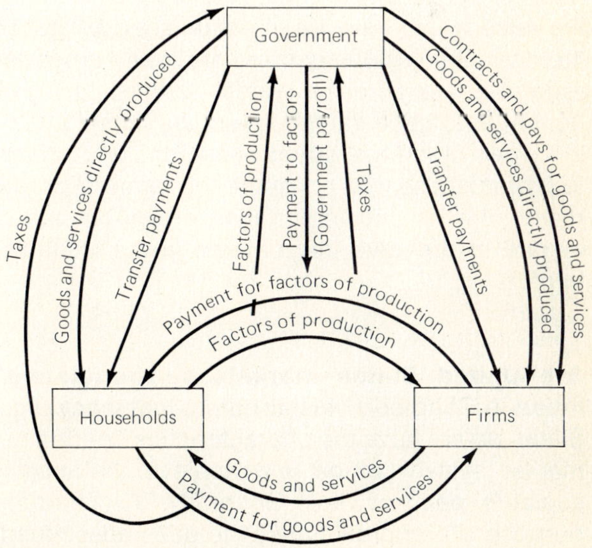

Figure 9-2 Flow of activity in an economy with a government sector. Government also receives income from a tax on the stock of wealth held directly by the households and on wealth held indirectly by households by virtue of their ownership of the firms. Also, households and firms sometimes pay directly for some of the goods and services they receive. This payment is frequently less than the cost of supplying the goods and/or services.

DECISION MAKING IN THE PRIVATE SECTOR

Economic theory attempts to explain the decision-making process in an economy. However, there is no single theory which can adequately explain the current decision-making process in the mixed economy of the United States.

Before proceeding with the discussion, it would probably be worthwhile to state the assumptions that underlie it. First, it is assumed that the ultimate purpose of all economic activity is to improve the well-being of the people. Thus, it is crucial to organize the economic activity in a way which will achieve this end. The second assumption is that the existing economy is something that has evolved over time and that it probably has not reached a stage that we should attempt to preserve; rather, the process of economic evolution is a continuing one. The real question that arises is whether we should attempt to control the pattern of change to fit some preconceived idea of the way the economy should operate, or whether we should allow the direction of change to be determined by the interplay of the existing forces in the economy. It is very probable that the best decision-making process is mixed, that is, one which includes both market and planned techniques. The problem is to find the best combination of the two. However, since the economy is continually changing, it seems highly probable that the "best" decision-making process will also be continually changing.

The decision-making process in the private sector of the United States, which accounts for 75 percent of our output, can best be described as a modified market mechanism. The system of markets through which decisions are made is regulated by government, and the limits of the activity which can take place in each are often prescribed by the rules which have been established by government. For example, in the agriculture industry there are many crops for which the government regulates the acreage which farmers can grow. The purpose of the control is to raise the income of the farmers. Government also regulates the types of fertilizers and pesticides which farmers can use in an effort to protect those who consume the farmers' product. There are also many restrictions on the importation of agricultural products which are designed to preserve the markets in the United States for United States farmers.

Are United States markets self-regulating? Reviewing the point made in Chapter 8, it is apparent that many of the markets in the United States do not have the characteristics needed to assure a self-regulating market system which will achieve the most desirable results from society's point of view. Generally, the characteristics needed for this purpose are approximately the ones associated with pure competition:

1. A standardized product
2. Many buyers and sellers
3. Freedom of entry into and exit from the market
4. Equal access to relevant market information.

When these characteristics are present, the prices of the goods and services that are exchanged in the market will reflect the total cost of producing them. In the competitive market the producers only make what economists call *normal profit*. Normal profit is the amount of return to the factors of production necessary to keep them employed in the production of a good or service. If the return falls below the normal return, the resources will be shifted to the production of something else. If the return to factors is greater than the normal profit, the producer is receiving *economic profit*. However, under pure competition the producer cannot make an economic profit in the long run because other resources will be shifted to the production of the good or service where the economic profit is being made. This has the effect of driving the price of the good or service down until only a normal profit is being realized by the producers of the good or service. The economic profit is removed because there is freedom of movement into the market under pure competition. In many markets in the United States there are barriers which prevent the free movement of resources. Once the free movement of resources from one market to another is inhibited, much of the ability of the market system to achieve desirable results through a self-regulating mechanism is lost.

In fact, many of the markets in the United States lack one or more characteristics of pure competition. Much of the output of the United States economy is exchanged in markets in which there are only a few producers. Such markets are called *oligopolies*. The auto industry is an example of an oligopoly. Another type of market that is common in the United States is one which economists call *monopolistic competition*. In this type of market the producers are able to get consumers to differentiate among similar, or in some instances identical, products. This differentiation is achieved primarily through advertising. For example, in the aspirin market consumers differentiate among different brands of aspirin which are actually identical. This enables the producers of the aspirin which are falsely identified as superior to receive a higher price for their product, even though it is identical to other aspirin on the market. Another type of economic market which is found in the United States is the monopoly. A monopoly market is one in which there is only one producer. This type of market is most commonly associated with public utilities and transportation. A problem with the monopoly market appeared early in the history of the United States in connection with the railroad. In many communities the only transportation available to ship the goods being produced in the community was the railroad which served the community. The owners of the railroad frequently took advantage of their monopoly position and used discriminatory pricing policies which worked undue hardships on those who were dependent on the railroad. Many of the monopolies in the United States today are regulated.

Under conditions of oligopoly, monopolistic competition, and monopoly the forces which regulate the markets to assure desirable results are absent. Regulation is frequently necessary to ensure that these markets will operate efficiently. Without regulation the producers who operate in these types of markets would be able to exert market power, and the output of the economy would not represent the preferences of the people. The organization of many of the markets in the United States has eliminated the alternative of completely relying on a system of self-regulating markets in the private sector.

APPROACHES TO THE ROLE OF GOVERNMENT

What the proper role of government in the United States economy should be is rather controversial. Much of the controversy results from non-economic considerations. Basically, the Jeffersonian idea that that government governs best which governs least has been applied to the role of government in economic activity. If we limit the activities of government to those that it already performs, then in the future the relative importance of government in the United States economy will be determined by the relative importance of these functions (i.e., police officer, producer of public goods and services, etc.) in the total economy. It seems probable that the functions which are currently being performed by government are going to grow in relative importance in the future. Thus, it seems likely that government's role in the United States economy is going to be enlarged. The impact that this probability has on an individual depends greatly on that individual's philosophy concerning the proper role of government. However, the total impact of an even larger and more responsible role for government in the economy will be determined primarily by the effectiveness of the leaders who are responsible for directing the activities of the government.

Least-government approach There are three possible approaches to the role of government in economic activity. One of these is to limit the activities of government to those functions that cannot be performed by private businesses. This implies that the government would be involved in the production of collective goods. Collective goods are things such as national defense which cannot be "consumed" by an individual alone, but rather are consumed by the group as a whole. How could national defense be divided into units for individual consumption? Obviously, this would be impossible.

Under the least-government principle there would also be a need for government involvement when there is a difference between private and social costs and/or benefits. An example of a difference between social cost and private cost is the situation where a producer is dumping wastes from the production process into a river and polluting it. It is obvious that this is an easy and inexpensive way for the producer to dispose of the wastes. The question of public costs arise when we consider alternative uses for the river. It is possible that the pollution might be so bad that the river would be destroyed as a source of recreation. Or, perhaps some city depends on the river for its water. The citizens of this city may have to bear additional costs to prepare the polluted water for consumption. It is quite clear that in this type of situation there are costs of production that the producer is not forced to pay. The question then arises, "How much does it cost society to produce the good of our hypothetical producer, when we consider both the costs paid by the producer and the costs paid by the public?"

A situation in which the benefits of an economic activity might be greater than the direct rewards is the construction of a dam on a river. The people living downstream may reap enormous benefits from the flood control that results from the construction of the dam. The question arises as to a private business's ability to assess and collect a price from those who benefit. It is quite possible that this type of project would not be profitable for a private business because the business would never collect for many of the benefits that were being provided. However, from society's point of view, this might be a very profitable and worthwhile project. This means that government will have to become involved if this project is to be undertaken. Government does not necessarily have to build the dam because it can achieve the same thing by providing a subsidy to a private business in order to encourage it to undertake the project. Education is another situation in which there is a divergency between private cost and public benefit. Everyone benefits from living in a society with a well-educated citizenry. Thus, people who have no children in school benefit from the taxes they pay to support the schools.

A third area of government involvement under the least-government approach is research and development in areas in which the risk is great and the profits and benefits do not necessarily accrue to the person conducting the research. Examples of this type of research are rapid transit systems, giant computers, and the space program. Many technological advances have resulted from the space program, and society benefits from these. However, it is difficult to imagine any private business undertaking such a project. This area presents one of the most difficult problems facing the decision makers in the planned sector. They must evaluate all potential projects and select the ones that will provide the greatest benefits to society. There is a great danger that special interest groups will have undue influence in the selection of projects of this type, and these groups are likely to be more concerned with personal benefit than with society's benefit.

Under this principle the government would also be involved when conditions of *natural monopoly* exist. A natural monopoly is a production situation in which there would be economic waste if more than one firm were producing. An example of this would be the production of electricity for a particular neighborhood. There would be an enormous waste if two companies competed because this would involve building two sets of power lines and facilities when one set could adequately do the job. Not only would there be a waste, but also, the consumer of electricity would have to pay a higher price for the electricity that he used because the cost to the firm supplying the service would be much greater if there were two firms. In the United States, firms are frequently granted a monopoly where conditions of natural monopoly exist. In a situation such as this, one firm is granted a monopoly to operate in a particular area and no other firm is allowed to come in and compete with it. Situations of this type are frequently referred to as *franchise monopolies.* The firm operating under conditions of natural monopoly is then regulated by the government. The government sets the price the franchise monopoly is allowed to charge, and the firm must supply all people in that particular area at the price set by the government regulatory agency. If the firm's profits are too low, the firm will be permitted to raise the price of the good or service being supplied, and if profits are too high, it will be forced to lower the price.

Another situation that might call for the involvement of government in the economy under the least-government approach is one in which the intervention of government would provide additional convenience and lower cost to the consumer. Also, there is a need for government intervention when the situation is such that the government must exercise its *power of eminent domain.* The power of eminent domain is the government's power to force people to sell private property when it is needed for public use. Government also becomes involved in protecting and ensuring the economic welfare of those who, for various reasons, cannot provide for themselves. Finally, under this criterion the involvement of government for the prevention of depression and inflation is justified.

It should be apparent to the reader that the principle of least government in the area of economic activity is the principle that has been followed during most of the history of the United States. The principle has been followed in the United States on the assumption that there are forces operating in the economy that ensure a more efficient operation of the economy than could be achieved by government intervention.

Socialist approach A second approach to the role of government in the economy is the socialist approach, which is the opposite of the least-government approach. In this type of situation the factors of production are owned and controlled by government. The assumption is that if other things are equal, the activity should be public rather than private. The rationale of this approach is the Marxian doctrine that private ownership and control of the means of production will inevitably lead to the exploitation of the workers. Implicit in this doctrine is the assumption that there are no forces operating in the economy that will protect the workers from those who own and control the factors of production other than labor, and that these owners will be able to use their power to exploit the owners of labor, i.e., the workers. Also, a major aim of those who favor the socialist approach is the prevention of gross inequalities in the distribution of income and wealth. There are some who believe that for many underdeveloped countries this is the only technique which will enable them to achieve the type of economic growth and development they desire.

Intermediate approach A third possible approach to the role of government calls for a more active role for the government than the least-government approach and a less active role than the socialist approach. In a sense, it is based on the assumption that under many conditions there are forces operating in the economy that enable it to function more efficiently without government intervention. However, this approach recognizes that these forces may not always ensure that the economy will function in a desirable manner, and calls for government intervention if they do not.

The advocates of this approach in the United States are increasing. They contend that it is frequently necessary for the government to assume the initiative in many areas of economic activity. The government has been particularly active in providing the initiative for research and development in the United States. For example, of the $23.7 billion spent on research and development in 1967, approximately 60 percent was provided directly by government. The remainder was subsidized indirectly through the tax structure.

There are many people who suggest that government should use its power to influence the pattern of consumption in the United States. One of the ways in which this is currently being done is through the use of the tax structure. Placing heavy excise taxes on various goods and services increases the price that consumers must pay for them, thereby discouraging the consumption of them. Another way that the government encourages a certain type of consumption is by using selective techniques, such as those used by the Federal Housing Administration. The major function of the FHA is to encourage home ownership, and it does this by making home financing easier. Those who contend that government should take a more active role in influencing the pattern of consumption in the United States frequently argue that private business, through the use of advertising and various types of market control, has distorted the pattern of consumption in the United States. Hence, there is a need for government intervention to counteract the influence of business.

Another governmental activity that is favored by those who support a more active role for government is involvement in the determination of the distribution of income in the United States. The technique most commonly suggested is the manipulation of the tax structure. The two types of taxes most commonly recommended to achieve a redistribution of income in the United States are the progressive income tax and the negative income tax. The progressive income tax is designed to level income by taking larger amounts from those with higher incomes and the negative income tax is designed to level the distribution of income by raising the incomes of those with low incomes. Another technique that is commonly used to control the distribution of incomes is the subsidy. Subsidies range from those given to the poor, such as rent subsidies, to those given to farmers and landowners, who are frequently quite wealthy.

GOVERNMENT VERSUS THE MARKETPLACE

When we evaluate the role of the government, we are actually comparing economic decision making via the ballot box with economic decision making via the marketplace. There are five factors relative to government that should be considered when comparing the merits of the action of government with the operation of the marketplace.

First, government decisions must be supported by everyone once they are made. This is because the government's operation is supported by tax revenue, and all people must pay taxes to support the government whether they like what the government is doing or not. At least, in the market the consumer can choose not to support the producer by not consuming.

Second, there is no assurance that people are receiving benefits which are greater than the cost of production for a particular good or service. This is because the people do not purchase each good or service from the government separately. This means that, if the goods and services were offered to the public at the cost of production, the public might not purchase them. The determination of whether benefit is equal to cost of production is more difficult for some types of goods than for others.

Another problem is that the political process tends to be a rather insensitive choice mechanism. This is because the voters are able to assess only a relatively small number of issues in an election. There is also a problem because the individual must vote for all the views of a candidate. In actual practice, the voter's position may be different from the positions of all the candidates for a particular office. Thus, a voter who casts a ballot for a particular candidate has no way of telling that candidate which ideas he or she supports and which ones he or she opposes.

A fourth problem associated with the political process as an economic decision-making unit is that, as often as not, the decisions reflect the distribution of political power as much as the views of the majority of the voters. This results from the fact that political power is frequently associated with regional groups, special interest pressure groups, etc. Finally, there is the consideration of the number of votes that each person has. In the marketplace an individual has as many votes as dollars, whereas each individual has only one vote at the ballot box. This means that an individual with an income of a million dollars a year has equal say with an individual with a $5,000 income in selecting the people who make decisions, if one considers only the number of votes the individual has to cast. In reality, this is probably not a valid reflection of the two individuals' relative influence on political decisions because the wealthy individual may be able to have a greater influence on political decisions by using his wealth to influence other voters and politicians and because of the prestige that is associated with the possession of wealth in the United States.

A word of caution to the reader who wishes to examine the relative merits of making economic decisions through the political process. One should not compare the weaknesses associated with the political process with the strengths of the market process or compare the strengths associated with the political process with the weaknesses of the market process. Any evaluation should consider the strengths and weaknesses of both decision-making techniques. This may well cause one to come to the conclusion that each technique has advantages. Thus, the "best" decision-making process will include elements of both. This means that the mixed decision-making process that we have in the United States is probably better than one which relies on a single technique to make economic decisions. The problem that remains is one of selecting the decision-making process that includes the correct "mix" of elements of each technique.

ECONOMIC POLICY

One of the major reasons for studying economics is to gain a better understanding of the "how's" and "why's" of economic policy. Economic policy refers to the things that are done or not done in an effort to control the operation of the economy. The reader should note that not doing anything, as well as actively attempting to control the economy, is defined as economic policy.

Often when one considers economic policy, it is helpful to divide the discussion into two parts. First, one must consider the types of things that implementation of a policy is designed to achieve (economic goals). And secondly, one must decide what techniques are to be used to achieve the desired results.

It is with respect to economic policy that the relationship between economics and the other social sciences becomes most obvious. It is impossible to select economic techniques and/or goals without also considering the social and political consequences associated with these techniques and with the achievement of the goals. For instance, rarely are taxes manipulated in order to generate employment or to reduce inflation without consideration of the political and social impact of this action. In 1968, for example, a much-needed tax increase to control inflation was delayed until August of that year because it was an election year. The members of Congress did not want to increase taxes because tax increases are generally unpopular, and many members of Congress felt that supporting a tax increase would hurt their chances for reelection. It was not until public-opinion polls reported that the electorate strongly favored a tax increase that Congress acted.

Economic policy goal selection Any discussion of economic goals must come to grips with two problems. First of all, of the possible goals that might be included in the discussion, which ones should be included? The ones selected should include those that are most important to the operation of the economy and to society. Once the goals are selected, it is essential to establish priorities, i.e., when it is impossible to achieve all the goals, which ones are to be achieved now and which ones are to be achieved later? Goals which a policymaker might consider are: (1) full employment, (2) price stability, (3) satisfactory economic growth rate, (4) economic efficiency, (5) removal of poverty, (6) satisfactory balance of payments, (7) a "fair" distribution of the burden of government, (8) environmental problems, and (9) problems associated with urban areas. The economic goals included in the list and the ordering of these in terms of priorities will change depending on the existing economic and social conditions.

At this stage of the discussion the reader should stop and relate the discussion of economic policy to the basic functions of an economic system. Remember that the five basic functions of an economic system are determining the composition of output of goods and services, allocating productive resources, providing for economic growth, distributing the output of the economy, and adjusting consumption to match the available supply in the short run. One of the purposes of economic policy is to enable an economy to perform these functions more smoothly than otherwise would be the case. One of the dangers that the economic policymaker faces is the possibility that improper or unwise policies and/or techniques may have undesirable effects on the economy.

Another function of economic policy is to alter the results that would be obtained if the economy were allowed to operate without any type of interference. There are many policies of this type. Schemes which involve a redistribution of income are examples of efforts to change the results that would be produced by the unrestricted operation of the economic system. The major problem involved in altering the way the economic system is operating is that there are normally some people who benefit and some who lose as a result of the change.

There is a problem involved in the consideration of economic policy that is directly related to political philosophy. It results from one's view of the proper role of the government in the economy. Some people assume that government should stay out of things altogether and, hence, deny the government any effective role in economic policy. For the purposes of this discussion we shall assume that government has a "right" and a "responsibility" to participate in controlling our economy. Differences in political philosophy will be reflected in the choice of techniques to be used to implement economic policy decisions. Noneconomic factors play an important role in the selection of economic goals and techniques. It is fairly common to make the selection on the basis of noneconomic factors and then attempt to justify the selection on economic grounds. This does not mean to imply that noneconomic criteria are not valid in the choice of economic goals and techniques. However, it is important to recognize the real reasons for their selection and to evaluate them on the basis of these reasons.

Policy agents and techniques The agents of economic policy in the United States are the government and the Board of Governors of the Federal Reserve System (Fed). Economic policy techniques are of two types. First, there are those techniques which control the general level of economic activity. These measures work by affecting the level of demand (aggregate demand) for goods and services in the economy. The Fed affects the level of aggregate demand for goods and services in the economy by manipulating the money supply and thus influencing interest rates and conditions of credit generally. An increase in the money supply tends to drive down the interest rate and ease credit, which increases the aggregate demand for goods and services and thus stimulates the economy. A contraction of the money supply has the opposite effect.

The federal government is the only level of government that attempts to control the level of aggregate demand in the economy. The federal government affects the level of aggregate demand by manipulating its income (taxes) and expenditures. Increases in government expenditures represent a direct and immediate increase in the level of demand for goods and services, whereas decreases have the opposite effect. However, increasing or decreasing government expenditures is not as simple as it might first appear. There is almost always disagreement among the members of Congress as to which expenditures should be reduced or expanded. Even when the members of Congress pass legislation designed to change the level of government expenditures, there is no assurance that it will not be vetoed by the President. A large part of the conflict results from the fact that different groups of people are not all affected equally by any particular change in government expenditures. Suppose, for instance, that the decision has been made to increase government expenditures by $5 billion to stimulate the economy. If this additional $5 billion is spent on new military equipment, the group who will benefit most is a different group than the one who would benefit if the additional expenditures were on urban renewal projects.

There is an incorrect assumption frequently associated with government expenditures. This is the assumption that the prosperity of the United States economy is dependent on large military expenditures. Some even go so far as to say that it is necessary to have a war to keep the economy prosperous. This is a lot of nonsense. What this argument really implies is that it takes large government expenditures to keep the economy prosperous. An expenditure of $1 billion on cancer research would stimulate the economy just as much as $1 billion spent on the development of new types of "germ warfare"; and $1 billion spent on cleaning up the environment would stimulate the economy as much as $1 billion spent on bombs. In the long run nonmilitary expenditures tend to yield a greater benefit to society than do expenditures on the military. Thus, expenditures on the military must be justified on grounds other than the economic benefit to society.

A decrease in taxes raises the level of aggregate demand by increasing the disposable income of the people, which will cause them to increase their purchases of goods and services. An increase in taxes has the opposite effect. Manipulation of taxes for purposes of economic control is frequently more difficult than manipulation of government expenditures. Generally, it is easier to get a tax reduction to stimulate the economy than a tax increase to control the level of aggregate demand. The reason, of course, is that tax changes are made by politicians, and it is politically more popular to lower taxes than to raise them. There is also the question of whose taxes to increase or decrease when manipulating taxes for purposes of economic control. Obviously, not all people will be affected to the same degree by any single change in taxes.

Problem of the national debt One of the major contributions of the "New Economics" is the concept of the full-employment budget. With a full-employment budget, the federal government plans its budget (expenditures and taxes) for any given fiscal period, on the basis of the state of the economy rather than on the basis of the private concept of budgeting, which involves balancing income and expenditures. Many people tend to think of such an approach to budgeting as irresponsible, and they point to the national debt as the product of such irresponsibility. Most economists do not consider the national debt a problem and usually do not even consider it when formulating policy proposals. An examination of some of the common misconceptions associated with the national debt will help clarify the seemingly irresponsible attitude of economists.

Many people think that the accumulation of a national debt means that we are "living high" and passing the burden on to our grandchildren. If one thinks in terms of real income, i.e., goods and services, this question takes on a different perspective. For instance, how can we consume something today that will not be produced until later? Since a large part of the national debt was accumulated financing World War II, we might ask, "How many of the bombs that were dropped in 1945 were produced after 1945?" The only way we can steal from our grandchildren is to do things that will later limit their consumption. It is difficult to argue that the creation of the national debt has had this effect. In fact, a good argument can be made that the things that were financed with the national debt have greatly benefited the "grandchildren." *The question that is relevant in the case of the national debt is whether or not there might have been a better way to finance the expenditures that were financed by the national debt.*

Another thing that upsets people is the size of the national debt. Table 9-3 shows the size of the national debt for selected years. As can be seen from the table, the national debt was larger than the GNP in 1945, whereas in 1972 it was only about 39 percent as large as the GNP. It is apparent that the relative size of the national debt has been

TABLE 9-3 HOLDERS OF NATIONAL DEBT

Year	GNP	National debt	Government accounts	Fed	Private	Total National debt as percent of GNP
1945	211.9	278.1	23.9	24.3	230.0	131.2
1946	208.5	259.1	27.4	23.3	208.4	124.3
1950	284.8	256.7	36.0	20.8	199.9	90.1
1955	398.0	280.8	49.0	24.0	207.0	70.5
1960	503.7	290.2	52.8	27.4	210.0	57.6
1965	684.9	320.9	59.7	40.8	220.4	46.8
1970	974.9	389.2	97.9	62.1	229.9	40.0
1972	1,152.1	449.3	116.9	69.9	262.5	39.0

Source: *Economic Report of the President,* 1973.

decreasing. It does not seem likely that a national debt 39 percent as large as the GNP would have as much effect on the operation of the economy as a national debt that is larger than the GNP.

One other feature of the national debt that bears mentioning is its composition, i.e., who holds the national debt? An examination of Table 9-3 reveals that the amount of the national debt held by private individuals has not increased much since 1945. Since it is debatable whether or not the part of the national debt held by government accounts and the Fed should actually be counted, an argument can be made that the actual dollar value of the national debt increased only slightly between 1945 and 1972.

It seems unlikely that the United States will ever need to pay off the principal of the national debt; instead, it can continually refinance the debt when it comes due. The debt is issued in such a way that only a small part of it ever comes due at any one time, thus making it easier to refinance. Most of the debt is in the form of Treasury bills and bonds, and the person who holds this type of debt cannot demand payment of the debt until it comes due. Since government debt represents "investment" to individuals in the private sector, the government should be able to refinance the debt as long as people desire to maintain investments of the type represented by government debt.

The real burden of the national debt is the payment of the interest on it. In 1972 the interest on the national debt was over $20.6 billion. This represented 1.79 percent of the GNP. The burden of the interest payments is not one that greatly affects the operation of the economy. This is because the national debt is internally held. Thus, payment of interest involves taxing the people and then using the taxes collected to pay the holders of the national debt their interest. The burden, then, is the expense incurred in refinancing the debt and the redistribution of income associated with payment of the interest. The redistribution of income results from the fact that those who hold the national debt are not necessarily the same people as those who pay the taxes to service the debt.

In view of the preceding discussion, it does not seem that the existence of a national debt or the fear of increasing it should act as a constraint when formulating economic policy. The policymakers should be guided by the economic conditions and the problem that they are attempting to alleviate when they make their selection of policy techniques.

There are other measures which government can take to deal with economic problems which do not respond to manipulation of the level of aggregate demand by the Federal Reserve System and government. These include wage and price guidelines and/or direct controls to limit inflation which cannot be controlled by manipulating aggregate demand, and labor market policies designed to help those workers who are unable to find employment when there is sufficient aggregate demand because they do not possess skills which are needed by the economy. The government can also use selective credit controls to encourage certain types of economic activity. The Federal Housing Administration, whose major purpose is to encourage home ownership, is an example of this. The government can negotiate trade agreements with foreign countries or manipulate tariffs and/or currency exchange rates to control the foreign sector of the United States economy. This list of economic policy measures could easily be expanded. However, the diversity of measures used by government to control the economy should be apparent by now.

THE ENERGY CRISIS

A topic which no discussion of economic policy can ignore today is the energy crisis. Assessment of the extent of the energy shortage and formulation of measures to deal with it are major problems facing policymakers today. The assessment of the extent of the shortage is complicated because of the lack of good data on the available reserves. There are some who speculate that the recent energy shortage was contrived by the major petroleum companies in order to reduce competition by driving smaller independent producers out of business and to reduce the pressures from environmentalists which have led to restrictions on the activities of the petroleum industry. It is, in fact, true that the recent shortage has probably tended to reduce the potential competition from smaller independent producers and has caused a major setback to the environmentalists. Examples of the latter effect include the easy passage of legislation approving the construction of the Alaskan pipeline, reduced pollution standards for industries, and postponement of pollution standards for automobiles. However, this is not proof that the petroleum shortage was contrived by the large petroleum producers. These effects were to be expected regardless of the source of the shortage.

There were several difficulties involved in attempting to solve the rationing problem associated with the recent shortage. These exist independent of the question of determining the source of the shortage. As discussed earlier, the two major techniques which might be used to achieve rationing are direct controls, which limit the amount consumers can purchase, and the market mechanism, which involves allowing the price to rise to a level high enough for demand to be reduced to the level of current supply. If questions of equity and long-run effects could be ignored, the simplest solution would be to allow the price to rise and thereby reduce the quantity demanded until it was equal to supply. However, this has the effect of placing most of the burden on low income groups. Since low income groups already have difficulty competing in society, anything which reduces their ability to compete seems extremely inequitable to the authors. Thus, we find ourselves in a situation in which the way the economy is performing one function, distribution of income, can cause gross inequities if the market mechanism is allowed to determine the way another function will be carried out, i.e., adjusting to a short-run shortage. Considerations of equity, therefore, dictate the use of some type of direct rationing of quantities which consumers could purchase.

If the energy crisis turns out to be the long-run problem that many economists believe it to be, the long-run solution will require policy measures considerably different from those needed to deal with the recent crisis. If it becomes serious enough, it may lead to drastic changes in the structure of the economy and of society generally. It seems that, at the very least, we are going to have to reshape our economic system so that we base its operation more on renewable supplies of energy. In the past our desire for economic growth and profit have caused us to expand our output without concern for the efficiency with which natural resources were being utilized. In an article in *The Los Angeles Times,* for example, Barry Commoner estimated that the efficiency with which nitrogen fertilizer is converted into food and fiber has decreased by 90 percent since 1946. Nitrogen fertilizer is made from natural gas. He points to the fact that a 1400 percent increase in fertilizer use had yielded only a 50 percent increase in crop output nationwide. This seems particularly distressing when one realizes that a large part of the inefficiency in the use of nitrogen fertilizer has been the result of government programs designed to limit farm production. For instance, as government restricted the acreage which farmers could plant, the farmers attempted to maintain high yields by applying more fertilizer to the smaller acreage. This results in smaller increments in output for each additional unit of fertilizer used.

A large buying public competing for scarce gasoline made inflated prices unavoidable during the recent shortage. *(George W. Gardner)*

Another example of inefficiency, Commoner points out, that has resulted from the unconstrained desire for growth and profit is in the transportation area and is directly related to the energy crisis. Since 1946 truck freight has grown at a 7 percent annual rate, compared with 0.8 percent for rail freight. Trucks use four to six times as much fuel per ton-mile of freight as trains. Transportation economists have been arguing for a long time that hauls of over 100 miles could be handled more efficiently by rail than by truck even without considering the efficiency with which fuel is consumed. Despite this, long-haul trucking has experienced faster growth than rail transportation. A large part of this seemingly unexplainable growth of the trucking industry can be explained by the rate structures established by government agencies, which have been favorable to the trucking industry.

It seems fair to conclude that, regardless of whether the recent energy crisis is real or contrived, there will be a real crisis in the future as our oil and other natural resource reserves are depleted if we continue to base our system on the assumption that we have unlimited supplies of natural resources. Measures which will lead to a more efficient use of our nonrenewable resources will have to be taken, and programs to encourage greater reliance on renewable resources will have to be developed. For example, some members of Congress are currently demanding the passage of legislation which would prohibit the production of automobiles which got less than 20 miles per gallon of gasoline. There are some observers who believe that fuel shortages will ultimately curtail the operation of automobiles so much that it will cause drastic changes in the life-style of many Americans, a life-style dependent on relatively inexpensive auto transportation.

SUMMARY

For purposes of analysis, the American economy is frequently divided into three sectors, the household, the firm, and the government. The households are the consumer units, and they also supply the labor force.

Firms, the production units, are classified according to the way they are legally organized. The three types are the proprietorship, the partnership, and the corporation. The overwhelming majority of firms are proprietorships; however, in 1967 corporations accounted for 82 percent of business receipts. The franchise is a variant form of business organization in which an individual operates a business under the name of some larger company. A franchise may be either a proprietorship, a partnership, or a corporation. The importance of the franchise relationship is that the company that starts the franchise network, rather than the owner who operates the individual franchise business, makes many of the business decisions.

The government sector consists of the activities carried on by the government at all levels—federal, state, and local. The functions performed by government fall into one of six categories: (1) police officer, (2) producer of public goods and services, (3) regulator of the private economy, (4) administrator of the public domain, (5) ensurer of a satisfactory rate of growth, and (6) redistributor of income.

The flow of economic activity in the United States actually consists of two flows, a financial flow and a real flow. It is important to distinguish between the two flows.

The decision making in the private sector of the United States economy can best be described as a modifed market mechanism. The system of markets which exists in the private sector operates under government regulation. The presence of oligopoly, monopolistic competition, and monopoly markets in the United States means that desirable results frequently cannot be achieved through self-regulation.

There are three possible approaches to the role of government in the economy. These are the least-government approach, the socialist approach, and the intermediate approach.

Under the least-government approach the activities of the government are restricted to those which private businesses cannot perform. In the socialist approach the means of production are owned and controlled by government, and private businesses are only allowed to do those things which government cannot do. The intermediate approach lies somewhere between the other two. It is based on the assumption that in some situations the economy will function more effectively without government, but that in other situations government intervention increases the effectiveness of the functioning of the economy.

When attempting to evaluate government versus the marketplace as a source of economic performance and decision making, it is necessary to consider such things as the insensitivity of choice associated with government, the problems of equating costs and benefits, forced support of government decisions, representativeness of government, and the democracy of the marketplace versus that of the ballot box. One must be aware of the dangers of comparing the strengths of one to the weaknesses of the other when evaluating the relative merits of the government and the marketplace as sources of economic performance and decision making.

Economic policy refers to those things that are done or not done in an effort to control the economy. The formulation of economic policy consists of selecting both goals and the techniques to be used to achieve the selected goals. An important aspect of the goal selection process is the establishment of priorities. The major problem involved in altering the way the economic system is operating is that there are normally some people who benefit and some who lose as a result of a change.

The agents of economic policy in the United States are the Federal Reserve System and the federal government. The Federal Reserve System implements its policy decisions primarily by manipulating the money supply. The federal government implements its decisions by manipulating taxes and expenditures. The federal government also uses various other techniques to deal with problems which do not respond to manipulation of taxes and expenditures.

Many people are concerned with economists' seemingly irresponsible attitude toward the fiscal position of the federal government, especially their attitude toward the national debt. However, an examination of the nature of the national debt reveals that the concern is unjustified. The confusion results because people compare the debt of the federal government to their private debt or to that of private businesses. Such comparisons are examples of false analogies.

A current problem facing economic policy makers is the energy shortage. The solution of this problem will require an accurate assessment of the extent of the problem and determination of whether it is a short-term or long-term shortage. Equity considerations complicate the short-run solution.

REVIEW QUESTIONS

1. What are the three sectors of the United States economy? What is the function of each?
2. Discuss the three major types of business organizations in the United States. What is the basis for this classification?
3. Why is it possible for one person to argue that the United States is a land of small businesses and for another to argue that the United States economy is dominated by large businesses, and both to be partially correct? Do you think big business is too powerful in the United States? Discuss.
4. What is a franchise business? How does it differ from other forms of business organization?
5. What are the six major functions performed by government in the United States economy? Do you think government shoud expand any of these functions? Add new ones?
6. What are the two types of flows of economic activity in the United States economy?
7. Briefly describe the circular flow of economic activity in the United States economy.
8. What assumption was made in this chapter concerning the ultimate purpose of all economic activity? Discuss the relevance and implications of this assumption.
9. What is the best decision-making approach for the United States economy? Explain.

10. What conditions are necessary if the results that are achieved in a market are to be "desirable" from society's point of view? Do the markets in the United States possess the necessary conditions? Explain. What is the meaning of "desirable"?
11. What is the least-government approach to the role of government in the economy? Give some examples of government involvement in the economy which would be called for under this approach. What is the rationale underlying the least-government approach?
12. What is the socialist approach to the role of government in the economy? What is the rationale underlying the socialist approach?
13. What is the intermediate approach to the role of government in the economy? Give some examples of government involvement in the economy which would be called for under this approach. What is the rationale underlying the intermediate approach?
14. What things should be considered when evaluating economic decision making and performance of government versus that of the marketplace? Evaluate the effectiveness of government versus that of the marketplace in the United States.
15. What is economic policy? What are the two aspects of economic policy?
16. What are some of the factors that must be considered when selecting economic policy goals? What role do value judgments play in economic policy?
17. What are the two economic policy agents in the United States? How does each implement its policy decisions? Describe how the techniques used by each works.
18. What is a "full-employment budget"?
19. Is the national debt a serious problem? Discuss.
20. What is the real burden of the national debt?
21. What are some measures which government can take to deal with problems that do not respond to manipulation of aggregate demand?
22. Do you think there is any energy crisis in the United States? Discuss.

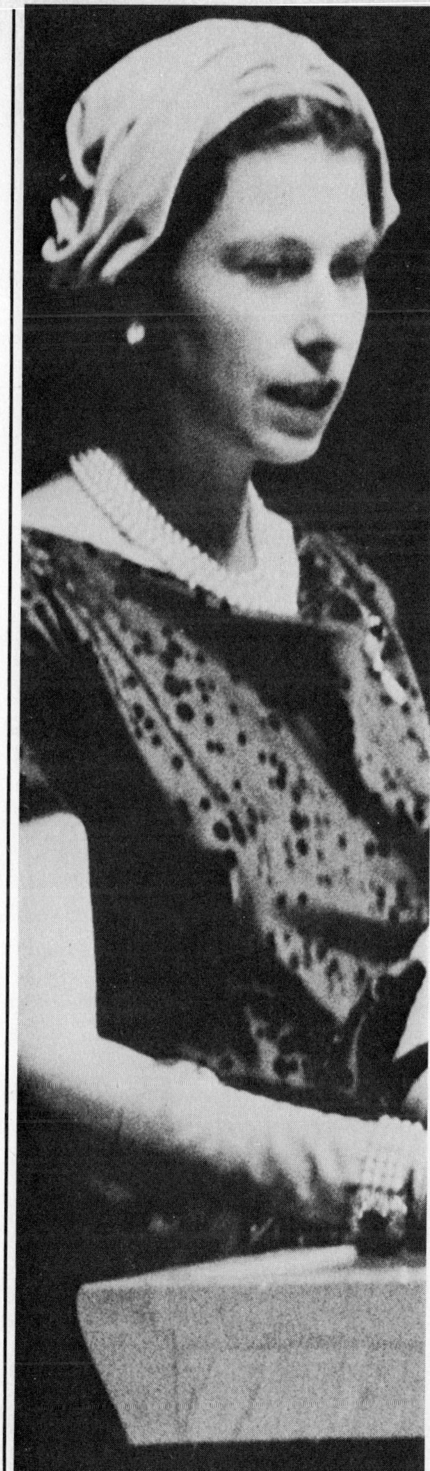

PART FOUR
POLITICAL SCIENCE

Political science is the study of political systems. A political system is all the institutions and processes which are involved in governing a society. Governing is the process through which people deal with those problems which they cannot solve on an individual basis. In a sense, then, the political system can be viewed as the organization which people have developed to handle problems which arise from the functioning and interaction of individuals and organizations.

Government is frequently called upon to cope with those problems which are the focus of the social sciences. The role of the social scientist is to unearth and investigate problems and provide information which will enable government to make intelligent decisions. For example, it is the function of the economist to discover the types of economic organization and behavior which are harmful to society. Once this has been done, government assumes the responsibility for preventing such organization and behavior. The antitrust laws and various regulatory agencies represent government efforts to this end.

Sociologists and psychologists are concerned with discovering the causes and effects of certain types of deviant behavior. Once they have discovered the cause-and-effect relationships, they decide how best to deal with that part of society. However, the responsibility for instituting and administering programs to control socially harmful behavior falls to government. Prisons and mental hospitals are reflections of government efforts to control such behavior.

Thus the political system is on one hand the focus of the study of social scientists, and on the other the agent to which social scientists look to implement programs which they deem beneficial to society. A properly organized and run political system can greatly improve the functioning of a society and greatly enhance the quality of life of the members of that society. However, when used improperly, the power that is vested in government can be used for the benefit of only some of the members of society and thereby reduce the quality of life of the other members.

FOR FURTHER READING

It is more difficult to specify general "text-type" books for those who wish to explore political science beyond the material contained in the chapters in this section than it was for the other social science areas covered in this book. This is the case because political scientists do not agree among themselves as much as do other social scientists as to the proper material to include in an introductory course. However, *A History of Western Political Theory,* by Gerald Runkle (Ronald Press, 1968), provides a good survey of the historical development of political theory in textbook form. Runkle traces the development of Western political theory from Plato to the present. James Gould and Willis Truitt in *Political Ideologies* (Macmillan, 1973) use series of readings to explore the meaning of various political ideologies. Each section begins with a short introduction to the ideology covered in that particular section. This book gives the reader a feeling for the complexity and scope of the different ideologies.

The reader whose major interest is American politics will find *Power and Politics in America,* by Leonard Freedman (Duxbury Press, 1971), an extremely useful source. The book deals with controversial topics and offers contrasting perspectives on whether or not government in the United States is capable of coping with the major issues that confront us. *Political Behavior in the United States*, edited by Fred Grupp, Jr., and Marvin Maurer (Appleton-Century-Crofts, 1972), provides a good selection of readings which deal with the various aspects of political behavior in the United States. The readings contained in this book deal with such aspects of political behavior as political participation, interest groups, and political communication.

There are many fiction books which focus on the problem of governing society. Aldous Huxley's *Brave New World* and George Orwell's *1984* remain the classics among those dealing with the potential of government for suppressing individual freedom.

GLOSSARY

anarchist one who believes there is no need for formal government because the governmental functions can be performed by voluntary associations

authoritarianism a form of government in which the majority of the people do not participate in the governmental process

capitalism a system in which the factors of production are all privately owned

Carlyle theory a "great man" theory of history which holds that the history of man is nothing more than a history of what great men have accomplished

collectivist one who believes that government should be deeply involved in all aspects of the functioning of society

delegated powers those powers enumerated in the U.S. Constitution that are to be exercised by the federal governmental process

democracy a government in which the masses of the people participate in the governmental process

export (import) quota restriction on the amount of a good which can be sent out of (brought into) a country

government all those agencies

and processes through which the state conducts its activities

individualist one who believes that government is a necessary evil but that it should be restricted as much as possible

laissez faire an economy in which government limits its role as much as possible

legitimacy the recognition by a group of people of an organization's right to rule them

politics the process through which power is employed to achieve certain goals

progressive tax a tax whose rate increases as income increases

proportional tax a tax whose rate remains unchanged as income increases

regressive tax a tax whose rate decreases as income increases

regulationist one who thinks government should perform more than the minimum functions prescribed by the individualist but should stop short of the pervasive role envisioned by the collectivist

seniority system the system used in the United States Congress to determine committee membership, etc.

socialism public or collective ownership of the factors of production, capital and natural resources

state a social organization which possesses a territory, a people, a government, and independence

tax base anything which a tax is levied against

tax loophole an indirect subsidy given to a group via the tax structure

tax rate the percentage of the tax base which must be paid in taxes

Tolstoi theory a theory of history which holds that history is an unfolding of the homogeneous, infinitesimal elements that regulate the masses

totalitarian system one in which every aspect of society is molded to fit the political ideology of the state

welfare state a state in which the government assumes responsibility for the material well-being of individuals

SOMETHING TO THINK ABOUT

Why do governments exist?

Can a citizen or group "fight city hall"?

Is the United States becoming a welfare state?

Does the United States have a government of laws and not of people?

Can a government legislate morality?

Should a state or the federal government be given the primary responsibility for providing for citizens?

Can you believe the information you receive from government?

Why is a democratic government better than an authoritarian government?

Why has governmental activity expanded so much in the United States during this century?

What is the urban problem?

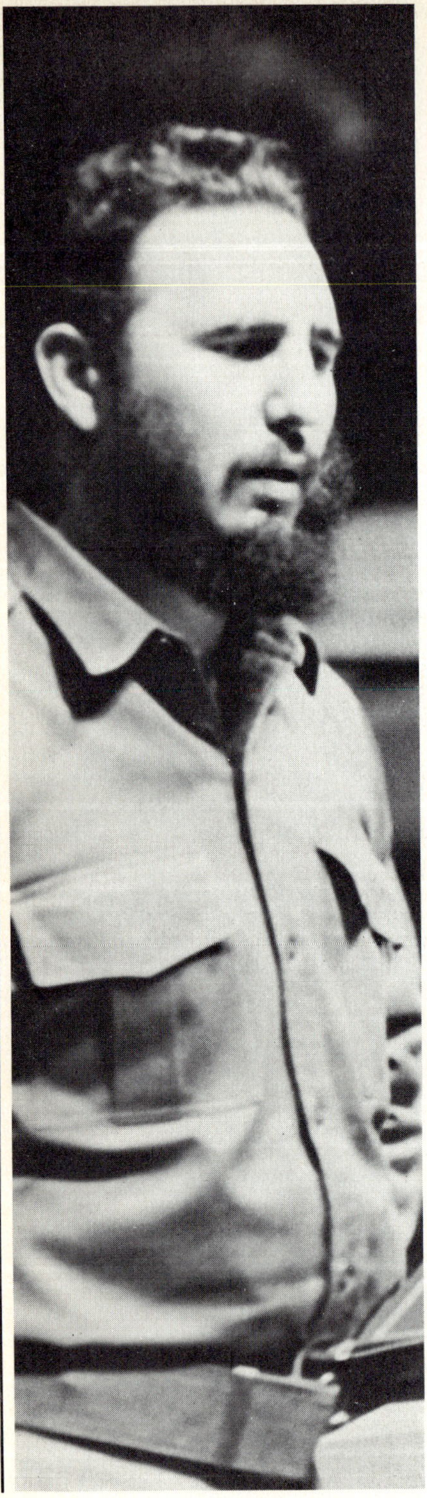

CHAPTER TEN
GOVERNING SOCIETY

IDEAS AND CONCEPTS

government
all agencies and processes through which the state conducts its activities

legitimacy
the recognition by a group of people of an organization's right to rule them

politics
the process through which power is employed to achieve certain goals

state
a social organization which possesses a territory, a people, a government, and independence

The existence of government reflects the existence of social problems which must be solved. Government is a social institution which people have developed to solve problems which they could not cope with on an individual basis. These problems frequently involve conflict between individuals, groups, and/or nations, and hence government's role has often been viewed as an agent of last resort to solve problems. However, there is growing recognition that government also has a positive function to perform: providing goods and services which are essential to fulfill material wants. The responsibility which government has assumed for the economic welfare of people in the United States has greatly increased in the last forty years. This controversial welfare role of government in the United States will be explored further in the next chapter.

Perhaps the major reason that the provision of goods and services by government in the United States is so controversial is that the other social institutions which provide goods and services view government as a competitor. They frequently use the power at their disposal to try to convince people that government should not be involved in supplying goods and services. Other social institutions which, along with government, attempt to satisfy needs for goods and services include the family, the church, the private educational system, and business enterprise. In the United States it has been business enterprises that have been particularly concerned about government's expanded role in supplying goods and services to the people. This is because the production of material goods and services has been almost exclusively the domain of business enterprise in the United States since the industrial revolution. The business community fears that the encroachment of government into their domain will reduce their power and importance in society and their profits.

Social institutions other than government not only perform certain functions for people, as does government, but also serve as regulatory agents in society. For instance, business enterprise provides material goods and services, and in so doing it acquires the power to greatly influence such things as the types of goods and services available, their quality, their prices, and their distribution among the people. Thus the study of government involves not only the structure of governmental institutions and the way they function, but also the interaction of government with other social institutions to determine the domain of each, the way government is influenced by the operation of other institutions, and the impact that the operation of government has on other institutions.

An important point to note at this time is that provision of additional goods and/or services by government or increased regulation by government does not necessarily imply that there is an increase in the supply of goods and services equal to the additional amount being supplied by government. Also, it does not mean that total regulation of society has increased by the amount of the additional regulation responsibilities assumed by government. It may be simply that government has assumed functions previously performed by other social institutions. The evaluation of the impact of a shift of functions from one social institution to another is a complex topic that will be examined in a later section of this chapter.

GOVERNMENT VERSUS POLITICS

The government or political system consists of all those agencies and processes through which the state conducts its activities, that is, through which governmental decisions are made and the functions of the state are carried out. The state (or nation) in this context refers to a social organization which possesses a territory, a people, a government, and independence. In the United States the governmental function is performed by different government units, each of which has specialized functions that it performs. Needless to say, the functions of the different units frequently overlap. These different government units are classified as federal, state, or local.

Politics is a general term which refers to the process through which power is employed to achieve certain goals. Power as used here refers to possession of the means of getting others to behave in the manner desired by the individual or group who is exercising the power. Power may stem from an elective or appointive position in government or some other social organization, the possession of wealth and prestige, etc. Thus, the term politics can be used to describe the exercise of power in many personal relationships or social organizations. For example, it is not uncommon in business, particularly at the management level, to hear that a person got a particular position by playing politics. The implication of this is that the individual has successfully used power to secure the position. The assumption frequently implicit in such a situation is that the individual did not receive the position strictly on the basis of merit.

Government, therefore, is the machinery which has been set up by a society through which the state performs its functions, and politics refers more specifically to the process which is involved when this governmental machinery is used to carry out governmental activities. It is fairly obvious that not all government leaders would use the machinery in the same way, and that even if two leaders did attempt to use it in the same way, they would not necessarily be equally effective in achieving their goals. Different Presidents of the United States, for instance, have had very different views as to the proper relationship between the office of the President and Congress. These differences in the views of our Presidents greatly influence the use of power involved in conducting the activities of the state, and it is important to recognize the distinction between the political process and the machinery of government.

A failure to distinguish between the political process involved in government and the governmental machinery can cause considerable confusion and often a complete breakdown in communication. For example, failure to make this distinction causes many people to misunderstand much of the criticism that is leveled at government in the United States today. One group of critics complains that the political process is not being conducted properly, but they do not object to the existing structure of government. The other group of critics contends that there is a need for a change in the governmental structure. The first group might object to such things as the way the President views the relationship between his office and Congress or the fact that a President has appointed only members of his own political party to positions of importance. Thus, they are objecting to the way the power associated with the Presidency is being used, but not to the power itself. The second group's criticism of the government goes beyond the way the governmental machinery is being used and is directed at the structure of government. This group, for example, might argue that the problem with the way Congress is functioning today is not with the way power is being used in Congress, but rather with the way Congress is organized. They might point to the use of the seniority system as a technique for selecting committee chairmen as one of the sources of the problem and suggest changing the organizational structure of the committees in Congress as a way of improving the functioning of Congress.

TYPES OF GOVERNMENT

Different classification systems have been developed to describe the various types of government organization. Classification systems usually concentrate on some specific aspect of government as the basis for distinguishing between types of governmental organization. Systems are based on such things as the role of government in the economy, the technique for selecting leaders, the system of ownership of property (capital and natural resources), and the ideology underlying the system. If we assume that the ideology of the society is consistent with the way the government is organized and operates, we can concentrate on the other three characteristics used in classifying governments.

Authoritarian The types of government in which the masses of the people do not participate in the selection of the leaders include absolute monarchies, rule by dictators, and rule by small minorities. (The latter type includes aristocracies and oligarchies. An oligarchy is a form of government in which the ruling power belongs to a few persons.) *Governments of these types in which the masses of the people do not* *directly participate are frequently called authoritarian.* Under an authoritarian regime the decisions of the government are law. The citizens are not entitled to challenge governmental decisions; that is, the citizens have no claim to *due process of law* as they do in the United States.*

Since the authoritarian regime is not bound by due process of law, it can use force as it desires in order to gain the cooperation of the people. However, authoritarian governments have historically relied strongly on tradition to gain the compliance of the people, and in recent years they have used the state monopoly of information to conduct widespread propaganda programs to convince the people to submit. Mao Tse-tung's government in Red China is a good example of an authoritarian government which has used propaganda programs very effectively.

In the twentieth century, authoritarian governments have frequently evolved into totalitarian systems, that is, systems in which every aspect of society is molded to fit the political ideology of the state. Such a development requires effective use of force and propaganda. Nazi Germany under Hitler and Mao's regime in Red China are excellent examples of authoritarian governments that effectively developed totalitarian systems. In such systems the economy, the family, etc., are shaped to conform with and to support the political ideology of the state.

Democratic *Those governments in which the masses of the people do participate in the political process are called democracies. Democracies are of two basic types, those in which people are directly involved in the governmental process and those in which they participate indirectly through elected representatives.* Democracies of the second type are frequently referred to as representative democracies or republican governments. The Greek city-state and the early New England communities which were run through town meetings are examples of direct participation by the people in the governmental process. The United States and most of the countries of Western Europe today are examples of representative democracies.

In a democratic system both the government and the people are subject to the rule of law or due process of law. The limits of governmental authority in a democracy are usually well defined, either in a constitution or in law. Government leaders are supposed to carry out the will of the people, and if they do not, new leaders will be selected to conduct the affairs of government.

Problems of classifying governments When we introduce the relationship between government and the economy into a classification system for political systems, a great deal of ambiguity is created. *The two possible extremes for government's role in the economy are laissez*

* Authoritarianism has been the most common form of governmental organization since the development of political states.

faire, in which the government limits its role in economic activity to the minimum possible, and totalitarianism, in which the government is involved directly or indirectly in every aspect of the economic activity of a society. However, there is no direct relationship between the technique used to select government leaders and the role of government in the economy. In addition, there is not necessarily a direct relationship between the system of property ownership in a society and the technique for selecting government leaders and/or the role of government in the economy.

For example, socialism—which is usually defined as public or collective ownership of the factors of production, capital and natural resources—can be associated with either authoritarianism or democracy. Also, the private ownership of property does not necessarily imply any particular technique for selecting leaders or any specific role for government in the economy. In Germany under Hitler and Italy under Mussolini most of the factors of production were privately owned although there was extensive state control of the economy, and both were authoritarian regimes. On the other hand, the United States has always had almost complete private ownership of the factors of production, a democratic political process, and limited government participation in the economy.

Since the different classifications of political systems are frequently based on a single characteristic, there are often misunderstandings about the total system being referred to. Saying that the political system of a particular country is authoritarian, or democratic, or socialistic, or liberal conveys only limited information about the nature of that country's political system. If one is interested in understanding aspects of a particular political system other than those on which the classification is based, it is necessary to look beyond the label associated with that political system.

SOVEREIGNTY VERSUS LEGITIMACY OF GOVERNMENT

Sovereignty refers to a government's claim to make decisions which affect the state, and the source of a government's sovereignty is its legitimacy. The sovereign government has the right to impose its will upon persons and organizations within its political boundaries and to establish and conduct relationships with other sovereign governments. Sovereignty does not necessarily imply the power to implement the decisions once they are made. De Gaulle's Free French government of France during World War II is an example of a sovereign government which did not possess the power to carry out its decisions. History is full of examples of weak rulers who did not possess the power to implement their decisions even though they were recognized as sovereign, i.e., as the legitimate rulers.

Legitimacy is a concept which refers to a group of people's recognition of the right of an organization to rule them. Government is not the only organization to possess legitimacy, but it is the only organization to possess sovereignty. The church, political parties, labor unions, etc., all possess legitimacy. Each of these organizations is recognized by its members as having the right to establish rules which they are expected to follow. However, only government has the right to impose its will upon people and other organizations within the political boundaries of the state. Since government has the final or supreme authority over the people and other organizations within its boundaries, ultimately only it has a right to rule.

In times of great social turmoil within a country there may be powerful political groups competing for the people's consent to their rule. When this occurs, legitimacy is being contested, and there is no group which is sovereign. The Civil War period is an example of a time when competing political groups were struggling to establish the right to govern. The political area being contested was those states which constituted the Confederacy. The period of the American Revolution is another example of a period when two political groups were competing for the right to govern. Vietnam is a place where powerful political groups are currently competing for the right to rule. In all three of these examples violence has been involved in the ultimate determination of which political group was legitimate. The question which arises is, "Does might make right?" That is, does legitimacy follow automatically from the possession of the power to govern? This raises the question of whether or not there are restrictions on the valid ways in which legitimacy and thereby sovereignty can be acquired.

SOURCES OF LEGITIMACY

The authorization of government by the people can come from various sources; that is, there are channels through which governments can acquire the legitimacy necessary to confer sovereignty on them. These are (1) legal or rational legitimacy, (2) traditional legitimacy, and (3) charismatic legitimacy. This classification of the sources of legitimacy is based on a system developed by Max Weber.

Legal or rational legitimacy *Legal or rational legitimacy stems from the belief that government is based on objective, rational principles and that these have usually been incorporated into law.* A government which is based on rational legitimacy is regulated by the legal framework within which it operates. In the United States there is a strong belief that ours is "a government of laws, and not men." The question, of course, is where the laws that serve as the rational basis of government come from. In the United States it is commonly believed that the laws represent or should represent the will of the people. The importance which people in the United States put on a formalized set of rules or laws is reflected by the fact that even in many voluntary associations, one of the first acts of business when the association is formed is to draw up a set of by-laws or a written constitution. It is important to note that if the laws which regulate the political process are in fact a reflection of the will of the people, you have "a government of the people."

It is possible to have rational legitimacy in which the laws or principles which regulate the government are not based upon the will of the people. For example, the British philosopher Thomas Hobbes argued that kings ruled by divine right and that kings were the instruments of God to establish order in an otherwise chaotic and violent state. Thus, the rational legitimacy of kings to rule, according to Hobbes, was the will of God. Also, there are those who believe that there are certain absolute laws of nature which can be discovered by the scientific process and which, when discovered, serve as the source of rational legitimacy for a government. Karl Marx is an example of one who falls into this latter category.

Governments which are based on rational legitimacy are expected to act upon the principles and laws which serve as the basis for their legitimacy. Governments which fail to do so leave themselves open to attack on the grounds that they are violating their authority and failing to perform their duties. In the United States government units which wish to pursue activities not covered by existing law must get legislation passed which legitimizes these activities. Ultimately, the test of whether or not government units in the United States can legitimately engage in any given activity is the Constitution of the United States.

The argument is frequently made that our system leaves the power to determine the legitimacy of governmental actions and policies to those justices who constitute the Supreme Court, and that these justices are sometimes prone to decide what they believe should be and then interpret the Constitution accordingly. The decisions of the Court related to public school segregation are often cited as examples of this. If Supreme Court decisions are arrived at in this manner, and this element is certainly involved in many of their decisions, what many see as the source of the rational legitimacy of the government has been violated and our government becomes one of people and not one of laws. This is not particularly disturbing when you realize that the Constitution of the United States was produced by people and as such is subject to revision by people. Historically, the Supreme Court's interpretation of the Constitution has been a major technique used to alter the meaning associated with the general language of the Constitution so that it is relevant to existing political and social circumstances. Probably, the relevant argument in this instance is whether or not this is the appropriate way to initiate the change.

Traditional legitimacy *Traditional legitimacy develops from precedent; that is, the right of government to perform certain tasks stems from the fact that it has performed these tasks in the past.* The kings who governed European countries in the past are examples of rulers whose source of legitimacy was traditional. In feudal Europe tradition was so strong that it served as almost the entire source of the legitimacy of those who governed. Traditional legitimacy has always been weak in the United States. In fact, the arguments used by those who led the American Revolution were to a large extent based on the idea that tradition was not a valid source of legitimacy. Jefferson believed that each generation should write its own constitution. He believed in leadership based on "ability" rather than on rank and birthrights. There is growing concern in the United States that we are moving toward a situation in which the country will be run by a wealthy elite who derive their positions of power and influence through inheritance. A survey by the Federal Reserve Board in 1962 revealed that approximately 2 percent of the household units in the United States owned 65 percent of the investment assests. (Investment assets are publicly traded stock, marketable securites other than stock, mortgage assets, investment real estate, business investments not managed by the consumer unit, and company savings plans.)[1] It is frequently argued that the wealthy elite is becoming an increasingly closed group. Ferdinand Lundberg, a well-known expert on income distribution in the United States, contends that: "Nearly all the current large incomes, those exceeding $1 million, $500,000, or even $100,000 or $50,000 a year, are derived in fact from old property accumulations, by inheritors—that is, by people who never did whatever one is required to do, approved or disapproved, creative or noncreative, in order to assemble a fortune."[2] One of the major issues in the 1972 Presidential election was the influence that those who controlled the wealth in the United States were having on the political process.

One of the major ways in which the wealthy influence the political process in the United States is through contributions toward the campaign expenses of those running for public office. The investigations of the Watergate Committee in 1973 to 1974 revealed how extensively those who control the wealth in the United States were involved in attempting to influence the Presidential election in 1972. The investigations also revealed the potential for corruption which is associated with the way campaigns are currently financed. There is strong support in the United States today for the passage of legislation which would provide for government financing of the campaigns of those running for national office. Those who favor such legislation argue that it would reduce the influence of the wealthy on the political process and reduce the corruption associated with campaigns for public office.

Tradition is an important element in determining the willingness of people to accept the legitimacy of governmental organization, even in a society that is as rationally oriented as the United States. For instance, a large part of the opposition to the federal government's involvement in public education stems from the fact that public education has traditionally been the domain of state and local governments. Also, the solution to the urban problems in the United States is hampered because it is impossible to establish the governmental organization needed to deal with the problems, and a major reason for the inability to establish the needed organization is the unwillingness of the people to accept nontraditional political organization.

Charismatic legitimacy *The third form of legitimacy, charismatic legitimacy, stems from certain leaders' possession of some seemingly magical quality which causes people to bestow upon them the right to govern.* (In Christian theology, charisma implies a divinely inspired gift or talent for something such as prophesying or healing.) Political leaders in modern times who have possessed this quality are Franklin Roosevelt, Mahatma Gandhi, Fidel Castro, Adolf Hitler, Mao Tse-tung, Martin Luther King, Jr., and John F. Kennedy. Rarely does one find pure charismatic legitimacy. Of the leaders listed above, Mahatma Gandhi is the one whose power was most dependent on charismatic legitimacy. Frequently, the early leadership of new movements is based on charisma; however, as the movements grow, rational and traditional legitimacy become increasingly important.

Charisma is an important factor in determining the extent to which political leaders will be restricted by the traditional and rational legitimacy which serves as the basis for the authority of the positions they hold. For example, Franklin Roosevelt was able to overcome a century and a half of tradition when he ran for a third term. This feat would have

The force and effectiveness of Martin Luther King, Jr's, civil disobedience movement in the 1960s depended greatly upon his personal appeal to large numbers of Americans, black and white. *(World Wide Photos)*

probably been impossible for someone with less charisma. The possession of charisma frequently enables political leaders to get people to accept social and political changes which other political leaders would have been condemned for attempting to bring about.

In most instances the legitimacy of governments is not derived from any single form of legitimacy but from some combination of the three. Even though most people would argue that in the United States, the government is based on rational legitimacy, it is obvious that at times tradition and the charisma of the leaders are important factors in determining the scope of the activities which the people consider valid for government. However, there have been situations in which government did not possess legitimacy from any of the three sources; that is, there have been illegitimate governments. The most common type of illegitimate government is one in which an outside political power forces the people to accept the government. The Vichy government's rule of France during World War II is a good example of this. The government of Mao Tse-tung in China did not possess traditional or rational legitimacy when it first came to power in 1949. The United States' official acceptance of Mao's government as the legitimate government of China did not come until President Nixon's visit to Red China in 1972 even though Mao's government possessed charismatic legitimacy from the beginning. Most of the other countries of the world had accepted Mao's government as the legitimate government of China long before the United States did. This was because Mao's government had been successful in gaining the general acceptance of the people of China and establishing new patterns of laws and beliefs long before 1972. The United States' acceptance was delayed because we had earlier recognized Chiang Kai-shek's exiled government on Formosa as the legitimate government of China, and we were hesitant to deny the claim of legitimacy of an ally.

THE PROPER ROLE OF GOVERNMENT IN SOCIETY

The question as to the "proper" role(s) of government is one which continually plagues social scientists. There are four general theoretical views as to the proper role of government in the social organization of a society. These are (1) anarchist, (2) individualist, (3) collectivist, and (4) regulationist. The last three of these directly parallel the three approaches to the role of government in the economy discussed in the last chapter.

Anarchist view *The anarchist approach assumes that there is no need for formal governmental organization.* Anarchists contend that the functions which government performs can be performed by voluntary associations of people. In its pure form Marx's communism is a form of anarchy. Marx believed that in advanced stages of social development, people would become socially responsible and government would "wither away." Unless there emerges such a society—i.e., one in which the state withers away because there is no need for coercion, since there is no exploition, no conflict, and no crime—anarchy does not seem like a very acceptable substitute for some form of governmental organization. Besides, it seems almost certain that any voluntary association that arose to perform such functions as the protection of life, liberty, and property would quickly evolve into a formal governmental organization.

Individualist view *Individualists, like anarchists, dislike government; however, individualists believe that government is a necessary evil which must be tolerated.* Individualists adhere to the Jeffersonian view that, "That government is best which governs least." This group reflects the ideology that dominated the United States from its founding until this century. Individualists believe that governmental activities should be restricted to the protection of life, liberty, and property, and that, whenever possible, functions which can be carried out through nongovernmental social organizations should be. Governmental organization as a technique for solving problems is looked upon as an inferior "last resort" by this group.

Collectivist view *Collectivists (or socialists) believe that government should be deeply involved in the functioning of society.* For example, they view government as the only social organization capable of equitably managing the economic resources of a society. Socialists believe that the government should own and control all the nonlabor inputs used in the production and distribution of the economic goods and services of the society. Thus government would own and control such things as natural resources; capital used in production, such as factories and equipment; financial institutions; the transportation systems; and public utilities such as gas and electricity. The collectivists believe that a properly run government is the social institution which can best ensure fair and equal treatment for all members of society, if not the only one that can do this.

Regulationist view *Regulationists take a position somewhere between individualists and collectivists; that is, they see government performing more than the minimum functions of protection prescribed by the individualists but stopping short of the pervasive role envisioned by the socialists.* The regulationist view best describes the government in the United States today; however, there are many people who philosophically adhere to the individualist approach and yearn for the "good old days" when government restricted itself to protection of life, liberty, and property. It is debatable if the "good old days" ever did exist except as wishful thinking. The New Deal of Franklin Roosevelt in the 1930s ended any effort to pursue the individualist approach. During the Roosevelt administration the government assumed a more active role in the regulation and supervision of the national economy and undertook broad social programs that would never have been seriously considered by previous government officials. These included such things as the social security program and programs to ensure adequate housing and full employment. Many of the programs started by Roosevelt have been continued and enlarged, and additional social programs have been added. The guaranteed annual income which is currently being considered represents an extension of the welfare philosophy of the New Deal.

In the United States, government has recently assumed a new role in relation to other institutions. It has always served as a regulatory agency or check to protect individuals or groups against overt activities of social organizations which were potentially harmful. However, since the 1950s, government, particularly the federal government, has been attempting to control institutional practices which discriminate against certain groups of people. The social institutions which have been the primary targets of these governmental policies are the educational system and business enterprises. Governmental policies have been aimed primarily at ending practices on the part of these organizations which discriminated against some racial and ethnic groups, certain age groups, and women. Government has been attempting to eliminate dual, segregated school systems which lead to inferior education for such groups as blacks and Mexican-Americans. Also, government has been attempting to eliminate such business practices as discrimination in hiring, in determination of wage scales, and in promotion policies. In the next chapter we shall discuss further the shift from the individualist approach to the regulationist approach in the United States.

FUNCTIONS OF GOVERNMENT

The functions which are performed by government can all be put into one of five general categories: (1) providing external security, (2) maintaining internal order, (3) ensuring justice, (4) promoting the general welfare, and (5) protecting individual freedom. Government is not totally responsible for all these functions in society. The extent to which government assumes the responsibility for these functions depends in large part on the society's approach to government, that is, anarchist, individualist, etc.

Providing external security This means protecting the society from threats by other societies. In order to perform this function governments engage in political relations in order to settle disputes that arise among different societies. The purpose of maintaining political relations with other governments is to provide a channel through which disputes can be resolved by nonviolent means. However, an examination of history reveals that states have not always been able to successfully resolve their disputes peacefully. Because states have not developed techniques that enable them to peacefully resolve all their disputes, governments devote large amounts of their resources to maintaining military establishments to safeguard their security.

In the United States this function is almost totally the responsibility of the federal government, and in 1970 over 80[3] percent of the goods and services purchased by the federal government were for national defense. This is the most costly function performed by government in the United States today. The only involvement of state and local government units in providing for external security in the United States is the maintenance of state militias (National Guard) which come under national control in times of emergency or war and are subject to Congressional authority in peacetime. However, the National Guard performs a dual role in that it is frequently called upon to help maintain internal order as well as to be available for national defense.

Maintaining internal order The second function performed by government, maintaining internal order, involves maintaining order within the domestic society. This means protecting the rights and property of the members of society and providing a means for members of society to settle disputes without resorting to violence. In order to perform this function, laws are developed to regulate human interaction, and machinery is created to enforce the law. We have developed an elaborate legal system to enforce the laws that have been passed. In the United States, government units at the federal, state, and local levels are involved in carrying out this function.

Ensuring justice This is a function which is difficult to define specifically, but it implies that the interaction of the members of society is regulated in a manner which ensures that the society is characterized by a sense of fairness and decency. The concepts of fairness and decency imply normative considerations which are almost certain to result in conflicting interpretations. A large part of the conflict can be resolved by separating any consideration of justice into two categories, legal justice and social justice.

Legal justice Legal justice involves the establishment of laws and the machinery to administer these laws in a fair and impartial way. Ideally human disputes would be settled through an impartial process which is operated on the basis of a fixed set of rules. However, it is important to recognize that any process which is regulated by a set of rules that people have developed is almost certain to be influenced by value judgments which reflect the cultural views of the society. Thus, the supposedly impartial process through which legal justice is dispensed may not be so impartial. In the United States, for example, there is frequently differential treatment of the sexes in the legal process, and the amount of money that a person has is important in determining the access that that individual has to certain aspects of the legal process, and therefore the type of treatment received. Despite the fact that legal justice frequently falls short of the ideal in practice, the fairness with which disputes are settled in society is enhanced by the existence of government.

A question that has recently arisen is whether or not the President and the Vice President are subject to the legal process in the same manner as other citizens. With respect to the Vice President, former Vice President Agnew avoided having this question taken up by the courts when he resigned. The issue involved was whether or not Agnew could be indicted for alleged misconduct which occurred while he was an elected official in Maryland. The alleged misconduct was "kickbacks" that he supposedly received during his tenure in public office. The issue of whether or not President Nixon can be indicted for his alleged activities in the events associated with Watergate is currently being debated. The general feeling seems to be that he cannot be unless he is impeached and found guilty by Congress first.

Social justice Social justice implies a fair distribution of the amenities available in a society among the members and a fair system for the sharing of any undesirable aspects associated with the functioning and/or survival of the society. Since social justice is defined in terms of fairness, it is by its very nature a normative issue. Thus, the value system of the society is the source of the criteria for determining what constitutes social justice. In laissez faire capitalist societies, for example, it is commonly believed that each member's share of the amenities available should be based on his or her contribution, whereas in many socialist societies it is believed that each person should contribute according to his or her abilities and share in the amenities to an extent determined by his or her needs.

The laissez faire capitalist view is the one which has historically been adhered to in the United States, philosophically if not in practice. However. in the last half century there has been a growing recognition that individual contribution was not an adequate explanation of the way the amenities were being distributed in the United States. In fact, in a complex society such as that of the United States, it is frequently impossible to measure the contribution of a single individual, or even of a group of people, for that matter, to the well-being of society. It is often an individual's membership in a particular group which receives preference in society or the ability to manipulate aspects of the system, not contributions to the well-being of society, that determine what share of the amenities that individual receives.

Because America's value system has changed over the last hundred years, so that we no longer accept laissez faire capitalism as a measure of social justice, government has intervened in the operation of society and has undertaken measures to correct the imbalance that existed. These measures include such things as unemployment insurance, old-age assistance, minimum wage laws, and more recently measures to prevent discrimination against people because of their race, ethnic origin, or sex.

Perhaps the only major undesirable aspect of society in the United States that has not been forced primarily upon those who lacked wealth and power is service in the military. Even this is a relative recent phenomenon, because prior to this century it was common for those with wealth to pay other people to fulfill their military obligations. In fact, there are some who oppose an all-volunteer army because they believe that the wealthy and their families would almost certainly be excluded. Their reasoning is that the all-volunteer army would be achieved by making the earnings of those in the military high enough to attract sufficient personnel to meet the military needs of the country, and it is almost certain that since the rank at which one can enter the military is restricted, the earnings would not ever be high enough to attract large numbers from the upper income groups of our society. Hence the real effect of an all-volunteer army would be to create an army composed primarily of people from the lower income groups, thereby enabling the wealthy to avoid military service completely. If this should in fact be the effect of an all-volunteer army, which has not been proven, it is debatable whether or not social justice would be served by such an army.

Promoting the general welfare The fourth function which government performs is promoting the general welfare. In this role government assumes the responsibility for promoting the material well-being of the members of society. Prior to Roosevelt's New Deal of the 1930s, this function consisted primarily of creating an environment conducive to private economic activity in the United States. Governmental activities included such things as tariffs to protect domestic producers from foreign competition, subsidies to private businesses to encourage them to undertake activities deemed essential to the development of the economy (the subsidies given to the railroads are an example of this), manipulation of the monetary system, the general regulation of private economic activity designed to prevent private businesses from engaging in activities that might prove harmful to the successful operation of the economy.

It was not until the New Deal that government began to play a major, positive role in directly promoting the material welfare of individuals within society. Measures which have been taken toward this end include such things as old-age maintenance programs, the institution of a massive social security system, provision of unemployment benefits, and child-welfare programs such as providing hot lunches to school children from low income families. Government assumption of responsibility for the material well-being of individuals is often referred to as welfarism, and governments which assume this responsibility are called welfare governments. The development of the "welfare state" in the United States is a highly controversial issue today. The question is primarily one of determining how far government should go in assuming responsibility for the material well-being of the individual. Currently the major controversy associated with this question is whether or not individuals should receive a guaranteed annual income. Also, there is the problem of determining whether or not there are any feasible alternatives which promote individual welfare that do not involve direct government participation.

Protecting individual freedom The final function performed by government is protecting the freedom of the individual from oppression by other people or groups within society. Associated with this function in the United States is the assumption that government exists to serve the people. This is an assumption that is restricted to the democratic countries of the world.

A question that has plagued philosophers and political scientists for centuries is how best to resolve the conflict between government's regulation of people's affairs and the individual's right to do as he or she pleases. Government should obviously restrict its activities to those that promote freedom and avoid those that encroach upon it. An example that is often used to illustrate this seeming conflict is regulations on the use of automobiles. Individuals are forced to obey traffic regulations, which would appear to be a restriction on their right to use their automobiles as they please, but in fact their mobility is enhanced by the traffic regulations because it would frequently be almost impossible to move from place to place without the regulations. The enhancement of individual freedom by governmental regulation is not always as clear-cut as in this example.

There is growing recognition in the United States that all too often government has incorporated into its regulation, or at least failed to sufficiently restrict, practices in society which encroach upon individual freedom. Practices which were condoned by government in the past but which are today illegal include Negro slavery, primogeniture applied to the transfer of land, and suppression of the rights of women. Government has also attempted to restrict institutional organization of the economy, which would have harmful effects on the individual, and to restrict the activities of groups such as the Ku Klux Klan when they encroach upon individual freedom.

Any casual observer of society in the United States can see that government has not been 100 percent successful in its efforts to protect individual freedom. However, government is continuing its efforts to extend equal opportunities to all members of society.* Recent efforts have been concentrated on assuring everyone an equal opportunity to an education, equal access to public accommodations, equal access to the occupational opportunities in society, and equal opportunity to participate in the governmental process. Success in these efforts would certainly lead to more individual freedom in society than there was previously. A case can be made against government's involvement in society which would point out that such things as government snooping and invasions of privacy have led to a reduction of individual freedom. Such an argument does not invalidate the use of governmental authority to expand individual freedom, it simply indicates that unrestrained power in the hands of government officials can lead to abuses. The implication is that continual vigilance is necessary in situations in which governmental authority is being exercised.

IMPLEMENTING GOVERNMENTAL DECISIONS

Once governmental decisions have been made, various techniques can be used to implement them. However, all these techniques fall into one of three general categories: (1) economic control, (2) force, and (3) education. It is quite likely that in most instances some combination of techniques from more than one of these categories will be used when implementing governmental decisions.

The selection of techniques to use in implementing any specific governmental decision is extremely important because governmental activity cannot be viewed as simply a set of end results. Rather, governmental activity is a continual process, and it is the techniques which government uses that determine the impact that the process has on individuals and on society generally. In fact, one of the issues that political scientists and social scientists generally are continually faced with is determining the extent to which desirable end results can serve as a justification for the use of techniques which would be considered undesirable if evaluated on their own merit. For example, many of those who have historically favored the use of violence to achieve "good goals" have contended that they abhorred violence but that it was necessary in order to achieve certain highly desirable end results. This

* Individual freedom has been given an operational definition: that all individuals be given not only the right to do certain things, but also a realistic opportunity to do them.

same issue is involved in such decisions as determining the use of such things as wiretapping and forced service in the military. Needless to say, this issue is rarely resolved in a manner which receives unanimous approval.

It is not possible to say that any of the techniques government uses to implement its decisions are good or bad per se. Almost any technique can be justified under certain circumstances, and any technique can be used improperly. However, it is very important to distinguish between goals and techniques. Failure to do so can lead to considerable confusion. For instance, if the goal is undesirable it makes little sense to discuss the merit of the techniques being used to achieve it. This type of situation caused some confusion in evaluating the United States role in the Vietnam war. Many people failed to recognize that the opposition to our participation in the Vietnam war came from two very different sources. First, there were those who were opposed to the war because they felt that our goal, or reason for being involved in Vietnam, was wrong, and to this group the techniques being used to conduct the war were of secondary importance in explaining their opposition to the war. Another large group who opposed the United States involvement did so because they felt that the techniques being used to conduct the war were not adequate to win it, and they did not approve of involvement in a war unless techniques which would ensure victory could be used. To this latter group, our reasons for getting involved were of secondary importance. Any attempt to explain the opposition of the people in the United States to the war in Vietnam which does not distinguish between these two different sources of opposition would be incorrect.

Economic control Many government decisions, particularly in the United States, are implemented through economic manipulation. Most of the techniques of economic control fall into one of four general categories: (1) government expenditures and direct subsidies, (2) taxation, (3) regulation of the monetary system, and (4) regulation of the private sector of the economy. In any given situation, government decision makers may use a combination of economic measures from two or more of these categories.

Government expenditures and subsidies are as diverse as government activity itself. Education and military expenditures are examples of government decisions implemented by direct expenditures. That is, it has been decided in the United States that it is the responsibility of government to make certain that there is adequate military protection and educational opportunity, and government implements the decisions by providing these things directly. The highway system is another example of the implementation of a government decision through direct expenditure. In fact, in 1970, military, education, and highways accounted for approximately 70 percent of direct government expenditures at all levels, i.e., federal, state, and local.[4] Government also provides direct payment of subsidies to such groups as farmers and the merchant marine in order to achieve its goals. However, most of the subsidies in the United States are indirect and are administered by manipulating the tax system.

Manipulation of the tax system has long been a technique used by government to get people to engage in activities which are deemed desirable. This has been achieved by providing special tax benefits (indirect subsidies) to those who did certain things. These special tax benefits are frequently referred to as tax loopholes. They include concessions to those who are engaged in such things as extracting natural resorces, to those who purchase houses instead of renting, to those who purchase bonds sold by state and local governments, and to business for new investments. For instance, all income earned from state and local government bonds is exempt from federal income tax. Such loopholes in the tax structure permit many individuals with large incomes to pay little or no federal income tax.

It is frequently argued that much of the existing tax structure does not reflect a system of incentives to encourage behavior that would be beneficial to our nation, but rather it reflects the efforts of special interest groups who have been successful in gaining tax provisions for their own interests. In fact, reform of the existing tax structure was one of the major issues in the Presidential election in 1972.

The federal government can also manipulate the monetary system in pursuing its goals. However, such manipulations have a general impact, and other measures are normally needed in order to achieve goals which do not involve the entire country. The federal government has created a monetary system called the Federal Reserve System, the control of which is in the hands of the Board of Governors of the System. This board is made up of seven members, each appointed by the President and approved by the Senate for a term of fourteen years. One new member is appointed every two years, and no member can serve more than one term. The Board of Governors of the Federal Reserve System is not directly accountable to anyone in the government. Because of this they have at times been referred to as the fourth branch of the federal government, i.e., judicial, legislative, executive, and monetary.

The fourth economic technique government uses to achieve its goals is regulation of the private sector of the economy. This has become one of the most-used economic techniques. However, this technique has been used more often in a negative than in a positive sense, i.e., to prevent activities which government considers undesirable, rather than to help achieve positive goals. Regulation by government of business organizations, of credit requirements, of quality standards for products, and of advertising, and more recently efforts to regulate wages and prices, are examples of regulatory activities which have been undertaken in order to prevent practices in the private sector of the United States which could prove harmful to the public. Governments at all levels are currently in the process of establishing restrictions on activities which would destroy our environment.

Another area in which government regulation plays an important role in economic activity is in the area of international trade. Virtually all economic activity which involves a party that is from another sovereign country is subject to some form of government regulation. This regulation includes such things as reciprocal trade agreements, tariffs, export and import quotas, and control of exchange rates between the currencies of the different countries.

At this point it must be fairly obvious that the scope of the economic techniques which government uses to implement its decisions is great. There are very few aspects of American society that are not influenced in some way or another by the economic controls and/or activities of government. Each of the economic activities of government can be directly attributed to attempts by those charged with making governmental decisions to implement their decisions. The use of economic controls to implement governmental decisions in the United States has greatly increased in the last forty or fifty years.

Force Force, which is the direct exercise of power, is one of the most effective techniques government uses to implement its decisions. It is in almost all instances the monopoly of government. That is, only government has a legitimate right to physically force people to comply with its demands. Unauthorized use of force, i.e., by private individuals or groups, is usually classified as violence. The exception to this is that in most societies the use of force by the head of the household is condoned in certain situations. However, it is common for the government to establish restrictions on the use of force by the head of the household.

The fact that government can legitimately use force to implement its decisions is often a major reason why economic and educational measures are effective. The people comply with economic measures because they know the government can use force if they fail to comply. The payment of taxes is an illustration of such a situation.

In many modern societies economic and educational measures are preferred to force as techniques for implementing domestic governmental decisions. In these societies force is usually considered a last resort. The Soviet Union under Stalin and Germany under Hitler are glaring examples of situations in which force was frequently considered the preferred technique for carrying out governmental policies. History is full of such examples, and in some societies force is still commonly used and accorded the same status as economic manipulation and education as a technique for implementing governmental decisions.

In the United States authorities normally attempt to use other techniques before resorting to force. An elaborate court system has been developed to provide the public with a source of appeal against the illegitimate use of force by the state. However, the existence of large numbers of jails and prisons in the United States is proof that force is an important technique used by government to gain compliance.

There is currently a controversy in the United States over what techniques are valid when the state is using its coercive powers against the public. The controversy centers around the use of such techniques as wiretapping, entry and search without court order, surveillance of public figures, etc. This controversy is part of a larger issue commonly referred to as the "law and order issue." The law and order issue involves the question of what constitutes the proper use of force in dealing with criminal activities and political dissent in the United States. The use of force when dealing with the latter is a particularly touchy issue.

This discussion has not meant to insinuate that all Americans are opposed to the use of force by the state to carry out its policies. This was apparent from the divided reaction to the incident at Kent State when several students were wounded or killed by the National Guard during a rally opposing the Vietnam war. Many people felt that this represented an extreme abuse of government's authority to use force.

In international affairs, i.e., relationships between nation-states,

Given the destructive consequences of modern warfare, pressure mounts for nations to find techniques other than force to settle international disputes. *(United Press International Photos)*

force has generally been used with less restraint. For instance, to achieve its goals in Vietnam, the United States was willing to use techniques that were certain to cause many innocent people to suffer, such as extensive bombing and defoliation. This is quite a contrast to our internal situation in which the court system is designed to provide every possible benefit to the innocent.

The United States has frequently attempted to achieve its international goals through such forms of economic manipulation as gifts, loans, and technical assistance and through education programs. However, the fact that the United States annually spends many times as much on the military as on other techniques reflects its unwillingness to rely too heavily on techniques other than force in pursuing its international policies.

Education Political education refers to efforts by government to persuade people to accept and conform to its policies by providing them with information and using psychological techniques of persuasion. Political education is considered a legitimate technique for implementing governmental decisions in all societies. When political education is misused, it is often called propaganda.

In practice it is frequently difficult to distinguish between political education and propaganda because so many governmental decisions involve normative considerations, and those who disagree with a decision frequently view political education which is used to gain support for it as propaganda. In some instances government leaders actually distort the information they provide in order to gain support for their policies. Such use of political education is obviously improper and represents the lowest form of propaganda. There is also a danger that government will use its power to squelch information which is unfavorable to it or which contains elements it does not like. The Nixon-Agnew attacks on the press are frequently viewed as efforts to squelch unfavorable information. Also, Nixon's rejection of commission reports on pornography, population, and the process of justice is an example of efforts to squelch information distasteful to the Administration. One can be quite certain that these reports would have been treated very differently had their findings been to Nixon's liking.

In a democratic society political education is more than a technique for gaining support for government policies. It is a process for providing the public with information so that they can become effectively involved in the decision-making process. This involvement, of course, is in the form of participation in open and free elections. Thus, the political education process must function properly if there is to be a freely functioning marketplace of ideas in which the people can select the ones that they deem most desirable. For instance, in order for the people to decide the role that they want government to play in the United States economy, they must be provided with all relevant information as to the possible roles that government might take and the potential effects of each. Obviously government leaders cannot be expected to supply all this information. One of the major functions of social scientists in society is to help provide it. One example of the implementation of this function is public opinion polls such as those conducted by Gallup, Harris, and Lubel.

The techniques used by government to provide political education include making printed materials and audio-visual materials available to the the public, usually free or for a nominal fee. Also, political leaders have made effective use of magazines, newspapers, radio, and television in providing political information to the public. Franklin D. Roosevelt was the first president of the United States to effectively use radio as a medium for gaining public support for his policies. Today television is frequently used by political leaders as a technique to provide political information to the people. All recent Presidents of the United States have used television in efforts to gain support for policies that they deemed important. This has particularly been true when they felt that their policies might be misunderstood or encounter strong opposition from other political leaders or influential segments of society.

Unlike force, political education is not a monopoly of the state in all societies. Political education is a monopoly of the state only in totalitarian societies, whereas in democratic societies any individual or institution can use this technique to attempt to persuade people. States such as Nazi Germany and today Red China, where political education is a state monopoly, have successfully used it to gain extensive public support for governmental policies. In both these instances the government leaders were succesfully able to manipulate the political information people had available, and by so doing gain support for their policies and develop a strong feeling of loyalty to the state among the people. Needless to say, political education as a technique for gaining support for governmental policies is not as effective in democratic societies where it is not a state monopoly. However, a comparison of the quality of the information provided the people reveals that the information received by the people in a democratic society is far better than in a totalitarian society, i.e., it is more extensive and accurate.

Some rather controversial situations related to the dissemination of political information have arisen recently in the United States. One of these concerns the question of how much the public should be told about what is going on in government, and the other involves agencies within the government which engage in political education activities that are beyond those which are legitimate for those agencies.

The question of how much the public should know about what is going on in government revolves around two major issues. The first issue is the classification of government information as "top secret" and withholding it from the public. Also related to this is the question of how accessible government files should be, and to whom they should be accessible. The use of the "top secret" classification to restrict information available to the public has primarily been associated with the federal government, whereas limited access to government files is a problem which exists at all levels. A related issue is that of determining which government meetings should be open to the public. Given the need of the people for political information in the decision-making process in a democratic society, it seems rational to attempt to have as much information as possible available and to make it as easily accessible as possible. Thus, it would seem desirable to have government meetings and files open to the public generally, and any time the public is denied access to these to place the burden of justifying this denial on government officials. The use of the "top secret" classification should be limited to information that directly involves national security or which would have harmful effects on innocent people. The thing that must be kept in mind when deciding which information should be available to the public is that a democratic system cannot function without a free flow of information.

The role which has been assumed by some government agencies in the political education process has been subjected to sharp criticism. Perhaps the best example of this is the program of political information that has been used by the Pentagon. In a television special on CBS in 1971, *The Selling of the Pentagon*, it was revealed that the military was engaged in providing speakers and audio-visual and printed materials which were designed to gain support for the views of those in the military. In addition, the military was providing entertainment for public and private events, conducting community leaders' conferences in which influential residents of communities were brought in and given a thorough presentation of the military point of view, and conducting open-houses on military installations which were designed to sell the military. The reason for criticizing these activities was that the military was attempting to influence aspects of political decision even though they did not have legitimate authority to participate in that aspect of the decision-making process.

We may conclude from our discussion that even though political education is a legitimate technique for implementing governmental decisions, its use must be restricted in a democratic system. Otherwise, the control of political information can become a technique of limiting the free flow of information which the people need if they are to participate effectively in the system.

SUMMARY

The existence of government reflects the existence of social problems which cannot be coped with on an individual basis. In the past government has frequently been viewed as a "last resort," but there is a growing recognition that government can perform a positive function in society.

Other social organizations frequently view government as a competitor in supplying goods and services. The growth of government has been in part a result of government's assumption of responsibilities formerly held by other social institutions.

The *government* consists of all those agencies and processes through which the state conducts its activities. States possess a territory, a people, a government, and independence. *Politics* refers more specifically to the process which is involved when the governmental machinery is used to carry out government's activities. A failure to recognize the distinction between government and politics can lead to confusion.

Most governments are classified on the basis of such things as the role of government in the economy, the technique for selecting leaders, the system of ownership of property, and the ideology underlying the system. Governments in which the people do not directly participate are classified as authoritarian governments, and those in which the people do participate in the political process are classified as democracies. Since the different classifications of political systems are frequently based on a single characteristic, the use of classification labels to describe political systems often leads to misunderstandings.

Sovereignty refers to a government's claim to make decisions which affect the state. The source of a government's sovereignty is its legitimacy. *Legitimacy* refers to a group of people's recognition of the right of an organization to rule them. The three types of legitimacy are (1) legal or rational, (2) traditional, and (3) charismatic. Governments generally derive their legitimacy from some combination of these three.

The four general theoretical views as to the proper role of government in society are (1) anarchist, (2) individualist, (3) collectivist, and (4) regulationist. The anarchist argues that there is no need for formal government and that the governmental functions can be performed by voluntary associations. Individualists believe that government is a necessary evil which must be tolerated but which should be limited as much as possible. Collectivists think that government should be deeply involved in the functioning of society. The Regulationists take a position somewhere between the those of individualists and collectivists.

The diverse functions performed by government fall into one of five general categories: (1) providing external security, (2) maintaining internal order, (3) ensuring justice, (4) promoting the general welfare, and (5) protecting individual freedom.

The three general techniques used by governments to implement their decisions are economic control, force, and education. Some combination of these techniques will usually be used to implement any single decision. The technique used to implement any governmental decision is very important because it determines the impact of the continuing governmental process on the individual. A question associated with the selection of techniques is, "Does the end justify the means?" Any of the techniques used to implement governmental decisions can be used either properly or improperly. Thus, it is impossible to classify any technique as good or bad per se. Economic control techniques used include (1) government expenditures and direct subsidies, (2) taxation, (3) regulation of the monetary system, and (4) regulation of the private sector of the economy. Force is always the monopoly of the government. Unauthorized use of force is classified as violence. Misuse of political education is called propaganda. Political education is extremely important in a democratic society because it provides the information which the members of society need to function effectively in the political process.

REVIEW QUESTIONS

1. What does the existence of government imply? Discuss.
2. Why do other social institutions view government as a competitor?
3. What is the difference between the concept of government and the concept of politics? How can failure to distinguish between these concepts cause confusion?
4. What serves as the basis for classifying types of governments?
5. What is the major difference between an authoritarian government and a democratic government?
6. What is a totalitarian social system?
7. What are the two major types of governments based on the relationship of government to the economy? Briefly describe each.
8. What is sovereignty? How does a government acquire sovereignty?
9. What is legitimacy? What are the sources of legitimacy? Describe each. Are there circumstances in which traditional legitimacy is best? Charismatic legitimacy? Legal-rational legitimacy?
10. What is the source of legitimacy of the United States government? Explain.
11. Are governments the only social institutions which have legitimacy? Explain.
12. What are the four theoretical views of the proper role of government in society? Discuss and evaluate each.
13. Which one of the four theoretical views of the proper role of government in society has predominated in the United States? Explain.
14. What are the five general categories into which the functions performed by government fall? Discuss each.
15. What are the three types of techniques used by government to implement its decisions? Discuss and evaluate each.

16. Why is political education so important in a democratic society?
17. Do you think government financing political campaigns would help. Why?

CHAPTER ELEVEN
THE EXTENT OF GOVERNMENT INVOLVEMENT IN THE UNITED STATES

IDEAS AND CONCEPTS

delegated powers
power of the federal government as defined by the constitution

progressive tax
a tax in which the rate increases as the taxpayer's income increases

revenue sharing
state and local governments would increase their income by developing a formula with the federal government to share the revenue collected by the federal government

social overhead capital
those facilities which are used jointly by those engaged in economic production and include such things as services, streets, and the communication system

In this chapter we shall examine the pattern of government in the United States and the factors which have contributed to the rapid expansion of governmental activity in this century. In so doing it is important to realize that there are certain factors that influence the limits of governmental activity in all societies and which are not peculiar to the American experience. In addition, we shall briefly survey the elements of the urban problem, one of the largest challenges facing government in contemporary society. However, it is important to recognize that the urban problem, like most of the problems facing us today, is not simply a political problem or an economic problem or a sociological problem; rather, it is a problem that involves all aspects of the functioning of society. Any attempt to find a solution to the urban problem is going to require the joint efforts and skills of people from many areas of specialization.

In some respects, the bias against governmental activity in the United States is hampering our efforts to solve many of the problems confronting our society. Ask yourself, what are the most important social problems facing us today? How many of these can be resolved without governmental intervention? As the United states became a mature industrial society, many social institutions were unable to continue to successfully perform the functions that they had performed in the past. An examination of existing social institutions does not reveal any developments which would alter the trend toward a more prominent role for government in society.

PATTERN OF GOVERNMENT IN THE UNITED STATES

Government is not a monolithic agency in the United States. When the United States was founded it was decided that governmental functions would be performed by many semi-independent units. Government units in the United States are usually classified as federal, state, or local. There are only one federal government, fifty state governments, and thousands of local government units. Many of the local units perform very specialized functions. For example, there are government units whose only function is to dispose of sewage or to provide fire protection for a specified area. The St. Louis metropolitan area has 474 local government units,[1] and some other metropolitan areas have several times this many.

In many instances today the solutions to problems are hampered by the existence of competing government units. For instance, the St. Louis metropolitan area is governed by two different state governments, Illinois and Missouri, although it is a single economic unit. Between 1970 and 1972, when the area was attempting to select a site for a new airport, locations in both Missouri and Illinois were considered. Conflict arose

The House and the Senate compete for power in the legislature branch of the government at the federal level. At the local level an increasing number of semi-independent units of government, such as school boards, function to keep power from becoming too centralized at the federal level while promoting greater involvement of the entire population. *((a) Sygma/Jean Pierre Laffont (b) George W. Gardner)*

because there were factions in each state that wanted to make certain that that state got the airport. The major consideration should have been which site would best serve the transportation needs of the entire urban area, provided that it had no particular shortcomings such as harmful ecological effects. Thus, the existence of competing government units complicated the selection of a site for an airport in St. Louis and reduced the chance that the best site would be selected.

WHO DOES WHAT?

In addition to the problem of determining what government should do in the United States, there is also the difficulty of determining which government unit should perform a task once it is decided that it should be done. The framers of the United States Constitution attempted to resolve the problem by limiting the powers of the federal government to those enumerated in the Constitution. These are usually referred to as *delegated powers.* All powers not specifically given to the federal

government are reserved for the states. However, not all undelegated powers can be exercised by the states because the Constitution prohibits the states from exercising certain powers. In some instances the federal and state governments are permitted to exercise certain powers concurrently. In order to prevent conflict over the exercise of certain powers, Article VI, paragraph 2, specifies that if a state constitution or law conflicts with a treaty, an act of Congress, or the national Constitution, the federal law overrules the state law.

The powers not delegated to the federal government are divided between state and local governments. The way the division is made varies somewhat from one state to another, but in each instance this division is spelled out in a state constitution.

The much debated issue of "states' rights" in the United States centers around the division of governmental activities between the federal government and state (local) governments. Those who take a strong states' rights position favor restricting the activities of the federal government as much as possible. Frequently a strong states' rights position is identified with the Southern states. This is because in the past states' rights has been used as a phony issue by those who were attempting to perpetuate first slavery and later racial inequality. Also, at one time states' rights was defended by the railroads because they could buy state legislatures more easily than Congress. The use of states' rights as a phony issue to advance socially unacceptable goals is unfortunate because the issue which should be involved is the allocation of the governmental functions. This should be determined by which unit can best perform the functions and still retain the checks against abuse of governmental power which have been built into our system.

Table 11-1 shows the division of direct government expenditures between the federal government and state and local governments for selected years. It also shows the percentage of total economic activity which government expenditures represented. It is the dramatic increase, both absolute and relative, in government activity in this century which we shall attempt to explain in this chapter. However, Table 11-1 represents only the aggregate purchase of goods and services by government and does not tell us specifically what government is doing. An examination of the actual outlays of government and the sources of its income should help us focus more specifically on this.

FEDERAL GOVERNMENT EXPENDITURES AND INCOME

The expenditures of the federal government can be classified in two ways: by the function to which the expenditures are allocated and by the technique used by the government to carry out the function. Table 11-2 shows the allocation of federal government expenditures by function and Table 11-3 by technique used to implement those functions. The figures in these tables are *not* the same as those in Table 11-1. The reason is that the figures in Table 11-1 reflect only government purchases of goods and services.

Note that only 43 percent of the federal government's expenditures involved the direct purchase of goods and services. Direct government

TABLE 11-1 GOVERNMENT*
(In billions of dollars)

Year	Total government	Percent of GNP	Total federal	Percent of all government	Percent of GNP	Total state and local	Percent of all government	Percent of GNP
1960	99.6	19.8	53.5	53.7	10.6	46.1	46.3	9.1
1962	117.1	20.9	63.4	54.1	11.3	53.7	45.9	9.6
1964	128.7	20.4	65.2	50.6	10.3	63.5	49.4	10.1
1966	156.2	20.8	77.8	49.6	10.4	70.0	50.4	10.4
1968	197.7	22.8	99.5	50.6	11.5	100.7	49.4	11.3
1970	219.4	22.5	97.2	44.3	10.0	122.2	55.7	12.5
1972	254.9	22.1	105.9	41.5	9.2	148.9	58.5	12.9

*Source: *Economic Report of the President*, U.S. Government Printing Office, Washington, D.C., 1973.

TABLE 11-2 FEDERAL GOVERNMENT EXPENDITURES, 1972*

Function	Dollar amount, billions	Percent of total expenditures
National defense	78.3	32.7
Space research and technology	3.4	1.4
General government; interest	25.5	10.6
International affairs and finances	3.7	1.6
Education	9.7	4.0
Health, labor, and welfare	82.0	34.2
Veterans' benefits and services	10.7	4.5
Commerce, transportation, and housing	15.4	6.4
Agriculture, agriculture resources	7.1	3.0
Natural resources	3.8	1.6
Total	239.6	100.0

*Source: *Economic Report of the President*, U.S. Government Printing Office, Washington, D.C., 1973.

expenditures occur when government actually provides goods and services to the public. They include things as highways, the military, education, and police protection. Transfer payments are a transfer of income from government to the public. It is important to make a distinction between direct government expenditures and government transfer payments, because each has a different impact. For instance, a direct expenditure by government will directly affect the composition of the output of the economy; national defense is an example of this. A decision to spend on national defense may mean the production of jets,

TABLE 11-3 FEDERAL GOVERNMENT EXPENDITURES, 1972*

Technique	Dollar amount, billions	Percent of total expenditures
Purchases of goods and services	104.4	42.7
Transfer payments and net interest paid†	96.3	39.4
Grants-in-aid to state and local governments	37.7	15.4
Subsidies less current surplus of government enterprises	6.1	2.5
Total	244.5	100.0

*Source: *Survey of Current Business*, U.S. Government Printing Office, Washington, D.C., July 1973.

†Most of the transfer payments are part of the social security progress and net interest paid is interest on the national debt.

tanks, or ships. On the other hand, social security payments are transfer payments and the recipients can spend the money they receive in the marketplace for any goods and services that they desire. The price mechanism is the vehicle used to determine the combination of goods and services produced. (Interest on the national debt is another example of a government outlay that has no direct effect on the composition of the output of the economy.) Veterans' benefits and services are examples of a category that involves both expenditures that directly affect the composition of the output of the economy and expenditures that have no direct effect on the composition of output. Veterans' pensions are usually paid to the recipients without any restrictions on how the money is to be spent, but other veterans' benefits, such as GI Bill payments, may require the recipient to attend college or some type of training program which directly affects the composition of output. Such programs also have a direct impact on resource allocation.

Most government expenditures affect the distribution of goods and services in some way. For instance, subsidies paid to farmers have the effect of redistributing the output in favor of the recipients. There is increasing pressure for the government to intervene in the income distribution process and to add some type of guaranteed annual income to the list of government expenditures in order to ensure a "fairer" distribution of income.

Other federal expenditures are for the specific purpose of ensuring a satisfactory rate of economic growth. The federal government finances much research and education for this purpose. These are necessary activities if our economy is to continue to grow.

It should be apparent from the preceding discussion that not all government expenditures have the same impact. It is therefore important to avoid bringing all expenditures together and treating them as if they did. It is also important to recognize that the techniques government uses to collect the revenue needed to finance its activities have important effects on society. The distribution of these effects shall be deferred to a later section of this chapter; however, Table 11-4 shows the sources of income of the federal government in 1972.

STATE AND LOCAL GOVERNMENTS' INCOME AND EXPENDITURES

Table 11-5 shows the sources of income of state and local governments, and Table 11-6 shows the type of expenditures incurred by these governments. An examination of Table 11-6 reveals that most state and local government revenue goes to direct expenditures, as a relatively small percentage goes to transfer payments. Students are frequently surprised to find that public welfare constitutes such a small percentage of the expenditures of state and local governments. Because of the

TABLE 11-4 FEDERAL GOVERNMENT INCOME, 1972*

Source	Dollar amount, billions	Percent of total income
Personal tax	107.9	47.2
Corporate profits tax	37.8	16.5
Indirect business tax	19.9	8.7
Contributions for social insurance	63.0	27.6
Totals	228.6†	100.0

*Source: *Survey of Current Business*, U.S. Government Printing Office, Washington, D.C., July 1973.
†The difference between income and the expenditures in Table 11-2 and Table 11-3 represents addition to the national debt.

inordinate amount of publicity this category receives, it is generally thought to represent a large portion of their total expenditures.

Everything said about the impact of federal expenditures on the economic system applies to the expenditures of state and local governments. Determining the total size of state and local expenditures and the composition of these expenditures are relevant problems in any discussion of the finances of state and local governments.

TAXES

Almost all government income is from some type of tax, all of which have a *base* and a *rate.* The tax base is the thing the tax is levied against, such as income, property, or sales. The tax rate refers to the percentage of the base that the taxpayer must pay in tax. Any discussion of a particular tax

TABLE 11-5 STATE AND LOCAL INCOME, 1972*

Source	Dollar amount, billions	Percent of total
Property taxes	42.7	24.1
Sales taxes	35.6	20.1
Individual income taxes	17.5	9.9
Corporation profit taxes	4.8	2.7
Revenue from federal government	37.7	21.3
All other†	38.9	21.9
Totals	177.2	100.0

*Source: *Survey of Current Business*, U.S. Government Printing Office, Washington, D.C., July 1973.
†Includes licenses and other taxes and charges and miscellaneous revenue.

TABLE 11-6 STATE AND LOCAL EXPENDITURES, 1970–71*

Type	Dollar amount, billions	Percent of total
Education	59.4	39.5
Highways	18.1	12.0
Public welfare	18.2	12.0
All other†	54.9	36.5
Total	150.6	100.0

*Source: *Economic Report of the President*, U.S. Government Printing Office, Washington, D.C., 1973.

†Includes expenditures for health, hospitals, police, local fire protection, natural resources, sanitation, housing and urban renewal, local parks and recreation, general control, financial administration, interest on general debt, and other unallocable expenditures.

should include some consideration of the technique that is used to determine the size of the base as well as the rate.

Progressive tax In general, the various types of taxes can be classifed according to what happens to the tax rate as the income of the taxpayer changes. First, there is the progressive tax. A *progressive tax* is one in which the rate increases as the taxpayer's income increases. The federal income tax is an example of a progressive tax. Table 11-7 is a portion of the federal income tax schedule for one group of United States taxpayers. The base is the taxable income in column I and the rate is the percent in column II.

With the above schedule, as with nearly all progressive taxes, the individual never pays more than 14 percent on the first $500 of taxable income. This means that an individual with a taxable income of $200,000 only pays 14 percent on the first $500 of taxable income. Something that

TABLE 11-7 SINGLE TAXPAYERS, 1974

I If taxable income is	II The tax is
Not over $500	14% of taxable income
Over $500 but not over $1,000	$70 plus 15% of the excess over $500
Over $1,000 but not over $1,500	$145 plus 16% of excess over $1,000
Over $1,500 but not over $2,000	$225 plus 17% of excess over $1,500
.	.
.	.
.	.
Over $90,000 but not over $100,000	$46,190 plus 69% of excess over $90,000
Over $100,000	$53,090 plus 70% of excess over $100,000

is very important in determining how much income tax an individual has to pay is the way in which the base is determined. In the United States, people do not legally have to pay tax on all of their income. Everyone is allowed so much tax-exempt income for each dependent, and an additional part of income is also tax exempt. This additional part is called a *standard deduction.* Not everyone takes the standard deduction, however, because there are other provisions which for various reasons exempt certain types of income and expenditures from the payment of tax. These exemptions are often referred to as *loopholes.* Tax loopholes include the exemption from taxation of all income earned on state and municipal bonds, 22 percent of income received from the sale of oil, and half of the income received from long-term capital gains. Also, an unlimited amount of interest expenses and taxes on private housing can be deducted from the tax base, as can all taxes paid to state and local governments. Those with high incomes derive almost all the benefits associated with these loopholes. As a result of the existence of loopholes in the federal income tax structure, the real federal income tax is frequently not as progressive as the schedule would make it appear. It is difficult to find any valid arguments to justify the exemption of income received from some sources if similar exemptions are not given income received from all sources. Why should income received from interest on state and municipal bonds be exempted from federal taxation and not income received as wages for working in a factory? To see how unlimited deductions for interest expenses and taxes on private housing can reduce the progressiveness of the federal income tax, one only has to look at a hypothetical example. Suppose we have two families of four living in apartments, one earning $10,000 per year and the other $100,000 per year. Both families are taking the standard deduction. This means that the current federal tax bill of family I is $758 and that of family II is $52,040. Family I buys a house for $20,000 and Family II buys one for $100,000. In order to simplify the example, we will assume that both pay the same interest rate on their loans. The current interest rate is 9 percent. We will also assume that the property tax paid by each is proportional to the value of the house and that the respective taxes are $600 and $3,000. We will make the same assumption with respect to the amount of the principal payment on the loans. The principal payments are $300 and $1,500 respectively. Thus, the total annual payment for the house of Family I is $2,700 and that of family II is $13,500. The gross cost of the house of family II is 5 times that of family I, which is proportional to the prices of the two houses. However, family I's federal tax bill is reduced by $291 because it bought the house and family II's tax bill is reduced by $8,210. This assumes that the other deductions of the two families (other than for housing) are equal to their standard deduction. Therefore, the net annual cost of family I's house is $2,408, and family II's net cost is $5,290. Family II is thus able to get a house with a price five times that of family I for a net cost of slightly more than twice as much. The high-income family is able to reduce its total federal tax bill from 55 percent of its income to less than 44 percent by purchasing high-priced housing, whereas the low-income family's federal tax bill is only reduced by 3 percent. Of course, the family which rents housing is even worse off because it receives no reduction in federal taxes. It seems to the authors that a fairer method would be to allow everyone a fixed deduction for housing similar to the fixed deduction allowed for dependents, regardless of the type of housing.

Regressive tax A second type of tax is the regressive tax. A *regressive tax* is one in which the rate decreases as income increases. Property taxes are regressive. The percentage of a person's income that goes to pay the property tax decreases as the person's income increases. Take a situation in which two individuals own identical houses in a housing development, and each homeowner pays $500 property tax. If one of the homeowners has an income of $10,000, then that person's real tax rate is 5 percent, whereas if the other has an income of $20,000, the real tax rate is only 2.5 percent. It would be difficult to find a tax for which the base the tax is levied against was regressive.

Proportional tax The third type of tax is the proportional tax. A *proportional tax* is one in which the rate remains constant as income changes. It is difficult to find an example of a proportional tax. The sales tax on goods that exists in many states is proportional in terms of its base; that is, the rate remains constant as the dollar amount purchased of the taxable items changes. Most of these taxes are regressive in terms of the taxpayer's income. The sales tax is regressive because the proportion of a family's income that is spent on goods declines as income rises, and therefore the percentage of income which is paid in tax also declines as income rises.

Many people do not really count some of the taxes they pay as taxes; they tend to include the tax as a part of the price of the thing that is being taxed. For example, do you divide the amount you pay when you purchase gas into the amount that goes toward the actual purchase of the gas and the amount that goes to the government as taxes? This same situation applies to the purchase of tires, movie tickets, cigarettes, alcoholic drinks, food where there is a sales tax, cosmetics, etc. Thus, we have a tax system in which large amounts can be collected that are not directly identified as taxes by those who are paying. The items included in the above list are things that are purchased by people in the lower income groups, whereas many of the items purchased mainly by people in the upper income groups, such as services, are exempt from sales and excise taxes. This frequently puts a relatively heavy burden on the poor.

Part of the difficulty inherent in the existing tax structure results from the fact that there is no single tax structure but rather one for each level of government. Each level of government develops a tax system that will enable it to collect the revenue it needs to operate, often without much consideration of the various taxes levied by the other governments. Thus, there is need not only for a revision in the existing tax structures, but also for greater coordination between the tax collections of the various governments in order to relieve the relative burden that has been placed on low-income families. (It has been suggested that families below a certain income level be completely exempt from federal income taxes, but this would provide very little relief to low-income families because most of the taxes that they pay are other types, and they would have to continue to pay these.)

Criteria for determining the best type of tax One important factor that must be considered when determining what type of tax to use to collect revenue is the *technical* aspect of the tax. This refers primarily to the precision with which the tax can be assessed and the cost involved in collecting it. For instance, it is much easier to assess the amount of a sales tax than the amount of a property tax, since in the case of the property tax the size of the base is more difficult to determine. One must also consider the cost involved in the collection of the tax, because it is the net tax which is available for government use. The federal government has developed a very economical method for collecting income taxes. They have the employer do the work and send the collected tax to the government.

Another aspect that should be considered is the effect of the tax on the taxpayer. The federal income tax is collected in an almost painless manner; that is, most people pay their taxes before they receive their income. Many people do not even consider the money they pay in federal taxes as ever having belonged to them. It would be interesting to see what would happen if people received all their income and then had to pay the entire year's taxes at one time.

A second criterion that is frequently used is that the tax should be *proportionate to the benefit received.* An example of a tax that is almost entirely based on benefit received is the tax paid on gasoline. Most of the revenue collected from the tax on gasoline is used for the construction or repair of highways.

Another criterion for determining the best type of tax is the *ability to pay.* It would be unwise to levy a tax if the people who were supposed to pay it could not do so. An example of a situation in which this criterion was originally intended as a major rationale is the federal income tax. The personal exemption allowance was made to ensure every individual enough tax-free income to pay for his basic needs. Thus, the amount of the personal exemption allowance for single persons, that is, tax-free income, ranged from $3,000 to $1,000 between 1913 and 1937. During World War II the personal exemption allowance for single persons was reduced to $500 as a part of the efforts associated with financing the war. By 1974 the personal exemption allowance had only been increased to $750. However, in order to be consistent with the principle of the ability to pay, this figure should be increased to a higher, more realistic amount.

The final two criteria are economic. First, can the tax be manipulated in ways which will enable the government to control the level of economic activity? The second consideration is the impact of the tax on the way the economy performs the basic economic functions. For example, what is the effect of the tax on the composition of the output, or how does it affect workers' willingness to supply labor?

EXTENT OF GOVERNMENT INVOLVEMENT

Think it over, to what extent should government get involved in setting society's limits? Before examining the factors which have led to the expanded role of government in the United States, an examination of the factors which generally determine the limits of governmental activity is in order. There are three major elements which are important determinants of the scope of governmental intervention in society. These are: (1) the organization of the state and the efficiency of the government officials, (2) the complexity of the economy and other social organizations, and (3) the ideological or cultural attitudes of the people.

Organization and efficiency Government is certainly more deeply involved in society in a totalitarian system, in which the government attempts to mold society to conform to the political philosophy of the state, than in one with a laissez faire attitude toward governmental activity, that is, one in which people feel that governmental activity should be limited as much as possible. Obviously there is a large number of possibilities between these two extreme positions. The efficiency of government officials will be an important element no matter what type of government organization exists in a society. The efficiency of the government officials will be determined in large part by the procedure used to select them and the general attitude of society toward them. A selection procedure in which the applicants for a government job are evaluated on the basis of merit will certainly lead to a more efficiently administered government than one in which positions are filled on the basis of political patronage or in which candidates are selected for any reason other than their ability to perform the duties associated with the job. The attitude of the people toward government employees is important because it greatly influences the quality of those who select government service as a career.

In the United States many government positions are still filled on the basis of political patronage, particularly at the state and local levels. Also, at the federal level many of the higher-level administrative positions are filled by noncareer appointees. Many capable individuals may not select government service as a career because they know that the top positions frequently go to noncareer people. The methods used to select government employees have probably reduced the efficiency of the government in the United States. However, until recently efficiency has not been a high priority of those who control government, despite the fact that they would have had you believe otherwise. In fact, an inefficient government is the best argument those who oppose government intervention in society have against such intervention. They, therefore, are not likely to undertake measures which would greatly increase the efficiency of government. The following quote from a one-time United States Chamber of Commerce official best summarizes this situation. "The best public servant is the worse one. A thoroughly first-rate man in public service is corrosive. He eats holes in our liberties. The better he is and the longer he stays, the greater is the danger."[2] Only recently has there been any extensive acceptance of the point of view that an efficiently administered government can expand rather than limit freedom.

Complexity of the economy and society The second factor, complexity of the economy and other social organizations, is especially important since almost all contemporary societies are characterized by increasing complexity. The major factor contributing to the increasing complexity of societies is the shift from simple subsistence or traditional economies to more complex industrial ones which require more interdependence and interaction among members of society. The increased interdependence and interaction is directly attributable to the complexity of the division of labor and specialization necessary for an industrial economy to function.

In an industrial economy new tasks develop and the ability or willingness of existing organizations to perform old ones is diminished. Frequently, government is the only existing institution capable of performing many of the new tasks or assuming the older ones which other institutions fail to perform. For example, the concentration of people in urban centers which is associated with industrialization creates an increased demand for services which only government is capable of satisfying. Also, industrialization changes the family structure in such a way that the family is unable to effectively perform many of its previous functions, such as caring for the older members of society. This topic will be explored further in the next section of this chapter.

Ideological or cultural attitudes Finally, a society's ideological or cultural attitudes are important in determining the extent of government intervention in that society. Societies are sometimes classified on the basis of community attitudes concerning politics, economics, mating customs, etc. Some societies are highly competitive, others are individualistic, and still others are highly cooperative and integrated. Societies which are basically competitive would certainly have different attitudes toward government involvement in society from those that are inherently cooperative.

American society obviously falls into the competitive category. Because of the fact that American society is highly competitive, the individual is exalted. However, individualism is encouraged only as long as it is consistent with the competitive framework of our society. In addition, Americans are very practical as opposed to theoretical and believe very strongly in the inevitability of progress. The American concept of progress is vague and not generally applied uniformly to all aspects of society. For instance, progress as applied to the technical and physical aspects of society is generally viewed as being basically good and having beneficial consequences. However, the "impact" of technical progress in areas such as economic production, communications, transportation, and medical research on values and social organization is often considered bad. A large part of the condemnation of the social impact of technical progress stems from a cultural lag, that is, a failure of social change to keep face with technical progress. Many people fail to see the link between technical and social change, and they therefore often identify much of the social change with moral deterioration.

Role of the leader A factor that has not specifically been discussed with any of the factors above is the importance of the role of the leader in determining the extent of government involvement in society. Social scientists frequently hold opposite views as to the impact of leaders. Thomas Carlyle developed the "great man" theory of history, which holds that human history is nothing more than a history of what the great have accomplished. Leo Tolstoi, on the other hand, developed a theory of history which holds that history is an unfolding of the homogeneous, infinitesimal elements that regulate the masses. In Tolstoi's view, the accomplishments of such men as Napoleon, Washington, and Mao Tse-tung were simply the consequences of vast social forces over which they had no control. Tolstoi's view of history serves as the philosphical basis for Marxian societies, which glorify the role of the masses and idealize a classless society. Carlyle's theories, on the other hand, frequently lead to an exaltation of the leaders. It should not come as a surprise that many of the most devout believers in the Carlyle view have been the great themselves. Hitler and Mussolini, for example, were enthusiastic supporters of the Carlyle view.

The view that an individual who tries can overcome all obstacles and succeed, which is held by many people in the United States, is an extension of the Carlyle view of history to the functioning of the individual within a society. Those who hold this view deny that an individual can fail because of the existence of social forces in the society which are beyond his control. To this group, failure to succeed is strictly the fault of the individual. They may admit that at times chance circumstances might cause some individuals to fail, but they would deny the existence of any systematic social forces which would prevent individual success.

It seems to the authors that both the Carlyle and the Tolstoi views of history have something to contribute toward an understanding of human development. There is little doubt that individual effort and social forces are both important in explaining the functioning of individuals in a society. The relative importance of each probably varies greatly from one individual to another and from one time and place to another. A parallel conclusion is that individual political leaders can undoubtedly reduce or increase the amount of governmental intervention in a society at any given time. However, the limits of the reduction or increase are probably set by forces which exist within the society and which are beyond the control of the leader.

EXPANSION OF GOVERNMENT IN THE UNITED STATES

The organization of government and the ideological attitudes of society have not been the factors providing the impetus for the expansion of governmental activities in the United States during this century. If anything, these two factors have acted as checks limiting governmental expansion. Almost all the expansion of governmental activities is attributable to the increased complexity of the economy and society generally.

Most of the expansion is linked, either directly or indirectly, to one of the following: (1) military and international commitments, (2) increased government responsibility for the economy, (3) more government responsibility for the welfare of the individual, and (4) increased complexity of society. Each of these will be discussed separately for pedagogical reasons, but it should not be assumed that clear-cut distinctions among them exist in the world.

Military and international commitments The most obvious result of the military and international commitments is the large expenditures of the federal government on national defense. In 1972 over 75 percent of the goods and services purchased by the federal government were for the military. This expenditure alone was more than 9 times as much as total expenditures of government at all levels in 1929.[3] In addition to direct expenditures for national defense, there are many other programs which might not have been undertaken, or at least not on as large a

An Atlas-Centaur rocket soars on a $25 million mission to test a four hour weather watching camera, a new electric jet, and radio relay gear. This mission failed when the satellite was stranded in the wrong orbit. United States international commitments provided the impetus for this and other programs. *(United Press International Photo)*

scale, had it not been for the impetus provided by the United States' international commitments. These include such things as expenditures on education (especially through the National Defense Education Act), the construction of an interstate highway system, and the space program.

There have also been many instances in which individual freedom has been greatly restricted in the name of national defense. The best-known example of this was during the late 1940s and early 1950s when committees in the House of Representatives and the Senate of the United States held public hearings in which people were literally accused and condemned of being agents in a world-wide Communist conspiracy without being given the benefit of due process of law. (This period is frequently referred to as the McCarthy era after Joe McCarthy, the most notorious of the chairmen of the Congressional investigation committees.) As a result many innocent people suffered severe hardships in the form of lost jobs and social ostracism simply because they appeared before one of the Congressional committees investigating Communism. The attitude associated with the Congressional investigations permeated the entire country, and people felt intimidated everywhere. They were very careful about what they said or wrote or did for fear that they would be accused of being Communists. The right to dissent was restricted more during the McCarthy era than at any other time during this century in the United States. Many social scientists compare the Congressional investigations into Communism to the Salem witch trials. Both were conducted in an atmosphere of fear and hysteria, with little if any concern for the rights of those accused. Also, both were periods of guilt by association; that is, to speak out in defense of those accused was to risk becoming one of the accused.

Other instances of governmental involvement in society which can be directly or indirectly be linked to our military and international commitments include the activities of the CIA, many restrictions on United States citizens traveling abroad, restrictions on international trade for national defense purposes, domestic surveillance of political dissenters, and the equipping of science laboratories in public schools. The examples given in this section are not intended to be an exhaustive list of the ways that military and international commitments have influenced government's role in the United States, but rather to suggest the wide scope of governmental activities that can directly or indirectly be attributed to this source.

Responsibility for the economy Since World War II the government has accepted increasing responsibility for ensuring satisfactory performance of the United States economy. As mentioned previously, this management of the economy was officially declared the responsibility of the government with the passage of the Employment Act of 1946. Until the late 1960s there was considerable debate as to whether or not the government should actively attempt to manage the economy; however, by the 1972 Presidential election the issue was how well the Nixon administration had managed the economy, not whether or not it should have managed it. Governmental activities aimed at controlling the economy have expanded the role of government in society into areas which had previously been considered outside the realm of governmental authority, except possibly in times of national emergency. For example, wage and price controls were used by the Nixon administration in the early 1970s in order to control inflation and this was the first time such measures had been used in relatively "normal" times.

Responsibility for individual welfare Since the 1930s the role of government in society has expanded rapidly because government has been assuming more and more responsibility for the welfare of the individual. When a state assumes the responsibillity for individuals, rather than relying on other institutions, it is referred to as a *welfare state.* Since the 1930s there has been a steady increase in the number of programs undertaken by government to ensure the protection of individual welfare. Many of these programs are designed to fill a void which has resulted from changes in the structure of the family. For instance, several programs have been developed to specifically provide for the aged, a responsibility formerly assumed by the family.

Another major reason that government has become increasingly concerned with providing for the welfare of the individual is that there have often been gaps between what the society was capable of providing and what it actually was providing. For example, the economy was producing a surplus of food, yet people were going hungry. In fact a major source of dissatisfaction with the way our system is operating today is that people are being denied "necessities," such as adequate medical care and adequate housing, which the system has the potential to provide. It seems very likely that the government is going to play an increasingly important role in the future in assuring the welfare of individuals when there is a gap between what is being achieved by the system and the real potential of the system.

Complexity of society Finally, societal complexity has increased rapidly during the past 100 years, especially during the last half century. This increased complexity has resulted from such things as a large population, resource exhaustion, the development of a modern industrial economy, and the rapid rate of change associated with the development of modern technology. As society has become increasingly complex it has been necessary for government to become more involved, particularly as a regulatory agent. This has taken the form of such things as regulation of air travel and the communication system, passage and enforcement of quality and safety standards, and protection of the environment. Any casual examination of the regulatory functions performed by government in the United States is enough to convince anyone that ours is not a self-regulating society. As a society becomes increasingly complex and impersonal, there seems to be no acceptable alternative to increased government regulation.

The problem of waste disposal, one of the by-products of the modern city, is increased by population growth, developing technology, and a lack of environmental control. This mound of garbage litters the landscape of the East River across from the United Nations. *(J. Paul Kirouac)*

THE URBAN PROBLEM

The urban problem really is not a single problem; rather, the term refers to a number of complex problems that have arisen as a result of the large concentrations of people in relatively small geographic areas. In this section we shall explore some of these problems which together constitute the "urban problem." It is generally agreed that the solution to the urban problem is dependent on the initiative and extensive participation of government. To understand how far we are from an effective solution to the urban problem, it is only necessary to realize that current government organization is one of the factors contributing to the problem.

The difficulty is that the political organization of urban areas creates jurisdictional conflicts which make it impossible to develop a comprehensive program to deal with the many aspects of the urban problem. There are usually several distinct government units in a single urban area, and these units often compete with each other when they should be cooperating.

As was mentioned earlier, the St. Louis metropolitan area, with 474 local government units, is an example of this problem. Many of these government units are supplying the same public goods and services to the people who live in their area of political jurisdiction; that is, such things as educational services and police and fire protection are being provided by several government units, and this leads to wasteful duplications. Perhaps more important than the waste, however, is the difference in the quality and the availability of the goods and services being supplied by the different units. These differences are frequently the result of a differential in the financial resources of the different government units.

Finance The financial position of many metropolitan areas is critical. The financial problems result in large part from the types of taxes that the government units must rely on. Most of the tax revenue of local governments in the United States must come from property taxes. In 1971, for example, city governments collected $15 billion in taxes, and $10 billion, or 67 percent, of this came from property taxes.[4] A property tax is a poor revenue raiser, since there is often a limit on the rate which local governments can levy against the property base, and to raise the rate often requires voter approval; furthermore, the base, that is, the value of the property, does not respond to rising prices. This means that the dollar revenue that can be collected from a property tax is not responsive to inflationary conditions which raise the costs of urban governments.

Since the major way for a local government to increase its income is to add to the value of the property within its taxing areas, the local units in metropolitan areas frequently manipulate zoning restrictions and building codes to promote high-tax producing uses for the land located within their areas. They also use these techniques to control the types of businesses that will be located within their domain. The municipalities that typically run the central city vie for the "clean" industries and high-revenue producing residential housing, which will not generate too much additional cost for the local government. For example, suburban political units welcome high-income housing units which tend to consume larger tracts of land because they increase the revenue while not significantly increasing the costs of the local government units by adding to expenditures on police, fire protection, and education. Low-income housing units, on the other hand, tend to generate less income per unit and to significantly increase the costs of the local governments because of the greater danger of fire associated with the cheaper units and because of the larger number of children per unit, whose education must be paid for in large part by the local government.

The financial problems of urban governments are not equally shared by all the political units. The central city is almost always in trouble because frequently much of the property in its tax base has deteriorated, and quite often large segments of the property are not taxable because they are owned by tax-exempt organizations such as churches, because they are involved in government programs which exempt them from taxation, or because they are under the control of other government units, which makes them tax exempt.

In the government units that ring the central city, the financial status varies, depending to a large extent on how successful the government unit has been in controlling the way in which the land within its taxable boundaries is being used. In the St. Louis suburban area in the school year 1970–1971, for example, one public school district had to stop operations for a time because of financial difficulties, while another in the area was able to have a low tax rate and still maintain a large contingency fund.

Race and poverty A national problem that is accentuated in the cities is the concentration of poverty among blacks. Table 11-8 shows the relationship between the income of white and black families in the United States in 1971.

The striking figures in Table 11-8 are the percentages for incomes under $3,000 and over $10,000. The fact that 19.4 percent of the black families had incomes of less than $3,000 compared with 6.9 percent of the white families indicates that the burden of poverty falls relatively more heavily on blacks than on whites in the United States. Also, the fact that 54.4 percent of the white families had incomes of over $10,000 compared with 30.0 percent of black families indicates that affluence is relatively more common among whites than among blacks. A figure that even more clearly demonstrates the relative economic positions of black and white families is the median family income of each group. The median income is the middle value, which means that half of the families had greater incomes than the median and half of the families had less. In 1971 the median family income of whites was $10,672; of blacks, $6,714.

No matter what definition of poverty one selects, there can be little doubt that a larger percentage of black than of white families live in poverty. For purposes of our discussion we shall use the definition of the Social Security Administration, which takes into account both family size and places of residence. The dollar values shown in Table 11-9 are

TABLE 11-8 MONEY INCOME IN THE UNITED STATES, 1971*

Family income	Percent of white families	Percent of black families
Under $3,000	8.9	19.4
$3,000–$6,999	20.1	32.8
$7,000–$9,999	18.6	17.8
$10,000 and over	54.4	30.0

**Statistical Abstract of the United States*, U.S. Government Printing Office, Washington, D.C., 1973, p. 328.

TABLE 11-9 AVERAGE POVERTY LEVELS BY SIZE OF FAMILY AND RESIDENCE, 1968*

Number of family members	Nonfarm income	Farm income
1 member		
Under 65	$1,797	$1,545
65 and over	$1,667	$1,422
2 members		
Head under 65	$2,333	$1,990
Head over 65	$2,102	$1,787
3 members	$2,774	$2,352
4 members	$3,553	$3,034
5 members	$4,188	$3,577
6 members	$4,706	$4,021
7 or more members	$5,789	$4,916

*Statistical Abstract of the United States, U.S. Government Printing Office, Washington, D.C., 1970, p. 327.

based on 1968 prices. (It is generally agreed that the definition of the poverty level for various family sizes used by the Social Security Administration is a very conservative one, and many put the poverty level considerably higher than the figures shown in Table 11-9.

Based on the definition of poverty in Table 11-9, the percentage of the population below the poverty level in the United States dropped from 22 percent in 1957 to 12.8 percent in 1968. However, an examination of Table 11-10 reveals that national statistics do not show the true circumstances of blacks living in metropolitan areas. Table 11-10 shows that a black living in the central city is 3 times as likely to be living in poverty as a white living in the central city, and that a black living in a suburban area is 4 1/2 times as likely to be living in poverty as a white living in a suburban area.

The migration of blacks to metropolitan areas has changed the racial composition of these areas, particularly the central cities. Table 11-11 shows how the relative distribution of whites and blacks in the United States changed between 1950 and 1966. It is important to note that 56 percent of the blacks lived in the central cities in 1966 compared with 43 percent in 1950, whereas there was a decline in the percentage of whites living in the central cities from 34 percent in 1950 to 27 percent in 1966. Blacks were moving into the central cities from small cities, towns, and rural areas, and whites were moving into urban fringes from the central cities and from smaller cities, towns, and rural areas.

The improvement of the economic situation of those living in the central city is made more difficult by the general trends in the location of

TABLE 11-10 PERSONS BELOW POVERTY LEVEL*

	Number below poverty level (in millions)				Percent below poverty level			
		Metropolitan areas				Metropolitan areas		
Race	Total U.S.	Central cities	Suburban rings	Outside metropolitan areas	Total U.S.	Central cities	Suburban rings	Outside metropolitan areas
All races	25.4	7.8	5.1	12.5	12.8	13.4	7.3	18.0
White	17.4	4.4	4.1	8.9	10.0	9.8	6.2	14.2
Negro	7.6	3.2	0.9	3.5	34.7	26.2	28.3	54.6

*_Statistical Abstract of the United States_, U.S. Government Printing Office, Washington, D.C., 1970, p. 329.

economic activity in metropolitan areas. During the past twenty years, many types of manufacturing that were formerly located in the central cities have moved to suburban areas, and in many large metropolitan areas the actual number of jobs available in manufacturing in the central cities has declined. Of course, the movement of people to the suburbs has caused many retail and wholesale businesses to move to the suburban areas, and it is quite likely that there has been a decline in the absolute number of jobs available in wholesale and retail occupations in United States central cities. This decline may have been as much as 400,000 in the last twenty years.

The central cities are faced with the enormous problem of attacking poverty at a time when their financial position is not only at a low point, but likely to continue to deteriorate unless the federal and state governments are willing to bear some of the costs associated with the solution. The problem is complicated because a large number of those who need

TABLE 11-11 PERCENT DISTRIBUTION OF POPULATION BY LOCATION*

	Negro		White	
	1950	1966	1950	1966
United States	100	100	100	100
Metropolitan areas	56	69	59	64
Central cities	43	56	34	27
Urban fringe	13	13	26	37
Smaller cities, towns, and rural areas	44	31	41	36

*The New York Times edition of _Report of the National Advisory Commission on Civil Disorders_, p. 250.

help are black, and the patterns of racial discrimination, both personal and institutional, that exist in the United States hamper efforts to solve the problem. In addition, small improvements in the economic conditions in the central cities tend to accelerate the migration of blacks to them from smaller cities, towns, and rural areas.

The solution to poverty in the central city is going to require the removal of the patterns of discriminations that deny blacks equal access to jobs. For example, unions are going to have to open their membership equally to all, regardless of race. Training will have to be provided for blacks and whites who lack the skills demanded by our modern economy, and job opportunities will have to be provided. There are three possible ways to make jobs available to the black and white poor of the central cities. First, industries can be encouraged through subsidies to locate near areas where the poor live. The second possibility is to open suburban areas to the poor, both black and white. This will require fair housing laws and government subsidies to provide low-cost housing in most suburban areas. The final possibility is to create transportation systems that will provide the poor easy access to jobs.[5]

Housing, social overhead capital, and public services The central cities in the United States suffer because of the existence of substandard housing, functionally obsolete social overhead capital, and low-quality public services. *Social overhead capital* refers to those facilities which are used jointly by those engaged in economic production and consumption and includes such things as services, streets, and the communication system. The obsolescence of social overhead capital and low-quality public services are related conditions which have resulted in large part from the financial plight of the cities. They have contributed to the exodus from the cities. The suburban areas which ring the central city typically offer better educational opportunities, fire protection, etc.

Much of the housing in the central cities is substandard and still deteriorating. There is little incentive for the owners of slum areas in the central city to do anything to improve the dwellings located there. A large part of the blame for this lack of incentive has been placed on absentee slum landlords, the contention being that the slum landlords make high profits because there is a ready supply of tenants no matter what the condition of the dwellings and that the governments of the central cities have not forced landlords to meet minimum standards for their rental property. These arguments are valid, but the root of the problem goes even deeper and affects those who own their homes as well. The value of residential housing depends in large part on the total environment within which it is to be consumed. Thus, there is little incentive for a homeowner or landlord to make expensive repairs to housing units in slum neighborhoods if no one else does. The external

Outmoded physical facilities and a shrinking tax base make the central city a district of decay and decline. When high commercial taxes force industries to leave, buildings are left to deteriorate or are left for occupancy by small transitory businesses providing services to the poor. *(Marcia Weinstein)*

effects which are associated with living in a slum cannot be removed without a total effort from the entire affected neighborhood.

Patterns of urban renewal One of the decisions that must be made by those charged with solving the problems of urban areas is the form which urban renewal should take. Should the cities be restored in their existing form, or should renewal plans attempt to achieve a better utilization of the land in the urban area? For example, should slum housing be replaced with modern housing, or should the people living in slum areas be relocated and the areas that are currently slum housing be converted to industrial ones? Intelligent planning is necessary to prevent the reoccurrence of mistakes like the Pruitt-Igoe project in St. Louis. The Pruitt-Igoe project was a shocking case in which modern apartments replaced former urban blight, and the apartments had to be razed a few years later.

There are two factors which tend to force renewal along existing patterns: racial prejudice and the different political units within the urban area. Most government units in an urban area view the determination of how to use the land within their political boundaries as a prerogative that they are unwilling to surrender. Therefore, it is impossible to develop a "master plan" for land utilization in the urban area. Because of this difficulty, the patterns of land usage frequently found in urban areas are far from optimum.

Even within a single government unit, however, it is often difficult to ensure optimum land utilization because of political and social pressures within the community. Perhaps the major source of these pressures is the pattern of racial discrimination that exists in almost all urban areas of the United States. The relocation of people from slum areas would almost certainly involve moving large numbers of blacks to areas where there are currently few, if any, blacks living.

It seems fair to conclude that extensive institutional and attitudinal changes are going to be required before a satisfactory solution to the urban problem can be expected. These changes are likely to occur more slowly than many of us would like. This means that we will have to be satisfied with partial solutions to the urban problem until these changes occur. This is sometimes the most frustrating aspect of studying social science—to realize that even though a problem has been identified and analyzed and potential solutions found, the solutions will not be undertaken or will be undertaken in a piecemeal fashion which will make them ineffective or effective only after a long period of time.

Resources versus responsibilities The solution to the urban problem and many other public problems cannot be handled within the existing political framework because of the imbalance between the resources and responsibilities of different government units. The imbalance has become one of the major issues of our day.

During the past several years the demand for social goods and services from state and local governments has been increasing at a much more rapid rate than the revenue of these governments. A large part of this increased demand has resulted from the expansion of the educational system and from the demand for increased social goods and services (improved streets and highways, urban renewal, public welfare, police and fire protection) in the urban areas of the United States. However, the federal government has tended to monopolize the two major sources of tax revenue, personal income and corporate profits, and it is generally agreed that techniques must be developed to give state and local governments greater access to revenue if they are to adequately discharge the increased responsibilities which have been thrust upon them. One of the techniques most often suggested for dealing with the problem is *revenue sharing.* Under revenue sharing the federal government would continue to collect the taxes, but some formula would be developed to share the revenue collected by the federal government with state and local governments.

The alternative to developing ways to give state and local governments greater access to revenue is an expansion of the activities of the federal government. In this case the federal government would assume responsibility for some of the activities currently being performed by the state and local governments. The issue thus becomes one of deciding whether to develop techniques which will ensure state and local governments the resources they need to meet their increasing responsibilities or to expand the already massive activities of the federal government. At present we seem to be moving in the latter direction.

SUMMARY

Government in the United States is not a monolithic agency. Government units are classified as federal, state, and local. Many of the local units perform very specialized functions. One difficulty is determining which government unit should do what. The framers of the Constitution attempted to resolve this problem by restricting the powers of the federal government to those enumerated in the Constitution. However, changes in social and economic integration and different interpretations of the Constitution have clouded the issue.

All taxes have both a base and a rate. The base is the thing that the tax is levied against, and the rate refers to the percentage of the base that must be paid. Taxes can be classified as progressive, regressive, or proportional, depending on what happens to the rate as the size of the base or the income of the taxpayer changes.

The most commonly used criteria for evaluating a tax are (1) the technical soundness of the tax, (2) the relationship between those who pay the tax and those who receive the benefits resulting from the tax, (3) the ability of those being taxed to pay, (4) the impact of the tax on the operation of the economy, and (5) the ability of government to use the tax for economic control.

The three factors which generally determine the limits of governmental activity are (1) the organization of the state and the efficiency of the governmental officials, (2) the complexity of the economy and other social organizations, and (3) the ideological or cultural attitudes of the people.

People's attitudes toward government are sometimes influenced by their view of history. One such view, the Carlyle view, holds that human history is nothing more than a history of what the great have achieved. Leo Tolstoi, on the other hand, developed a theory of history which holds that history is an unfolding of the homogeneous, infinitesimal elements that regulate the masses.

Most of the expansion of governmental activity in the United States is attributable to one of four factors: (1) military and international commitments, (2) increased government responsibility for the economy, (3) more government responsibility for the welfare of the individual by government, and (4) increased complexity of society.

The urban problem is really not a single problem; rather it includes a number of complex problems that have arisen as a result of the large concentration of people in relatively small geographic areas.

The existence of different government units in an urban area frustrates efforts to solve the problems of the area. In fact, the existence of competing political units frequently contributes to existing problems and adds new ones.

The financial situation of many of the governments in the metropolitan areas is at a crisis stage. A large part of the difficulty results from the dependence of local governments on the property tax as their major source of revenue. The property tax is a particularly poor source of revenue during inflationary periods like those the United States has suffered periodically since World War II. The financial problem is not shared equally by all the government units in the urban areas, however. Some government units are quite prosperous, while others are near bankruptcy.

The national problems of race and poverty are accentuated in the central cities. This is due in large part to the growing concentration of blacks in the central cities of the United States as a result of the migration of blacks from smaller cities, towns, and rural areas into the central cities. Migration into the central cities takes place because the economic and social condition of blacks in central cities is probably better than in the areas they are leaving. The solution of the poverty problem in the cities is complicated by the patterns of racial discrimination that exist in the United States and the general trend in economic activity in the urban areas. In order to solve the poverty problem in urban areas, jobs are going to have to be made accessible to the poor, and training will have to be provided when vocational skills are lacking.

The central cities suffer the additional burden of having a large percentage of substandard housing and obsolete social overhead capital, and they are typically unable to provide public services of as high quality as the other government units in the metropolitan area. These conditions tend to create a vicious circle.

Urban renewal is complicated because it is impossible to develop a "master plan" for urban areas. This is so because of the existence of different political units and of racial discrimination within the urban area. These factors prevent optimum utilization of urban land.

REVIEW QUESTIONS

1. Describe the structure of government in the United States.
2. How does the structure of government in the United States complicate the determination of which government unit shall do what? How is this issue resolved?

3. What are the major expenditures of the federal government? What types of taxes are its major source of revenue?
4. Why is it important to distinguish between direct expenditures and transfer payments?
5. What are the major expenditures of state and local governments? What types of taxes are their major source of revenue?
6. What is a tax base? A tax rate?
7. What are the three classifications of taxes based on what happens to the rate as the taxpayer's income increases?
8. What difficulty is inherent in the existing tax structure?
9. What are five criteria commonly used in the determination of the best type of tax? Discuss and evaluate each.
10. What are the three factors which are important in determining the extent of government involvement in a society? Discuss the merits of each.
11. What are the Carlyle and Tolstoi theories of history? How might one's view of history influence one's attitude as to the proper role of government in society?
12. What are the four factors which have been important in determining the expanded role of government in the United States? Discuss each.
13. Do you think there are viable ways of dealing with many of society's current problems which do not involve increased government activity? Discuss.
14. What is the "urban problem"?
15. How does the political organization of urban areas affect urban problems?
16. What is the major reason for the financial plight of many urban governments? Are all governments affected equally?
17. How has the financial condition of urban governments influenced their attitudes toward the way the land within their political boundaries is utilized?
18. Describe the relationship between race and poverty in urban areas.
19. How have changes in the location of economic activity affected the poverty problem in urban areas?
20. What can be done to help alleviate poverty in urban areas?
21. What is the condition of housing, social overhead capital, and public services in the central cities? What factors contribute to this?
22. What would you suggest doing to alleviate the lack of jobs for the indigent in the cities?
23. What are the major issues associated with determining patterns of urban renewal?
24. Do you think expanded federal government activity is the best way to deal with many of the current public problems? Discuss.

REFERENCES

CHAPTER ONE

1. Roethlisbeyer, F.J. and W.J. Dirkson: *Management and the Worker*, Harvard, Cambridge, Mass, 1939.
2. *Final Report of the Graduated Work Incentives Experiment*, Institute for Research on Poverty, Madison, Wis. December 1973. Inquiries concerning this report should be directed to Ms. Angela Keyon, Institute for Research on Poverty, University of Wisconsin, Madison, Wisconsin 53706.

CHAPTER TWO

1. Rosenberg, B.: *The Province of Sociology,* Thomas Y. Crowell, New York, 1972.
2. Faris, Robert E.: "The Discipline of Sociology" in Robert E. Faris (ed.), *Handbook of Modern Sociology,* Rand McNally, Chicago, 1964, pp. 1–35.
3. Ibid.
4. Blake, Judith, and L. Davis: "Norms, Values and Sanctions" in Robert E. Faris (ed.), *Handbook of Modern Sociology,* Rand McNally, Chicago, 1964, pp. 426–455.
5. Lenski, G.: *Human Societies.* McGraw-Hill, New York, 1970, p. 9.
6. Anderson, C. H.: *Toward a New Sociology: A Critical Review,* Irwin, Dolsey Limited, Homewood, Ill., 1971.
7. Ibid.
8. Davis, J. (ed.): *The American Indian: The First Victim,* Morrow, New York, 1972, pp. 85–86.
9. Graves, T.: "Acculturation, Access, and Alcohol in a Tri-ethnic Community," *American Anthropologist,* 1967, **69**, 118–124.
10. Ferguson, Frances: "Navaho Drinking: Some Tentative Hypotheses," *Human Organization,* 1968, **27**, 159–167.
11. Bahr, H. M.: *Native Americans Today: Sociological Perspectives,* Harper, New York, 1972.
12. Ibid.
13. Rosenberg: op. cit.
14. Anderson: op. cit.
15. Durkheim, E.: *Suicide,* Free Press, New York, 1951.
16. Fromm, Erich: *Escape From Freedom,* Holt, New York, 1941.
17. Anderson: op. cit.
18. Svalastoga, L.: "Social differentiation," in Robert E. Faris (ed.), *Handbook of Modern Sociology,* Rand McNally, Chicago, 1964, pp. 530–575.
19. Mayer, K. B., and W. Buckley: *Class and Society,* Random House, New York, 1970.

20. Ibid.
21. Ibid.
22. Hollingshead, A. B.: "Selected Characteristics of Classes in a Middle Western Community," *American Sociological Review,* 1947, **12**, 385–395.
23. Dunkin, O.: "Occupational Mobility in the U.S.," *American Sociological Review,* 1969, **30**, 498.
24. Anderson: op. cit., p. 105.
25. Phillips, B. S.: *Sociology: Social Structure and Change,* Macmillan, London, 1969.
26. Ibid.
27. Glazer, N., and D. D. Moynihan: *Beyond the Melting Pot,* M.I.T., Cambridge, Mass., 1963.

CHAPTER THREE

1. Appelbaum, R. P.: *Theories of Social Change,* Markham Publishing Co., Chicago, 1970.
2. Spencer, H.: *Sociology,* vol. I, Appleton, New York, 1892.
3. Durheim, E.: *Suicide.* Free Press, N.Y., 1951.
4. Applebaum: op. cit., p. 16.
5. Durkheim: op. cit.
6. Dahrendorf, R.: "Toward a Theory of Social Change," in Amitai Etzioni and Eva Etzioni (eds.), *Social Change,* Basic Books, New York, 1964.
7. Spengler, O.: "The Life Cycle of Cultures," in Amitai Etzioni and Eva Etzioni (eds.), *Social Change,* Basic Books, New York, 1964.
8. Appelbaum: op. cit.
9. See Goode, W.: "Family Disorganization," in Robert K. Merton and Robert Nisbet (eds.), *Contemporary Social Problems.* Harcourt, Brace Jovanovich, New York, 1971, pp. 481–482, 486, 497, 500–501.
10. Ibid.
11. Goode, W.: *After Divorce,* Free Press, New York, 1956.
12. Ibid.
13. Adopted in part from Goode: *Family Disorganization.*
14. Bettelheim, B.: *Children of the Dream.* Macmillan, New York, 1970.
15. Ibid., p. 105.
16. Ibid.
17. Ibid., p. 123.
18. Bronfenner, U.: *Two Worlds of Childhood: U.S. and U.S.S.R.* Basic Books, New York, 1972.
19. Sidel, R.: *Women and Child Care in China,* Hill and Wang, Inc., New York, 1972, p. 82.
20. Mead, M.: "New Designs for Family Living," *Redbook,* October 1970, pp. 22–25.

21. Kincade, K.: "Commune: A Walden Two Experiment," *Psychology Today,* January and February, 1973, p. 174.
22. Ibid.
23. Ibid.
24. Glick, P.: "Marital Stability as a Social Indicator," *Social Biology,* 1969, **16**, 158–166.
25. Bird, C.: *Born Female,* McKay, New York, 1968.
26. Watson, G.: "Psychological Aspects of Sex Roles," in G. Watson (ed.), *Social Psychology: Issues and Insights,* Lippincott, Philadelphia, 1966.
27. See U.S. Department of Labor, Wage and Labor Standards Administration, Women's Bureau publication *Handbook on Women Workers,* 1969, Bulletin 294 and President's Manpower Report, 1972.
28. See U.S. Department of Labor, Wage and Labor Standards Administration, Women's Bureau; *Fact Sheet on Earnings Gap,* February 1970.
29. Millett, K.: *Sexual Politics,* Avon, New York, 1969.
30. Ibid.
31. Freeman, J.: "The Origin of the Women's Liberation Movement," in Joan Huber (ed.), *Changing Women in a Changing Society,* University of Chicago Press, Chicago, 1973.
32. Ibid.
33. Ibid.
34. *Yale Law Review,* 1972, **86**, 871, 985. Reprinted in *Women,* U.S. Government Printing Office, Washington, D.C., April 1973.
35. *Population and the American Future*, Signet, New York, 1972, p. 1.

CHAPTER FOUR

1. See vol. 20, pp. 191–198.
2. *Worker Adjustment Problems: High School to Work,* Ohio State Center for Vocational Technical Education, Columbus, 1972.
3. Ibid.
4. Seymour, W. N.: *The Young Die Quietly,* Morrow, New York, 1972, pp. 13–14.
5. Brotman, R., and F. Suffet: *Youthful Drug Use,* U.S. Department of Health, Education, and Welfare, Washington, D.C., 1970.
6. Ibid.
7. Ibid.
8. Ausubel, D.: *Drug Addiction,* Random House, New York, 1958.
9. *Guide Post,* Feb. Washington, D.C.: American Personnel and Guidance Association, 1973, p. 1.
10. De Fleur, L.B., and G. R. Garrett: "Dimensions of Marijuana Usage in a Land Grant University," *Journal of Counseling Psychology,* 1970, **17**, 468–476.
11. Sutton, H.: "Drugs: Ten Years to Doomsday?" *Saturday Review,* 1970, **53**, 18–21.

12. Ibid.
13. *Measures for Prevention and Control of Drug Abuse and Dependence,* World Health Organization, Regional European Office, Copenhagen.
14. *Report of the National Commission on Violence,* U.S. Government Printing Office, Washington, D.C., 1970.
15. Ibid.
16. Sutherland, E. H., and R. Cressey: *Principles of Criminology,* Lippincott, Philadelphia, 1970.
17. Glueck, S., and E. Glueck: *Predicting Delinquency and Crime,* Harvard, Cambridge, Mass., 1959.
18. McCord, W., J. McCord, and I. Zola: *Origins of Crime,* Columbia, New York, 1959.
19. Merton, R. K.: "Anomie, Anomia, and Social Interaction: Context of Deviant Behavior," in M. B. Clinard (ed.), *Anomie and Deviant Behavior,* Free Press, New York, 1964.
20. *Report of the National Commission on Violence,* p. xxiv.
21. Cressey, D. R.: "The State of Criminal Statistics," *National Probation and Parole Association Journal,* 1957, **3**, 230–241.
22. Schur, E. M.: *Our Criminal Society,* Prentice-Hall, Englewood Cliffs, N.J., 1969, p. 159.
23. "Crime in the U.S.," *Uniform Crime Reports,* U.S. Government Printing Office, Washington, D.C., 1972.
24. Blum, Lahava D., and P. H. Rossi: "Social Class Research and Images of the Poor: A Bibliographic Review," in D. P. Moynihan (ed.), *On Understanding Poverty,* Basic Books, New York, 1969.
25. Ibid.
26. The President's Commission on Income Maintenance Programs, U.S. Government Printing Office, Washington, D.C., 1969.
27. Ibid.

CHAPTER FIVE

1. Fitch, S. K.: *Insights into Human Behavior,* Holbrook Press, Boston, 1970, p. 77.
2. Kalish, R. A.: *The Psychology of Human Behavior,* Brooks/Cole, Belmont, Calif., 1972, p. 57.
3. Coleman, J. C.: *Abnormal Psychology and Modern Life,* Scott Foresman, Chicago, 1964.
4. Maslow, A.: *Toward a Psychology of Being,* Van Nostrand, New York, 1962.
5. Kubler-Ross, Elizabeth: *On Death and Dying,* Macmillan, New York, 1969.
6. Watson, J. B.: *Behaviorism,* Norton, New York, 1925, 1930, p. 82.
7. Jensen, A. K.: "How Much Can We Boost IQ and Scholastic Achievement?," *Harvard Educational Review,* 1969, **39**, 1, 1–123.
8. Coleman, J. S., et. al.: *Equality for Educational Opportunity,* Depart-

ment of Health, Education, and Welfare, Washington, D. C., 1966.
9. Sheuy, A. M.: *The Testing of Negro Intelligence,* 2d ed., Social Science Press, New York, 1966.
10. Jensen, A. K.: op. cit.
11. Shockley, William: "Dysgenics, Geneticity, Raceology," *Phi Delta Kappan,* 1972, **52**, 297–307.
12. Gage, N. L.: "IQ Heritability, Race Differences, and Educational Research," *Phi Delta Kappan,* 1972, **52**, 308–312.
13. Gage, N. L.: "Replies to Shockley, Page and Jensen: The Causes of Race Differences in IQ," *Phi Delta Kappan,* 1973, **53**, 442–427.
14. Hudson, L.: "Intelligence, Race, and the Selection of Data," *Race,* 1971, **12**, 283–292.

CHAPTER SIX

1. Freud, S.: *New Introductory Lectures on Psycho-Analysis,* Norton, New York, 1933, p. 11.
2. Erikson, E. H.: *Childhood & Society,* Norton, New York, 1950, pp. 226–228.
3. Munroe, Ruth L.: *Schools of Psychoanalytic Thought,* Holt, New York, 1955.
4. Ibid., p. 251.
5. Freud, Sigmund: *The Interpretation of Dreams,* trans. James Strachey, Avon, New York, 1965.
6. Jung, C. G.: *Collected Works, Vol. 7. Two Essays on Analytical Psychology,* Pantheon, New York, 1953.
7. Dreikurs, R.: *Psychology in the Classroom,* 2d ed., Harper & Row, New York, 1968.
8. Bischof, Ledored J.: *Interpreting Personality,* 2d ed., Harper & Row, New York, 1970.
9. Dinkmeyer, Don, and R. Dreikurs: *Encouraging Children to Learn,* Prentice-Hall, Englewood Cliffs, N.J., 1963.
10. Dreikurs: op. cit., p. 75.
11. Rogers, Carl: "Toward a Science of the Person," in T. W. Wann (ed.), *Behaviorism and Phenomenology,* The University of Chicago Press, Chicago, 1964, 110–118.
12. Combs, A. W., and D. Snygg: *Individual Behavior: A Perceptual Approach to Behavior,* 2d ed., Harper & Row, New York, 1959.
13. Rogers, C. R.: *Client Centered Therapy,* Houghton Mifflin, Boston, 1951.

CHAPTER SEVEN

1. Heidbreder, Edna: *Seven Psychologies,* Appleton Century Crofts, New York, 1933.
2. Hilgard, E. R., and G. H. Bower: *Theories of Learning,* 3d. ed., Appleton Century Crofts, New York, 1966.
3. Heidbreder: op. cit.

4. Skinner, B. F.: *Behavior of Organisms: An Experimental Analysis,* Appleton Century Crofts, New York, 1938.
5. Skinner, B. F.: *Science and Human Behavior,* Macmillan, New York, 1953.
6. Bandura, A.: *Principles of Behavior Modification,* Holt, New York, 1969.
7. Keller, F. S.: *Learning Reinforcement Theory,* Random House, New York, 1954.
8. Watson, J. B., and Rosalie Rayner: "Conditioned Emotional Reactions, *Journal of Experimental Psychology,* 1920, **3**, 14.
9. Bandura, op. cit.
10. Lovaas, O. I., G. Frestag, V. G. Gold, and I. C. Kassorla: "Experimental Studies in Childhood Schizophrenia: Analysis of Self-destructive Behavior," *Journal of Experimental Psychology,* 1965, **2**, 67–74.
11. Skinner, B. F.: *Science and Human Behavior.*
12. Skinner, B. F.: "The Technology of Teaching," *Proceedings of the Royal Society,* The Royal Society, London, 1962.
13. Unwin, P.: "An Organizational Approach for Certain Retention and Correlational Factors in Comparison between Two Teaching Methods," *Programmed Learning,* Vol. 3, 1966.
14. Portes, A.: "On the Emergence of Behavior Therapy in Modern Society," *Journal of Consulting and Clinical Psychology,* **36**, 3, 303–313, 1968.
15. Eysenck, H. J.: "The Effects of Psychotherapy: An Evaluation," *Journal of Consulting Psychology,* 1952, **16**, 319–325.
16. "Screams, Slaps, and Love," *Life,* May 7, 1965, pp. 90A–95.
17. Skinner, B. F.: *Walden Two,* MacMillan: New York, 1948.
18. Skinner, B. F.: *Science and Human Behavior,* pp. 426–427.
19. Skinner, B. F.: *Beyond Freedom and Dignity,* Knopf, New York, 1971.
20. Eysenck, H. J.: "Behavior Therapy as a Scientific Discipline," *Journal of Consulting and Clinical Psychology,* 1971, **36**, 314–319.
21. Skinner, B. F.: "The Technology of Teaching."
22. Skinner, B. F.: *Science and Human Behavior.*
23. Eysenck: op. cit., p. 316.

PART THREE

1. Broom, Leonard and Philip Selznick, *Sociology,* Harper & Row, New York, p. 3.
2. Beals, Ralph and Harry Hoijer, *An Introduction to Anthropology,* MacMillan, New York, 1959, p. 6.

CHAPTER EIGHT

1. Tuckman, Howard P., *The Economics of the Rich,* Random House, New York, 1973, pp. 18–22.
2. Becker, G. and B. Cheswick, "Education and the Distribution of Earnings," *American Economic Review,* May 1966, pp. 358–369.

3. For an excellent discussion of this topic see Leonard J. Kirsch, *Soviet Wages: Changes in Structure and Administration Since 1956,* MIT Press, Cambridge, Mass., 1972.

CHAPTER TEN

1. Tuckman, Howard P., *The Economics of the Rich,* Random House, New York, 1973, p.22.
2. Lundberg, Ferdinand, *The Rich and the Super Rich,* Bantam, New York, 1969, p. 155.
3. *Economic Report of the President,* U.S. Government Printing Office, Washington, D.C., 1971. This percent includes only direct expenditures by the federal government.
4. *Ibid.*

CHAPTER ELEVEN

1. Advisory Commission on Intergovernmental Relations, *Urban America and the Federal System,* Washington, 1968, p. 85.
2. Alfred De Grazia, *The Elements of Political Science,* Knopf, New York, 1952, p. 49.
3. *Economic Report of the President,* U.S. Government Printing Office, Washington, D.C., 1973.
4. *Statistical Abstract of the United States,* U.S. Government Printing Office, Washington, D.C., P. 431.
5. These suggestions are based on those made in the *Report of the National Advisory Commission on Civil Disorders.*

NAME INDEX

SUBJECT INDEX